OXFORD WORLD'S CLASSICS

THE OXFORD SHAKESPEARE

General Editor · Stanley Wells

The Oxford Shakespeare offers new and authoritative editions of Shakespeare's plays in which the early printings have been scrupulously re-examined and interpreted. An introductory essay provides all relevant background information together with an appraisal of critical views and of the play's effects in performance. The detailed commentaries pay particular attention to language and staging. Reprints of sources, music for songs, genealogical tables, maps, etc. are included where necessary; many of the volumes are illustrated, and all contain an index.

H. J. OLIVER, the editor of *The Taming of the Shrew* in the Oxford Shakespeare, was Professor of English in the University of New South Wales, Australia. He edited *The Merry Wives of Windsor* and *Timon of Athens* in the new Arden Shakespeare, *As You Like It* in the New Penguin Shakespeare, and two plays by Christopher Marlowe in the Revels series.

THE OXFORD SHAKESPEARE

All's Well that Ends Well
Anthony and Cleopatra
As You Like It
The Comedy of Errors
The Complete Sonnets and Poems
Coriolanus
Cymbeline
Hamlet
Henry V
Henry IV, Part 1
Henry IV, Part 2
Henry VI, Part One
Henry VI, Part Two
Henry VI, Part Three
Julius Caesar
King Henry VIII
King John
King Lear
Love's Labour's Lost
Macbeth
Measure for Measure
The Merchant of Venice
The Merry Wives of Windsor
A Midsummer Night's Dream
Much Ado About Nothing
Othello
Pericles
Richard II
Richard III
Romeo and Juliet
The Taming of the Shrew
The Tempest
Timon of Athens
Titus Andronicus
Troilus and Cressida
Twelfth Night
The Two Gentlemen of Verona
The Two Noble Kinsmen
The Winter's Tale

OXFORD WORLD'S CLASSICS

WILLIAM SHAKESPEARE

The Taming of the Shrew

Edited by

H. J. OLIVER

OXFORD
UNIVERSITY PRESS

Great Clarendon Street, Oxford OX2 6DP

Oxford University Press is a department of the University of Oxford.
It furthers the University's objective of excellence in research, scholarship,
and education by publishing worldwide in

Oxford New York

Auckland Bangkok Buenos Aires Cape Town Chennai
Dar es Salaam Delhi Hong Kong Istanbul Karachi Kolkata
Kuala Lumpur Madrid Melbourne Mexico City Mumbai Nairobi
São Paulo Shanghai Taipei Tokyo Toronto

Oxford is a registered trade mark of Oxford University Press
in the UK and in certain other countries

Published in the United States
by Oxford University Press Inc., New York

First published by the Clarendon Press 1982
First published as a World's Classics paperback 1994
Reissued as an Oxford World's Classics paperback 1998
Reissued 2008

British Library Cataloguing in Publication Data

Data available

Library of Congress Cataloging in Publication Data

Shakespeare, William, 1564–1616.
The taming of the shrew.
(Oxford World's classics)
Bibliography: p. Includes index.
I. Oliver, H. J. (Harold James). II. Title.
III. Series: Shakespeare, William, 1564–1616. works 1982.
PR2832.A204 1984 822.3'3 83–193710

ISBN 978–0–19–953652–8

13

Printed in Great Britain by
Clays Ltd, St Ives plc

CONTENTS

Introduction 1

The play in the First Folio 3

The Quarto: The Taming of A Shrew 13

The relation of Quarto and Folio 22

The story of Christopher Sly 34

The Bianca subplot and 'supposes' 43

Katherine and Petruchio 48

The style 57

The play on the stage 64

Editorial Principles 77

THE TAMING OF THE SHREW 85

APPENDIX A

The Christopher Sly scenes from The Taming of A Shrew 233

APPENDIX B

The Song at 4.1.36 236

Index to the Commentary 237

INTRODUCTION

THE playgoer who sees *The Taming of the Shrew* for the first time, or the reader who opens the play for the first time, having known in advance only that the story is about the taming of a termagant Kate by a swashbuckling Petruchio, must be startled to find that it begins, in the standard (First Folio) text, not with Petruchio or Kate or her family but with a drunken tinker, one Christopher Sly, who is being thrown out of an inn for refusing to pay his debts. It is true that Christopher also once calls himself 'Christophero' and that he is so named in one stage direction, but he has acquaintances in Burton-heath and is well known to '*Marrian Hacket* the fat Alewife of Wincot'. Most unusually for a Shakespeare play (the only other may be *The Merry Wives of Windsor*), we are, without subterfuge, in the England of Shakespeare's own time – indeed, apparently not far from Stratford;[1] and Petruchio and his Italy must wait.

An unnamed sporting Lord finds Sly in a drunken stupor and advances the plan of dressing him up as a nobleman while he is unconscious and leading him to believe when he awakes that he has been suffering for many years from delusions but can now, with care, resume his rightful aristocratic role. The plan is carried out, and Sly, now 'aloft' with his attendants, is persuaded that, as part of the medical treatment during his 'amendment', and to avert 'melancholly', he should allow himself to be entertained with a comedy. Sly does not even know what a comedy is but condescends to watch it, in company with his supposed wife; and the play 'proper' (which is thus a 'play within a play') then begins, with the story of Baptista and his daughters Katherine and Bianca and their various suitors.

Sly watches the first scene, apparently without much interest or even understanding (he does not know whether it has finished and he has indeed been 'nodding'); he makes the immortal remark ''Tis a verie excellent peece of worke, Madame Ladie: would 'twere done'; the stage direction in the First Folio says '*They sit and marke*'; and then we hear or see nothing more of him. A producer has to make up his mind what to do about him (and the most frequent solution is to let him fall asleep again and be quietly carried off, or have curtains drawn, across him and his group, in the hope, either way, that the

[1] See notes on Induction 2, ll. 17, 18, 20, and 91.

audience will forget him – although it is not unknown for him to be left on the stage till the very end of the play and then removed, a device that does little or nothing either for Sly or for the taming story).

It is, then, doubly interesting to find that there is another version of *The Taming of the Shrew*, somehow distantly related to it, in which the Sly story is carried through to the bitter end. This is the version – not known at all to the general reader and acted on the modern stage if at all only as a curiosity – printed in Quarto format in 1594 as 'A Pleasant Conceited Historie, called The taming of a Shrew. As it was sundry times acted by the Right honorable the Earle of Pembrook his servants' (but perhaps it was not acted at all). In this text, Sly is tricked as in the other version, and begins to watch the play-within-the-play; but he shows interest in it, particularly in the clown (called 'Sander', 'Saunder' or 'Saunders' but with the same function as Grumio). '*Sim*', he says to the Lord at one point (sig. C1^{v}), 'when will the foole come againe?' and is assured that 'Heele come againe my Lord anon'. After some time, he asks for confirmation of his (seemingly strenuous) attempt to understand what is going on (sig. E4):

> SLIE *Sim* must they be married now?
> LORD *I* my Lord.
> Enter *Ferando and Kate and Sander.*
> SLIE Looke *Sim* the foole is come againe now.

Then, most amusingly, he tries to interfere with the action, when the character corresponding to Lucentio's father Vincentio, who has just learnt of the deception perpetrated by his son and servant, orders that they be sent to prison (sig. F2):

> SLIE I say wele have no sending to prison.
> LORD My Lord this is but the play, theyre but in jest.
> SLIE I tell thee *Sim* wele have no sending,
> To prison thats flat: why *Sim* am not I *Don Christo Vary?*
> Therefore *I* say they shall not go to prison.
> LORD No more they shall not my Lord,
> They be run away.
> SLIE Are they run away *Sim?* thats well,
> Then gis some more drinke, and let them play againe.
> LORD Here my Lord.
> *Slie* drinks and then falls asleepe.

Before the final scene (in which the fully tamed Kate wins her husband's wager for him), the Lord orders that the sleeping Sly be carried back to the place where he was found, outside the 'alehouse', and be again dressed in his own 'apparell' (sig. F3); and after the Katherine play is over, we see these orders being obeyed and watch Sly's awakening (sigs. G2, G2^{v}):

SLIE *Sim* gis some more wine: whats all the
Plaiers gon: am not I a Lord?
TAPSTER A Lord with a murrin: come art thou dronken still?
SLIE Whose this? *Tapster*, oh Lord sirra, I have had
The bravest dreame to night, that ever thou
Hardest in all thy life.
TAPSTER I marry but you had best get you home,
For your wife will course you for dreming here to night,
SLIE Will she? I know now how to tame a shrew,
I dreamt upon it all this night till now,
And thou hast wakt me out of the best dreame
That ever I had in my life, but Ile to my
Wife presently and tame her too
And if she anger me.
TAPSTER Nay tarry *Slie* for I'le go home with thee,
And heare the rest that thou hast dreamt to night.
Exeunt Omnes.

FINIS.[1]

(Even now it may be noted that the Tapster's final words may imply his doubts whether what Sly has learnt, from the imaginary world of a play, about taming shrews will be of practical use when it comes to taming a 'real-life' wife.)

One must ask 'whose is this full Sly story?' Does it, or something like it, really belong in *The Taming of the Shrew*? Is a producer entitled to import it into a production of the Shakespeare play? These are only the most interesting of many questions to which a more confident answer would be given if there were certain knowledge of the relationship between the two texts.

The play in the First Folio

The play now found in collected editions of Shakespeare – the one, substantially, that is printed in this volume and that may for the

[1] A full text of all Sly scenes from the Quarto not found in the Folio is given in this edition, in modern spelling, as Appendix A.

moment be called, however optimistically, the 'true' Shakespeare text – was not printed until the first collected edition of his dramatic work, the First Folio ('F1') of 1623, some seven years after the playwright's death. It is called in head-title and running-titles as well as in the 'catalogue' of contents, '*The Taming of the Shrew*'; and it is the eleventh of the Comedies, coming – in the unpredictable order of the Folio – after *As You Like It* and before *All's Well that Ends Well*, on pp. 208–29, S2ᵛ–V1. It would seem to have been set up in type by three different compositors – the one known nowadays as 'B', who set most of it; 'C' (who set T1, T1ᵛ, T2, T2ᵛ – i.e. 2.1.260 to 4.1.13); and 'D' (T5, T5ᵛ, T6, T6ᵛ – 4.3.189 to 5.2.131).[1]

There was apparently an interruption during the printing of the play: quires S and T were probably printed in the months April–mid-July 1622, but the last page (with other pages in quire V) not until September or later.[2] Fortunately, however, this delay does not seem to have any textual implications; nor do surviving copies of the Folio have in *The Shrew* variant readings of any importance (the six variants on S5ᵛ being obvious corrections of typographical errors and that on V1 involving only the signature).[3]

The evidence strongly suggests that *The Taming of the Shrew* was set up by the Folio compositors from author's manuscript – not a transcript of it, or a prompt-copy used in the theatre; and no error in the text makes necessary a theory that dictation was involved at any time (although Dover Wilson argued to the contrary when he prepared the New Cambridge edition in 1928).

There is, first, the evidence of the speech prefixes. Line 98 of the Folio (Induction 1. 85, the reply to the Lord when he recalls that he had previously seen one of the players, on the stage) has the speech prefix '*Sincklo*' where one would expect '*Player*' or '1. *Player*'. John Sincklo, or Sincler, is known to theatre historians as a minor actor of the last ten or twelve years of the sixteenth century and the first decade of the seventeenth.[4] His name, along with the names of Burbage and others, is found in the 'plot' of *The Second Part of the Seven Deadly Sins*, which can probably be dated 1592 (the MS is preserved

[1] Charlton Hinman, *The Printing and Proof-Reading of the First Folio of Shakespeare*, 2 vols. (Oxford, 1963), ii. 446–62, 514–18; T. H. Howard-Hill, 'The Compositors of Shakespeare's Folio Comedies', *Studies in Bibliography*, 26 (1973), 61–106.

[2] Hinman, ii. 446–62.

[3] Hinman, i. 262–3.

[4] See, for example, Allison Gaw, 'John Sincklo as one of Shakespeare's Actors', *Anglia*, 49 (1926), 289–303.

at Dulwich College). It occurs again in F1 *3 Henry VI* l. 1396: '*Enter Sinklo, and Humfrey . . .*', and some subsequent speech prefixes. (In modern editions (3.1) Sinklo and Humfrey become the anonymous deer-keepers who capture the king.) In the 1600 Quarto of *2 Henry IV* (5.4) 'Sincklo' is found both in a stage direction and in speech prefixes – and here his part is that of a beadle who is addressed by Doll Tearsheet as 'you thin man in a censer', 'you filthy famished correctioner', 'Goodman death, goodman bones' and by Mistress Quickly as 'you starved bloodhound' and 'thou atomy' (or skeleton). Then in the Induction (probably written by Webster) to Marston's *Malcontent* (printed in 1604), several of the King's Men, including Sincklo and Burbage, appear under their own names and again there seems to be a jocular allusion to Sincklo's thinness. Apparently Sincklo was easily recognized; and his reply to the Lord in *The Shrew* 'I think 'twas *Soto* that your honor meanes' would have had significance for an Elizabethan audience, reminding them of a distinctive role that the actor had taken.[1] Shakespeare must have had Sincklo in mind when he wrote this part for the otherwise unnamed 'Player' – and used the appellation in the speech prefix by an easy slip of the pen. (The name of an actor would hardly appear thus in a prompt-book, in one line and not in another, where it could cause only confusion.) The case is parallel, then, to the famous stage direction '*Enter Will Kemp*' in the second (1599) Quarto of *Romeo and Juliet* (sig. K3^v: 4.5.99.1) and to the speech prefixes '*Cowley*' and '*Kemp*', for Verges and Dogberry, in the 1600 Quarto of *Much Ado about Nothing* (G3^v, G4, G4^v: 4.2): in all these instances the dramatist in the process of composition momentarily identifies a character with the member of the acting company who is to play the part.

Another actor's name is probably in l. 1376 of the First Folio text of *The Shrew* (3.1.80), where – after the stage direction '*Enter a Messenger*' – the speech prefix for the messenger's announcement is '*Nicke*' (but there is no need to equate this 'Nicke' with Petruchio's servant Nicholas in 4.1; and the identification of 'Nicke' with Nicholas Tooley, later a sharer in the King's Company and a leading actor, is pure guesswork, or wish-fulfilment). The theory[2] that Gabriel, Curtis, and Peter, among Petruchio's servants in 4.1, are actors' names must be rejected as unproven and improbable (as Greg

[1] See also note on Induction 1.84.

[2] *The Taming of the Shrew*, ed. by Sir Arthur Quiller-Couch and John Dover Wilson (Cambridge, 1928), pp. 116–17.

says, what of Nathaniel, Joseph and Sugarsop?[1]); but certainly '*Peter*' in the curious stage direction of l. 2253 may be the name of the actor playing Lucentio.[2] Another speech prefix '*Fel.*' at l. 2047 (4.3.63), where one would expect '*Haberdasher*', or an abbreviation of it, may be another actor's name (Dover Wilson suggested William Felle) but is more probably an abbreviation of '*Fellow*', and either way would again seem to suggest an author's casualness, not a prompter's interference.[3]

A special problem is created by the speech prefix '*Par.*' at l. 1924 (4.2.71), where no speech prefix seems to be needed, the line in question being apparently the last of a five-line speech by Tranio. Even if there is merit in the explanation that this is an actor's name written in the margin (perhaps the actor playing the Pedant, who enters immediately after the line) and that it was misunderstood by the compositor as a speech prefix, we cannot know whether it is the author's jotting or an annotation at some later stage (any time before 1622) by a 'book-keeper'. If the name is that of William Parr (as Dover Wilson conjectured, p. 116), then it cannot refer to early performances of the play (although he would have liked to think so) unless G. E. Bentley is wrong in his plausible suggestion that William Parr was not born until 1581.[4] One addition by a prompter, however, would not in any case mean that the manuscript on which the jotting was made was not an author's manuscript. It is certainly improbable that damage to such a script would be risked by *regular* use in the theatre, but, as Greg points out, prompters sometimes marked up the author's manuscript before the transcript was made from it.[5]

At least twice in the Folio text of *The Shrew*, there is another kind of confusion in the speech prefixes. Before l. 1341, 3.1.46, the second line of a speech by Hortensio and the beginning of an aside, is the prefix '*Luc.*' and l. 1344 is continued to him, although clearly it should be spoken by Bianca. Lines 1345–6, belonging to Lucentio, are given to '*Bian.*'; and the following five lines, belonging to Bianca, are given to '*Hort.*' The explanation may be that Shakespeare used a

[1] W. W. Greg, *The Shakespeare First Folio* (Oxford, 1955), p. 166, note F.

[2] See note on 4.4.65–72.

[3] '*Fel.*' occurs again as a speech prefix, twice, in the 'good' Second Quarto of *Romeo and Juliet* (K1v–4.4.15 and 18)–thought to have been printed from author's MS–and obviously stands for 'fellow', because Capulet has called the speaker 'fellow' in the preceding speech.

[4] G. E. Bentley, *The Jacobean and Caroline Stage*, 7 vols. (Oxford, 1941–68), ii. 520.

[5] Greg, *First Folio*, p. 109 and n. 4.

speech prefix before l. 1341, because it was an aside, and that the compositor took it to mark a new speaker and so started to go wrong; and as Dover Wilson suggested (p. 102) the error would have been doubly easy if Shakespeare happened to be writing '*lit.*' (for '*Litio*') as the speech prefix for the disguised Hortensio: '*lit*', '*luc*', and '*bia*' (or '*li*', '*lu*', and '*bi*') would readily be mistaken for one another in most secretary scripts and could certainly be so mistaken in such a script as that found in the part of *Sir Thomas More* generally thought to be in Shakespeare's handwriting. It may be added that speech prefixes were often aligned incorrectly in Elizabethan dramatic manuscripts, and perhaps bad alignment alone will explain the confusion. What is not credible is Dover Wilson's theory that the errors were the result of 'editorial interference' in a transcript. Any 'editor', one is tempted to quip, would have to see the error; and necessarily it would have had to be tidied up in a prompt-book.

There is a second instance of, apparently, the same misreading. In the Folio, l. 1850 (4.2.4) is given to '*Luc.*' when it should be spoken by Hortensio/Litio – and what makes it more likely that the dramatist would have written '*Li.*' or '*Lit.*' is that Hortensio has been addressed by Tranio as 'friend *Lisio*' only three lines earlier. Faced then with an entry for Bianca and Lucentio immediately afterwards (l. 1853; 4.2.5.1) the compositor omitted Lucentio because he thought Lucentio was already on stage, and proceeded to give Lucentio's next two prefixes to Hortensio (i.e. misreading '*luc.*' or '*lu.*' as '*lit.*' or '*li.*').[1]

Many of the stage directions also read like author's directions and most of them can readily be distinguished from what would be expected in a prompt-book or any other transcript. For example, the dramatist reminds himself, as it were, of the relationship of his characters to one another: '*Enter Baptista with his two daughters, Katerina & Bianca, Gremio a Pantelowne, Hortensio sister* [almost certainly a compositor's error for '*suitor*'] *to Bianca*' (1.1.47.1) or '*Enter Lucentio, and his man Triano*' (1.1.0.1 – another compositor's error since the name '*Tranio*' is correct in the very next line). He adds the proper name as an afterthought: '*Enter Begger and Hostes, Christophero Sly*' or simultaneously tells the story, as it were, and gives instructions to the company on their costumes, by a kind of shorthand: '*Enter a Lord from hunting, with his traine*'. If for the minute he

[1] For another possible confusion, see the headnote to 4.4 and the notes on 4.4.5 and 4.4.6.

thinks of a character as having a certain function or being in a certain state, reference to that function or state will do, and consistency and names do not matter: so we have '*Enter aloft the drunkard with attendants, some with apparel, Bason and Ewer, & other appurtenances, & Lord*' (Induction 2) and near the end of 1.1 '*The Presenters above speakes*'. He can even for the minute forget Biondello's name: '*Enter . . . Petruchio with Tranio, with his boy bearing a Lute and Bookes*' (ll. 897–9; 2.1.38.1–4). He can be extremely casual or just careless: this same stage direction omits Hortensio, who must enter here.[1] The stage direction at ll. 1387–8 (3.2.0.1–2) omits Lucentio – who does not speak until l. 137 of that scene; Grumio is omitted from the entrance at l. 1565 (3.2.182.2–3) – it is, so to speak, taken for granted that he waits on Petruchio; and at the beginning of the final scene, Petruchio and Katherine are omitted, presumably because they have just left the stage (perhaps they *follow* the others on again) and Hortensio is overlooked (after all, his bride comes on and he must too!) but Tranio's name is repeated: '*Enter . . . Tranio . . . and Widdow: The Servingmen with Tranio bringing in a Banquet*', possibly because while writing the direction, the dramatist remembered that a banquet had been allowed for in the dialogue.

If, however, a particular costume or stage-picture is important, the playwright will be specific, in his own unorthodox theatrical language. So, '*Enter Tranio brave*' – i.e. dressed as Lucentio (l. 786; 1.2.213.1); '*Enter . . . Lucentio, in the habit of a meane man*' (l. 897; 2.1.38.1–2) – even though he has already appeared in this disguise in an earlier scene; '*Enter Hortensio with his head broke*' (l. 1007; 2.1.140.1); and '*the Pedant drest like Vincentio*', followed a few lines later by '*Pedant booted and bare headed*' (ll. 2180, 2200–1; 4.4.0.1–2 and 4.4.18.1–2) – where there may have even been a false start and the first eighteen lines perhaps intended for deletion.[2]

Stage movement and position, too, are sometimes specified, examples being '*Lucen. Tranio, stand by*' (l. 349; 1.1.47.3); '*They sit and marke*' (l. 564; 1.1.252.1); '*He rings him by the eares*' (l. 584; 1.2.18.1); '*Flies after Bianca*' (l. 887; 2.1.29.1); and '*Pedant lookes out of the window*' (l. 2397; 5.1.13.1). Particularly interesting is the direction of ll. 2379–80 (5.1.0.1–2): '*Enter Biondello, Lucentio and*

[1] But on Hortensio, see later, pp. 10–13.

[2] For all these reasons, R. B. McKerrow's classification of *The Taming of the Shrew* among the plays with consistency in naming characters (and thus likely to be from a transcript) must be rejected. ('A Suggestion regarding Shakespeare's MSS', *Review of English Studies*, 11 (1935), 459–65.)

Bianca, Gremio is out before' where '*Gremio is out before*' is surely not 'an afterthought by someone, evidently not the author, who has discovered, on reaching line 6, that Gremio has been on stage all the time, though hitherto he has said nothing'[1] but an idiosyncratic shorthand instruction that Gremio should enter first and *stand aside* so that Biondello, Lucentio, and Bianca do not see him.

Again, one's impression that '*Exit Biondello, Tranio and Pedant as fast as may be*' (l. 2490; 5.1.100.1) is Shakespeare's own wording is supported by the occurrence of an identical phrase in the Folio text of *The Comedy of Errors*, '*Exeunt omnes, as fast as may be*' (l. 1447; 4.4.144.1) where also there are good reasons for thinking that the printer's copy for the play was some kind of author's manuscript.

Finally, there is a point to be made about the placing of the stage directions. Whoever wrote them – and of course the argument is that it can only have been the author – knew exactly how he wanted the entrances to be timed. If he wrote, for Petruchio, 'But heere she comes, and now *Petruchio* speake' *followed* by '*Enter Katerina*' (ll. 1050–1; 2.1.180 and 180.1), it was no doubt to avoid the platitudinous or bathetic effect of Petruchio's telling the audience what it could see for itself. A superfluous announcement can bring an unfortunate laugh in the theatre, and Shakespeare removes that possibility by having Petruchio see Katherine approaching, off-stage, before the audience sees her. But when he writes '*Enter Gremio and Lucentio disgu*[*i*]*sed*' followed by Grumio's 'Heere's no knaverie. See, to beguile the olde-folkes, how the young folkes lay their heads together. Master, master, looke about you: Who goes there? ha' (ll. 703–6; 1.2.135.1–138), the whole point is that the audience sees Gremio and Lucentio *before* Grumio sees them and so can enjoy an even better example of 'beguiling' than the one Grumio is commenting on: he is wiser than he knows. There are other examples, recorded in the notes (and there may be a few exceptions); and such subtleties would be spoilt by the 'normalizing' of a prompter and are often spoilt by the practice of modern editions.

One other kind of evidence has been used in the attempt to decide the status of the Folio text. Dover Wilson counted over forty lines in the play that he considered metrically imperfect – 'ruined by the omission, or less often by the addition, of some small word or

[1] *The Taming of the Shrew*, ed. G. R. Hibbard, the New Penguin edition (Harmondsworth, 1968), p. 246.

words'[1] – and thought that the best hypothesis to explain this was that the compositors were working from a faulty transcript. There are three answers to this, two of which he alluded to himself without seeing their full force. The first is that his theory of scansion is far too limited: some of the lines that he thought imperfect scan very well when spoken with natural stressing and pauses ('As before imparted to your worship', for example). The second is that an author himself can easily omit an unimportant word, particularly if writing at speed, and can use an abbreviation that a compositor fails to expand correctly (for instance, in 'Wilt please your Lord drink a cup of sacke', Shakespeare probably wrote 'Lo.', the common Elizabethan abbreviation for either 'Lord' or 'Lordship', and the compositor used the wrong expansion). The third is that, as in the example just quoted, compositors can be responsible for many such mistakes, and Dover Wilson's argument is self-defeating: he notes that Act 3 Scene 2 contained about a quarter of the relevant lines that he considered defective whereas 2.1 was 'hardly affected at all' – and this whole scene 3.2 is now attributed to a different compositor, 'C', from the one, 'B', who set the greater part of 2.1.

The assumption must be, then, that *The Taming of the Shrew* was set up in print from Shakespeare's own manuscript. The problem is, unfortunately, that this manuscript apparently bore signs of change of mind – not only during composition (as perhaps in the 'false start' to 4.4, discussed in the headnote to that scene) but also after a period of time, whether that period extended over only months or over years.[2]

The evidence relates almost entirely to Hortensio – and, to anticipate, suggests a theory that Hortensio did not, in the first intention, woo Bianca in the disguise of Litio, and that lines originally given to, or meant for, him had either to be omitted or to be transferred to Tranio when Hortensio, as a result of his wooing disguise, became, as it were, unavailable for other duties. (There would have been a music master in the first version of *The*

[1] op. cit. p. 97.

[2] In the ensuing discussion, no great importance is attached either to Florence Ashton's outdated attempt to infer revision from her judgments of good and bad verse and prose, and supposed interpolations and omissions ('The Revision of the Folio Text of *The Taming of the Shrew*', *Philological Quarterly*, 6 (1927), 151–60) or to R. A. Houk's attempted refutation of that ('Strata in *The Taming of the Shrew*', *Studies in Philology*, 39 (1942), 291–302); and indeed sometimes the differences of opinion between them are more apparent than real.

Shrew, or a pretended one – but if the latter, it must have been Tranio, not Hortensio.[1])

Hortensio is introduced, in 1.1, as a suitor to Bianca (indeed, that is the actual wording of the F1 stage direction if an apparent misprint is corrected). He is Gremio's rival but is content to join forces with him in finding a suitable husband for Katherine, to 'set' Bianca 'free'. In 1.2 it is specifically said that he is an old friend of Petruchio and of Grumio; and with due warnings about Kate's shrewishness, he will help Petruchio to marry her if that is what Petruchio wishes. Since Baptista (1.1.92–9) has asked both Gremio and Hortensio to introduce to him any suitable instructors for Bianca (in particular) in music or poetry, Hortensio now takes advantage of Petruchio's proposed suit to Katherine and asks Petruchio to present him to Baptista as a possible music master, 'That so I may by this device at least | Have leave and leisure to make love to her, | And unsuspected court her by her selfe' (1.2.129–35). His first pupil is Katherine, who breaks the lute over his head; and he now finds that he has another apparent rival, in Tranio disguised as Lucentio (and does not then know that his real rival is Lucentio, disguised as the schoolmaster Cambio).

By the end of 2.1, however, everybody seems to have forgotten that Hortensio ever was a suitor to Bianca in his own right.[2] A marriage for Katherine has been arranged, and Bianca is available to the highest bidder, but only Gremio and the disguised Tranio state their claims, and Hortensio's name is not even mentioned. An explanation that this is because Hortensio has gone off as Litio and could hardly re-enter so soon in his own person is inadequate (there are over a hundred intervening lines); and in any case the explanation does not cover Tranio's omission of Hortensio from the full list of rivals and opponents in 3.2.144–7 or Lucentio's failure to mention Hortensio to Bianca in 3.1.34–6 when he tells her that the supposed Lucentio is really the servant Tranio, 'bearing my port . . . that we might beguile the old Pantalowne' (i.e. Gremio). The original plan involved fooling Hortensio too.[3]

Then in 3.2 Tranio, who cannot be an old acquaintance of Petruchio's, suddenly becomes knowledgeable about Petruchio's

[1] See p. 27 later, the discussion of a corresponding scene in *A Shrew*.

[2] This has often been noted – perhaps first by P. A. Daniel, *A Time-Analysis of the Plots of Shakspere's Plays* (*New Shakspere Society Publications*, Ser. I, London [1879]).

[3] Many of these points are well made by G. I. Duthie, '*The Taming of A Shrew* and *The Taming of the Shrew*', *Review of English Studies*, 19 (1943), 337–56.

habits, in a way that would have been appropriate for Hortensio – and this time it was theatrically impossible to give the lines to Hortensio in his own person for he has just left the stage as Litio.[1] (There are other signs of dislocation and change of mind in 3.2 – see note on ll. 127 ff.) Then the dramatist remembers to bring Hortensio on again at l. 182.2, apparently as himself (F1 does not distinguish in its stage directions between the 'real' Hortensio and Hortensio as Litio, but the music master would be the less likely wedding-guest); yet he is not given a single word to say, in some seventy lines of dialogue. It is again as if his original function as a rival, in his own name, to Gremio for the hand of Bianca has become meaningless; one wonders whether lines of dialogue may not have been written for him and later expunged.

In 4.2, when the suspicions of Hortensio/Litio about Bianca's 'inconstancy' have been confirmed, Hortensio reveals his identity to Tranio, who acknowledges having heard of Hortensio's suit and 'entire affection to Bianca'. When they make a bargain that both will forswear her, Hortensio suddenly declares – to the astonishment of reader or audience – that within three days he will marry a wealthy widow who has loved him as long as he has loved Bianca and he goes off. Tranio promptly announces this to Bianca and Lucentio and incongruously adds that Hortensio has gone to Petruchio's 'taming schoole'. But Hortensio has mentioned only the plan to marry the widow; and again it seems that something relevant has been accidentally omitted – perhaps, as Duthie ingeniously suggests, in the process of tying up the ends of the story of the Litio disguise.

In 4.3 Hortensio is at Petruchio's house (he does not marry the widow until after 4.5) and sees the final stage of the taming – he has now reverted to his original status as Petruchio's friend – but there is one minor final inconsistency when in 4.5.74 he supports Petruchio's statement to Vincentio in ll. 60–3 that Vincentio's son has already married Bianca. The audience has not been told how Petruchio learnt of the marriage, but in the theatre has no time to care; and Hortensio's confirmation of Petruchio's announcement would hardly matter *if* Hortensio had never been 'Litio'. Even in the theatre, however, the objection is bound to be raised: since in his

[1] The attempt by R. A. Houk to defend the appropriateness of these lines to Tranio is desperate: he has to postulate ways in which Tranio *might* have learnt about Petruchio's way of life ('The Integrity of Shakespeare's *The Taming of the Shrew*', *Journal of English and Germanic Philology*, 39 (1940), 222–9).

disguise as Litio he made a bargain with the man he supposes to be Lucentio that neither of them would in any circumstances marry Bianca, he ought to be contradicting Petruchio, not agreeing with him. Again the inconsistency is between the Hortensio who is the friend of Petruchio (and the open rival to Gremio) and the Hortensio who passes himself off in disguise as Litio.[1]

In short, the First Folio text of *The Taming of the Shrew* was almost certainly printed from Shakespeare's manuscript, but that manuscript shows signs of change of mind; and that change proves to be relevant to, and important for, any attempt to establish the relationship between the Folio and the Quarto texts of the play.[2]

The Quarto: The Taming of A Shrew

On 2 May 1594, there was entered on the Stationers' Register, to Peter Shorte, 'a booke intituled A plesant Conceyted historie called the Tayminge of a Shrowe';[3] and Short published the play in the same year, for the bookseller Cuthbert Burby, as a quarto, under the title (already cited) *A Pleasant Conceited Historie, called The taming of a Shrew*. (Only one copy of this 1594 edition survives – the Devonshire copy, now in the Huntington Library in San Marino, California.) It has become convenient for scholars to refer to this Quarto as *A Shrew* and to the Folio text as *The Shrew* (and this shorthand will be adopted in the remainder of this Introduction and in the Commentary); but there is no evidence whatever that the Elizabethans themselves made this distinction and some evidence (given later) that they did not make it: they probably knew one play – whether they called it *The Taming of the Shrew* or *The Taming of a Shrew* – and perhaps also took it for granted, if they paused to think about it, that the only text in print, the Quarto, was less than perfect. What Shakespeare himself thought of it is not on record.

'P.S.' – Peter Short – published another edition for Burby in 1596.

[1] One other possible sign of change of mind may be added: F1 omits Hortensio from the stage direction at 897–9 (2.1.38.1–4) which is his first entrance in disguise as Litio. Presumably Shakespeare forgot to go back to put him in.

[2] The probability that the Folio text retains a false start in the first eighteen lines of 4.4 is not relevant here: that alteration may easily have been made during continuous composition. (See headnote to the scene.) Nor need there be any textual significance in Petruchio's mention of his Cousin Ferdinand. (See 4.1.136 and note.)

[3] The publishing history is summarized from, *inter alia*, E. K. Chambers, *William Shakespeare*, 2 vols. (Oxford, 1930), i. 322–3 and W. W. Greg, *A Bibliography of the English Printed Drama to the Restoration*, 4 vols. (London, 1939–59), i. 203–5.

Then on 22 January 1607, after Short's death (in 1603), a further entry on the Stationers' Register transferred the rights in *A Shrew* and two other 'copies' (*Romeo and Juliet* and *Love's Labour's Lost*) to Nicholas Linge 'by direccon of A Court and with consent of Master Burby under his handwrytinge'. There seems to have been in this an attempt to clear muddy waters and it was apparently successful, for no objection was recorded when in the same year 'V.S.' (Valentine Simmes) published 'for *Nicholas Ling*' a third edition. Ling must have died very soon afterwards, for on 19 November 1607 another entry on the Register transferred to John 'Smythick' (Smethwick) *A Shrew* and other 'bookes ... Whiche dyd belonge to Nicholas Lynge' (*Romeo and Juliet, Love's Labour's Lost*, and *Hamlet*). There was no further entry before the publication of *The Shrew* in the 1623 Folio: obviously Smethwick's rights to *A Shrew* were taken to cover any other version of what was regarded as the same play; and 'W.S.' published for Smethwick another Quarto in 1631 – this time as '*The Taming of the Shrew*' and indeed this Quarto is a reprinting of the Folio text, not of that of the 1594, 1596, and 1607 Quartos.

With hindsight one can see that it was inevitable that for hundreds of years *A Shrew*, being the first of the two versions of the story to be published, and being clearly inferior, should have been assumed to be the first composed and to be, in whatever sense, the source of the Folio play, *The Shrew*. Opinions differed on whether Shakespeare had anything to do with the 'earlier' version (Capell attributed it to him, as did Frey) but it was taken for granted that he had set out to improve on it (whatever reservations there might be about the 'incomplete' Induction). Nor was any evidence produced to the contrary until Samuel Hickson, in a series of brief articles in *Notes and Queries* in 1850,[1] pointed out not only that there were 'a dozen instances' in *A Shrew* of lines almost identical with lines from Marlowe's *Tamburlaine* (both Parts) and *Dr Faustus* (e.g., the first four lines of the Lord's speech in the 'Induction') but also that in 'passages which were identical, or nearly so' in *A Shrew* and *The Shrew*, 'the original conception was invariably to be found' in *The Shrew*.

For instance, he quoted the part of the exchange between Grumio and the tailor which goes, in the Folio:

[1] 'Marlowe and the old *Taming of a Shrew*' (pp. 194, 226–7); '*The Taming of the Shrew*' (pp. 345–7).

GRU. Thou hast fac'd many things.
TAIL. I have.
GRU. Face not mee: thou hast brav'd manie men, brave not me; I will neither bee fac'd nor brav'd

(ll. 2108–11; 4.3.122–5)

and demonstrated that the Quarto version preserves the words, by and large, but misses the puns on 'braved' and 'faced', and loses 'the spirit', so that 'the tailor's admission becomes meaningless':

SAN. Doost thou heare *Taylor*, thou hast braved
Many men: brave not me.
Thou'st faste many men.
TAYLOR Well sir.
SAN. Face not me Ile nether be faste nor braved
At thy handes I can tell thee

(sig. E2v).

Again, Hickson asked whether Quarto's version of Kate's address to the strange man whom her husband insists on treating as a woman

Faire lovely lady ...
As glorious as the morning washt with dew

(sig. F1)

could be anything other than a not quite successful attempt to recapture, from *The Shrew*, Petruchio's plan to manage Kate:

Say that she frowne, Ile say she lookes as cleere
As morning Roses newly washt with dew

(ll. 1041–2; 2.1.171–2)

the crucial 'roses' having been forgotten.[1]

Even more convincingly, he quoted from *A Shrew* the answer to Kate's

For I will home againe unto my fathers house.
FERAN. I, when you'r meeke and gentell but not
Before

(sig. D4v)

[1] This is admittedly not *quite* certain: 'the morning washed with dew' does make sense as a somewhat extravagant image. (The point was made, by J. W. Shroeder, '*The Taming of a Shrew* and *The Taming of the Shrew*: A Case Reopened', *Journal of English and Germanic Philology*, 57 (1958), 424–42, but he overstated his case.)

and compared from *The Shrew*:

> KATE Ile have no bigger, this doth fit the time,
> And Gentlewomen weare such caps as these.
> PET. When you are gentle, you shall have one too,
> And not till then
> (ll. 2053–6; 4.3.69–72)

to show how the author of *A Shrew* had half-recalled a witty retort but had missed the 'cue' that made it witty.

Similarly he noted that *A Shrew* stupidly gave, as the tamer's motive for insisting on plain clothes, not ''tis the minde that makes the bodie rich' (l. 2155), which is the 'justification' for his conduct throughout the scene with the tailor and haberdasher, but the feeble

> Our purses shallbe rich, our garments plaine,
> To shrowd our bodies from the winter rage
> (sigs. E2v–E3).

To mention one other of Hickson's remaining two or three examples, the lines in *A Shrew*

> My mind sweet *Kate* doth say I am the man,
> Must wed, and bed, and marrie bonnie *Kate*
> (sig. B3)

– where 'marrie' is a pointless repetition of 'wed' – can only be a failure to reproduce from a different context in *The Shrew* Gremio's reference to any man who 'would thoroughly woe her, wed her, and bed her, and ridde the house of her' (ll. 445–7; 1.1.140–2).

Unfortunately the conclusion that Hickson wished to draw from his evidence was that *A Shrew* was hurriedly written at some time after Shakespeare's *The Shrew*, by Marlowe. It is, however, particularly interesting, in view of theories propounded much later – and in view of what has already been said in this Introduction – that Hickson added, as a kind of postscript, 'At the same time, though I do not believe Shakespeare's play to contain a line of any other writer, I think it extremely probable that we have it only in a revised form, and that, consequently, the play which Marlowe imitated might not necessarily have been that fund of life and humour that we find it now'.

Hickson's arguments seem to have fallen on deaf ears; at any rate, none of the many editors of *The Taming of the Shrew* during the next sixty years appears to have been influenced by them.[1] But once A.W. Pollard had demonstrated that the reference by the compilers of the First Folio, Heminge and Condell, in the prefatory address 'To the great Variety of Readers', to previously published 'stolne, and surreptitious copies' of Shakespeare's plays was to a certain kind of corrupt quarto, and not to all earlier quartos; and once W. W. Greg had shown that the Quarto of *The Merry Wives of Windsor*, for example, was an attempt to reconstruct the authentic text, from memory, and Peter Alexander that *The First Part of the Contention* and *The True Tragedy of Richard Duke of York* were not early versions but memorial reconstructions of the second and third parts of *Henry VI*, Hickson was rediscovered; and Alexander himself, starting from Hickson's evidence as supplemented by Creizenach, now drew a new conclusion from it and classified *A Shrew* among the 'Bad Quartos' – it being, like Q1 of *Romeo and Juliet* and Q1 of *Hamlet*, to give other examples, an attempt by actors or persons unknown to remember what had been spoken on the stage in performances of the genuine Shakespearian texts (though the latter were not published until *after* the Bad Quartos, sometimes a year or so later, sometimes – as with *Henry VI* and *The Shrew* – not until 1623).[2]

Not all the arguments that Alexander advanced in 1926 are convincing. For example, following Creizenach, he reasoned that there was no motive in *A Shrew* for the decision by the lover of the younger sister to disguise himself, since access to that sister is not forbidden or restricted, and so concluded that the disguise was another pointless half-reminiscence from *The Shrew*. In fact the motive that Alexander dismissed as 'possible' but improbable is quite clearly implied in *A Shrew*: the lover Aurelius thinks his rank as son of the Duke of Sestos is too high to promise successful wooing and so arranges to be introduced as a wealthy merchant's son. It may still be true that this is only an inferior version of Lucentio's motive for disguise in *The Shrew*; and Alexander's main argument is valid: *A Shrew* sometimes

[1] Wilhelm Creizenach, however, saw the force of Hickson's evidence and added that the sub-plot of *The Shrew* was closer than was *A Shrew* to the source, *Supposes* (*Geschichte des neueren Dramas*, 1909, iv. 694).

[2] The principal references are A. W. Pollard, *Shakespeare Folios and Quartos* (London, 1909) and *Shakespeare's Fight with the Pirates* (Cambridge, 1920); *Shakespeare's 'Merry Wives of Windsor'* ed. W. W. Greg (Oxford, 1910); Peter Alexander, '*The Taming of a Shrew*', *The Times Literary Supplement*, 16 September 1926 (and earlier articles 9 October, 13 November 1924); B. A. P. van Dam, '*The Taming of a Shrew*', *English Studies* (Amsterdam), 10 (1928), 97–106; and Alexander, *Shakespeare's 'Henry VI' and 'Richard III'* (Cambridge, 1929).

has actions without motives where *The Shrew* gives the motives, which have apparently been forgotten by the 'reporters'.

Since 1926 a great deal of evidence has accumulated about the derivative nature of *A Shrew*. Chambers's statement that there are only 'half a dozen practically identical verse lines' in the two plays may be literally true but gives a completely false impression of the number of parallels.[1] There are scores of lines in the two plays that are so alike as to demand explanation. From the Induction alone, for example, may be cited:

(i) Folio Ile pheeze you infaith (l. 4)
Quarto Ile fese you anon (sig. A2).

(ii) F. Carrie him gently to my fairest Chamber (l. 50)
Q. beare him to my house, . . .
And in my fairest chamber make a fire (A2[v]).

(iii) F. Procure me Musicke readie when he wakes,
To make a dulcet and a heavenly sound (ll. 54–5)
Q. Let heavenlie musicke play about him still,
. . . when he dooth awake . . .
With heavenlie musicke sounding in his eares (A2[v]).

(iv) F. Some one be readie with a costly suite.
And aske him what apparrel he will weare (ll. 63–4)
Q. And I will aske what sutes he meanes to weare (A3).

(v) F. Upon my life I am a Lord indeede (l. 224)
Q. By the masse I thinke I am a Lord indeed (A4).

An example taken at random from 4.1 is:

F. Where is the foolish knave I sent before? (l. 1754)
Q. Wheres that villaine that I sent before (D3)

and from 4.3 may be cited, also at random:

(i) F. this kindnesse merites thankes.
What, not a word? (ll. 2022–3)
Q. what ist not worthie thankes (D4[v]).

(ii) F. KATE [to Petruchio] Belike you meane to make a puppet of me.
PET. Why true, he [the tailor] meanes to make a puppet of thee. (ll. 2088–9)

[1] *William Shakespeare*, i. 325.

Q. KATE belike you,
Meane to make a foole of me.
FERAN[DO] Why true he meanes to make a foole of thee (E2).

Obviously one text is indebted to the other, and the main reason for believing that the Quarto is the later must continue to be those passages in Q, such as Hickson cited and as Hart has shown to be the distinguishing feature of the 'Bad Quarto',[1] that make sense only if one knows the F version from which they must have been derived. Duthie chooses perhaps the best example, the soliloquy in *A Shrew* in which Ferando announces his plan of action for taming his wife:[2]

This humor must I holde me to a while,
To bridle and hold backe my headstrong wife,
With curbes of hunger: ease: and want of sleepe,
Nor sleepe nor meate shall she injoie to night,
Ile mew her up as men do mew their hawkes,
And make her gentlie come unto the lure,
Were she as stuborne or as full of strength
As were the *Thracian* horse *Alcides* tamde,
That King *Egeus* fed with flesh of men,
Yet would I pull her downe and make her come
As hungry hawkes do flie unto there lure
(sigs. D3–D3^{v}).

If this is compared with the Folio text (ll. 1822–45; 4.1.175–98 in this edition), it will become clear that the 'author' of *A Shrew* is trying to recall phrases he does not even understand. For example, the keeping awake of the haggard has nothing to do with 'mewing', which is the technical term for locking the hawk up during moulting; and mewing similarly has nothing to do with teaching the bird to come to the lure. The taming of horses by feeding them is a most curious analogue to the taming of haggards by starving them; and in fact the three lines about the horses are cribbed from *2 Tamburlaine*, 4.3.12–16 ('The headstrong jades of Thrace Alcides tamed, | That King Aegeus fed with human flesh, | And made so wanton that they knew their strengths, | Were not subdued with valour more divine, |

[1] Alfred Hart, *Stolne and Surreptitious Copies* (Melbourne, 1942), particularly Ch. XIII (but Hart seems to have been in two minds about *A Shrew*: he treats it as a source of *The Shrew* but also calls it a 'Bad Quarto').

[2] Duthie, *Review of English Studies*, 19, 338–42 – but Duthie quoted from the second, 1596, edition of *A Shrew*. The text of the first, 1594, is given here.

Than you by this unconquered arm of mine') and Duthie offers the explanation that the reporter's memory was started along the wrong track, as it were, by the occurrence of the word 'headstrong' in the passage from *The Shrew*. 'Headstrong' in association with taming was quite enough to suggest the Marlowe passage to him. (Marlowe seems to have been particularly *memorable*; lines from his plays are common in 'Bad Quartos', and the latest count would estimate some seventeen or eighteen passages from his work in *A Shrew*.)

Duthie also pointed out that 'ease' is most ineptly used in the third line of the soliloquy: 'it is not *ease* but the reverse which is to be used as a *curb*' (but perhaps the reporter thought of it as a kind of ellipsis – 'curbes of . . . ease' – although to say this may be devil's advocacy). Duthie might have added that the word 'humor' (applied by Petruchio in *The Shrew* to Kate's shrewishness) is inappropriate when transferred in *A Shrew* to the tamer's own carefully thought-out strategy.

Finally, Duthie showed how lines from other parts of *The Shrew* – such as 'And therefore has he [Baptista] closely meu'd her up' (l. 486; 1.1.180) – have been remembered, or misremembered, and transferred to and conflated with the speech from the good text that uses similar imagery in this later scene. (Other examples of this curious tendency to transpose have been cited earlier, in the section on Hickson; yet another is the inept transferring of a character's ignorance of what a comedy is, from Sly in *The Shrew* to one of the Players in the Quarto.)

The result of all these processes, it will be obvious, is a passage of no literary merit at all. With the weaknesses in meaning go most incompetent versification and a slackness in diction that allows the speech to end with 'flie unto there lure' as if the words were a magnificent climax and not a bathetic echo of 'come unto the lure' some five lines before.

Feeble repetition of words is one of the many characteristics that *A Shrew* shares with acknowledged 'Bad Quartos'. A further instance is the willingness to begin several successive lines with 'and' – that being perhaps the reporter's or reporters' notion of rhetoric. (Somebody involved in the report has also been impressed by Marlowe's extravagant similes and his habit of saying 'more than', for example, where another writer would say 'as much as'.) Attempting to soar, the reporters constantly fall flat; their blank verse is execrable, except when they get right odd lines from the authentic text and other plays; and there is complete incongruity between, on the one hand, the prosaic quality of much of the language and of the unamusing 'gags' of the clowns and, on the other, the grandiose words that close an agreement about a marriage contract: 'Eternallie this league of peace shall last, | Inviolet and pure on either part' (sig. E1ᵛ).

The story-telling also in *A Shrew* is particularly incompetent. Several times the story is given away in advance (for example, with the hint that one of Kate's sisters will have to be tamed): it is as if those reconstructing the text could not resist giving to a character the knowledge that they themselves had of what was to happen later. They also retain such an incident as Petruchio's beating of his domestic servants but lack the intelligence to perceive that the action has no point when Kate is not there to see it. They have Sly, the assumed lord, ask his wife's name – but do not provide an answer, let alone allow him to make further blunders over it. Not only do they not explain why Polidor (Hortensio) did not send for Ferando to become a suitor to Kate before Aurelius came into the picture, but also they have Ferando arrive already committed to wooing Kate *before* Polidor has said a word about her to him.

There are, too, a few – but perhaps not as many as elsewhere – of the characteristic superfluous stage directions of the 'reported' texts, such as

KATE Ile first begin
And lay my hand under my husbands feete
She laies her hand under her husbands feete
(sig. G1ᵛ)

or 'Then *Slie* speakes' (F2) or '*Ferando* speakes to the olde man' (E4ᵛ) – which is a 'stage direction' for a *reader*, to avoid confusion when the old man is addressed as a woman (the audience would see what was happening).

One curious feature of the stage directions of *A Shrew* is that there is no indication that any of the Sly scenes are on an upper stage or upper level of any kind. At the point now usually marked as the beginning of 'Induction 2', when the Folio has '*Enter aloft the drunkard with attendants . . .*', the Quarto reads 'Enter two with a table and a banquet on it, and two other, with *Slie* asleepe in a chaire, richlie apparelled, & the musick plaieng' (sig. A3ᵛ). This has been taken as evidence that the reporters were recalling performances – for example, when they were on tour away from London – where no upper stage was available; or it may mean, *if* one believes that Bad Quartos were intended as acting texts, that they were envisaging such performances in the future. The play they were publishing was not likely to be acted by the London company that had the rights in the genuine text, or openly by companies in competition with it.

Like the other reported texts, *A Shrew* is almost certainly too short to appeal to a leading company or to a London audience. It has some 1480 lines (interestingly, among the Shakespearian Bad Quartos only *The Merry Wives of Windsor*, which may be a parallel in other ways, is shorter – about 1420 lines; the extremely corrupt Marlowe tragedy *The Massacre at Paris* has about 1260). The truncating affects the length of single speeches; reporters can rarely manage a speech of more than twenty or thirty lines, and the longest in *A Shrew* are one of 28 lines by the Lord (broken by some stage action) and Kate's final oration of 29. Perhaps too much should not be made of this, for *The Shrew* has not many long speeches either – but the Lord runs to 37 lines and Kate to 44. What does matter is the way so many exchanges are reduced to the barest minimum: the interview of Kate's suitor with his intended father-in-law before he meets Kate herself is but 12 lines – and for that reason alone, if for no other, would be unintentionally absurd; and the first sparring match between Kate and the tamer is only 16 lines and does nothing to suggest how the girl could possibly become interested (or interesting) – and the 'author' tries to cut the Gordian knot by giving Kate the aside:

> But yet I will consent and marrie him,
> For I methinkes have livde too long a maid,
> And match him to, or else his manhoods good
> (sig. B3).

The relation of Quarto and Folio

The analysis in the preceding pages of parts of the text of *The Taming of a Shrew* has demonstrated that in some way the play must be a reconstruction, from memory, of another that we know in the form in which it appears in the First Folio as *The Taming of the Shrew*. It is still necessary, however, to ask another two questions: is the *entire* play *A Shrew* such a reconstruction? and is it possible that the play being reconstructed, although in many ways identical with that in the Folio, was different from it in others?

To the second of these questions, Duthie gave an impressive affirmative answer – one that has been rejected by some scholars for inadequate reasons. When Richard Hosley, for example, writes that 'the theory of a lost Shrew play is *merely a postulate* [my italics] by textual scholars designed to explain the unusual variations between Shakespeare's *Taming of the Shrew* and the bad-quarto text of *The Taming of a Shrew*',[1] he is overlooking the fact that Duthie was also working from the inconsistencies in *The Shrew* itself. Duthie has shown – and an earlier part of this Introduction (pp. 10–13) has tried to show – that without any reference whatever to *A Shrew*, the text of *The Shrew* reveals signs of change of mind and is indeed self-contradictory. At the very least there must have been a 'form' of *The Shrew* in which Hortensio was not disguised as the music teacher Litio and in which he remained in open, undisguised, competition with Gremio for the hand of Bianca – and the probability is that it was the earlier form, the difficulties arising from the endeavour to complicate the plot. There is no reason at all for thinking that it was by somebody other than Shakespeare (and therefore it is best not called '*the Ur-Shrew*'). And it is that version of *The Shrew* that *A Shrew* is attempting to recapture.

In the section of *A Shrew* corresponding to 3.2, for example, where Tranio shows unexpected knowledge of Petruchio's habits and suddenly becomes his equal,[2] the relevant lines are given not to Valeria (who is, in so far as anyone is, the equivalent of Tranio) but to Polidor (the counterpart of Hortensio). It is Polidor who offers an explanation of the bridegroom's delay:

> His Tailor it may be hath bin too slacke,
> In his apparrell which he meanes to weare,
> For no question but some fantasticke sutes
> He is determined to weare to day . . .

and it is Polidor who rebukes the groom for arriving 'baselie attired', and offers to lend him clothes (sig. C3^{v}).

Then whereas in 4.2 of *The Shrew*, Tranio so surprisingly announces (what he cannot know) that Hortensio 'is gone unto the taming schoole' (l. 1905), *A Shrew* has Polidor/Hortensio specifically state that he is going to see whether the tamer is succeeding:

[1] Richard Hosley, 'Sources and Analogues of *The Taming of the Shrew*', *Huntington Library Quarterly*, 27 (1964), 292.

[2] See pp. 11–12 of this Introduction.

> Within this two daies I will ride to him,
> And see how lovingly they do agree
> (sig. D2)

and so another character (Aurelius), who has heard this, can logically affirm of Polidor

> Faith he's gon unto the taming schoole (sig. D4).

This part of Duthie's case is watertight; and in so far as *A Shrew* is a reported version not of the text that survives in the Folio but of a slightly different form of it, there is a parallel, which Duthie overlooked, with *The Merry Wives of Windsor*, where the 'Bad Quarto' seems to be an attempt to reconstruct from memory not the Folio version of the play (which preserves a text written for a special occasion) but an adaptation of that for the public stage.[1] Of one play (*The Shrew*), the Folio apparently gives a later form of the text that the Quarto 'reports'; of the other (*The Merry Wives*) it gives an earlier – but fortunately discussion of *The Merry Wives* has not been muddied by talk of an *Ur-Merry-Wives*.

Where Duthie and others probably went wrong was in their belief that because so much of *A Shrew* is memorial reconstruction, the rest of it almost certainly is. In particular, he seems to have erred in postulating that because Katherine has two sisters in *A Shrew* (and only one in *The Shrew*), the reporters were trying to reconstruct an earlier form of *The Shrew* in which also there were three sisters. There is not a shred of evidence for this theory – and much to be said against it.

The 'Bad Quartos' that are now seen to be 'reported' texts, in which reconstruction from memory was a large part of the process of composition, have many 'common factors' (those that have been dealt with in the discussion of *A Shrew* above, pp. 14–22). These texts are not, however, alike in all respects. They are produced not by faulty tape-recorders but by human agency, trying to fabricate something saleable, for reading or for acting or both; and even after one reporter has dictated (or written down) – or several reporters have dictated (or written down) – what can be remembered of a play, somebody has to put those reminiscences together. There is room for considerable variety not only in the process of recalling but also in the process of putting together; and the degree of originality shown in the latter would depend both on the amount of material that the

[1] *The Merry Wives of Windsor*, the new Arden edition (London, 1971), pp. xiii–xxxvii.

'editor' (let us call him) had to work with *and* on his own ability. Here was a chance for any man who fancied his literary talents – and that certainly does not exclude one of the reporters or another actor; or here was the opportunity for the reporters, or their potential publisher, to bring in any would-be dramatist, or hack-writer, who would 'make a play' out of the given material for not too heavy a fee. (The interesting suggestion was made some years ago that Henry Chettle, who was one of John Danter's associates and also a minor writer, was called in thus as 'reporter-versifier' of the Bad, 1597, Quarto of *Romeo and Juliet*.[1]) It has been argued above that Hosley was wrong to reject entirely Duthie's theory of an earlier version of *The Shrew*; but in his rejection of the proposed *Ur-Shrew* with a sub-plot different from *The Shrew*'s, he was surely right. *A Shrew* is not 'simply a bad Quarto of *The Shrew*', but we should indeed 'concede that it is of rather a different type from the bad quartos of other Shakespearean plays – an "abnormal" type, that is to say, which involves a good deal more conscious originality on the part of its author or authors than is usually to be observed in bad-quarto texts'.[2]

Perhaps it should be added that 'conscious originality' in such instances does not exclude a great deal of literary borrowing or even plagiarism. The reporters who supplied the 'editor' of *The Taming of a Shrew* with reminiscences of the play in which they had acted certainly contaminated these with lines from other plays in which they had acted (including, of course, some by Marlowe); but the 'editor' himself may also have had a taste for Marlowe, and some inferior 'Marlovian' passages may be his. Similarly, it may have been he rather than the reporter who apparently introduced, into Katherine's final speech, lines from the Sylvester translation of Du Bartas.[3] There are so many *kinds* of composition in a text such as *A Shrew* that no method of analysis is likely to be able to distinguish them all from one another.

It is possible that the reporter of *A Shrew* was more familiar with the Induction and the main plot of *The Shrew* than with the Bianca story – possible, for example, that as H. D. Gray conjectured, the

[1] H. R. Hoppe, *The Bad Quarto of 'Romeo and Juliet'* (Ithaca, N.Y., 1948), p. 220; Sidney Thomas, 'Henry Chettle and the First Quarto of *Romeo and Juliet*', *Review of English Studies*, N.S. 1 (1950), 8–16.

[2] Hosley, 'Sources and Analogues', p. 293.

[3] The borrowing was pointed out by George Coffin Taylor, 'Two Notes on Shakespeare', *Philological Quarterly*, 20 (1941), 373–6.

reporter (if there was only one) took the role of the Tailor, and that he was also one of Petruchio's servants.[1] It is certainly true that the scene with the tailor is better reported than most others in *A Shrew* (though still often 'wrong'); on the other hand, a curious similarity in the wording of at least one stage direction may suggest that the reporter was familiar not simply with an actor's part but with a written form of the main text. *A Shrew*'s 'He [Slie] fals asleepe. | Enter a Noble man and his men | from hunting' (sig. A2) looks like a memorial reconstruction of the author's written *stage direction* and not merely an inference from the dialogue or a recollection of the scene on the stage: F1 has '*Falles asleepe. | Winde hornes. Enter a Lord from hunting, with his traine*' (ll. 17–18). This might suggest that the reporter had served as 'book-holder' or prompter (but there is nothing to say that actors did not share that duty too).

There may seem to be a further problem, in van Dam's claim that the opening stage direction of the play-within-the-play, 'Enter two yoong Gentlemen, and a man and a boie' is that of 'a note-taker ... not yet acquainted with the names of the characters', writing down what he *saw* (van Dam would say, somebody making 'stenographic notes ... during the performance of a play')[2] – but this is exceptional, and the conclusion is not inevitable: the 'editor' beginning to compose – and he *was* composing most of the subplot – could have jotted this down before *he* had decided what names to give to his characters (and he did vary the names from those in *The Shrew*).

In any case, whoever the reporters were, it would not have been difficult for the 'editor' to build a superstructure on their reminiscences and to invent a second sister for Kate. When Hosley argues that 'we need not search for a source or analogue involving three sisters',[3] he is saying that we need not seek them in an *Ur-Shrew* – but even reporters or their editors may be influenced by analogues, or use 'sources', and this is one way in which the Danish and Spanish folk tales, of men who had three daughters, may be of some relevance.[4] For that matter, girls in fairy-story who turn out to

[1] H. D. Gray, '*The Taming of the Shrew*', *Philological Quarterly*, 20 (1941), 329.

[2] *English Studies*, 10, 104.

[3] 'Sources and Analogues', p. 295.

[4] See, e.g., *The Taming of a Shrew* ed. F. S. Boas (London, 1908), Introduction. J. W. Shroeder, 'A New Analogue and Possible Source for *The Taming of a Shrew*', *Shakespeare Quarterly*, 10 (1959), 251–5, unconvincingly adds the tale of Queen Vastis in Caxton's 1484 translation of *Book of the Knight of La Tour Landry* – which concerns only one woman, not three. J. H. Brunvand, 'The Folktale Origin of *The Taming of the Shrew*', *Shakespeare Quarterly*, 17 (1966), 345–59, although more concerned with the taming story, discusses other interesting analogues.

be thoroughly desirable often have two sisters who are at first preferred to them – Cinderella, for one.

Perhaps, then, because not enough 'recollected' material had been given to him to work on, and perhaps because he thought he could go one better than Shakespeare, the 'editor' of *A Shrew* seems to have introduced the third sister on his own initiative to fill out the subplot.[1] In doing this, he had the aid, probably, of folk-tales; and he would have been assisted by the reporter's few vague memories of what had happened in the subplot of *The Shrew*. Presumably this is why he had Valeria sent as a music master to Kate – quite forgetting that Valeria has already been instructed to impersonate his master, Aurelius. He provided a motive, though a weak one (to keep Kate occupied while her sisters were courted); but Kate's threat to break the lute over Valeria's head has little point when Petruchio's counterpart, Ferando, is not there to see it. (Behind this, one infers, was a scene in Shakespeare's first version of *The Shrew* in which, to Petruchio's delight, Kate treated a supposed music master – Tranio, perhaps – as she now treats Hortensio in Act 2 Scene 1.)

If the above argument is correct – that is, if *A Shrew* is a report of an earlier, Shakespearian, form of *The Shrew* in which Hortensio was not disguised as Litio but in which Katherine had only one sister, Bianca, *and* if the third sister never was in any version of the play except *A Shrew* – then most of the difficulties that have been found in other theories disappear.[2] E. K. Chambers's question, why there should be a difference in the names of all the characters except Sly and Kate in the two texts,[3] may perhaps be answered by the suggestion that this time the reporters – and the 'editor' – did see themselves as composing something different from, and better than, the original (and having altered the subplot, they may have felt free to transfer the action from Padua to another seat of learning, Athens, and change the names of the characters as well – not to something Greek but, in the subplot at least, to something more

[1] The discarding of Gremio probably followed from the decision to have three sisters each with one suitor.

[2] S. Thomas, 'A Note on *The Taming of the Shrew*', *Modern Language Notes*, 64 (1949), 94–6, saw another difference between *The Shrew* and *A Shrew* in that (so he said) Grumio is short, Sander not – and suggested that since reporters would not misremember such a fact, there was here confirmatory evidence for an *Ur-Shrew* in which Grumio was *not* short. The evidence will not bear the weight of the argument. The exchange between Sander and the Boy (sigs. C4v–D1v) is conventional stuff, and the boy's threat to cut Sander's leg off has nothing to do with relative tallness.

[3] *William Shakespeare*, i. 327.

obviously romantic, like Phylema, Emelia, Polidor, and Aurelius). Similarly, Alfred Hart's statistics are not odd but are what we should expect: *A Shrew* has fewer words in common with *The Shrew* than, say, Q1 of *Romeo and Juliet* has with Q2, both because the text being recalled is not exactly that of the Folio (and again *The Merry Wives* is the perfect parallel) and because there is in *A Shrew* a greater proportion of original composition. Most important, the doubts of Alexander, Hosley, and J. C. Maxwell about theories that required Shakespeare to have gone back to Gascoigne's *Supposes* for the subplot after the '*Ur-Shrew*' had altered it from that of *Supposes* are shown to be fully justified: nobody but Shakespeare used *Supposes* as a source and it was, as they argued all along, *A Shrew* that made these alterations.[1] But there was an earlier version of *The Shrew*, different from the Folio in *other* ways.

The most interesting question of all, however, remains unanswered and perhaps unanswerable. Did the 'editor' of *A Shrew* 'complete' the Induction by having Sly comment on the action from time to time and by ending the play with him – in the same spirit of 'improving' Shakespeare as that in which he added the third sister? Or was there a full Sly framework in the earlier form of *The Shrew* that *A Shrew* 'reported', and did Shakespeare change his mind about it as he changed his mind about Hortensio (and perhaps – though not necessarily – at the same time)?

There is little evidence on which to base a judgement. Karl Wentersdorf has pointed to what he takes to be two reasons for believing that the full Sly plot was once in the Shakespeare play.[2] One is Sly's announcement in *A Shrew* (sig. C1^{v}) 'O brave, heers two fine gentlewomen' when in fact the two characters who enter are Kate and the supposed music master, Valeria; and the argument is that Sly's words are a reminiscence of the beginning of what is now called Act 2 in the Folio text, where it is Kate and *Bianca* who enter. It may be so – but the order of the action is not quite the same in the two texts at this point and it would seem too stupid even for a reporter to keep 'gentlewomen' and not notice that it was wrong. An alternative explanation remains possible: Sly was to be represented as befuddled once again. The second proffered 'error that bears witness' is the re-

[1] Hart and Hosley as cited; Peter Alexander, 'A Case of Three Sisters', *The Times Literary Supplement*, 8 July 1965; J. C. Maxwell, '*The Shrew* and *A Shrew*: The Suitors and the Sisters', *Notes and Queries*, N.S. 15 (1968), 130–1.

[2] Karl P. Wentersdorf, 'The Original Ending of *The Taming of the Shrew*: A Reconsideration', *Studies in English Literature*, 18 (1978), 201–16.

entry of Katherine, Petruchio, and Grumio at the beginning of 5.2 although they did not leave the stage until the very end of 5.1, particularly as time must be assumed to pass between the two 'scenes'; and the proposed inference is that there was originally a Sly scene in between, as there is in *A Shrew*. Again an alternative explanation may be given of the breaking of what has come to be known as the 'law of immediate re-entry' (itself perhaps a fiction): as is suggested later, in the headnote to 5.2 in this edition, the re-entry of Petruchio and Katherine (and if necessary Grumio) can be slightly delayed. And if Shakespeare was finally prepared to have the immediate re-entry after the excision of the Sly scene, why would he not have been prepared to have it in the first place? The verdict must be 'not proven'. Nor, unfortunately, is there enough material in the Sly scenes that are peculiar to *A Shrew* on which to base a judgement whether, for example, their imagery is likely to have been originally Shakespeare's.

It is, of course, possible to convince *oneself* that the 'additional' Sly scenes of *A Shrew* are too good to have been the invention of a reporter, or – granting that they will have been partly spoilt in the reporting – to be sure that one hears in them from time to time the 'true Shakespearian note' (many readers would cite Sly's refusal to have the culprits sent to prison, quoted earlier in this Introduction on p. 2). What should, however, be resisted is the temptation to believe that if the fuller form of the Induction is held to be the *better*, Shakespeare must necessarily have written it.

It appears reasonably certain that the parts of the Sly story that are not in *The Shrew* were not simply lost. The problem is not of one single leaf missing at the end: there are all the other Sly interpolations to be accounted for. If, then, Shakespeare finally had an 'incomplete' Induction in his play, it would seem to mean *either* that he never had any other, *or* that, having tried the full framework, he afterwards preferred to discard part of it. The reasons for which he might have made that decision are discussed later (pp. 40–3); but it may be suggested even now that a producer of the play in the modern theatre should accept what appears to be Shakespeare's decision, and either leave Sly there silent or, better, somehow get rid of him after 'Act 1 Scene 1'.

Date of composition, the acting companies, and the first performances

Once it is accepted that *A Shrew* is a reported text, it becomes certain that the play of which it is a report must have been acted before the first date on which *A Shrew* is mentioned – namely, the date of entry on the Stationers' Register, 2 May 1594. The statement on the title-page of the first edition of *A Shrew* in 1594 (repeated in the 1596 edition) 'As it was sundry times acted by the Right honorable the Earle of Pembrook his servants' does not necessarily or even probably mean that this company had acted *A Shrew*, any more than the claim on the title-page of the 'Bad' 1597 Quarto of *Romeo and Juliet* 'As it hath been often (with great applause) plaid publiquely, by the right Honourable the L. of Hunsdon his Servants' means that Shakespeare's own company had used the corrupt text and not the authentic one (and the title-page of the 'good' Quarto of 1599 duly notes 'As it hath bene sundry times publiquely acted, by the right Honourable the Lord Chamberlaine his Servants' – the same company under another name). The publishers of Elizabethan title-pages are not on oath, and indeed title-pages were used as advertisements and posted up outside booksellers' shops (they were often therefore printed last and in greater numbers than the other sheets of the book). Even if an attempt had been made in the printed text to improve on the acting version, the publisher was keen to profit from any success the play had had on the stage – and would have been no less anxious to do so when he knew his text to be inferior.

That *The Shrew* had been acted by the Earl of Pembroke's Men probably puts the composition of the play even earlier than 1594. The records of Pembroke's Men are incomplete, and conjecture about them continues but, briefly, the company is first heard of when touring in 1592 and may have been a branch of, or 'splinter group' from, either the companies with which Edward Alleyn was associated (the Admiral's and Strange's) or the Queen's Men.[1] The provincial tour was during a period, the second half of 1592, when the London theatres were closed. Back in London, Pembroke's Men acted at Court on 26 December 1592 and 6 January 1593; but when the theatres were closed a second time, by plague, at the end of

[1] Chambers, *The Elizabethan Stage*, 4 vols. (Oxford, 1923), ii. 129 and *William Shakespeare*, i. 46–55; G. M. Pinciss, 'Shakespeare, Her Majesty's Players, and Pembroke's Men', *Shakespeare Survey* 27 (Cambridge, 1974), 129–36; Scott McMillin, 'Casting for Pembroke's Men: the *Henry VI* Quartos and *The Taming of A Shrew*', *Shakespeare Quarterly*, 23 (1972), 141–59, and 'Simon Jewell and the Queen's Men', *Review of English Studies*, N.S. 27 (1976) 174–7; Karl P. Wentersdorf, 'The Origin and Personnel of the Pembroke Company', *Theatre Research International*, 5 (1979–80), 45–68.

January, they went touring again, as far as Bath and Ludlow. By 28 September, however, they had been back in London for some time and were financially ruined, for Philip Henslowe on that day wrote to his son-in-law Alleyn, himself then on tour with Strange's Men, 'as for my lorde a penbrockes wch you desier to knowe wheare they be they are all at home and hauffe ben this v or sixe weackes for they cane not saue ther carges [i.e. charges] wth trauell as I heare and weare fayne to pane [i.e. pawn] ther parell for ther carge'.[1] (There are later sporadic references to a Pembroke's company in 1595 and 1596, and other references from 1597 to 1600, but this may be a reorganized or different group.) It seems that the original Pembroke's Men, bankrupt, had to break up; and it can hardly be coincidental that four plays bearing their name on the title-page were published in the period July 1593–1595. A fifth, *The First Part of the Contention*, 1594, a 'Bad Quarto' of *2 Henry VI*, does not mention them by name but seems to belong with the other four. The four are Marlowe's *Edward II* (entered on the Stationers' Register 6 July 1593); *Titus Andronicus* (published 1594); *The True Tragedy of Richard Duke of York* (1595 – the reported version of *3 Henry VI*) and *The Taming of a Shrew*. The natural assumption is that all were sold to publishers by actors who desperately needed money;[2] and presumably *The Taming of the Shrew* had been in the possession of Pembroke's Men before they began their country tour late in January 1593, for there is no record of their playing after their return and little likelihood that any new play would have come into their possession then.

There is no call for elaborate theories about companies constructing alternative versions of plays for provincial performances or selling good texts and publishing corrupt ones. Two of the published Pembroke plays, *Edward II* and *Titus Andronicus*, are in fact very good texts, though the other two or three are reported. If the actors had access to a full text, presumably they sold that; if they hadn't, they made one up. When companies disbanded, some arrangement must have been made about the ownership of plays (which companies bought outright from authors) but it is not known what those arrangements were. Apparently the ownership of *The Shrew* went

[1] *Henslowe's Diary*, ed. R. A. Foakes and R. T. Rickert (Cambridge, 1961), p. 280.

[2] *Orlando Furioso* and *The Famous Victories of Henry the Fifth*, both printed in 1594, are other corrupt texts published at the same time, apparently for the same reasons, but perhaps not sold by the same actors.

either to the Admiral's Men or more probably to the Chamberlain's who, as it were, crystallize out as a separate group under a new name at about this time (and there is nothing against the theory that Shakespeare himself was a member of the Pembroke company before he became one of the Chamberlain's Men). Philip Henslowe noted a performance (not marked 'new') at Newington Butts on 11 June 1594 (assumed to be an error for 13 June):

> begininge at newing ton my Lord Admeralle men & my Lorde chamberlen men As ffolowethe 1594
> ... 11 of June 1594 Rd at the tamynge of A shrowe IX s.[1]

(Henslowe's entry may mean that the two companies acted on alternate days or by some special arrangement, rather than that they had combined.) This performance would have been of the genuine Shakespeare play – since Shakespeare's own company is somehow involved – and not of what we mean by *A Shrew*; and *The Shrew* would then have remained continuously in the possession of that company (which later became the King's Men) until the text was published with their full consent in the First Folio of 1623.

Unless there is a flaw in the arguments already advanced, then, *The Taming of the Shrew* cannot be later, in its original Shakespearian form, than 1592. Accordingly, there is no difficulty in accepting the theory that there is an allusion to the play in the line 'He calls his *Kate*, and she must come and kisse him' in the poem by Anthony Chute, *Beawtie Dishonoured written under the title of Shores Wife*, entered on the Stationers' Register on 16 June 1593 – and the reference would be to *The Shrew*, which Chute must have seen acted before the theatres closed in January 1593, for the relevant lines do not appear in *A Shrew*.[2]

It is also possible to believe with Marco Mincoff, if one wishes, that *The Taming of the Shrew* preceded *The Comedy of Errors* – but the date of the latter is most uncertain, and what Mincoff took for greater maturity in the characterization of the submissive wife in it might rather be seen as treatment in a different tone, with a different purpose.[3] The two plays may well belong to the same early period in Shakespeare's career (it has often been noted, for example, that they

[1] *Henslowe's Diary*, pp. 21–2. Nine shillings, incidentally, made a very poor day's takings.

[2] W. H. Moore, 'An Allusion in 1593 to *The Taming of the Shrew?*', *Shakespeare Quarterly*, 15 (1964), 55–60.

[3] 'The Dating of *The Taming of the Shrew*', *English Studies*, 54 (1973), 554–65.

share an occasional tendency to break into rhymed doggerel). What 'internal' evidence would suggest, however, is that neither was his first comedy and that *The Two Gentlemen of Verona*, so elementary in its dramatic techniques, preceded both.[1]

That Francis Meres does not mention *The Taming of the Shrew* in the list of Shakespeare's plays that he gave in *Palladis Tamia* in 1598 is of no significance. It can no longer be strongly argued that Meres did mention it, under the title '*Love labours wonne*': a list made by an Exeter bookseller Christopher Hunt in 1603 included both '*loves labor won*' and '*taming of a shrew*'. These were, then, different plays – and the former has yet to be satisfactorily identified with some other Shakespearian comedy;[2] it may even be a play since lost. What can be said is that Meres was not claiming to name all Shakespeare's plays or even all those known to him: he was listing those that he could neatly pair, and balance against Plautus and Seneca (and, for what it is worth, although he included *Romeo and Juliet*, available in print in 1598 only in a Bad Quarto, he omitted, as well as *The Shrew, Henry VI*, of which two parts had been published but only in reported versions).

Little weight can be given to the suggestion that for the music scene of *The Shrew* (3.1 – where Hortensio presents his gamut to Bianca) Shakespeare relied on Thomas Morley's *A Plaine and Easie Introduction to Practicall Musicke*, published in 1597.[3] Useful as Morley's book is to us for our understanding of Elizabethan music theory, it was not necessary to Shakespeare, and there is nothing in the music scene of *The Shrew* that would not have been commonplace to any Elizabethan with the least smattering of music. There were, too, other, earlier, books on the subject readily available. Even if there were anything in the argument that Shakespeare was indebted to Morley's treatise, what would follow would be only that Shakespeare's change of mind over Hortensio, when he gave Hortensio in disguise the role of the music teacher Litio, was in 1597 or later.[4] Since, however, the evidence is so weak, it may be preferable

[1] See, for example, Stanley Wells, 'The Failure of *The Two Gentlemen of Verona*', *Shakespeare Jahrbuch* (Heidelberg), 99 (1963), 161–73.

[2] *All's Well* and *Much Ado* have been proposed; both seem unsuitable. See, e.g., T. W. Baldwin, *Shakspere's 'Love's Labor's Won'* (Carbondale, 1957).

[3] J. H. Long, 'Shakespeare and Thomas Morley', *Modern Language Notes*, 65 (1950), 17–22.

[4] It would also follow that the less complicated version of the Hortensio story – that reported in *A Shrew* – cannot have been the later.

to rely on impressions of style, and say that since the Litio parts are not distinguishable in manner from the rest of the play, the revision of *The Shrew* more probably took place very early in its history – perhaps as early as 1594 or 1595. (And the hypothesis is that Shakespeare's original 'foul papers' remained in his possession and were used for the revision.)

That the 1594 Quarto, corrupt as it was, was republished in 1596 and 1607 is evidence of the play's popularity but there are not many early references to it. One of these may be Anthony Chute's line, already quoted; another is unimportant, Samuel Rowlands's 'The chiefest Art I have I will bestow | About a worke cald taming of the Shrow'.[1] The most interesting is John Harington's allusion in *The Metamorphosis of Ajax*, 1596: 'For the shrewd wife, reade the booke of taming a shrew, which hath made a number of us so perfect, that now every one can rule a shrew in our countrey, save he that hath her'.[2] Harington is obviously thinking of the published book, *A Shrew*, and has captured the tone of its concluding lines (which is also the tone of the authentic play): the story of the taming is for our amusement; and the world of farce in the theatre is not the 'real' world, nor would any man in his senses think of applying the standards of one to the other.

It is the function of the Induction to make this quite clear.

The story of Christopher Sly

No one source for the 'Induction' of *The Taming of the Shrew* has yet been found, and none need be sought: Shakespeare may well have first heard at his mother's knee some version of the universal tale of how a sleeper or drunken man, when he awoke to find himself dressed in fine clothes, was deceived into believing that he was really a lord, or of some such high rank, and that what he thought to be his memories of his earlier life were delusions. The form of the story most widely known today is that in *The Arabian Nights*, where the Caliph Haroun al Raschid plays the trick on Abu Hassan (and although *The Arabian Nights* as such was not known in Europe until the eighteenth century, it is perhaps worth recalling that the stories in it may have

[1] Quoted by, e.g., Chambers, *William Shakespeare*, i. 328, from *A Whole Crew of Kind Gossips* (1609).

[2] John Harington, *The Metamorphosis of Ajax*, ed. Elizabeth Donno (London, 1962), pp. 153–4.

been collected as early as the fourteenth and in origin may go back many centuries before that).

Discussion of Shakespeare's acquiring of this fable was put on the wrong track years ago when Thomas Warton stated in his *History of English Poetry* (1774–81) that Shakespeare found the story in a collection of prose tales made by Richard Edwards in 1570. Then in the papers of the Shakespeare Society in 1845, H. G. Norton, from loose printed leaves in his possession, published such a tale, calling it 'The Waking Mans Dreame' and assuming that it came from the book by Edwards, of which no copy had ever been seen. In 1913 A. E. Thiselton demonstrated that the tale printed by Norton supposedly from Edwards's (hypothetical) volume was in fact one of a collection of anecdotes, *Admirable Events*, translated by S. Du Verger from the French of J. P. Camus and not published until 1639; but this demonstration went almost unnoticed and the point had to be made again by Charles C. Mish in 1951.[1] The Edwards collection is apparently a 'ghost' – but it haunts many scholarly discussions of Shakespeare's sources written even since 1951.

It is, then, still necessary to say that no printed version of the story has been found earlier than Shakespeare's except the one in Latin by Heuterus, in *De Rebus Burgundicis*, 1584, which Shakespeare is not likely to have known: it was not translated into French, by Goulart, until about 1600, or into English until 1607, by Edward Grimeston. Grimeston's, the version printed by Geoffrey Bullough in his *Narrative and Dramatic Sources of Shakespeare*,[2] tells how Philip the Good, Duke of Burgundy, found 'a certaine Artisan' very drunk in the street, had him carried home to the palace, dressed in fine clothes, conducted to the Mass, waited on there, taken hunting and hawking, and entertained with 'a pleasant Comedie', before being carried back, drunk again, to where he was found. The tale is told in a completely different tone from Shakespeare's, to draw moral lessons about the vanity of state – but one suspects that if it were not safely dated 1607, somebody could long since have 'proved' by verbal parallels that Shakespeare used it. Perhaps some day an earlier translation will be found.

It may be difficult to name a source for the Sly scenes, but it is not

[1] A. E. Thiselton, *The Mystery of the Waking Mans Dreame revealed*, (London, 1913); Charles C. Mish, letter in *The Times Literary Supplement*, 28 December 1951.

[2] *Narrative and Dramatic Sources of Shakespeare* (London, 1957, repr. 1961), i. 109–10.

difficult to appreciate them. From the moment of the entry of Sly and the Hostess – an opening sure to capture the attention of an audience, particularly if Sly reels on to the stage as if he has been thrown out of the alehouse – the pace does not slacken. The tinker's drunken recalcitrance is caught in just a few sentences; his intellectual limitations are well established by his references to Richard Conqueror and Saint Jeronimy and by his fondness for the catch phrases from *The Spanish Tragedy*. Within a few minutes the Lord and his train have come on, and their knowledgeable discussion of the hounds, in technically correct language – but in only fourteen lines – has made the necessary contrast with the peasant and has also added to the already convincing details of life in a 'real' countryside. The plan to deceive Sly is outlined in the firmest of language – noticeable particularly are the precise active verbs, 'take him up', 'carry him', 'hang it round', 'balm his foul head', and so on – and the audience is eager to see what will happen. Not many plays have openings as competent, theatrically, as this: it is, albeit in a completely different tone, comparable with the magnificent beginning of the much later *Othello*.

The entry of the players provides further variety in stage 'action' before plans are worked out both for their share in the tricking of Sly and for the share of the page who is to be Sly's wife. The exchange about Soto makes a private joke with the audience and so helps to maintain its feeling of complicity, in however small a way. Sly is brought forward again, 'aloft', and the interest now is in the psychological changes as he is faced with the new situation. The first mood, after he wakes calling 'For God's sake, a pot of small ale', is the surliness, the truculence that has already been seen: 'call not me "honour" nor "lordship". I ne'er drank sack in my life . . . Ne'er ask me what raiment I'll wear . . . ' and so on. Surliness is succeeded by plain anger, that he should be made a victim of what he naturally assumes to be their mockery of him: 'What, would you make me mad? Am not I Christopher Sly . . . ?' (and there follows the sequence of local allusions, to 'Burton-heath' and Marian Hacket and Wincot, which certainly builds up 'atmosphere', even if Shakespeare is amusing himself at the same time). Then there is a period while the others talk *at* Sly, and he remains silent and presumably perplexed; when he does speak, it is to announce his decision to make the best of it and enjoy both the small ale (he is still, of course, continually giving himself away) and the company of his 'lady'. As Hazlitt delightedly – and delightfully – put it, 'we have a great predilection' for him.[1]

Detailed comment would be superfluous on Sly's guarded dialogue with the servants, or his blunder over the aristocratic way to address a wife ('"Al'ce madam", or "Joan madam"? . . . Madam wife, they say . . . ') or his willingness to watch the comedy to be played before him, though he is none too sure what a comedy is. There is, however, some need for comment on the search for 'meaning' in the Sly section, and on its dramatic function.

Whereas once there would have been general agreement with F. A. Marshall's opinion that *The Taming of the Shrew* 'is the one of Shakespeare's plays most devoid of serious interest, not excepting the *Comedy of Errors*',[2] it has become orthodoxy to claim to find in the Induction the same 'theme' as is to be found in both the Bianca and the Katherine–Petruchio plots of the main play and to take it for granted that identity of theme is a merit and 'justifies' the introduction of Sly. Such a claim is seen in its extreme form in the statement that the three segments of the play 'are all linked in idea because all contain discussion of the relations of the sexes in marriage'.[3] So do *Othello*, and *Hamlet*, and *Macbeth*, and even *King Lear*. The situation is not saved by the statements that *The Shrew* deals with 'different ways of wooing and holding a wife' and portrays 'different kinds of wives and husbands. *The Shrew* becomes thereby a drama with more social and intellectual substance than *The Comedy of Errors*, but in presenting shrewishness and preaching morality it resembles that play.'[4] What *The Shrew* has to say about wooing a wife can be – and in the play itself is – put in a few sentences; and if one were to read the comedy – or *The Comedy of Errors* or for that matter any early Shakespearian comedy – for its 'social and intellectual substance' or to see what it preaches, then – if Dr Johnson's famous phrase about reading the novels of Samuel Richardson for the story may be adapted – 'your impatience would be so much fretted that you would hang yourself'. If, as Meredith said in his *Essay on Comedy*, the test of *true* comedy is that it should awaken *thoughtful* laughter, probably *The Taming of the Shrew* qualifies – but only just.

[1] William Hazlitt, '*The Taming of the Shrew*' in *Characters of Shakespear's Plays* (1817). (*Complete Works*, ed. P. P. Howe, 21 vols., London 1930–4, iv. 345.)

[2] Introduction to the play in *The Works of William Shakespeare*, ed. Henry Irving and F. A. Marshall (New York and London, [1888]), Vol. 2.

[3] Bullough, *Sources*, i. 58.

[4] Ibid.

It is also debatable whether discussion is much advanced by the more widely held theories that the Induction, the Bianca story, and the taming form a unified play because each deals with 'assumptions about identity' and 'assumptions about personality'.[1] An alternative version is that the plots are all based on 'supposes' – the 'counterfeit supposes' of 5.1.106, with the implied reference to Gascoigne's *Supposes*, the source of the Bianca plot.[2] Such theories seem to derive from D. A. Stauffer's suggestion that the play demonstrates that people can become – or, indeed, are – what others think they are or treat them as being. Sly is compared with Katherine: 'there is something deeper than humor, however, in Petruchio's calling Katherine affable, modest, and mild: in the outcome, thinking makes it so'.[3] Is it too late in the day to insist that it is *not* 'thinking' that makes it so – neither Petruchio's nor Katherine's – and that Sly does *not* become what others pretend him to be?

The terms used in all these interpretations are far too wide: the sense in which Sly (for the minute) 'assumes a new personality' is quite different from the sense in which Kate is thought to assume one. Does she in fact ever assume one? Perhaps she merely learns that in certain circumstances certain kinds of behaviour do not work. Bianca, of course, does not assume a new personality at all: Lucentio finally sees her in her true colours, as the audience, if it has any acuity or theatrical experience, will have predicted from the first scene in which she appears. Assumptions about identity and assumptions about personality may be wildly different things. And it is simply not true that 'Sly's story is in effect "finished" when, like Kate, he has been persuaded to accept a new personality'.[4] He remains in the play after that, to watch a comedy – and not only to watch it but also to comment on it: ''Tis a very excellent piece of work, madam lady: would 'twere done!' – and Sly's *attitude to* the play within the play is crucial to the attitude

[1] *The Taming of the Shrew* ed. Richard Hosley, the Pelican Shakespeare (Baltimore, 1964), p. 24. Similarly, Maynard Mack, 'Engagement and Detachment in Shakespeare's Plays', in *Essays on Shakespeare and Elizabethan Drama in honour of Hardin Craig*, ed. Richard Hosley (London, 1963), pp. 279–80. Equally unacceptable is Alexander Leggatt's 'Petruchio, Katherina and the Lord have a special vision, an awareness of life as a game . . . ' (*Shakespeare's Comedy of Love* (London, 1974), p. 62).

[2] C. C. Seronsy, '"Supposes" as the Unifying theme in *The Shrew*', *Shakespeare Quarterly*, 14 (1963), 15–30.

[3] *Shakespeare's World of Images* (New York, 1949), p. 46.

[4] Hosley, Pelican edition (1964), p. 24.

to it of the audience in the 'real' theatre. The Sly Induction does not so much announce the theme of the enclosed stories as establish their *tone*.

There are many reasons for telling a story indirectly or putting it within a framework – as, for example, a play can be enclosed within a play. Sometimes, as in Defoe, the main tale is wrapped up in discussion about the narrator, and the author's knowledge of the veracity of the narrator and so on, as a kind of camouflage, with the aim of causing a reader to quibble, if at all, about what does not matter so that the main story will remain unchallenged. It is a method of making the enclosed story more realistic, more credible. Something similar, although far more sophisticated, is seen in the novels of, say, Joseph Conrad; if Conrad tells us about Marlow who helps with others to tell us about Lord Jim (or Kurtz, in *Heart of Darkness*), it is, partly, that we may believe more readily in the 'truth' of the story and also that attention may be given to the analysis of the complex moral issues that the story raises: Marlow's opinion, among others, is accepted, rejected or modified by the reader only because he for the minute accepts the 'reality' of both Marlow and Jim. The moral or intellectual debate in a sense presupposes the reality of the characters. Similarly, in a less complex and indeed unsophisticated use of the technique, a film or play will start with an 'I remember' followed by a dramatization of what is remembered – the aim again being greater conviction.

More often, however, the 'enclosing' technique works in exactly the opposite way. If in a film the characters go to see a film, the film they see is quite remote: it is at one further move from the 'reality' of the audience in the 'real' cinema. Similarly if a play on a small scale is put within a play, what happens in the enclosed play is not 'believed' at all. Examples would be 'The Mousetrap' in *Hamlet* and 'Pyramus and Thisbe' in *A Midsummer Night's Dream* – both of which, of course, are further 'distanced' by other methods and notably by a deliberately artificial and old fashioned style. Since, however, these are short and in some ways special, it may be better to look for a parallel to the technique of *The Shrew* in a play in which the enclosed story is the longer and the enclosing story apparently no more than a way of introducing it. Just such a play is George Peele's *The Old Wives Tale*, the exact date of which is uncertain but which undoubtedly belongs within a few years of *The Shrew*. In Peele's play as in Shakespeare's the audience is introduced in the Induction to realistically drawn rustics who are contrasted with more aristocratic and intellectual types; and Peele's delightfully down-to-earth Old Wife, Madge, begins to tell a typical old wife's tale which is then, as it were, acted out for her by the players, with all the inconsecutiveness and the crossed lines of the story as it would be if she told it. And, of course, we do not 'believe' a word of it, and have been told not to believe it – and enjoy it the more. *The Taming of the Shrew* is in some ways very similar: the enclosed story is not told by an uninformed and unimaginative rustic but it is put on to amuse one; we 'believe' in Sly but do not really believe in Lucentio, or Bianca – or Petruchio. The phenomenon of theatrical illusion is itself being laughed at; and the play within the play makes Sly drowsy and probably soon sends him to sleep. Are we to let *that* play 'preach morality' to us or look in it for 'social and intellectual substance'? The drunken tinker may be believed in as one believes in any realistically presented character; but we cannot 'believe' in something that is not even mildly interesting to him. The play within the play has been presented only after all the preliminaries have encouraged us to take it as a farce (meaning by that not slapstick, but a broader kind of comedy not involving 'engagement' with the characters). We have been warned.

Why, then, having begun the Induction, might Shakespeare have decided not to continue with it to the end; or – what is for this purpose much the same question – if he did at first continue with it, in a form of which *A Shrew* gives us some idea, albeit inadequate, why might he have changed his mind and decided to cut it short?

There are, in the first place, some purely practical, theatrical, considerations that may have weighed with him. It has been suggested, for example, that there was a staging problem because the presence of Sly and the 'presenters' 'aloft' made the use of the 'upper stage' for another purpose difficult; and the raised acting area does seem to be needed again in 5.1 when, as F1 has it, the '*Pedant lookes out of the window*' (l. 2397).[1] There may be something in this, although not enough is certain about the 'upper stage' in Elizabethan theatres for the argument to carry full conviction; it was not necessarily impossible to keep Sly's party well away from the 'window' required for the

[1] So, for instance, Bond, in the original (1904) Arden edition, p. 33. The New Cambridge editors were inclined to add 4.1 – surely unnecessarily (p. 142). For further discussion of the staging, see the headnote on Induction 2 in the present edition and, in a wider context, Richard Hosley, 'Shakespeare's Use of a Gallery over the Stage', *Shakespeare Survey 10* (Cambridge, 1957), 77–89.

Pedant. (Conceivably the form of the Induction in *A Shrew*, which has Sly on the main stage throughout, represents some intermediate, experimental version that tried to get over the problem of the differing uses of the area 'aloft'; alternatively, as has been suggested above (pp. 21–2), the compilers of *A Shrew* – *if* they were thinking that the text they compiled might be acted by, for example, touring companies – may have had in mind the limitations of stages and theatres *other than* those for which the Shakespeare play was written.)

The staging would not seem to have been so difficult as to make necessary by itself the decision not to continue the Sly story after Act 1 Scene 1. A greater difficulty was, perhaps, casting, although again it cannot be said that an Elizabethan company could not have coped with the problems of the full framework (including in that phrase both the carrying through of Sly's comments as in *A Shrew* and the alternative possibility of leaving him and others, even though they remain silent, in view of the audience throughout). If the actors of Sly, the Lord, and the Page in the Induction are not available to play other roles, then *The Taming of the Shrew* requires a cast of sixteen to play named parts (plus a few odd servants), of whom at least four would be boys (the Page, Kate, Bianca, the Widow) – five if a boy played Biondello; and it may have been necessary – if the company could not rise to this number – to introduce some doubling, not merely by ending the Sly story when it does end in the Folio text but also by getting him and his fellow presenters off the stage altogether.[1] One caveat may be entered: it has perhaps been too readily assumed that because the Lord remains on the stage with Sly in *A Shrew*, he must remain with Sly, if Sly remains, in *The Shrew*. This is not so. The Lord could leave the Induction for the last time at 2.114 and be available for Vincentio or any other role thereafter, unless he is made to be the 'Messenger' of Induction 2.125.1 (itself involving an almost impossibly rapid change of costume) and also the '1. *Man.*' who is one of the 'Presenters' still watching the play at the end of 1.1.[2] If these two very minor roles are given to a minor actor or hired man, then only

[1] Discussions of the casting include Richard Hosley, 'Was there a Dramatic Epilogue to *The Taming of the Shrew?*', *Studies in English Literature*, 1 (1961), 17–34; Karl P. Wentersdorf, 'The Original Ending of *The Taming of the Shrew*: A Reconsideration', *Studies in English Literature*, 18 (1978), 201–16; and William A. Ringler, 'The Number of Actors in Shakespeare's Early Plays', in *The Seventeenth-Century Stage*, ed. G. E. Bentley (Chicago, 1968), 110–36.

[2] See the notes on Induction 2.114.1 and 125.1 and 1.1.246.1.

Sly and the boy-Page-'wife' are being 'wasted' if they are kept on stage; but certainly if they are removed from the view of the audience, 'Sly' can play the Pedant later, and the boy can play the Widow in the final scene.[1] (Perhaps it should be added – in view of some rather wild theorizing about Sly's 'dream' – that the actor playing Sly cannot conceivably play Petruchio if the Folio text is adhered to; Sly must 'sit and marke', at least for a while, and the very first thing he is required to mark is the entrance of Petruchio.[2]) William Ringler's analysis of *The Two Gentlemen of Verona*, however, has suggested that Shakespeare as a young dramatist did not always use his actors economically, and has shown that he probably could count on twelve adult actors and four boys if he really needed them. It may therefore be wiser to look beyond the casting, as well as the stage, for explanations of the dramatist's final preference for the 'incomplete' framework and to consider the possibility that the final form of the play is in fact the better for aesthetic reasons.

If what has been argued earlier in this Introduction is correct, the main purpose of the Induction was to set the tone for the play-within-the-play – in particular, to present the story of Kate and her sister as a none-too-serious comedy put on to divert a drunken tinker. The artificial style of the beginning of 1.1 is perhaps further indication that we are not expected to become too involved in the Lucentio–Bianca–disguises plot; we are told that it more or less put Sly to sleep; and only then are we invited to watch also Petruchio's campaign to tame the shrew. As that tale goes on and especially when Kate is introduced, it gradually changes key and it does become, for a while, more realistic and convincing (and an attempt will be made later to justify this claim); but it never for long loses its basically farcical character, and it ends, perfectly logically for a farce, with the shrew not only tamed but also prepared to instruct the untamed wives on the social desirability of tameness. That last scene *has* been taken literally by, for example, G. I. Duthie, who wrote that 'What Shakespeare emphasizes here is the foolishness of trying to destroy order'.[3] He can take such a view, however, only because for

[1] One minor textual point may be made here. The Pedant is listed as entering in 5.2 but says not one word. Is that because he originally played a speaking part there, but was removed from the scene although accidentally left in the opening stage direction?

[2] Nevertheless it has been known for one actor to double the parts – notably Oscar Asche; and Jonathan Pryce played both, in a controversial Royal Shakespeare Company production, as recently as 1978.

[3] G. I. Duthie, *Shakespeare* (London, 1951), p. 59.

him the Induction is finally irrelevant (indeed, in this discussion he does not so much as mention its existence); for him, all the hints about the nature of theatrical illusion have been in vain; because Kate is straightfaced, he believes what she has said. Others, holding that 'the best in this kind are but shadows', as Shakespeare was to put it later, and remembering that this particular shadow was for the amusement of a shadow, will have their doubts.

The play as it stands is, in modern jargon, 'open-ended' – and it is made not more 'open' but less so by having Sly, in a final scene, convinced that he now knows how to tame a shrew and by having Sly's friend not so sure. The reintroduction of the presenters would also, as has been suggested by several modern critics, run the risk of anti-climax and, one might add, of seeming to gild the lily. One does not improve a farce by ending it with the reminder that it may have been only a farce; far better to let the audience make that judgement, if it wishes to make it.

Perhaps Shakespeare first tried the play with the full Sly framework, perhaps he did not; but at least one can say that he seems to have had very good reasons for his apparent decision to leave it 'incomplete' as it is now in the approved text and (probably) to get Sly out of view of the audience early in the play and let them forget him – until perhaps they have left the theatre and have time to wonder what happened to him and even, perhaps, what has happened to them.

The Bianca subplot and 'supposes'

At least there is no dispute about the main source for the part of *The Taming of the Shrew* that deals with Bianca and her suitors. Shakespeare even alludes to it, and paraphrases it, when he has Lucentio reveal his identity, with the words:

> Here's Lucentio,
> Right son to the right Vincentio,
> That have by marriage made thy daughter mine,
> While counterfeit supposes bleared thine eyne
> (5.1.103–6).[1]

The source was George Gascoigne's *Supposes*. Its title-page describes it as 'a Comedie written in the Italian tongue by Ariosto Englished by

[1] See notes on these lines.

George Gascoygne of Grayes Inne Esquire, and there presented 1566' (and there is an apparent record of a later private performance at Oxford, in Trinity College, in January 1582[1]). Gascoigne was translating Ariosto's *I Suppositi* in the original prose version in which it was acted at Ferrara in 1509 and at the Vatican in 1519 (although he may have known also Ariosto's rewriting of it in verse) and his translation is thought to be the first English drama in prose (it anticipates Lyly by nearly twenty years). Gascoigne's play was easily available to Shakespeare, particularly in the collections *The Posies of G. Gascoigne* (1575)[2] and *The Whole Woorkes of G. Gascoigne* (1587).

In the Ariosto–Gascoigne story, Erostrato [Shakespeare's Lucentio], after falling in love at first sight, has enjoyed for some time a secret liaison with Polynesta [Shakespeare's Bianca], daughter of Damon [Baptista]. Erostrato is able to arrange meetings because in disguise he has been employed by Damon as a servant, Dulipo, while Erostrato's real servant Dulipo [Tranio] pretends to be the master Erostrato. The feigned Erostrato pretends to woo the girl, as a way of frustrating a rival suitor, the aged Cleander [Gremio]. These two try to outbid each other with offers of lavish dowries; and to support his claim Erostrato persuades a travelling stranger [the Pedant] to impersonate his real father Philogano [Vincentio]. Erostrato arranges this both by pretending that because of a ducal decision it is dangerous for a Sienese to be found in Ferrara and by offering protection if the stranger will impersonate the father. Matters come to a head when Polynesta is found to be pregnant (Shakespeare altered this, of course: he obviously wanted for his second female character one who to appearance had all the marks of the romantic heroine). Dulipo is put into a dungeon (too 'serious' a fate for Shakespeare's kind of comedy); from Sicily[3] arrives 'the right Philogano the right father of the right Erostrato', to find both that Dulipo is impersonating Erostrato and that a stranger is impersonating Erostrato's father, namely himself; but finally all is solved, and true identities

[1] Chambers, *Elizabethan Stage*, iii. 321.

[2] This is the version printed by Bullough in *Narrative and Dramatic Sources of Shakespeare* i. 111–58 and quoted in the present edition.

[3] Incidentally – lest Shakespeare alone be thought guilty of ignorance of Italy – Philogano has come to Ferrara via Ancona, 'from thence by water to *Ravenna*, and from *Ravenna* hither, continually against the tide'. (The journey has to be made to appear onerous.)

revealed, and Cleander [Gremio] even discovers that Dulipo is the son he lost long ago after the battle of Otranto (and Shakespeare chose to avoid that improbability, which adds nothing of import to the story). For one character who looms large in the source but hardly affects the action – the typical parasite of classical comedy, Pasiphilo – Shakespeare found no place at all; nor did his Bianca (since she was not pregnant) need a confidant-nurse. His main addition, which perhaps he saw as an alternative to these superfluous characters, was to complicate the action by giving Bianca a third suitor, Hortensio; and then – on second thoughts, if the argument of the earlier part of this Introduction is correct – he complicated it further by having Hortensio assume the disguise of Litio to compete with Erostrato/Lucentio in disguise as Cambio. In short, he added still more 'supposes' to those of which Gascoigne already thought so highly that he put notes in the margin pointing them out lest the reader should miss any.[1]

Gascoigne, as part of a whole series of quibbles on his title, explained in his 'Prologue or Argument': 'But understand, this our Suppose is nothing else but a mystaking or imagination of one thing for an other. For you shall see the master supposed for the servant, the servant for the master: the freeman for a slave, and the bondslave for a freeman: the stranger for a well knowen friend, and the familiar for a stranger.' His audience is kept amused by the misconceptions of the characters – as in the Plautine comedies of which *Supposes* is a direct descendant[2] – and is not invited (unless it be by the strong *suspicion* of irony in the Prologue and the marginal notes) to wonder if it has misconceptions of its own. The interest, in short, is not in characterization but in plot, the audience watching to see what happens next and how the knots are untied.

The Bianca section of Shakespeare's play, for the most part, is no

[1] Still another 'suppose', in a sense, is Lucentio's wooing of Bianca while pretending to teach her Latin (3.1.27–43), a scene that Furnivall (and others since) thought to be borrowed from a speech in R. W[ilson]'s *Three Lords and Three Ladies of London* (1590). The speech in question is Simplicity's to Pleasure: 'O *singulariter nominativo*, wise Lord Pleasure: *genitivo*, bind him [Fraud] to that post; *dativo*, give me my torch; *accusativo*, for I say he's a usurer; *vocativo*, O give me leave to run at him; *ablativo*, take and blind me' (Dodsley's *Old English Plays*, revised W. C. Hazlitt, London, 1874, vi. 500). Shakespeare's certainly has more point, and more humour, and may have led in turn to the Latin lesson in *The Merry Wives of Windsor*. See also note on 4.1.130–1.

[2] See, e.g., R. W. Bond, *Early Plays from the Italian* (Oxford, 1911).

different.[1] It is the kind of comedy that he attempted also in *The Comedy of Errors*, with its two pairs of identical twins (this time beginning from Plautus' *Mostellaria*); he attempted it again – albeit in a very different tone – in the parts of *A Midsummer Night's Dream* that follow from the anointing of the wrong lover's eyes with the juice of the magic flower, so that Demetrius and Lysander are temporarily infatuated with the wrong women. Being Shakespeare, he carried it off. A reader's head sometimes spins as he tries to remember whether Lucentio is Cambio or Litio and momentarily confuses the names of Grumio and Gremio – but in the theatre all is clear, and the pace of the action is well maintained. Indeed it is increased towards the end and particularly in 5.1, where one seeming disaster after another falls on the bewildered Vincentio: he himself is being impersonated by a complete stranger; his son Lucentio's servant Biondello claims never to have seen him before; the other servant Tranio, whom he brought up in his own house, claims to be Lucentio; and for all this he, Vincentio, is threatened with imprisonment, until the problem is solved by Biondello's unfortunate entrance (unfortunate for Biondello) with Lucentio and Bianca, and his prompt exit with Tranio and the false father 'as fast as may be'. It is all very fast indeed.

Interestingly, it is in this scene that Shakespeare seems to have worked most closely from Gascoigne. He even borrows such a small detail as having the real father knock in vain at the door for admittance to his own son's dwelling and be greeted by a stranger looking out of the window (although in *Supposes* the stranger is a servant and not the feigned father). There are also verbal reminiscences, albeit of commonplace phrases. One example is Philogano's 'What hast thou done with my son villain?'; Vincentio's 'Tell me, thou villain, where is my son . . . ?' with the same expressed fear that the son has been murdered by his former servant. Another is Gascoigne's Philogano to his own servant: 'Do you not know me?' 'As farre as I remember Sir, I never saw you before'; Shakespeare's Vincentio: 'What, have you forgot me?' 'Forgot you? No, sir. I could not forget you, for I never saw you before in all my life.'

This last example, with its improvement on Gascoigne in its colloquial tone and the balance of its calculated repetitions, is

[1] It should be added that W. E. Harrold's analysis of the relationship of Plautus' *Mostellaria* to *A Shrew* and *The Shrew* fails to give reason for altering the generally accepted opinion that Shakespeare borrowed *directly* from Plautus only the names of Tranio and Grumio. ('Shakespeare's Use of *Mostellaria* in *The Taming of the Shrew*', *Shakespeare Jahrbuch*, Heidelberg, 1970, 188–94.)

sufficient warning against equating Shakespeare with his sources. It is also noticeable how he avoids the traps into which others fall: he will not slow up the scene just discussed, for instance, or falsify its tone, by introducing passages of self-pity amounting to attempted pathos, such as 'Alas, who shall relieve my miserable estate? to whom shall I complaine? . . . Alas, you might have some compassion of mine age . . . '. Nevertheless it remains true that it is the Gascoigne kind of comedy that he is writing in the Bianca scenes; and (although a few caveats to this judgement will be entered later, in the general discussion of the style) he does not attempt to alter that kind by elevating or enriching the language. It would not have been an improvement for Bianca to speak or be described in genuinely romantic terms; on the contrary, she must be seen, at first, as nothing but the conventional heroine sought by the hero of fiction, and in this capacity she will be contrasted with another type of woman, at first much less attractive, her spirited 'real-life' sister Kate.

Shakespeare is not content, however, to leave it at that. He does not merely contrast one sister with another: he uses the younger as part of the explanation of the acquired shrewishness of the elder, and so – for better or worse – also uses Bianca in a 'realistic' way. In particular there is psychological realism in the scenes in which Katherine resents not only Bianca's success with her 'pretty' tricks, and Baptista's treatment of his favourite, younger, daughter, so different from the way he treats the elder ('Why, and I trust I may go too, may I not?', 1.1.102) but also Bianca's very meekness. Words like 'what you will command me will I do, | So well I know my duty to my elders' (2.1.6–7), and the offer to pull off her 'raiment' if Katherine wants her to do so, might well, if a phrase from elsewhere in the play may be purloined, 'vex a very saint', let alone a girl of Katherine's 'impatient humour'; understandably, they infuriate her. The audience, moreover, has the opportunity of seeing Bianca 'in action' with her suitors Lucentio and Hortensio/Litio. (The suddenness of Lucentio's infatuation with her, incidentally, on the strength of her beauty, her 'dutiful' behaviour, and the four lines he has heard her speak may not be mere dramatic casualness: it may be part of Shakespeare's characterizing of the kind of lover other literature asks one to admire.[1]) In 3.1 it is a very self-possessed young lady who

[1] The casualness may be elsewhere – in having Lucentio refuse to give a reason for ordering Tranio to pretend to be a suitor to Bianca (1.1.244–6) – although it turns out to be a useful arrangement.

manages both Lucentio and Hortensio to her own satisfaction, insists on the right to please herself about her lessons, and gives Lucentio the encouragement that she could not in all modesty give if she were what she pretended to be in the earlier scenes. His 'reward' proves to be a wife who is not only 'disobedient' (to the extent of losing him his wager) but also capable of spitting at him 'the more fool you for laying on my duty'.

The second function of the Bianca story, then, is to help explain how Kate has *become* a shrew. It serves also to make us more sympathetic with Kate by contrast – and presumably that is what Shakespeare intended (although it may have landed him in difficulties of another kind, to be discussed later). And it is all done with amazing economy: has it always been realized how very few lines Bianca has in the play and how short her speeches tend to be?

On the level of mere narrative, the Bianca 'plot' connects with the Katherine story when Bianca's wooers support the suit of Petruchio because of their interest in having Kate married off first, that Bianca may become available; and the two groups of characters compete in the final scene. It is clear, however, that there are links of the other kinds, discussed above; and Dr Johnson may not have been exaggerating as much as is often thought, if he had those others in mind when he made his famous statement that 'of this play the two plots are so well united that they can hardly be called two without injury to the art with which they are interwoven. The attention is entertained with all the variety of a double plot, yet is not distracted by unconnected incidents.'

Katherine and Petruchio

Continuation of the search for a 'source' of Petruchio's taming of Katherine may well be pointless. There were shrews galore in literature long before Shakespeare – tamed and untamed. Petruchio himself refers to the wife of Socrates, Xanthippe, whom literary tradition rather than any ascertainable facts had made into the very symbol of the nagging wife; and in earlier English drama, tradition again seems to have determined that Noah's wife in the religious cycles should be a termagant and almost as great a trial to her husband as was the Deluge. There are shrews in Old English verse, and in Chaucer, in medieval tales, in Persian literature, in popular Italian stories, in Danish and other folklore; and probably there were shrews in many a stage farce. It is even possible to speculate whether there may not have been a stock costume to identify the character as soon as she appeared on the stage.

Peter Alexander and others were convinced that Richard Hosley had identified *the* source of the taming story when he again drew attention to a ballad that had been well known to earlier scholars such as Frey, W. C. Hazlitt, Boas, and Bond but rejected by them as the probable origin.[1] This is the verse tale *A Merry Jest of a Shrewde and Curste Wyfe, Lapped in Morrelle's Skin, for Her Good Behavyour.* The alleged parallels, however, can be overstated, and Hosley himself seems to have withdrawn to a more easily defensible position and is content to say in his edition of the play (in the Complete Pelican Shakespeare, 1969, p. 81) that the ballad perhaps 'suggested the basic framework' of Shakespeare's comedy. The verse tale has a shrew – likened to a fiend or devil – with a meek younger sister who is the father's favourite; after the wedding, the shrew returns with her husband to his house in the country; and after the taming the newly-reformed shrew's 'good behaviour' is a subject for surprise at a family dinner. But the verbal parallels seldom, if ever, go beyond the standard phrases that one would expect to find in such a story; and as Hosley is the first to point out, the method and spirit of Petruchio's taming of Kate is very different from that of the husband who tears off his wife's clothes, 'beats her with birch rods till the blood runs on the floor and she faints, and then wraps her in the skin of an old lame plough-horse, Morel, killed and flayed especially for the occasion' (p. 296).

A stronger case is made by J. H. Brunvand who argues most convincingly that Shakespeare did not *need* a literary source for his taming story and that he is much more likely to have drawn on oral tradition (although oral tradition may always be recorded in a printed text and perhaps one such has been lost). There is no incident in the Petruchio–Katherine story that Shakespeare needed to invent; on the contrary, the highest common factors, so to speak, of relevant folk-tales include the arrival of the groom at the wedding in poor clothes, the wife's having to learn to swear that black is white if her husband says it is, the wager on her obedience, and even

[1] Richard Hosley, 'Sources and Analogues of *The Taming of the Shrew*', *Huntington Library Quarterly*, 27 (1964), 289–308. The ballad is most easily found in W. C. Hazlitt's *Shakespeare's Library* (London, 1875), Vol. 4.

the treading on her cap as proof of it.[1] The further significance of this may be – how can one know? – that the Elizabethan audience came to see Shakespeare's play 'pre-conditioned', as we might say, to enjoy the spectacle of the taming of one on whom they would not expect to waste a moment's sympathy – just as they presumably came to see revenge-plays, not excluding *Hamlet*, knowing what the rough outline of the story would be, knowing that the revenger could not be allowed to survive, but still fascinated to see, *inter alia*, how the dramatist filled in the given outline.

Theories of minor sources that Shakespeare may have used also fall far short of proof. Of the three verbal parallels that have been found[2] with Erasmus's *Colloquies*, for example, two are actually listed by Tilley as proverbs. What works such as this really demonstrate, as Hosley also well points out (p. 299), is that 'the business of "training" a wife to accept a viable social relationship to her husband, as one would teach a colt to go through its paces or a hawk to fly to the lure, is a commonplace of humanist discussions of marriage'. Indeed, they probably all trace back to the Bible, from which Katherine more or less quotes in her final speech.

A reference to a suppressed ballad called 'The taminge of a shrewe' in the Stationers' Company's Decrees and Ordinances for 1596 is now suspected of being a forgery[3] and many of the other suggested sources or analogues seem much less likely after Brunvand's demonstration of the strength and detail of the oral tradition. It is clearly more profitable on all counts to consider what Shakespeare did with the taming story.

Literary tradition perhaps prepared Shakespeare's audience, going to *The Taming of the Shrew*, to expect a farce; the Induction certainly did not invite them to become deeply involved with the characters of the inset play; the very costume worn by the boy playing Katherine may have identified her as nothing but a shrew: in short, there may have been as much likelihood of the audience's sympathizing with Katherine, when she first appeared on the stage, as there is of a twentieth-century music-hall audience's feeling sorry for a mother-in-law. The very first words addressed to Kate also take

[1] J. H. Brunvand, 'The Folktale Origin of *The Taming of the Shrew*', *Shakespeare Quarterly*, 17 (1966), 345–59.

[2] W. S. Walker, *A Critical Examination of the Text of Shakespeare*, 3 vols. (London, 1860), iii. 70; Hosley, pp. 299–300; Kenneth Muir, *The Sources of Shakespeare's Plays* (London, 1977), pp. 20–1.

[3] Chambers, *William Shakespeare*, i. 328; ii. 391–2.

it for granted that she has no humanity: Gremio's reply to Baptista's invitation to court his elder daughter is 'To cart her rather. She's too rough for me' – which virtually calls Kate to her face a prostitute; Hortensio classes her among 'devils'; Tranio can believe only that she is 'stark mad, or wonderful froward'; Gremio brands her a 'fiend of hell'. Yet already a modern audience, at any rate, has made a mental reservation. Kate's own first words, to her father, 'I pray you, sir, is it your will | To make a stale of me amongst these mates' – with their resentment at Gremio's insult and their feeling that a father might well resent it too – seem reasonable enough and, what is more, deserving of sympathy.

That, in brief, is the main problem in understanding or interpreting the play. It is as if Shakespeare set out to write a farce about taming a shrew but had hardly begun before he asked himself what might make a woman shrewish anyway – and found his first answer in her home background. Just as, later, his portraits of Capulet, Lady Capulet, and the Nurse were to serve to arouse pity for the young Juliet, tragically thrown back on her own resources, so here the sketches of the spoilt younger daughter and of the father lacking in discernment (but perhaps not in good will – one may agree with R. B. Heilman that Baptista is not the villain of the piece[1]) help the audience to understand what Baptista does not – and *tout comprendre, c'est tout pardonner*. We sympathize with Katherine – and as soon as we do, farce becomes impossible. Just as Shakespeare, when he wrote *The Two Gentlemen of Verona*, tried to dramatize materials from prose romances which had been acceptable precisely because the characters had no character – and had made the story unacceptable as soon as he did introduce character (it is one thing for a puppet hero to offer to hand over his puppet-like beloved to his best friend but quite another for Valentine to offer *Silvia* to *Proteus*), so in *The Taming of the Shrew* he was dramatizing material from unrealistic literature that was perfectly acceptable on the level of the Punch and Judy show but ran the risk of embarrassing as soon as it rose above that level. We may laugh at Punch's hitting Judy on the head in the puppet play but it is not so easy to laugh at Petruchio's taming of Katherine. As M. R. Ridley put it: if it were all farce 'our subtler feelings would lie contentedly quiescent. . . . But Shakespeare, being Shakespeare, cannot restrain his hand from making Petruchio more

[1] 'The *Taming* Untamed, or, the Return of the Shrew', *Modern Language Quarterly*, 27 (1966), 147–61.

of a man, and Katharine more of a woman, than from the artistic point of view was wise; and so Petruchio's bullying of Katharine, funny though it would be if they were mere marionettes, and effective and indeed salutary though it is in its results, leaves a slightly unpleasant taste in the mouth.'[1] It is not necessary to agree with this in detail – for example, about Petruchio – in order to agree with it in general. In other words, Shakespeare was already too good a dramatist for the material he was dramatizing: characterization and farce are, finally, incompatible.

Finding itself in this dilemma, the average audience seems to decide to get as much enjoyment as it can from the farce – trying, as it were, to keep its sympathy with Katherine in a state of suspense (paradoxically, a suspension of belief, in the interests of enjoying what is not to be believed). And on the level of farce, *The Taming of the Shrew* is, generally, superb; and in so far as one can put sympathy aside and watch the taming of Kate as one might watch the taming of a falcon or wild beast (although even that presents problems to an audience more sensitive than Shakespeare's to cruelty to animals), one can 'enjoy' Petruchio.

He, of course, is the 'right' man for the task – and it is difficult to understand the objections to Peter Alexander's statement that the story is, among other things, a variation on 'the perilous maiden theme, where the lady is death to any suitor who woos her except the hero, in whose hands her apparent vices turn to virtues'.[2] As Curtis infers, hearing of Petruchio's behaviour, 'he is more shrew than she' (4.1.75); or as Grumio puts it, 'an she knew him as well as I do, she would think scolding would do little good upon him' (1.2.107–8); as Peter sums it up, 'he kills her in her own humour' (4.1.168) (and not, surely, as the sentimental modern orthodoxy believes, by *burlesquing* her behaviour, so that she sees herself as others see her, and finally 'sees the joke',[3] but by standing over her and proving that with him shrewishness simply will not work).

For his role as tamer, he has all the necessary attributes. For example, he is mature: 'Yet you are withered', Kate taunts him, and he replies ''Tis with cares' (2.1.238) – and although in most modern productions Kate is played by a sophisticated actress in her twenties

[1] *William Shakespeare. A Commentary*, Introductory Volume to the New Temple Shakespeare (London, 1936), p. 24.

[2] *Shakespeare's Life and Art* (London, 1939), p. 71.

[3] Hardin Craig, *An Interpretation of Shakespeare* (New York, 1948), p. 90.

or thirties, Shakespeare may well have thought of her as about sixteen. She is older than Bianca – but then on the evidence of other Shakespeare comedies Bianca would be thought marriageable at fourteen – and Kate's tantrums as well as Petruchio's treatment of them may seem rather more credible if she, too, in her own way is a spoilt child. However that may be, she certainly thinks of Petruchio, in the line just quoted, as older than she is. He also claims – and there is no reason to doubt the claim – a wide range of dangerous experience:

> Have I not in my time heard lions roar? . . .
> Have I not heard great ordnance in the field . . .
> And do you tell me of a woman's tongue . . .?
> Tush, tush, fear boys with bugs!

– and Grumio adds 'For he fears none' (1.2.196–206).

In the tradition of the best tamers, he is quite without sentiment:

> I come to wive it wealthily in Padua;
> If wealthily, then happily in Padua
> (1.2.74–5)

and insists that his prospective father-in-law come to the point:

> Then tell me, if I get your daughter's love,
> What dowry shall I have with her to wife?
> (2.1.118–19).

It is apparently not even beneath his dignity to bargain with Bianca's wooers that if they want Katherine out of the way, they shall pay the expenses of his courtship of her.

If he lacks sentiment, however, he is certainly capable of appreciating strength in a woman's character, including strength of resistance, and when he hears of Kate's breaking of the lute over Hortensio's head proclaims:

> Now by the world, it is a lusty wench;
> I love her ten times more than e'er I did.
> O how I long to have some chat with her!
> (2.1.159–61).

Love, of course, has nothing to do with the case, and there is no place for love in a farce; but he does admire, and he welcomes the challenge of prospective strong opposition. Kate is like him in that respect: the implication of their first meeting and its prolonged and rather tedious exchange of insults is that she is at least interested in him, almost in spite of herself, and welcomes his un-Hortensio-like refusal to cower.

Petruchio has one other quality invaluable in a tamer – the ability to make a plan, and to keep to it. Just before their first meeting he announces, in soliloquy, his proposed strategy of calculated opposition:

> Say that she rail, why then I'll tell her plain
> She sings as sweetly as a nightingale...
> If she deny to wed, I'll crave the day
> When I shall ask the banns, and when be marrièd
> (2.1.169–79);

he tells her to her face what he proposes to do:

> For I am he am born to tame you, Kate,
> And bring you from a wild Kate to a Kate
> Conformable as other household Kates
> (2.1.275–7)

and then, again in soliloquy, when the programme is in operation, explains exactly how he is carrying out the plan 'to man my haggard' (4.1.175–98). Nothing is accidental, nothing unpredicted; and Hazlitt summed it up perfectly when he said that 'There is no contending with a person on whom nothing makes any impression but his own purposes, and who is bent on his own whims just in proportion as they seem to want common sense. With him a thing's being plain and reasonable is a reason against it.... The whole of his treatment of his wife at home is in the same spirit of ironical attention and inverted gallantry.'[1]

Katherine learns that it is no use hitting him, as she might hit Hortensio, for 'I swear I'll cuff you if you strike again' (2.1.222); it is no use being shrewish when he has announced that it is their agreement that she shall be so in public; it is no use refusing to go with him after the wedding when he pretends that he is rescuing her from those who might help her to stay; it is no use claiming to be the injured party when he thanks the wedding guests who 'have beheld me give away myself | To this most patient, sweet, and virtuous wife' (3.2.193–4); it is no use complaining that food is denied when it is

[1] William Hazlitt, '*The Taming of the Shrew*', in *Characters of Shakespear's Plays* (*Complete Works*, iv. 343).

said to be bad for her health. Petruchio's campaign has already passed the point of possible failure when the assurance is given, in 4.1.68–70, that for the first time she was more concerned with somebody else – Grumio – than with herself ('how she waded through the dirt to pluck him off me'); and soon afterwards she is seen trying to defend the servants from her husband's (feigned) anger.

There is nothing to warrant an assumption that – at this stage, at any rate – Katherine and Petruchio are merely 'playing a game'. She *is* being *tamed*, and the spectacle would be acceptable if, but only if, Katherine had no feelings and the audience had no concern for *her*.[1] In fact, however, Shakespeare sometimes dramatizes Kate's genuine distress. No modern playgoer can fail to sympathize with her, part of the time at least, and – difficult as such questions are – it is not easy to believe that the Elizabethan audience was always on Petruchio's side.

A crucial scene is the wedding. Katherine's words when her bridegroom does not appear for the ceremony are bound to arouse compassion:

> No shame but mine . . .
> Now must the world point at poor Katherine
> And say 'Lo, there is mad Petruchio's wife,
> If it would please him come and marry her'
> (3.2.8–20).

Tranio is embarrassed ('Patience, *good* Katherine . . . '); and Baptista for once shows fatherly understanding:

> Go, girl, I cannot blame thee now to weep,
> For such an injury would vex a very saint,
> Much more a shrew of thy impatient humour.

They are both further concerned – not least for Katherine – when Petruchio arrives in his disarray ('See not *your bride* in these unreverent robes'). Most significantly of all: Gremio admits, in his account of the riotous marriage ceremony, that Katherine is 'a lamb, a dove' compared with Petruchio, and confesses 'I seeing this came thence *for very shame*'. If even Gremio can be ashamed, the audience cannot fail to be so too; it will feel that this is indeed 'a way to *kill* a

[1] The problem presumably disappears for anyone who agrees with Gareth Lloyd Evans that Petruchio 'is every woman's dream of a kind of ideal lover' (*Shakespeare I, 1564–1592*, Edinburgh, 1969, p. 109).

wife', and not 'with kindness'. The world of farce – for all the broad humour of Petruchio's antics – has been left behind, and Katherine has long ceased to be merely the subject of an experiment.

The audience's disquiet will probably continue in the scenes at Petruchio's house, when she is not only denied food but also allowed to be the victim of mockery by the very servants; and there will not be general agreement with the attempts by some twentieth-century critics to 'save' her by saying that she 'enjoys the game' in Act 4 Scene 5 when she declines any longer to have an opinion different from her husband's. The mood is rather weary resignation:

> . . . be it moon, or sun, or what you please;
> And if you please to call it a rush-candle,
> Henceforth I vow it shall be so for me
> (ll. 13–15).

Petruchio's victory, if it is a victory, is a very poor one indeed – and to say this is not to agree for one minute with H. C. Goddard's desperate claim that 'the play is an early version of *What Every Woman Knows* – what every woman knows being, of course, that the woman can lord it over the man so long as she allows him to think he is lording it over her'.[1] (As R. B. Heilman nicely put it, 'After three centuries of relative stability, then, Petruchio has developed rather quickly, first from an animal tamer to a gentleman lover who simply brings out the best in Kate, and then at last to a laughable victim of the superior spouse who dupes him'.[2]) In fact, Katherine never 'lords it' over Petruchio; in nearly every sense that matters she loses; and Goddard admits that his main reason for interpreting the play in this way is to bring it 'into line' with the other comedies because otherwise it would be 'an unaccountable exception' and a regression. It is not a regression but a young dramatist's attempt, not repeated, to mingle two genres that cannot be combined – and it may not even be exceptional if, as has been suggested earlier in this Introduction, *The Two Gentlemen of Verona* had also tried to blend incompatible literary modes, albeit modes different again from those in *The Taming of the Shrew*.

It is the logic of the farce in the play that demands that in the final scene the tamed shrew shall be shown to be tamer than both the

[1] *The Meaning of Shakespeare*, 2 vols. (Chicago, 1951, repr. 1963), i. 68.

[2] 'The *Taming* Untamed, or, the Return of the Shrew', *Modern Language Quarterly*, 27 (1966), p. 151.

seemingly meek sister and the worldly-wise widow; and the tone is certainly farcical as the husbands who have made the wagers on the wives' obedience urge those wives on exactly as if they were animals: 'To her, Kate!' 'To her, widow!' The lecture by Kate on the wife's duty to submit is the only fitting climax *to the farce* – and for that very reason it cannot logically be taken seriously, orthodox though the views expressed may be. If one does take the finale seriously, then one experiences some such difficulty as that felt by R. W. Bond, who protested solemnly that the order to Katherine to throw her 'cap' away and trample on it is 'a needless affront to her feelings, not excusable like former freaks as part of a wise purpose, but offered at the very moment when she is exhibiting a voluntary obedience' (p. lvii). (Treading on the cap, it should be remembered, is one of the elements common to the shrew-taming folk tales.) It is the same mistake, attempting to take the last scene as a continuation of the realistic portrayal of character; that leads some modern producers to have it played as a kind of private joke between Petruchio and Kate – or even have Petruchio imply that by now he is thoroughly ashamed of himself. It does not, cannot, work. The play has changed key again: it has modulated back from something like realistic social comedy to the other, 'broader', kind of entertainment that was foretold by the Induction. Hazlitt was perhaps for once wrong when he said that '*The Taming of the Shrew* is almost the only one of Shakespeare's comedies that has a regular plot, and a downright moral' (p. 341); the moral, if any, is light-hearted and it is the very irregularity and inconsistency – of the tone, if not exactly of the plot – that creates the problems, not only for the reader but also, if the truth be told, for the audience.

Shakespeare certainly plays with the subject of theatrical illusion, and through the Induction and elsewhere seems to warn his audience of the ambiguity of 'belief'; he perhaps illustrates – he certainly for the moment accepts, or pretends to accept – some of the commonplaces of the thought of his time on social behaviour and the desirability of conforming; but if the play is to be enjoyed, it must be enjoyed primarily for its fun, and the paradox is that this fun is cut across and indeed reduced by that other dramatic skill that makes a character credible or 'real'.

The style

J. W. Mackail once said of *The Taming of the Shrew* that, although 'brilliantly successful on the stage', 'it has no high quality as literature, and but a few touches of Shakespeare's magic or of his verbal and rhetorical felicity'.[1] It is not difficult to see why the comment was made, but Mackail shows a very limited concept of 'verbal felicity' and is almost certainly wrong about the absence of good 'rhetoric'.

To be sure, one will look in vain in *The Shrew* for the kind of 'magic' that often leaps from the Shakespearian page even as early as *The Two Gentlemen of Verona*. There are no memorable lines of the type of 'the uncertain glory of an April day' or verbal pictures of 'the current that with gentle murmur glides' and 'makes sweet music with th' enamelled stones, | Giving a gentle kiss to every sedge | He overtaketh in his pilgrimage'. Such romantic touches are ruled out by the subject matter of this very different play. There are, however, other kinds of poetic skill.

The comedy is not lacking in images (though Caroline Spurgeon counted only 92 in the whole play, an exceptionally low number[2]); indeed there is even iterative imagery – notably that of training the falcon which is, as it were, basic to Petruchio's theory of taming. K. Wentersdorf has shown not only that many of the images are characteristic of Shakespeare – the *noise* of hell, for example, and the noise of battle[3] – but also that they tend to recur (and how an image, such as card playing, can often be found both in a part of the play that the disintegrators were prepared to accept as Shakespeare's – 1.2.33 and 2.1.311 – and in another part – 4.2.57 and 2.1.387 – that they wished to allot to a collaborator).[4] With the possible exception of the falcons and haggards, however, there is no important pattern of imagery; and where one image is repeated in a later part of the play, the second rarely gains any added significance from the first. For example, it is difficult to see any *dramatic* significance in the fact that Vincentio's indignation with Tranio in 5.1.108–9 – 'Where is that damned villain, Tranio, | That faced and braved me in this matter

[1] *The Approach to Shakespeare* (Oxford, 1930), pp. 58–9.

[2] *Shakespeare's Imagery and What It Tells Us* (Cambridge, 1935), p. 361.

[3] See also, e.g., 1.2.199 and note, and note on 1.1.165–7.

[4] K. Wentersdorf, 'The Authenticity of *The Taming of the Shrew*', *Shakespeare Quarterly*, 5 (1954), 11–32. The caveats entered by Moody E. Prior, 'Imagery as a Test of Authorship', *Shakespeare Quarterly*, 6 (1955), 381–6, should not be disregarded; but if the 'authenticity' of the play is not further discussed in this Introduction, it is because there is no case to answer once the variations in style are seen to be functional.

so?' – repeats the pair of words on which Grumio chose to pun in his attempt to outface the tailor in 4.3.122–5. The repetition may be deliberate but is more likely to be unconscious and in itself meaningless.

Single images are vivid enough – such as the Lord's first picture of Sly, in the Induction, 'O monstrous beast, how like a swine he lies! | Grim death, how foul and loathsome is thine image!' or Hortensio's picture of himself after Kate has broken the musical instrument over his head, 'And there I stood amazèd for a while, | As on a pillory, looking through the lute' (2.1.154–5) or – one of several that may, as B. Ifor Evans has said, 'derive from a genuine rustic experience'[1] – 'Kate like the hazel-twig | Is straight and slender, and as brown in hue | As hazel-nuts and sweeter than the kernels' (2.1.252–4). It will be noticed, however, that the images tend to take the form of the self-conscious simile rather than the direct metaphor – 'as loud | As thunder', 'as rough | As are the swelling Adriatic seas', 'gives not half so great a blow to hear | As will a chestnut in a farmer's fire'. This is characteristic of the early Shakespeare, as, too, is an occasional tendency towards the literary, seen not only in Petruchio's 'as foul as was Florentius' love,| As old as Sibyl, and as curst and shrewd | As Socrates' Xanthippe' but also in Tranio's 'so devote to Aristotle's checks | As Ovid be an outcast quite abjured', in Sly's blunders about 'Saint Jeronimy' and 'Richard Conqueror' and his '*paucas pallabris*', and in the speeches to Sly of the Lord and attendants when he wakes in Induction 2.33–58.

The inflation in these last-mentioned speeches, however, may be deliberate – the Lord and those in league with him are playing, and even consciously over-playing, parts; and this is reminder enough that in any discussion of the style of *The Taming of the Shrew* one important caveat must be entered, namely that it is exceptionally difficult, when the language falls flat, or seems inflated, to be sure that the playwright is not deliberately making it so, for what may seem to him to be, and often still seem to be, excellent dramatic reasons.

The first example has already been given: the classical allusions in the second part of the Induction are probably a meaningful kind of overwriting, indicative of the pleasure taken by the intriguers in their intrigue, and their awareness of the glorious inappropriateness of references to Adonis, Cytherea, Io, and Daphne when addressing Christopher Sly. There is even the suggestion that the

[1] *The Language of Shakespeare's Plays* (London, 1952, repr. 1965), p. 29.

attendants are not fully successful in their attempts to reproduce the inflated language of the Lord.[1]

The style of the beginning of the play-within-the-play presents a similar problem. There can be little doubt that the exposition is blatant, that the verse sounds not much better than jog-trot, and that the line-endings 'Lombardy', 'Italy', 'company' add to the effect of jingle. But is this Shakespeare's relative incompetence or is he already trying by artificiality of language to mark off the play-within-the-play as less 'real'? Is this in short the same technique as he was to use – one is tempted to say 'more obviously' but perhaps should say 'more clearly' – when he began the play-within-the-play in *Hamlet* with the prologue 'For us, and for our tragedy, | Here stooping to your clemency, | We beg your hearing patiently'? One would like to be sure.

It seems reasonably certain that the language of Gremio and Hortensio in 1.1.105–42 is made up largely of proverbs and clichés not because Shakespeare can do no better but because he sees the characters as having commonplace minds; and when Lucentio speaks as he does about his falling in love at first sight with Bianca:

> I saw sweet beauty in her face,
> Such as the daughter of Agenor had,
> That made great Jove to humble him to her hand,
> When with his knees he kissed the Cretan strand
> (1.1.164–7)

– the rhyme may be significant – it is perhaps not because Shakespeare thinks that this is admirably romantic but because Lucentio is being presented as the traditional lover who thinks it so, the lover found in romantic drama, poetry, and fiction. (The case would admittedly be stronger if Lucentio had not addressed *Tranio* a few lines earlier as the confidant 'That art to me as secret and as dear | As Anna to the Queen of Carthage was'.)

Most interesting of all is the speech of the Pedant, who when he talks in his own character, on first meeting Tranio (4.2.72 ff.), uses regular blank verse but as soon as he has to play the part of Vincentio speaks to Baptista in verse that limps:

> and, if you please to like
> No worse than I, upon some agreement

[1] See notes on Induction 2, ll. 15, 29, and 46.

Me shall you find ready and willing
With one consent to have her so bestowed
(4.4.31–4).

There may be textual corruption – or is this Shakespeare's way of indicating that the Pedant is unsure of himself and improvising?[1]

The passages just discussed may all belong to the process of experimentation that may be seen again and again in the play. Experiment is clear, for example, in the use of rhyme. One is not surprised by rhyme when a statement is to sound platitudinous or vaguely ridiculous, as Marlowe had used it for the speech of Mycetes in *Tamburlaine* and as Shakespeare perhaps uses it in the lines of Lucentio quoted above (1.1.166–7), rhyming 'hand' and 'strand', and in the speeches by Hortensio and Gremio at 1.2.225–34. One also expects it when a statement is to be given the force of an epigram or is to sound conclusive, as in Petruchio's:

My father dead, my fortune lives for me,
And I do hope good days and long to see
(1.2.187–8)

(where it is not very successful) and, probably, in Katherine's:

To comb your noddle with a three-legged stool,
And paint your face, and use you like a fool
(1.1.64–5).

Tranio is presumably uttering a 'home truth' when a few lines later he comments on Kate:

Husht, master, here's some good pastime toward;
That wench is stark mad, or wonderful froward.

Lucentio's rejoinder, however, gives a subtler effect:

But in the other's silence do I see
Maid's mild behaviour and sobriety.

The rhyming of the fully stressed syllable with one stressed only lightly, if at all, allows Lucentio to sound convinced of his truth, too, but perhaps makes it sound less convincing to us; and it allows Shakespeare to modulate back to blank verse.

Rhymed doggerel also seems to be used in an attempt to obtain special effects. It is prominent, for example, on the first appearance of

[1] Compare note on 4.4.32–3.

Petruchio and Grumio, at the beginning of 1.2, and the impression given is, appropriately, of something clownish. What is perhaps different from uses in other early drama is that the rhymed lines are not continuous but are broken up with others – complete or half-lines or even prose; and if an editor's head spins, endeavouring to decide which is which, it may be because Shakespeare is trying out occasional rhymed prose. An example would be the speech by Grumio (1.2.29–35) which begins with colloquial prose and ends 'Whom would to God I had well knocked at first, | Then had not Grumio come by the worst' – which may be verse, or may not. The opposite process seems to occur in 2.1.74 ff., where Petruchio's 'O pardon me, Signor Gremio, I would fain be doing' is capped by Gremio's 'I doubt it not, sir, but you will curse your wooing' followed by several lines of prose. At least this avoids jingle and monotony.

A still more interesting use of rhyme is found in Petruchio's initial statement of his strategy (2.1.169–79). In the lines:

> Say that she rail, why then I'll tell her plain
> She sings as sweetly as a nightingale . . .
> If she do bid me pack, I'll give her thanks,
> As though she bid me stay by her a week.
> If she deny to wed, I'll crave the day
> When I shall ask the banns, and when be marrièd

it may not at first be apparent that 'rail' within the first line rhymes with 'nightingale' at the end of the second; 'pack' and 'week' are a kind of half-rhyme; and 'marrièd' rhymes with 'wed' in the middle of the line before. This interlacing, as it were, gives the whole passage the musical effect of lyric, and continuity, and a certain emphatic quality, without risking the monotony of a sequence of rhymed couplets that might have the added disadvantage of making Petruchio sound at this stage *too* confident or even ridiculous.

Also fascinating is Shakespeare's choice of prose or verse for different parts of the play. Sly, for example, normally speaks prose, of the most colloquial kind; but once he accepts the argument that he is 'a lord indeed', he adopts the more formal blank verse of those around him:

> Am I a lord, and have I such a lady?
> Or do I dream? Or have I dreamed till now?

(and soon adopts the royal plural!). Petruchio normally speaks in verse, but the best accounts of him are by speakers of prose.[1] (One exception is Gremio's description of the wedding – but that involves Kate too.) Presumably the verse gives him a certain status, forces the listener on the stage to take him seriously, as it were, while the prose passages prevent his seeming to the audience in any way heroic. The best instances, of course, are Biondello's description of Petruchio's horse and of his dress for the wedding (3.2.43–68) and Grumio's report to Curtis of what happened on the way home from the ceremony (4.1.58–74) – the latter, incidentally, also a splendid example of the art of narrative (as is Gremio's account of the wedding itself).

One other change from prose to verse, completely unexpected, is worthy of mention. Grumio, appropriately enough, usually speaks in prose, as colloquial as Sly's, if more fluent. Why then in 4.1, in answer to Petruchio's feignedly angry question why the servants did not meet him in the park, does he speak in very formal blank verse?

> Nathaniel's coat, sir, was not fully made,
> And Gabriel's pumps were all unpinked i'th' heel;
> There was no link to colour Peter's hat,
> And Walter's dagger was not come from sheathing;
> There were none fine but Adam, Ralph, and Gregory,
> The rest were ragged, old, and beggarly . . .

The effect, surely, is of something prepared, possibly learnt off verbatim – a warning to the audience, in fact, that Grumio is in league with Petruchio throughout the taunting of Katherine in this scene and 4.3.

Perhaps enough has been said to demonstrate that *The Taming of the Shrew*, *pace* Mackail, is very rich in verbal and other technical skills: and if one looks for 'rhetorical felicity', that is easily found – in Petruchio's 'Think you a little din can daunt mine ears? | Have I not in my time heard lions roar? . . .', for example (1.2.195–206), or Gremio's account of the riches with which he would be prepared to endow Bianca:

> My hangings all of Tyrian tapestry;
> In ivory coffers I have stuffed my crowns . . .
> I have a hundred milch-kine to the pail,

[1] Both points are made by, e.g., Milton Crane, *Shakespeare's Prose* (Chicago, 1951, repr. 1963), pp. 78–9.

> Six-score fat oxen standing in my stalls . . .
> If whilst I live she will be only mine
> (2.1.348–64)

or (let us not forget) in Sly's:

> . . . if you give me any conserves, give me conserves of beef. Ne'er ask me what raiment I'll wear, for I have no more doublets than backs, no more stockings than legs, nor no more shoes than feet . . .

This last passage is also sufficient reminder that there are verbal virtues other than the romantic or the rhetorical: directness, for instance, ready intelligibility, lifelikeness, sprightliness, and vigour – and all these abound in *The Taming of the Shrew*. It has its linguistic weaknesses, in the occasional flatness (subject to the caveats entered above) and in the over-long wit-combats of Grumio and Curtis and even of Petruchio and Kate, but for the most part it is superbly *written*, in both verse and prose; and the qualities it is said to lack would not necessarily be improvements.

The play on the stage

The title-page of the 1631 Quarto of *The Taming of the Shrew* claims that the play had been acted by the King's Men at both the Globe and the Blackfriars – which would mean that it remained in the repertoire after 1610, when the Blackfriars theatre was first regularly used by the adult company; and other evidence that the comedy did not quickly 'date' is found in Sir Henry Herbert's record that it was 'liked' when presented at Court before Charles I and Henrietta Maria on 26 November 1633.

Two days later the Court audience showed less judgement when a performance of Fletcher's sequel to *The Taming of the Shrew*, *The Woman's Prize, or, The Tamer Tamed*, was 'very well liked'. Fletcher attempts to cap Shakespeare's farce by telling how, after Kate's death, Petruchio meets more than his match in his second wife, Maria. Announcing, in the second scene, her programme of action, as he had announced his in Shakespeare's play, she is made to pick up and, as it were, reverse Shakespeare's imagery: tame wives, she says, are only 'eyasses', and the true woman is the 'free haggard' and will fly as she pleases, scorning both the quarry and the lure, till her keeper is 'glad to fling out trains, and golden ones, to take her down again'. Similarly, later, her threats are described by one of

Petruchio's friends – named 'Sophocles'! – as 'bug's-words' (1.3); presumably Fletcher is recalling Petruchio's 'Tush, tush, fear boys with bugs!' and suggesting that tamers may learn to respect 'bugs' after all. Again, Petruchio himself (2.5) compares his taming of Kate to the twelve labours of Hercules, having ignored that parallel when Gremio proposed it in *The Taming of the Shrew* (1.2.254–5). Petruchio has to accept his wife's conditions – the providing of coaches, and gifts of jewels and so on – but, not content with that, she locks him up, pretending that he is dying of plague, and otherwise out-manoeuvres him until, after a huddle of false contracts and feigned death, there is a final and implausible reconciliation. Fletcher's play works, if at all, only by sacrificing completely the character of Petruchio – as Shakespeare did not sacrifice the character of Kate – and so fails as an 'answer', even a jocular one.

On 9 April 1667, Samuel Pepys saw a play that he calls '*The Tameing of a Shrew*'. He thought it 'but mean', in spite of 'some very good pieces in it', and complained that he could not always understand the words. He saw it again on 1 November and pronounced it 'a silly play and an old one'. It was not, however, 'an old one', and not Shakespeare's, but an adaptation, all in prose, by John Lacy. ('The best part', Pepys thought, was Lacy's own 'Sawny'.) It was finally published in 1698 as *Sauny the Scott: or, The Taming of the Shrew: A Comedy. As it is now acted at the Theatre-Royal. Written by J. Lacey*; and the printed cast-list gives Powell as Petruchio, Bullock as Sauny, Mills as Winlove/Lucentio, Mrs Verbruggen as 'Margaret the Shrew' and Mrs Cibber as 'Biancha her Sister' (a cast which 'is compatible with the company at Drury Lane for this [1698] season'[1]).

Sauny, or Sauney, the Scot or Scott – the spelling varies – is Lacy's version of Grumio (the name presumably deriving from the 'Saunders' or 'Sanders' of *The Taming of a Shrew*); and the explanation of Pepys's failure to understand the words is that Sauny/Grumio speaks in the most atrocious Scottish dialect (Biondello, incidentally, becomes 'Jamy'). Shakespeare's Lucentio becomes Winlove (son of Sir Lyonell Winlove), who has come up from Warwickshire to London to live and learn; and Baptista is translated into a Restoration Lord Beaufoy. As in the Fletcher sequel, however, it is Petruchio who loses most – almost everything except his name. He is truly willing to marry anyone, for money; threatens to flog the shrew if she refuses to

[1] W. van Lennep *et al*, *The London Stage 1660–1800. Part I 1660–1700* (Carbondale, Ill., 1960), p. 485.

marry him; and completes her cure by claiming that she is dead, sending for bearers to put her on a bier and – not satisfied with that – having her tied on. Mercifully (for the modern reader, that is), on winning his wager for him she delivers only a two-line sermon; and in genuine Restoration style the play ends with a dance. (In 1698, it also had interpolated songs; two were subsequently printed.[1]) Its interest today can be only in the contrast its vulgarity provides with Shakespeare's Elizabethan directness and in the examination of the possible reasons for retaining some Shakespearian phrases and not others. One half-recognizes, for example, with vague discomfort, 'I am all fire, burn, pine, perish Tranio, unless I win her; Counsel me, and Assist me, Dear Tranio', and wonders who misread, misheard or altered what, when Winlove instructs Tranio that he 'must make one among these *Wars*' (Shakespeare's 'wooers') – again for no good reason given at the time. What is clear is why Pepys found it 'silly', but it was still being acted, at Lincoln's Inn Fields, in 1725, and at Goodman's Fields as late as 1732; and although Shakespeare's own *Taming of the Shrew* was among the plays 'allowed' to the King's Company in January 1669, there is no record that it was ever presented by them in its original form (or forms).[2]

Lacy solved the problems of the Christopher Sly Induction by omitting it altogether; two early eighteenth-century writers made short plays out of the Induction and omitted everything else. Charles Johnson and Christopher Bullock each wrote a farce called *The Cobler of Preston*. Johnson's, acted at Drury Lane, in February 1716, was published first, in the same year; and therefore Bullock, although his version was the first on the stage, being given at the Theatre Royal in Lincoln's Inn Fields late in January, had to insist that his work was independent. (He admits that he knew Johnson's play was being rehearsed and wrote his own hurriedly.) Both were acted several times during the year.

Bullock uses not much more than the initial idea of the trick played on the drunken 'cobler'. He calls him Guzzle, and allows him as a supposed justice to try sundry people, including his wife (he orders her to be ducked). Little of Shakespeare's phrasing is preserved. Johnson, too, retains a few words (the 'Madam wife' joke, for exam-

[1] Ibid.

[2] J. Genest, *Some Account of the English Stage*, 10 vols. (Bath, 1832), iii. 168; van Lennep, ii. 817; C. B. Hogan, *Shakespeare in the Theatre 1701–1800*, 2 vols. (Oxford, 1952–7), i. 414–22; van Lennep, i. 152.

ple) but makes the comedy topical, with references to Spain, and other political allusions, and also tries to carry it further, by having Sly attempt to convince his wife that he is indeed a lord. Bullock's farce lasted longer on the stage than Johnson's (a performance is recorded at Covent Garden in 1759[1]), and was popular enough to go into at least four editions; but neither of the plays adds anything to our understanding of Shakespeare.[2]

Another less-than-full-length offshoot of Shakespeare is James Wordale's two-act 'ballad-farce' *A Cure for a Scold*, acted in 1735 at the Theatre Royal in Drury Lane and published in the same year. (It was revived in 1750.[3]) It is clearly influenced by *Sauny the Scot* and misinterprets the character of the shrew in the same way: Wordale's version of her motivation 'Now, have I a mind to marry him, to try if I can't tame him', in spite of an apparent difference, is only too like Lacy's 'I have a good mind to marry him to try if he can tame me'; and the shrew is again 'Margaret' ('Peg'), though daughter of Sir William Worthy. (Mrs Clive played the part.) All the names are now brought into line: not only is Lucentio 'Gainlove' but also Petruchio is 'Manly' (it had to come). Some few Shakespearian phrases are retained, but they are lost amid Restoration and eighteenth-century platitudes, and there are many songs. The ending is new: there is no wager, but the shrew pretends to be dying and when her husband is willing to run for a surgeon, she announces that she is conquered, and cured. Once again the contrast with Shakespeare points up his complete refusal to spoil the logic of *his* comedy with any touch of sentimentality.

Wordale's version has no Induction; neither has the most famous and long-lasting of all the adaptations of *The Shrew*, David Garrick's *Catharine and Petruchio*. Garrick did without the subplot as well: his Bianca is already married, to *Hortensio*; and Baptista replaces Vincentio in the equivalent of Act 4 Scene 5 of Shakespeare's comedy and is thus the one addressed by Catharine, on demand, as a woman. This, though a three-act play, is still not full-length and was sometimes performed on the one programme with Garrick's cut version of *The Winter's Tale*; and the prologue, which covers both, claims

[1] C. B. Hogan, *Shakespeare in the Theatre 1701–1800*, ii. 615.

[2] Johnson's, with an added subplot, was turned into a kind of comic opera in 1817.

[3] G. C. D. Odell, *Shakespeare from Betterton to Irving*, 2 vols. (New York, 1920), i. 255; Hogan, i. 422.

that in this way not 'one drop' of Shakespeare is lost. (Genest understandably complained, although he was speaking specifically of *The Winter's Tale*, that Garrick 'has certainly lost a tun' of Shakespeare.[1]) No author is named on the title-page of the 1756 edition ('*Catharine and Petruchio*. A Comedy . . . As it is perform'd at the Theatre-Royal In Drury-Lane. Alter'd from Shakespear's *Taming of the Shrew*') but Garrick is named as the author of the prologue, and his authorship of the play is not in question.

The taming section of Shakespeare's text is at times reproduced exactly (the description of Petruchio's ill-garbed arrival on the broken-down horse, for example, is almost word for word, even when Shakespeare's language presents difficulties of comprehension today – 'near-legg'd before, and with a half-check'd Bit', for instance). Sometimes it is cut; sometimes it is adapted (Petruchio, 'Oh how I long to have a Grapple with her'!) – and in the process Garrick shows a very bad ear for blank verse; and sometimes, of course, it is replaced or supplemented. Briefly, Baptista tells Petruchio (before Petruchio has even seen Catharine) that he may have her, or she will be turned out of doors; she earns Petruchio's admiration when she first appears, for breaking the lute over the music master; and Baptista's attitude leaves her little choice over the marriage, though Petruchio does try to save her face. That the tradition of the Lacy travesty could not easily be shaken off is shown by her aside 'I'll marry my Revenge, but I will tame him'. The wedding-scene and the return to Petruchio's house form Act 2. Act 3 is made up of the scene in which Grumio taunts her by seeming to offer food; the exchange with the tailor and haberdasher; the debate over the sun and moon (not involving the Pedant); and Catharine's readiness to call a man a woman if Petruchio wants it thus. There is, however, no wager (there is nobody for Petruchio to bet *with*) – and so Catharine reads Bianca the lecture, on demand; Baptista gives her a second dowry; and Petruchio speaks up:

> Kiss me, my Kate; and since thou art become
> So prudent, kind, and dutiful a Wife,
> *Petruchio* here shall doff the lordly Husband;
> An honest Mask, which I throw off with Pleasure.
> Far hence all Rudeness, Wilfulness, and Noise,
> And be our future Lives one gentle Stream
> Of mutual Love, Compliance and Regard.

[1] Genest, *English Stage*, iv. 446.

Shakespeare's Katherine, one hopes, would have walked out, but Garrick's replies in all humility:

> Nay, then I'm all unworthy of thy Love,
> And look with Blushes on my former self

(and Petruchio concludes the play by addressing the audience with some of the phrases that Garrick has not already used from Katherine's oration to the other wives in *The Taming of the Shrew*). Shakespeare's comedy, it has been suggested, is open-ended; after Garrick's there is namoore to seye.

Presumably female honour was satisfied, for the travesty held the stage for a hundred years, and more, in America as well as in England.[1] It was probably the form ('a new Comedy in 3 acts'[2]) used for Mrs Pritchard's benefit performance in March 1754 (she played Catharine to Woodward's Petruchio); and it was acted many times between 1756 and 1760 – with Woodward as Petruchio, and Yates as Grumio, but with Mrs Clive now normally as Catharine – and often afterwards, always as an afterpiece. Mrs Siddons played Catharine to Kemble's Petruchio for his 'benefit' in March 1788, with a text slightly altered from Garrick's; and Kemble was still playing this Petruchio in June 1810, to his wife's Catharine.[3] Macready also used the Garrick version, slightly altered again, as late as 1842; and it was *Catharine and Petruchio* that was adapted as the libretto for Frederic Reynolds's opera in 1828, although it was supplemented by all kinds of material taken from Shakespeare's other works, including songs. (The playbill claimed that this was the first performance for 80 years with the Shakespeare text![4]) It was still the Garrick version, making up a full night's programme with two farces, in which the young Henry Irving as Petruchio and Ellen Terry as Catharine appeared, not very successfully, at the Queen's Theatre at the end of 1867.[5]

These various adaptations kept *The Taming of the Shrew* on the stage throughout the eighteenth century and for the first half of the nineteenth. Literally hundreds of performances are recorded for that period and (if they can count as Shakespeare) they demonstrate that

[1] The first performance in America was in Philadelphia in 1766.

[2] Genest, iv. 387.

[3] Kemble's text was published in 1810 as *Katharine and Petruchio*.

[4] Odell, ii. 144.

[5] Laurence Irving, *Henry Irving* (New York, 1952), p. 147. Beerbohm Tree, in a spirit of antiquarianism, revived Garrick's adaptation in 1897.

The Shrew was one of the ten or twelve most popular Shakespeare plays during those years.

In 1844 the complete Shakespeare play, with the Induction, was restored to the English stage, from which it had been exiled since before the closing of the theatres some two hundred years earlier.[1] J. R. Planché proposed to Benjamin Webster, who 'sanctioned it without hesitation', that the full comedy should be produced at the Haymarket Theatre in London in what was taken to be the Elizabethan manner. There were only two sets – one represented the outside of the alehouse and one the nobleman's chamber in which the strolling troupe performed the play proper. The main curtain was not lowered between acts; but other curtains and screens, with the help of written placards, still assisted with 'changes of scene' to, for example, 'a room in Baptista's house'. Planché, who gives this account in his *Recollections and Reflections* (London, 1872, Vol. 2), took particular pride in having restored the Induction: it was 'one of the events in my theatrical career on which I look back with greatest pride and gratification' (p. 86). Sly remained on stage throughout. Servants brought him 'wine and refreshments' during the act-intervals; while the fifth act was in progress he sank gradually 'into a heavy drunken stupor'; and he was silently carried off at a sign from the Lord to his 'domestics' as the final curtain slowly fell.

This production, which had been motivated in large part by the return of Mrs Nisbett to the stage after a short retirement, was revived in 1847 when she again played Katherine. That it had successfully re-established the Induction was further demonstrated by Samuel Phelps's performance as Sly in the next important interpretation of the play, in 1856. Henry Morley, in his *Journal of a London Playgoer* (London, 1866), has left a memorable account of Phelps's portrayal of Sly's stupidity and sensuality, though stressing that it always remained humorous. Phelps had Sly carried off at the end of Act 1; and Morley thought this successful: 'The Induction thus insensibly fades into the play, and all trace of it is lost by the time that a lively interest in the comedy itself has been excited' (p. 161). For the other problem presented by *The Shrew* to all its later producers – how to make Kate's final submission acceptable – Phelps's solution was to cut heavily, contrary to his practice with the

[1] There is a bare possibility that the Shakespeare play was revived in 1663, but firm evidence is lacking.

rest of the text. The last act, we are told, was 'much abbreviated' – and the adaptation had a mixed reception.

What Webster and Planché had done for England, Augustin Daly tried to do for the United States, when in 1887 in New York he reverted from Garrick's text to Shakespeare's – in a sense. His extremely popular production, which ran for more than one hundred and twenty performances and was afterwards brought to the Gaiety Theatre in London, kept the Induction; but Daly rearranged scenes elsewhere, particularly in Act 4: he began with the present Scenes 2 and 4 and then took 1, 3, and 5 consecutively and without a break. Theatrical 'convenience' had been served but even Odell found the result 'ridiculous': 'I could not help wondering why Katharine had been brought to her husband's house merely to spend a few minutes and depart again for the place whence she had just come' (ii. 406). Once again the superiority of the fluid Elizabethan staging had, inadvertently, been proved. Daly also cut Shakespeare's text quite fiercely (though he found room for scraps of Garrick's and for other variations);[1] and, all in all, the best aspect of the production would seem to have been the artistry of Ada Rehan, whose Kate has been ranked 'among the very few greatest Shakespearian representations, not only of that age but of all time'.[2]

The Shrew gave relatively few opportunities to the renowned actor-producers of the late-nineteenth and earlier-twentieth centuries who judged their success partly by the elaborateness of their scenery and spectacle. To be sure, F. R. Benson customarily led his Kate back towards Padua on live donkeys (though his company was constantly on tour) but the feature of his productions commented on even more frequently was his habit, as Petruchio, of carrying Kate off, thrown over his shoulder, 'kicking and squealing'.[3]

Unfortunately neither of the men who showed the way to more truly Elizabethan methods of performance – William Poel and Harley Granville-Barker – seems to have been tempted to put on the play, although Poel had some undefined influence on Martin Harvey's production in 1913. The twentieth-century stage history has as its principal interest the various attempts to solve the two great problems, of the 'unfinished' Induction and the lack of appeal of Kate's final tameness to audiences whose sympathies, even when

[1] W. Winter, *Shakespeare on the Stage*, Second Series (New York, 1915), p. 514.

[2] Odell, ii. 383.

[3] So, e.g., J. C. Trewin, *Benson and the Bensonians* (London, 1960), p. 65.

they are not exactly feminist, are unlikely to be with the taming of a wife.

Benson omitted the Induction; Martin Harvey kept Sly in view throughout, seated in the orchestra with his back to the audience;[1] Bridges-Adams at Stratford-upon-Avon in 1919 and later years – although he was renowned for not cutting texts – 'had conceived a strong aversion to Christopher Sly, and had him away altogether when he felt that he could do so with impunity';[2] Max Reinhardt, at the other extreme, convinced that the key was in the Induction, kept it and took it as his justification for having the rest of the play presented as rollicking farce – in *commedia dell' arte* style; Sir Barry Jackson, in a performance in modern dress at the Court Theatre in 1928, let Sly and the Lord remain till the end, seated in one of the boxes;[3] at the New Theatre in 1937, Sly 'watched everything from his bed' (and somehow doubled the part of the Pedant);[4] at the Old Vic in 1931 Harcourt Williams used the epilogue from *A Shrew*; at sundry performances at Stratford-upon-Avon and at Stratford, Ontario in the 1960s, the play ended with the strolling Players packing up and going off again;[5] and at the Oregon Festival in the late 1970s, it began not with the Sly Induction but with a Punch and Judy show.

Obviously the question of establishing the 'right' *tone* persists; and it is really this same question that is faced in the varying interpretations of the final scene. As early as 1908, in Melbourne, and 1914, in New York, Margaret Anglin is said to have spoken Kate's sermon on obedience 'as if it were mere mockery – implying that it is hypocritical, a jest, secretly understood between Petruchio and his wife'[6] – and one has the impression that this is the 'solution' most favoured today; in the Oregon production previously mentioned, Petruchio handed the cap back to Kate and gently stopped her from kneeling to place her hand beneath his foot (hardly likely to satisfy the feminists!); and at Stratford-upon-Avon in 1978, the oration was 'delivered in a spiritless, unreal voice and received without appreci-

[1] J. C. Trewin, *Shakespeare on the English Stage 1900–1964* (London, 1964), pp. 46, 80.

[2] *A Bridges-Adams Letter Book*, ed. Robert Speaight (London, 1971), p. 17.

[3] Trewin, *Shakespeare on the English Stage*, p. 112.

[4] Ibid., p. 156. Trewin was not amused. Hay Petrie had doubled Sly and the Pedant at the Old Vic in 1922. (This is simple if Sly is removed from view after Act 1.)

[5] At Stratford-upon-Avon, Sly 'wandered in their wake, ruminating about his wife in Sligo' – which Robert Speaight found 'rather touching'. (*Shakespeare on the Stage*, London, 1973, p. 278.)

[6] Winter, Second Series, p. 538.

ation by the men, and with smouldering resentment by the women'[1] – and, understandably, by many of the audience.

A different tone again is established in the modern – and modernistic – adaptation by Charles Marowitz that turns the Katherine–Petruchio story into 'Gothic tragedy', 'a kind of Grimm Fairy Tale world, a world of sinister archetypes and hopeless victims'. (The Induction is, necessarily, omitted, and so are Gremio and Hortensio; the Bianca–Lucentio sexual relationship is dramatized in a Noel-Cowardish prose of 'he' and 'she'.) By leaving out whatever is not adaptable; by transposing occasionally (for example, some of the lines spoken by the Page as Sly's 'wife', such as 'I am your wife in all obedience', are now given to Kate but spoken in a very different spirit); by supplying stage directions to help create the new mood; and by preserving an extraordinary number of Shakespeare's lines intact, Marowitz turns the taming of Kate (by a savage, perverted Petruchio) into an illustration of 'the modern technique of brainwashing . . . almost to the letter'. The effect is quite terrifying. This is certainly not Shakespeare's play but it may well confirm the suspicions of many readers that the ice on which Shakespeare dances so skilfully is dangerously thin.[2]

In spite of its problems, *The Shrew* remains popular in the theatre; indeed, it is generally said to be one play that is more popular with theatre-goers than with academic or other readers, and its stage-history includes the names of many famous actors and actresses in addition to those already mentioned: Lily Brayton and Oscar Asche, for example; Dorothy Green and Baliol Holloway; Sybil Thorndike and Lewis Casson; Lynn Fontanne and Alfred Lunt (129 consecutive performances in the 1930s – but there was much horseplay, and even a band, and songs). The stage tradition that Petruchio carries a whip is now rarely followed, and today the tailor will not necessarily have the conventional stammer; but more often than not the Katherine will still be what Martin Holmes has called 'a near-Wagnerian Amazon'. Convinced (perhaps too easily) that the part was first played by a boy 'small, brisk and incisive' – who was the regular foil to the boy of different talents who played Bianca and, for example, Helena in *A Midsummer Night's Dream* – Holmes pleads for

[1] Lorna Sage, 'The Shrew's Revenge', *The Times Literary Supplement*, 19 May 1978.

[2] Charles Marowitz, *The Marowitz Shakespeare* (London, 1978). The quotations are from the Introduction, p. 18.

'a little Hermia-type spitfire' as Kate, and there is much to be said for his view.[1]

The Taming of the Shrew has been produced 'in the round' and it has often been acted in modern dress (not only in England and the United States but also in Canada and Germany), with the dress varying from evening clothes to the Mexican or South American poncho; but although Shakespeare's 'fire' in Act 4 Scene 1 can be changed without undue difficulty to an electric one, there is the usual difficulty over mention of swords; the music lesson, for example, has to be reworded unless there is to be anachronism; and of course a modern setting only makes the problem of Kate's submission to Petruchio more acute.

The play has also been adapted for ballet, musical, film, and opera. The Stuttgart Ballet version and the Cole Porter musical of 1948, *Kiss Me Kate*, have no relevance here, but it may be appropriate to note that some of the films have sought answers to the same questions as are raised in the theatre.

A silent film, of some 1120 feet, was made of Benson's performance, on the stage of the Shakespeare Memorial Theatre at Stratford, as early as 1910 (unfortunately, it does not survive) and even this was preceded by David Griffith's 1908 American film (which is held in the Library of Congress, but cannot be screened). Of the Mary Pickford–Douglas Fairbanks version of 1929, the first 'talkie' of Shakespeare (though a 'silent' was made at the same time), it is interesting to learn that Kate's sermon was delivered 'with a wink to the other women';[2] and of Franco Zeffirelli's 1966 adaptation, with Richard Burton and Elizabeth Taylor, not only that the Lucentio–Bianca plot was heavily cut, but also that Petruchio arrived drunk for the wedding (a compliment to the ladies – or not?). There have been at least eight other films, made in England, Italy, France, Spain, Denmark, and even India.[3]

The second operatic version, with libretto by Victor Widmann and music by Hermann Goetz – first presented in 1874, in Mannheim – also deserves special mention, as possibly the only adaptation ever made in which the story of Bianca and her suitors was neither

[1] Martin Holmes, *Shakespeare and his Players* (London, 1972), pp. 36–7.

[2] Roger Manvell, *Shakespeare and the Film* (London, 1971), p. 24.

[3] R. H. Ball, *Shakespeare on Silent Film* (London, 1968); J. J. Jorgens, *Shakespeare on Film* (Bloomington and London, 1977); O. J. Campbell, ed., *A Shakespeare Encyclopaedia* (London, 1966), p. 227.

omitted nor abbreviated but played *up* – 'to give relief to Petruchio's blustering and to the exhibitions of temper by the Shrew'.[1] There, indeed, is further food for thought, and not only about the opera. Perhaps when he 'unnecessarily complicated' his story of taming a shrew, not only with an Induction but also with a subplot, Shakespeare took for granted what his adapters had to discover, that a Petruchio–Katherine story has not in itself either the substance or the variation of theatrical interest desirable in a full-length play.

[1] Gustav Kobbé, *The Complete Opera Book* (London, 1922), p. 773. On the operatic versions, see Winton Dean, 'Shakespeare and Opera', in *Shakespeare in Music*, ed. Phyllis Hartnoll, London, 1964. (There are at least five.)

EDITORIAL PRINCIPLES

THE following modern-spelling text of *The Taming of the Shrew*, together with the collations and commentary, has been prepared in accordance with the principles declared for the Oxford Shakespeare by the General Editor. (This does not mean that he necessarily agrees with decisions made on single words or lines.) The 'control-text' for this play is, of course, the First Folio; and wherever an interpretation of it is in any way open to question or where the Folio is departed from, its reading is given in the collations. (Such a collation as 'cur is] F1; cur, is GRANT WHITE' does not necessarily mean, however, that F1 *spells* 'cur is'; in fact it has 'Curre is'.) Otherwise the collations are selective, and emendations by earlier editors are not listed unless they seem at least defensible or have been adopted by later editions.

The conventional act and scene divisions are recorded in the margin of the text, but only to facilitate the use of glossaries, lexicons and other works of reference: they are not considered to be 'authoritative' or to have any theatrical significance. The eccentric act division of the Folio is noted in the collations. No scene locations are given nor are those invented by editors normally listed.

Stage directions that are implied by the dialogue are not attributed to the editor who may first have printed them; they are, however, collated as '*not in* F1'. The exceptions are the directions that lines are to be addressed to particular characters or are to be spoken as asides: all these are editorial in origin. Directions for action that seems probable but is not certain are printed in broken brackets (⌈ ⌉).

In the text, the 'stress-mark' is placed on 'ed' only in those verse lines where there seems to be no reasonable doubt that the vowel must be pronounced. There are many other lines (e.g. Induction 2.95) in which a reader, or actor, may well *prefer* to pronounce it. (A theory that author, or compositors, attempted to make, or to preserve, a distinction between syllabic and non-syllabic 'ed' receives very limited support, if any, from the Folio text of *The Shrew*: one even finds there 'That fac'd and braved me in this matter so'.)

The view has also been taken that since the several irregularities in Italian and Latin in the play cannot possibly all be blamed on the compositors, emendation would be tantamount to improving Shakespeare – and that this is no part of an editor's duty.

In citations of old-spelling printed texts, including the Folio and Quarto, not only in the collations but also in the commentary and Introduction, long 's' (f, ʃ) has normally been replaced by 's', without comment; and (except in the collations) the letters 'i' and 'j', 'u' and 'v' have been distinguished as in modern usage.

ABBREVIATIONS AND REFERENCES

THE following abbreviations are used in the collations and explanatory notes. The place of publication is London unless otherwise specified.

EDITIONS

A Shrew	*A Pleasant Conceited Historie, called The taming of a Shrew.* 1594.
F1	*Mr. William Shakespeares Comedies, Histories, & Tragedies.* 1623.
Q1631	*A Wittie and Pleasant Comedie Called The Taming of the Shrew. As it was acted by his Maiesties Seruants at the Blacke Friers and the Globe. Written by Will. Shakespeare.* 1631.
F2	*Mr. William Shakespeares Comedies, Histories, and Tragedies.* 1632.
F3	*Mr. William Shakespear's Comedies, Histories, and Tragedies ... The third Impression.* 1664.
F4	*Mr. William Shakespear's Comedies, Histories, and Tragedies ... The Fourth Edition.* 1685.
Rowe	*The Works of Mr. William Shakespear ... Revis'd and Corrected ... By N. Rowe, Esq.* 6 vols. (Vol. 2), 1709.
Rowe (1709b)	*The Works of Mr. William Shakespear ... Revis'd and Corrected ... By N. Rowe, Esq.* 6 vols. (Vol. 2), 1709.
Rowe (1714)	*The Works of Mr. William Shakespear ... With his Life, by N. Rowe, Esq.* 8 vols. (Vol. 2), 1714.
Pope	*The Works of Mr William Shakespear ... Collected and Corrected ... by Mr. Pope.* 6 vols. 1723–5 (Vol. 2), 1723.
Pope (1728)	*The Works of Mr William Shakespear. Publish'd by Mr. Pope and Dr. Sewell.* 8 vols. (Vol. 3), 1728.
Theobald	*The Works of Shakespeare ... Collated with the Oldest Copies, and Corrected; With Notes ... By Mr. Theobald.* 7 vols. (Vol. 2), 1733.
Tonson (1734)	*The Taming of the Shrew. By Mr. William Shakespear ... Printed for J. Tonson ...* 1734.
Theobald (1740)	*The Works of Shakespeare ... Collated ... and Corrected: With Notes ... By Mr. Theobald. The Second Edition.* 8 vols. (Vol. 2), 1740.

Hanmer	*The Works of Shakespear . . . Carefully Revised and Corrected by the former Editions.* 6 vols. 1743–4 (Vol. 2), Oxford, 1743.
Warburton	*The Works of Shakespear. The Genuine Text . . . settled . . . By Mr. Pope and Mr. Warburton.* 8 vols. (Vol. 2), 1747.
Blair	*The Works of Shakespear* [edited by Hugh Blair]. 8 vols. (Vol. 2), Edinburgh, 1753.
Johnson	*The Plays of William Shakespeare . . . To which are added Notes by Sam. Johnson.* 8 vols. (Vol. 3), 1765.
Capell	*Mr William Shakespeare his Comedies, Histories, and Tragedies* [edited by Edward Capell]. 10 vols. [1767–8] (Vol. 3), [1767].
Hanmer (1771)	*The Works of Shakespear. The Second Edition.* 6 vols. 1770–1 (Vol. 2), Oxford, 1771.
Steevens	*The Plays of William Shakespeare . . . To which are added notes by Samuel Johnson and George Steevens.* 10 vols. (Vol. 3), 1773.
Steevens (1778)	*The Plays of William Shakspeare . . . The Second Edition, Revised and Augmented.* 10 vols. (Vol. 3), 1778.
Reed	*The Plays of William Shakspeare . . . The third Edition, revised and augmented by the Editor of Dodsley's Collection of Old Plays.* 10 vols. (Vol. 3), 1785.
Rann	*The Dramatic Works of Shakspeare . . . with notes by Joseph Rann.* 6 vols. 1786–[94] (Vol. 2), Oxford, 1786.
Malone	*The Plays and Poems of William Shakspeare . . . With . . . notes . . . By Edmond Malone.* 10 vols. (Vol. 3), 1790.
Steevens (1793)	*The Plays of William Shakspeare . . . The Fourth Edition . . .* 15 vols. (Vol. 6), 1793.
Reed (1803)	*The Plays of William Shakspeare . . . The Fifth Edition. Revised and augmented By Isaac Reed.* 21 vols. (Vol. 9), 1803.
Reed (1813)	*The Plays of William Shakspeare . . . Revised and augmented by Isaac Reed . . . The Sixth Edition.* 21 vols. (Vol. 9), 1813.
Boswell	*The Plays and Poems of William Shakspeare with the corrections and illustrations of various commentators* [edited by James Boswell]. 21 vols. (Vol. 5), 1821.
Chalmers	*The Plays of William Shakspeare . . . Printed . . . by Alexander Chalmers. A New Edition . . .* 8 vols. (Vol. 3), 1823.
Singer	*The Dramatic Works of William Shakspeare. With Notes . . . by Samuel Weller Singer.* 10 vols. (Vol. 3), Chiswick, 1826.

Knight	*The Pictorial Edition of the Works of Shakspere. Edited by Charles Knight.* 8 vols. [1838–43] *Comedies.* (Vol. 1), [1839].
Collier	*The Works of William Shakespeare . . . with the various readings, notes . . . by J. Payne Collier.* 8 vols. 1842–4 (Vol. 3), 1842.
Hudson	*The Works of Shakespeare . . . with Introductions, Notes . . . by the Rev. H. N. Hudson.* 11 vols. 1851–6 (Vol. 3), Boston, 1851.
Collier (1853)	*The Plays of Shakespeare: The text regulated by the old copies, and by the recently discovered Folio of 1632, containing early manuscript emendations. Edited by J. Payne Collier.* 1853.
Halliwell	*The Works of William Shakespeare, The text formed . . . by James O. Halliwell.* 16 vols. 1853–65 (Vol. 6), 1856.
Singer (1856)	*The Dramatic Works of William Shakspeare. With Notes . . . by Samuel Weller Singer.* 10 vols. (Vol. 3), 1856.
Dyce	*The Works of William Shakespeare. The Text revised by the Rev. Alexander Dyce.* 6 vols. (Vol. 2), 1857.
Grant White	*The Works of William Shakespeare . . . edited . . . by Richard Grant White.* 12 vols. 1857–66 (Vol. 4), Boston, 1857.
Collier (1858)	*Shakespeare's Comedies, Histories, Tragedies, and Poems. Edited by J. Payne Collier. The Second Edition.* 6 vols. (Vol. 2), 1858.
Staunton	*The Plays of Shakespeare. Edited by Howard Staunton.* 3 vols. 1858–60 (Vol. 1), 1858.
Delius	*Shakspere's Werke. Herausgegeben von Nikolaus Delius.* 7 vols. 1854–[61] (Vol. 5), Elberfeld, 1859.
Cambridge	*The Works of William Shakespeare edited by William George Clark and William Aldis Wright.* (The Cambridge Shakespeare) 9 vols. 1863–6 (Vol. 3), Cambridge and London, 1863.
Keightley	*The Plays of William Shakespeare. Carefully edited by Thomas Keightley.* 6 vols. (Vol. 2), 1864.
Dyce (1866)	*The Works of William Shakespeare . . . Second Edition.* 9 vols. 1864–7 (Vol. 3), 1866.
Hudson (1871)	*The Works of Shakespeare . . . with Introductions, Notes . . . by The Rev. H. N. Hudson . . . Revised edition.* 6 vols. (Vol. 2), Boston, 1871.
Keightley (1874)	*The Plays of William Shakespeare. Carefully edited by Thomas Keightley.* 6 vols. 1874–9 (Vol. 1), 1874.

Dyce (1875)	*The Works of William Shakespeare ... Third edition.* 9 vols. 1875–6 (Vol. 3), 1875.
Frey	*The Taming of the Shrew edited by A. R. Frey.* The Bankside Shakespeare II. New York, 1888.
Marshall	*The Works of William Shakespeare. Edited by Henry Irving and Frank A. Marshall.* The Henry Irving Shakespeare. 8 vols. 1888–90 (Vol. 2), New York and London, 1888.
Cambridge (1891)	*The Works of William Shakespeare edited by W. A. Wright. The Second edition revised.* 9 vols. 1891–3 (Vol. 3), 1891.
Herford	*The Works of Shakespeare edited by C. H. Herford.* 10 vols. (Vol. 2), 1899.
Bond	*The Taming of the Shrew. Edited by R. Warwick Bond.* The Arden Shakespeare. 1904.
Neilson	*The Complete Dramatic and Poetic Works of William Shakespeare edited by W. A. Neilson.* Boston and New York, 1906.
Boswell-Stone	*The Taming of the Shrew edited W. G. Boswell-Stone.* The Old-Spelling Shakespeare. 1908.
New Cambridge	*The Taming of the Shrew. Edited ... by Sir Arthur Quiller-Couch and John Dover Wilson.* The New Shakespeare. Cambridge, 1928, 1953.
Ridley	*The Taming of the Shrew. Edited by M. R. Ridley.* The New Temple Shakespeare. 1934.
Kittredge	*The Complete Works of Shakespeare. Edited by George Lyman Kittredge.* Boston, [1936].
Harrison	*The Taming of the Shrew* [edited by] *G. B. Harrison.* The Penguin Shakespeare. 1951.
Alexander	*William Shakespeare The Complete Works ... edited ... by Peter Alexander.* The Tudor Shakespeare. 1951.
Sisson	*William Shakespeare The Complete Works ... Edited by Charles Jasper Sisson.* [1954].
Munro	*The London Shakespeare ... edited by ... John Munro.* 6 vols. (Vol. 1), 1958.
Hardin Craig	*The Complete Works of Shakespeare edited by Hardin Craig.* Glenview, Illinois, 1951, 1961.
Hibbard	*The Taming of the Shrew. Edited by G. R. Hibbard.* New Penguin Shakespeare. Harmondsworth, 1968.
Hosley	*The Taming of the Shrew. Edited by Richard Hosley.* The Pelican Shakespeare, revised edition, in *The Complete Works* (general editor Alfred Harbage). Baltimore, 1969.

Riverside	*The Riverside Shakespeare. Textual editor G. Blakemore Evans.* (Vol. 1), Boston, 1974.

OTHER WORKS

Abbott	E. A. Abbott. *A Shakespearian Grammar.* Third edition. 1873.
Baldwin	T. W. Baldwin. *William Shakspere's 'Small Latine & Lesse Greeke'.* Urbana, Illinois, 1944.
Brook	G. L. Brook. *The Language of Shakespeare.* 1976.
Bullough	Geoffrey Bullough. *Narrative and Dramatic Sources of Shakespeare.* (Vol. 1), 1957, repr. 1961.
Capell *Notes*	[Edward Capell]. *Notes and Various Readings to Shakespeare.* [1783].
Cartwright	Robert Cartwright. *New Readings in Shakspere.* 1866.
Collier *Notes*	J. Payne Collier. *Notes and Emendations to the Text of Shakespeare's Plays . . . The Second edition.* 1853.
Golding	*The .XV. Bookes of P. Ouidius Naso, entytuled Metamorphosis, translated oute of Latin into English meeter* [by Arthur Golding.] 1567.
Heath	[Benjamin Heath.] *A Revisal of Shakespear's Text.* 1765.
Hulme	Hilda M. Hulme. *Explorations in Shakespeare's Language.* 1962.
Kinnear	B. G. Kinnear. *Cruces Shakespearianae.* 1883.
Lilly	[William Lilly, John Colet, *et al.*], *A Shorte Introduction of Grammar.* 1549, 1557, 1577.
Madden	D. H. Madden. *The Diary of Master William Silence.* 1907.
Markham	Gervase Markham. *Markham's Maister-peece. Or, What doth a Horse-man lacke.* 1610.
Mason	J. M. Mason. *Comments on the Several Editions of Shakespeare's Plays.* Dublin. 1807.
Nares	Robert Nares. *A Glossary. New edition.* 1859.
Nashe	*The Works of Thomas Nashe,* Edited by Ronald B. McKerrow (1904–10) . . . With supplementary notes . . . by F. P. Wilson. 5 vols. Oxford, 1958.
Naylor	E. W. Naylor. *Shakespeare and Music.* Revised edition, 1931.
Noble	Richmond Noble. *Shakespeare's Biblical Knowledge.* 1935.
OED	*The Oxford English Dictionary, being a corrected reissue of* '*A*

	New English Dictionary upon Historical Principles'. 13 vols. Oxford, 1933, (and Supplements).
Onions	C. T. Onions. *A Shakespeare Glossary.* Second edition 1919, reprinted with enlarged addenda, Oxford, 1958.
Perring	Philip Perring. *Hard Knots in Shakespeare.* 1885.
Schmidt	Alexander Schmidt. *A Shakespeare Lexicon.* 2 vols. Third edition, revised Sarrazin, 1902; reprinted Berlin, 1962.
Sisson, *New Readings*	C. J. Sisson. *New Readings in Shakespeare.* 1956; reprinted 1961.
Theobald *S.R.*	Lewis Theobald. *Shakespeare Restored.* 1726.
Thomson	J. A. K. Thomson. *Shakespeare and the Classics.* 1952.
Tilley	M. P. Tilley. *A Dictionary of the Proverbs in England in the Sixteenth and Seventeenth Centuries.* Ann Arbor, Michigan, 1950.
Tillyard	E. M. W. Tillyard. *Shakespeare's Early Comedies.* 1965.
Turbervile	[George Turbervile]. *The Noble Arte of Venerie or Hunting.* [1575].
Tyrwhitt	Thomas Tyrwhitt. *Observations and Conjectures upon Some Passages of Shakespeare.* 1766.
Upton	John Upton. *Critical Observations on Shakespeare.* 1746, 1748.
Waldo and Herbert	T. R. Waldo and T. W. Herbert, 'Musical Terms in *The Taming of the Shrew*', *Shakespeare Quarterly*, 10 (1959), 185–99.
Walker	W. S. Walker. *A Critical Examination of the Text of Shakespeare.* 3 vols. (Vol. 3), 1860.
Wright	Joseph Wright. *The English Dialect Dictionary.* 6 vols. 1896–1905, reprinted Oxford, 1961.

The Taming of the Shrew

THE CHARACTERS OF THE PLAY

KATHERINA (also 'Katherine' and 'Kate') MINOLA, of Padua, the shrew

BIANCA, her younger sister

BAPTISTA, her father

PETRUCHIO, from Verona, Katherina's suitor, later her husband

GRUMIO, his servant

CURTIS, NATHANIEL, PHILIP, JOSEPH, NICHOLAS, PETER, and others: Petruchio's domestic servants

GREMIO, a wealthy old man, of Padua, one of Bianca's suitors

HORTENSIO, another suitor; part of the time disguised as LITIO, a teacher of music and mathematics

LUCENTIO, from Pisa, a younger suitor, eventually Bianca's husband; for much of the time disguised as CAMBIO, a teacher of languages

TRANIO, his servant; for much of the time impersonating LUCENTIO

BIONDELLO, another of Lucentio's servants

VINCENTIO, Lucentio's father

A SUPPOSED SCHOOLMASTER ('PEDANT'), from Mantua, tricked into impersonating VINCENTIO

A WIDOW, who becomes Hortensio's wife

A TAILOR

A HABERDASHER

AN OFFICER

OTHER SERVANTS, of Lucentio and Baptista

In the Induction

CHRISTOPHER (also 'Christophero') SLY, a drunken tinker and beggar

THE HOSTESS, perhaps MARIAN HACKET of Wincot

A LORD, his HUNTSMEN, his PAGE, and SERVANTS

A COMPANY OF STROLLING PLAYERS, who later act parts in the play-within-the-play

THE CHARACTERS OF THE PLAY] *first listed by* ROWE; *not in* F1

The Taming of the Shrew

Induction 1 *Enter Christopher Sly (a beggar) and the Hostess*

SLY I'll feeze you, in faith.

HOSTESS A pair of stocks, you rogue!

SLY You're a baggage, the Slys are no rogues. Look in the Chronicles, we came in with Richard Conqueror. Therefore *paucas pallabris*, let the world slide. Sessa! 5

Induction 1] POPE; *Actus primus. Scæna Prima.* F1 0.1 *Enter ... Hostess*] F1 (*Enter Begger and Hostes, Christophero Sly*); Enter a Tapster, beating out of his doores *Slie Droonken.* A SHREW 1 SLY] ROWE; *Begger* F1 (*and 'Beg.' throughout Induction*) 5 *paucas pallabris*] F1; *pocas palabras* DYCE 1875

Induction 1 Headings such as *'Actus primus. Scæna Prima.'* are set up, as a matter of routine, by the F1 compositors – even in plays such as *Antony*, where there is no subsequent act or scene division. In the F1 text of *Shrew*, the second division to be marked is *'Actus Tertia'*. See Editorial Principles, p. 77 and 4.3 Headnote. Pope first gave the Sly story the convenient name of 'The Induction'.

0.1 ***Enter ... Hostess*** F1's stage direction, with the odd placing of 'Christophero Sly', is just as likely to be an author's note as a relic of a prompter's marginal addition (as suggested by New Cambridge). Sly is again described as a 'beggar' by the Lord in l. 38, and his speech prefix in F1 is invariably *'Beg.'*. It is not inconsistent that he should say that his present occupation is 'tinker' (Induction 2.19): he adds that he is sadly behind with payment for the ale he has drunk. The name 'Sly' has been found in both Warwickshire and London records.

1 **feeze** 'do for' (a colloquial extension of the original meanings 'drive off' and 'frighten' that perhaps became a catch-phrase)

2 **pair of stocks** Presumably 'pair' because of the *two* holes in the wooden frame to confine the ankles of the person publicly punished (another two often confined the wrists). So also in *Errors*, 3.1.60.

3 **baggage** contemptible, or even loose, woman

4 **Richard Conqueror** Sly, having heard of William the Conqueror, has presumably inferred that 'Conqueror' is a surname – and then gets the Christian name wrong too. To claim that one's family 'came in with the Conqueror' is the proverbial protestation of the antiquity of one's lineage (Tilley C594).

5 ***paucas pallabris*** Although Sly later (Induction 2.134–5) does not know what a comedy is, his speech seems to include catch-phrases picked up, inaccurately, from the most popular of Elizabethan tragedies of blood, Kyd's *Spanish Tragedy*. Kyd's hero, Hieronimo, whose name causes Sly further confusion in l. 7, reminds himself not to give too much away, with the line *'Pocas palabras!* [i.e. few words] mild as the lamb!' (3.14.118).

let the world slide A proverb (Tilley W879): 'why worry?' Sly repeats it in the form 'let the world slip' (Induction 2.140). He (or Shakespeare) may have in mind the fuller versions 'Let the world wag, we must needs have drink' or 'Let the world slide, let the world go: | A fig for care, and a fig for woe! | If I can't pay, why I can owe, | And death makes equal the high and low.'

Sessa! Variously explained as 'a cry used by way of exhorting to swift running' (Schmidt, comparing German *sasa*); a cry of triumph following a hit at fencing; and an anglicization of French *cessez* (Halliwell), or Spanish *cesa*, 'stop', 'be quiet!' (Theobald), or even of *c'est ça* ('that's that'). Edgar's dual use of 'sessa' while playing the part of Poor Tom in *Lear* (3.4.99 and 3.6.73) gives some support to the first explanation, but Sly might rather be expected to affirm 'there's an end of the matter'.

HOSTESS You will not pay for the glasses you have burst?
SLY No, not a denier. Go by, Saint Jeronimy, go to thy cold
bed and warm thee.
HOSTESS I know my remedy, I must go fetch the head-
borough. *Exit* 10
SLY Third, or fourth, or fifth borough, I'll answer him by
law. I'll not budge an inch, boy. Let him come, and kindly.
He falls asleep. There is a winding of horns.
Enter a Lord from hunting, with his train
LORD
Huntsman, I charge thee tender well my hounds.

7 Saint] F1 (S.); *not in* Q1631 9–10 headborough] F1; Third-borough POPE 1728 (*conj.* THEOBALD *S.R.*) 10 *Exit*] *not in* F1 12.1 *He*] *not in* F1 12.1 *There is a winding of*] F1(*Winde*)

6 **burst** broken. There are similar uses in 3.2.58 and 4.1.71.

7 **denier** A small French coin of minimal value. Compare the modern '(not worth a) brass farthing'.

Go by, Saint Jeronimy Sly confuses St. Jerome (Hieronymus) with Kyd's Hieronimo, whose further counsel to himself 'Hieronimo, beware! go by, go by!' (*Spanish Tragedy*, 3.12.30) became proverbial and the subject of many gibes. Sly's confusion, incidentally, provides further evidence that the name of the character was pronounced 'Jeronimo' on the public stage, whatever spelling Kyd might use with his characteristic pedantry (and ignorance).

7–8 **go to thy cold bed and warm thee** Although Tilley does not record the phrase, the use of it by Edgar also (*Lear*, 3.4.47) may mean that it was proverbial. As Theobald suggested, however, the association in Sly's mind may again be with *The Spanish Tragedy* – Hieronimo's notorious 'What outcries pluck me from my naked bed?' (2.5.1). Sly presumably puts his advice to himself into practice and lies down on the cold earth in his drunken stupor (hence ll. 29–30).

9–10 **headborough** The common emendation to 'thirdborough', made because of Sly's rejoinder, is gratuitous: Sly's mind is quite capable of jumping from one word to the other, particularly as the two were for most purposes interchangeable, as the title of a petty constable. (Exceptionally, however, an Act cited by *OED* – 28 *Hen. VIII.* c. 10 – speaks of 'Every ... counstable, hedborowe, thyrd boroughe, borsolder, and every other lay officer'.) William Lambard explains in his *Eirenarcha*, 1581, sig.[B8], also quoted by *OED*: 'where each third Borowe onlie hath a Constable, there the officers of the other two Borowes, be called Thirdeborowes' (and he is speaking of Warwickshire and perhaps giving the popular, false, local etymology. It is more likely that 'thirdborough' derives from ME *fridborgh*, OE *friðborg*, a peace-surety (*OED*).) In *LLL*, the Constable (Dull) announces 'I am his graces Tharborough' (F1 ll. 195–6, 1.1.182); in *Much Ado* in a stage direction Verges is introduced as the 'Headborough' (3.5.0).

12 **boy** Frequently in Elizabethan use an insulting form of address to an individual – but not always so (see l. 16) and Sly is not speaking to anybody in particular. 'Not for anyone'.

and kindly and welcome! (an extension of the use of 'kindly' meaning 'agreeably', *OED adv.* II.3)

12.1 ***winding*** blowing, sounding calls

12.2 ***train*** Four actors would be the barest minimum; six or more are desirable. At least two servingmen remain after Sly has been carried off, perhaps by two other servants, at 70.1; and two huntsmen speak – and are still on stage after l. 127 (unless it is they who carry Sly out, and the lord is alone on the stage when he speaks ll. 128–35).

Breathe Merriman – the poor cur is embossed –
And couple Clowder with the deep-mouthed brach.
Saw'st thou not, boy, how Silver made it good
At the hedge corner, in the coldest fault?
I would not lose the dog for twenty pound.

FIRST HUNTSMAN

Why, Bellman is as good as he, my lord:
He cried upon it at the merest loss, 20
And twice today picked out the dullest scent;
Trust me, I take him for the better dog.

LORD

Thou art a fool: if Echo were as fleet,
I would esteem him worth a dozen such.
But sup them well, and look unto them all;
Tomorrow I intend to hunt again.

FIRST HUNTSMAN

I will, my lord.

LORD

What's here? One dead, or drunk? See, doth he breathe?

SECOND HUNTSMAN

He breathes, my lord. Were he not warmed with ale,
This were a bed but cold to sleep so soundly. 30

14 Breathe] SISSON (*conj.* MITFORD); Brach F1; Leech HANMER; Broach NEW CAMBRIDGE cur is] F1; cur, is GRANT WHITE 28] *as verse* Q1631; *as prose* F1 29–30] *as verse* ROWE 1714; *as prose* F1

14 **Breathe** This emendation of F1's 'Brach' makes better sense than 'broch' or 'broach', meaning 'bleed', and plausibly conjectures a compositor's misreading of 'breath', under the influence of 'brach' ('bitch') in the following line. 'Merriman' is a name for a dog, not a bitch; and the dog is to be 'breathed' (given time to recover its breath) while another, Clowder, takes its place in the leash with the better-conditioned unnamed bitch. Turbervile, in *The Noble Art of Venerie or Hunting* [1575], specifically recommends the coupling thus of a young hound and an old bitch: two males together would fight.
embossed panting and completely exhausted (a regular hunting term)

15 **couple** put on the leash (with a second animal). An inexperienced animal (such as Clowder apparently is, being held in reserve) was normally coupled with a more experienced one for training purposes.

15 **deep-mouthed** capable of baying with the deep note the Elizabethans valued in their hunting hounds (compare 'deep-mouth'd thunder', *K. John*, 5.2.173). Gervase Markham, in his *Country Contentments* (1615, and later editions), even gives advice on how to choose dogs so that their cries blend.

16 **made it good** i.e. picked up the scent

17 **in the coldest fault** i.e. even though there was a 'fault' (break in the scent) and the scent therefore lost, as 'cold' as it could be

20 **cried upon it** (first) bayed to proclaim that he had picked up the trail
merest 'Mere' meant 'absolute' (as in the famous 'mere oblivion' of the 'Seven Ages of Man' speech in *As You Like It*). Hence 'almost complete'.

LORD
O monstrous beast, how like a swine he lies!
Grim death, how foul and loathsome is thine image!
Sirs, I will practise on this drunken man.
What think you, if he were conveyed to bed,
Wrapped in sweet clothes, rings put upon his fingers,
A most delicious banquet by his bed,
And brave attendants near him when he wakes,
Would not the beggar then forget himself?

FIRST HUNTSMAN
Believe me, lord, I think he cannot choose.

SECOND HUNTSMAN
It would seem strange unto him when he waked. 40

LORD
Even as a flattering dream or worthless fancy.
Then take him up, and manage well the jest.
Carry him gently to my fairest chamber,
And hang it round with all my wanton pictures.
Balm his foul head in warm distilled waters,
And burn sweet wood to make the lodging sweet.
Procure me music ready when he wakes,
To make a dulcet and a heavenly sound.
And if he chance to speak, be ready straight
And, with a low submissive reverence, 50
Say 'What is it your honour will command?'
Let one attend him with a silver basin
Full of rose-water and bestrewed with flowers;

32 The line builds on the traditional description of sleep as the image of death, with perhaps special ironic reference to the biblical 'He giveth his beloved sleep' (Psalms 127: 2).

33 **practise on** 'to act upon, by artifice, so as to induce to do or believe something' (*OED* 'practise' *v.* 11)

35 **sweet** perfumed

36 **banquet** Not, in Elizabethan use, an elaborate full meal, but the fruit and sweetmeats that normally followed or ended one.

37 **brave** elaborately dressed in finery

39 Perhaps a witty adaptation of the proverb 'Beggars cannot be choosers' (Tilley B247).

41 **flattering** gratifying, or instilling confidence
fancy fantasy (of which 'fancy' is in fact a contraction)

44 **pictures** paintings – or possibly the painted cloth or woven tapestry then used for wall-covering, the latter in the houses of the wealthy. Compare Induction 2.47–58.

45 **Balm** anoint (here, with perfume distilled from, e.g., flowers); compare 'rose-water' in l. 53.

46 **sweet wood** aromatic wood, such as pine or juniper

48 **dulcet** sweetly melodious

49 **straight** straightaway, immediately

50 **reverence** (deep) bow

Another bear the ewer, the third a diaper,
And say 'Will't please your lordship cool your hands?'
Someone be ready with a costly suit,
And ask him what apparel he will wear.
Another tell him of his hounds and horse,
And that his lady mourns at his disease.
Persuade him that he hath been lunatic, 60
And when he says he *is*, say that he dreams,
For he is nothing but a mighty lord.
This do, and do it kindly, gentle sirs.
It will be pastime passing excellent,
If it be husbanded with modesty.

FIRST HUNTSMAN
My lord, I warrant you we will play our part
As he shall think by our true diligence
He is no less than what we say he is.

LORD
Take him up gently and to bed with him,
And each one to his office when he wakes. 70
Sly is carried out

61 he *is*, say] F1 (*without italics*); he's Sly, say NEW CAMBRIDGE (1928 *only*) (*conj.* JOHNSON)
70.1] *not in* F1; *Exeunt* two with *Slie*. A SHREW

54 **ewer** large jug or pitcher, once commonly placed in bedrooms, to hold water for washing
diaper hand-towel

58 **horse** Probably the old generic plural (now used only of troops, 'the foot and the horse'). In OE the plural was the same as the singular. Emendation to 'horses' is unnecessary.

59 **disease** Closer to the literal 'dis-ease': derangement or indisposition, of body or (as here) of mind.

61 **he *is*** i.e. that he is, must be, lunatic now, if he thinks he hears such nonsense correctly. Johnson's conjecture 'he's Sly' is not only unnecessary but also falsely assumes that the Lord knows Sly's name, which has not been mentioned in his presence. The many other emendations are too improbable to be worth listing.

63 **kindly** naturally – but Shakespeare often also uses the word to mean 'in a friendly way' (see l. 12 and note) and puns on the two senses in *Timon*, 2.2.217 and *Lear*, 1.5.14.
gentle sirs The phrase (even if 'gentle' means 'noble') is not inappropriate to the Lord addressing huntsmen, who duly agree to take part in the jest. Those who later trick Sly, however, seem to be mere servants (they are called 'attendants' in the stage direction and have speech prefixes like '1.*Ser*.' and '3.*Man*').

64 **passing** surpassingly (a common Elizabethan colloquial use – which indeed is found much later – without the distinguishing 'adverbial' termination 'ly'; Abbott 1)

65 **husbanded** managed prudently (*OED* 'husband' *v. trans.* 2)
modesty moderation, restraint (an almost obsolete but once normal meaning of the noun; compare l. 91). The adjective 'modest' can still mean 'moderate', as in 'a modest request'.

67 **As** so that, so as to ensure that (a regular use: Abbott 109)

69 **to bed with him** put him to bed

70 **office** allotted task

70.1 F1 gives no instruction for the removal of Sly but the servants (or huntsmen) must obey the Lord's command to put him to bed, and he is next said to '*Enter aloft*'.

Trumpets sound

Sirrah, go see what trumpet 'tis that sounds –

Exit Servingman

Belike some noble gentleman that means,

Travelling some journey, to repose him here.

Enter Servingman

How now? Who is it?

SERVINGMAN An't please your honour, players

That offer service to your lordship.

Enter Players

LORD

Bid them come near. – Now, fellows, you are welcome.

PLAYERS

We thank your honour.

LORD

Do you intend to stay with me tonight?

FIRST PLAYER

So please your lordship to accept our duty.

LORD

With all my heart. This fellow I remember 80

Since once he played a farmer's eldest son. –

'Twas where you wooed the gentlewoman so well.

I have forgot your name; but sure that part

Was aptly fitted and naturally performed.

SECOND PLAYER

I think 'twas Soto that your honour means.

70.2] *Sound trumpets* F1 71.1] *not in* F1 75.1] F1; Enter two of the players with packs at their backs and a boy. A SHREW; *Enter Players.* ROWE, *after 'near' in l.* 76 79 FIRST PLAYER] 2. *Player* F1 85 SECOND PLAYER] *Sincklo* F1; *Sin.* F2; *Sim.* F3

70.2 The sound of trumpets similarly announces the arrival of strolling players in *Hamlet* ('*Flourish for the Players*', F1 l. 1415; 2.2.364).

71 **Sirrah** A normal form of address to a servant or social inferior (and therefore in other contexts sometimes implying an insult).

72 **Belike** perhaps, or even 'probably'

75.1 F1's placing of the stage direction is not an error: on the deep Elizabethan stage, actors must often have entered from the rear, and been seen by the audience, before they were visible to other characters on the stage.

79 **So** if it

79 **duty** services (*OED* 5)

81 **Since once** Explained by Abbott 132 as meaning 'when once' but seems to mean rather 'since the time when . . .'.

84 **aptly fitted** well suited to you; i.e. you were well cast in it.

naturally realistically, convincingly.

85 **SECOND PLAYER** For comment on the F1 speech prefix '*Sincklo*', the name of an actor, see Introduction, pp. 4–5.

Soto A minor character named 'Soto' appears in Fletcher's heterogeneous play *Women Pleased*, but that is much later than *The Taming of the Shrew*, and the Lord's description of the part does not fit. (As Tyrwhitt first pointed out, Soto, a

LORD

'Tis very true; thou didst it excellent. –
Well, you are come to me in happy time,
The rather for I have some sport in hand
Wherein your cunning can assist me much.
There is a lord will hear you play tonight; 90
But I am doubtful of your modesties,
Lest, over-eyeing of his odd behaviour –
For yet his honour never heard a play –
You break into some merry passion
And so offend him; for I tell you, sirs,
If you should smile, he grows impatient.

FIRST PLAYER

Fear not, my lord, we can contain ourselves
Were he the veriest antic in the world.

LORD (*to a Servingman*)

Go, sirrah, take them to the buttery,
And give them friendly welcome every one. 100
Let them want nothing that my house affords.

Exit Servingman with the Players

– Sirrah, go you to Barthol'mew my page,

97 FIRST PLAYER] F1 (*Plai.*)

foolish servant, is a farmer's son but does not woo a gentlewoman.) No other is known, but Sir Walter Greg drew the attention of the New Cambridge editors to lines from the Oxford Twelfth-Night entertainment *Narcissus*, dated '*c.*1602': 'least you should counte me for a Sot-o I (A very pretty figure called pars pro toto)', which perhaps suggest a character who was physically small. Sincklo seems to have been very thin; and if the F1 speech prefix '*Sincklo*' derives, as is probable, from the author's manuscript, there is the greater likelihood that Shakespeare was referring jocularly to another part that Sincklo was generally known to have played. (New Cambridge conjectures that it was in a play revised by Fletcher for *Women Pleased*.)

86 **excellent** excellently (compare l. 64 above, and note)

87 **in happy time** opportunely

89 **cunning** acquired skill (the derogatory meaning was already known but was less common)

91 **modesties** discretion, self-control (compare l. 65 above, and note)

92 **over-eyeing of** witnessing, observing

93 **yet** as yet. As Abbott points out (76), the use *before* a negative was then as common as is the surviving use *after* one ('never yet' e.g.).

94 **merry passion** uncontrollable laughter. ('Passion': 'any . . . vehement, commanding, or overpowering emotion', *OED* 'passion' *sb.* III. 6.)

98 **veriest antic** truest, or most extreme, eccentric ('antic' is defined by *OED* as 'a parallel form' to 'antique' but 'distinct in sense': the adjective meant, originally, 'grotesque')

99 **buttery** store-room, for both liquor and food

101 **want** lack

102 **Barthol'mew** Then normally pronounced 'Bartlemy'.

And see him dressed in all suits like a lady.
That done, conduct him to the drunkard's chamber,
And call him 'madam', do him obeisance.
Tell him from me – as he will win my love –
He bear himself with honourable action,
Such as he hath observed in noble ladies
Unto their lords, by them accomplishèd.
Such duty to the drunkard let him do, 110
With soft low tongue and lowly courtesy,
And say 'What is't your honour will command
Wherein your lady and your humble wife
May show her duty and make known her love?'
And then with kind embracements, tempting kisses,
And with declining head into his bosom,
Bid him shed tears, as being overjoyed
To see her noble lord restored to health,
Who for this seven years hath esteemed him
No better than a poor and loathsome beggar; 120
And if the boy have not a woman's gift
To rain a shower of commanded tears,
An onion will do well for such a shift,
Which in a napkin, being close conveyed,
Shall in despite enforce a watery eye.
See this dispatched with all the haste thou canst;
Anon I'll give thee more instructions.

103 **suits** respects – but with awareness of another meaning ('suit of clothes')

106 **as he will** if he wishes to

107 **bear** is to bear, must bear (the use of the subjunctive after a verb implying command, Abbott 369)
honourable action the demeanour befitting a person of honour or rank. (For 'action', see ll. 128–9.)

109 **accomplishèd** carried out, performed

111 **lowly** humble
courtesy Elizabethans made no firm distinction between 'courtesy' and 'curtsy', at least in written English. Here the word is clearly trisyllabic, but the meaning 'curtsy' seems the more appropriate.

116 i.e. the pageboy is to bow his head as if to conceal tears. The division of the adjectival phrase ('declining into his bosom') so that the adjective comes before the noun but the adverbial phrase after it is frequent in Shakespeare (Abbott 419 a).

119 **esteemed him** believed himself to be (the Lord is putting into indirect speech the words the Page is to utter). The versification is irregular but the line may be spoken with three strong stresses on 'thís séven yéars'.

122 **commanded tears** tears produced when required

123 **for such a shift** as an expedient, to obtain the desired end

124 **napkin** (Probably) handkerchief (*OED* 2), as clearly in *Titus*, 3.1.140 (although in Shakespeare one cannot always be certain).
close conveyed secretly brought close to the eyes (another instance of the adverb without the suffix 'ly')

125 **in despite** notwithstanding the natural tendency to laugh; or, perhaps, the natural disinclination to weep

Exit Second Servingman

I know the boy will well usurp the grace,
Voice, gait, and action of a gentlewoman.
I long to hear him call the drunkard 'husband' 130
And how my men will stay themselves from laughter
When they do homage to this simple peasant.
I'll in to counsel them: haply my presence
May well abate the over-merry spleen,
Which otherwise would grow into extremes. *Exeunt*

Induction 2 *Enter aloft the drunkard (Sly) with attendants (some with apparel, basin and ewer, and other appurtenances) and Lord*

SLY For God's sake, a pot of small ale.

FIRST SERVINGMAN
Will't please your lordship drink a cup of sack?

SECOND SERVINGMAN
Will't please your honour taste of these conserves?

132 peasant.] BLAIR; peasant, F1; Peasant; ROWE 135 *Exeunt*] *not in* F1
Induction 2.0.1–3 *Enter ... Lord*] F1 (*omitting* '(*Sly*)'); Enter two with a table and a banquet on it, and two other, with *Slie* asleepe in a chaire, richlie apparelled, & the musick plaieng. A SHREW 2 FIRST SERVINGMAN] F1 (1. *Ser.*) lordship] Q1631; Lord F1

127 **Anon** very soon, without delay ('anon', like 'presently', has weakened in meaning)

128 **usurp** adopt, put on

131 **And how** There may be an ellipsis ('And *see* how') but 'hear how' also makes sense.

132 **simple** Perhaps 'insignificant', perhaps 'simple-minded' – or both.

133 **I'll in** In Elizabethan usage a verb of motion is often implied in such phrases. 'I'll go in'.
haply perhaps or (possibly) with good luck ('haply' and 'happily' were not always distinguished). Compare 1.1.8, 1.2.55, 4.4.53.

134 **spleen** impulse (the spleen was thought to be the seat of emotion). So too in 3.2.10.

Induction 2 F1's '*aloft*' would naturally refer to the 'upper stage' of the Elizabethan theatre, but there is some doubt whether so many characters could move with ease there, or be seen by the audience from all parts of the theatre. (It is not true, however, that there must have been space for a bed: Sly has presumably risen from the bed on which he was first placed; he is later – l. 35 – offered another.) The upper stage would possibly have the advantage of curtains that could be drawn to remove Sly from sight when he ceases to have any further part in the play. Alternatively, some temporary raised platform may have been used on the main stage, although there would have been some clumsiness if it had to be dismantled after 1.1. In either case, movement from a lower to an upper level, not necessarily within view of the audience, would allow the immediate (re-)appearance of the Lord without breach of the so-called 'law of re-entry'; there is therefore no need to emend the Folio stage direction.

1 **small** weak (and accordingly less expensive; all that Sly can reasonably demand)

2 **cup of sack** bowl of dry white wine, such as sherry ('sack' deriving from French *sec*, dry) – a more aristocratic beverage than small beer. It was imported from Spain and the Canaries.

3 **conserves** fruits preserved with sugar

THIRD SERVINGMAN

What raiment will your honour wear today?

SLY I am Christophero Sly, call not me 'honour' nor 'lordship'. I ne'er drank sack in my life; and if you give me any conserves, give me conserves of beef. Ne'er ask me what raiment I'll wear, for I have no more doublets than backs, no more stockings than legs, nor no more shoes than feet – nay, sometime more feet than shoes, or such shoes as 10 my toes look through the overleather.

LORD

Heaven cease this idle humour in your honour!
O that a mighty man of such descent,
Of such possessions, and so high esteem,
Should be infusèd with so foul a spirit!

SLY What, would you make me mad? Am not I Christopher Sly, old Sly's son of Burton-heath, by birth a pedlar, by education a cardmaker, by transmutation a bear-herd, and now by present profession a tinker? Ask Marian Hacket, the fat ale-wife of Wincot, if she know me not: if 20

3, 4 SECOND SERVINGMAN, THIRD SERVINGMAN] F1 (2. *Ser.*, 3. *Ser.*) 17 Sly's] F1 (Sies)

7 **conserves of beef** preserved (salted) beef

7–11 **what raiment . . . overleather** Shakespeare here has Sly elaborate picturesquely on the proverbial 'my wardrobe is on my back' (Tilley W61).

8 **doublets** coats, close-fitting, worn by men

11 **overleather** upper leather of the shoe

12 **cease** stop (the intransitive verb used as a transitive, according to Abbott, 291, but the transitive use was already known in Middle English)
idle foolish, or unprofitable; perhaps both
humour state of mind (one of several related meanings growing from the original idea that disposition was determined by the proportion of the four humours or fluids of the human body)

15 **infusèd with so foul a spirit** imbued with so unhealthy a disposition, or indisposition – but possibly with some notion of 'possession' by an evil spirit. That the Lord is deliberately speaking in pedantic terms is suggested by Hamlet's use of 'infusion', presumably to mean 'character', when he is parodying Osric's misuse of polysyllabic words (5.2.117).

17 **Burton-heath** Perhaps Barton-on-the-Heath, a dozen or so miles from Stratford-upon-Avon. It has even been conjectured that Shakespeare is amusing himself in this section of the play by referring not only to places in or near Warwickshire but also to people living there. See, e.g., notes on ll. 19–20, 20, 87, 91.

18 **cardmaker** maker of 'cards', iron-toothed instruments for combing wool. As Hibbard points out, it is a likely trade for one dwelling on the edge of the Cotswolds, famous in Shakespeare's day for producing sheep and wool.
bear-herd the keeper of a performing-bear led round the country

19–20 **Marian Hacket** It is not clear whether this is the Hostess of the opening lines of the play.

20 **Wincot** Probably the small village, partly in the parish of Quinton, only a few miles from Stratford – not to be confused with Wilmcote, the home-village of Shakespeare's mother Mary Arden, or with the Woncot (Woodmancote) of *2 Henry IV*, 5.1.37. Parish records mention a family named Hacket, in 1591.

she say I am not fourteen pence on the score for sheer ale,
score me up for the lyingest knave in Christendom. What,
I am not bestraught. Here's –

THIRD SERVINGMAN
O, this it is that makes your lady mourn.

SECOND SERVINGMAN
O, this is it that makes your servants droop.

LORD
Hence comes it that your kindred shuns your house
As beaten hence by your strange lunacy.
O noble lord, bethink thee of thy birth,
Call home thy ancient thoughts from banishment,
And banish hence these abject lowly dreams. 30
Look how thy servants do attend on thee,
Each in his office ready at thy beck.
Wilt thou have music? (*Music*) Hark, Apollo plays,
And twenty cagèd nightingales do sing.
Or wilt thou sleep? We'll have thee to a couch

24 THIRD SERVINGMAN] F1 (3. *Man.*) *and similarly throughout Induction 2* 25 SECOND SERVINGMAN] F1 (2 *Man.*) *and similarly throughout Induction 2* is it] F1; it is ROWE 33 *Music*] This edition; *at end of line* F1

21 **on the score** on the reckoning for debt. Alehouse debts were chalked up on a board – hence 'score me up' (in l. 22): 'post' me or list me as an offender.
sheer ale Rather than 'pure ale', this probably means the same as the 'small ale' of l. 1 (*OED* 'sheer' 5, 'thin, not containing much substance' – although *OED* overlooks the possibility of that meaning here and gives as its first illustration one of 1632). The alternative interpretation, accepted by *OED* (7), is 'ale alone, ale without food' – but this line is the first cited, and the others found before 1625 are not unambiguous; and 'shire' *adj.* 6 – a related word – is glossed 'Of beer: weak, "small"'.

22 **lyingest** Elizabethan English 'allowed', as Modern English does not, this form of the superlative of a present participle used as an adjective. Either 'most given to lying' or 'telling the greatest lies'.

23 **bestraught** distraught, out of my wits (the word existed and is not an error by Sly)
Here's Bond took this to be the beginning of a toast – and many editors therefore supply stage directions such as 'A servingman brings him a pot of ale' and 'He drinks'. The interruptions by the attendants lend this no support.

25 **droop** become dispirited. *OED* 'droop' *v.* 5.

26 **kindred shuns** May be explained *either* as the use of the singular verb after a generic noun *or* as the old 'Northern' plural formed by adding 's' to the verb stem, as in 'My old bones aches', *Tempest*, 3.3.2 (Abbott 333). Shakespeare elsewhere uses 'kindred' sometimes with a singular, sometimes with a plural verb; the *Middle English Dictionary* gives reason for thinking that it was then more often regarded as a singular noun.

27 **As beaten hence** i.e. feeling that they have been driven out

29 **ancient** former. A normal meaning of the word but the image is strained: throughout this speech Shakespeare is putting inflated language into the mouth of the Lord as he plays his part.

32 **in his office** according to his allotted function or responsibility
beck nod or other silent signal of command (as in the surviving phrase 'to be at [somebody's] beck and call')

33 **Apollo** i.e. the god of music himself

Softer and sweeter than the lustful bed
On purpose trimmed up for Semiramis.
Say thou wilt walk; we will bestrew the ground.
Or wilt thou ride? Thy horses shall be trapped,
Their harness studded all with gold and pearl. 40
Dost thou love hawking? Thou hast hawks will soar
Above the morning lark. Or wilt thou hunt?
Thy hounds shall make the welkin answer them
And fetch shrill echoes from the hollow earth.

FIRST SERVINGMAN
Say thou wilt course, thy greyhounds are as swift
As breathèd stags – ay, fleeter than the roe.

SECOND SERVINGMAN
Dost thou love pictures? We will fetch thee straight
Adonis painted by a running brook,
And Cytherea all in sedges hid,
Which seem to move and wanton with her breath, 50
Even as the waving sedges play with wind.

LORD
We'll show thee Io as she was a maid,
And how she was beguilèd and surprised –

51 with] F1; wi' th' ALEXANDER

36 **lustful** provoking sexual desire (but the word in Elizabethan use did not necessarily have the strongly pejorative connotation of the modern adjective)

37 **trimmed up** decorated; both prepared and adorned
Semiramis The Queen of Assyria, notorious – according to one tradition – for voluptuousness. In *Titus*, 2.1.21–3, Aaron similarly describes Tamora as 'this queen, | This goddess, this Semiramis, this nymph, | This siren that will charm Rome's Saturnine . . .'.

38 **bestrew the ground** lay rushes – or even carpets – to prevent the possible danger to an aristocratic foot. Compare the modern 'roll out the red carpet'.

39 **trapped** caparisoned ('trap' is an altered form of French *drap*, a covering)

43 **welkin** sky (the word was already 'poetical' and is used by characters like Armado). For the pride in the sounds of the hunting pack, compare 'deep-mouthed' in Induction 1.15 above.

45 **course** hunt hares

46 **breathèd** long-winded, as in *LLL*, 5.2.645 and *Timon*, 1.1.10 (not, as often, 'out of breath', 'exhausted'). The servants imitate, with less than complete success, their master's rhetoric.

46 **roe** the smaller species of deer. 'As swift as a roe' was proverbial (Tilley R158).

47–51 The 'pictures' – whether single paintings, painted cloth, or tapestry – are of standard erotic scenes derived from, particularly but not exclusively, Ovid. The first is of the infatuation of the goddess Venus (Cytherea) with Adonis; and Shakespeare imagines Venus, hidden in the sedges or rushes, spying on the naked Adonis bathing. As Thomson points out, however, Shakespeare seems to have conflated the Venus–Adonis story and an incident from Ovid's version of the story of Salmacis and Hermaphroditus (*Metamorphoses* IV. 285 ff.). The same confusion appears in *The Passionate Pilgrim* (6). The epithet 'Cytherea' is derived from the island Cythera, near which Venus was 'born' when she sprang from the sea.

50 **wanton** sway seductively

As lively painted as the deed was done.

THIRD SERVINGMAN

Or Daphne roaming through a thorny wood,
Scratching her legs that one shall swear she bleeds,
And at that sight shall sad Apollo weep,
So workmanly the blood and tears are drawn.

LORD

Thou art a lord, and nothing but a lord.
Thou hast a lady far more beautiful 60
Than any woman in this waning age.

FIRST SERVINGMAN

And till the tears that she hath shed for thee
Like envious floods o'errun her lovely face
She was the fairest creature in the world,
And yet she is inferior to none.

SLY

Am I a lord, and have I such a lady?
Or do I dream? Or have I dreamed till now?
I do not sleep: I see, I hear, I speak,
I smell sweet savours and I feel soft things.
Upon my life, I am a lord indeed, 70
And not a tinker nor Christopher Sly.
Well, bring our lady hither to our sight,
And once again a pot o'th' smallest ale.

71 Christopher] F1; Christophero F2

52 The second picture is of the rape of Io by Jupiter (Zeus) who concealed himself for the purpose under a thick cloud or mist.

54 **As ... done** painted with such animation that it perfectly represents the original act

55–8 The third picture is of the god Apollo, infatuated (because of Cupid's wilful interference) with Daphne. Cupid also ensured that Apollo's love would not be returned; Daphne escaped when by divine intervention she was turned into a laurel tree.

61 **this waning age** An allusion – deliberately pretentious – to the widely-held belief that the world had consistently deteriorated from the Golden Age (or, in the Christian version, the Garden of Eden).

63 **envious** malicious. 'Envy' in Elizabethan usage implies ill-will or even hatred, not jealousy. So 'an envious thrust from Tybalt', and Juliet's 'Can Heaven be so envious?', *Romeo*, 3.1.165 and 3.2.40.

63 **o'errun** overran. The common form of the past tense with 'u', as in 'sung', 'begun' (Abbott 339).

65 **yet** still, even now

66 Sly speaks in verse as he begins to believe himself a lord.

68–70 Again Shakespeare has Sly ring the changes on a proverb, 'seeing is believing' (Tilley S212).

71 **Christopher** Most editors adopt the F2 reading 'Christophero', to make the line 'metrical'. It reads quite well, however, with a pause after 'tinker'; and Sly has already called himself 'Christopher' as well as 'Christophero' (ll. 16, 5 above).

72 **our** Sly has amusingly adopted the 'royal plural'.

SECOND SERVINGMAN

Will't please your mightiness to wash your hands?
O how we joy to see your wit restored,
O that once more you knew but what you are!
These fifteen years you have been in a dream,
Or when you waked, so waked as if you slept.

SLY

These fifteen years! By my fay, a goodly nap.
But did I never speak of all that time? 80

FIRST SERVINGMAN

O yes, my lord, but very idle words,
For though you lay here in this goodly chamber,
Yet would you say ye were beaten out of door,
And rail upon the hostess of the house,
And say you would present her at the leet
Because she brought stone jugs and no sealed quarts.
Sometimes you would call out for Cicely Hacket.

SLY

Ay, the woman's maid of the house.

THIRD SERVINGMAN

Why, sir, you know no house, nor no such maid,
Nor no such men as you have reckoned up – 90
As Stephen Sly, and old John Naps of Greece,

91 Greece] F1; Greet HOSLEY (*conj.* HALLIWELL)

75 **wit** mental powers or understanding (regular Elizabethan meanings of the word)

77 **fifteen** The servant is bettering his instruction (compare 'seven years' in Induction 1.119).

79 **fay** faith
goodly considerable, long (*OED* 2)

80 **of** during (a regular use – Abbott 176 – as in, e.g., *LLL*, 1.1.43, 'And not be seen to wink of all the day')

83 **you, ye** Elizabethan usage with these pronouns varied, but it is odd to find both used as nominatives in the one line. Perhaps 'ye', the original nominative form (on the way to being replaced by 'you', originally the accusative) is attributed ironically to Sly because it was thought more aristocratic – but it is soon dropped (l. 85); perhaps a shortened or elided pronunciation is indicated.

84 **house** inn, tavern

85 **present her at the leet** accuse her in the court held by the lord of the manor. It had power not only to indict but also to punish summarily many minor crimes – including selling by short measure.

86 **Because . . . quarts** The stone jug, unlike the sealed (officially stamped) quart, gave no guarantee of quantity.

87 **Cicely Hacket** Presumably the daughter of Marian (named in ll.19–20) and her maid, if Sly's reply is to be so interpreted – but conceivably he means that Cicely would act as maid to any woman guest in the mother's ale-house.

90 **reckoned up** named, listed

91 **Greece** Perhaps 'John Naps' is an anglicization of a Greek name but more probably 'Greece' is Sly's variant of 'Greet', a small village in Gloucestershire and not far from Stratford. If Shakespeare wrote 'Greete', that may have been misread as 'Greece'.

And Peter Turf, and Henry Pimpernel,
And twenty more such names and men as these,
Which never were nor no man ever saw.

SLY
Now Lord be thanked for my good amends.

ALL Amen.

Enter Page, dressed as a lady, with attendants

SLY I thank thee, thou shalt not lose by it.

PAGE How fares my noble lord?

SLY
Marry, I fare well, for here is cheer enough.
Where is my wife? 100

PAGE
Here, noble lord; what is thy will with her?

SLY
Are you my wife, and will not call me 'husband'?
My men should call me 'lord'; I am your goodman.

PAGE
My husband and my lord, my lord and husband,
I am your wife in all obedience.

SLY I know it well. – What must I call her?

LORD 'Madam'.

SLY 'Al'ce madam', or 'Joan madam'?

LORD
'Madam', and nothing else, so lords call ladies.

SLY
Madam wife, they say that I have dreamed 110
And slept above some fifteen year or more.

PAGE
Ay, and the time seems thirty unto me,
Being all this time abandoned from your bed.

92 Turf] F1 (*Turph*) 96.1] F1 (*Enter Lady with Attendants*); *after l.* 97 CAPELL 98 etc. PAGE] F1 (*Lady, La.*) 99–101] *as verse* F1; *as prose* POPE 108 Al'ce] F1 (*Alce*) 110–11] *as verse* F1; *as prose* POPE

94 **nor no** A normal Elizabethan use of the 'double negative' for emphasis.

95 **amends** improvement in health, amendment

97 **it** Many editors believe that Sly is thanking an attendant for a proffered drink. He may be only acknowledging the good will of the joint 'Amen'.

99 **Marry** A mild oath, though a corruption of 'By Mary' (the Virgin).

99 **fare** Sly is punning: he 'fares' well because of the good 'fare' ('cheer'), probably the ale.

103 **goodman** husband (and again Sly is using a word that would come more naturally to a peasant than to a lord)

113 **abandoned** banned or banished (*OED* v. IV)

SLY

'Tis much. Servants, leave me and her alone.

Exeunt [Lord and] Servingmen

Madam, undress you and come now to bed.

PAGE

Thrice-noble lord, let me entreat of you
To pardon me yet for a night or two,
Or, if not so, until the sun be set,
For your physicians have expressly charged,
In peril to incur your former malady, 120
That I should yet absent me from your bed.
I hope this reason stands for my excuse.

SLY Ay, it stands so that I may hardly tarry so long. But I would be loath to fall into my dreams again. I will therefore tarry in despite of the flesh and the blood.

Enter a Servingman

SERVINGMAN

Your honour's players, hearing your amendment,
Are come to play a pleasant comedy,
For so your doctors hold it very meet,
Seeing too much sadness hath congealed your blood,
And melancholy is the nurse of frenzy. 130
Therefore they thought it good you hear a play
And frame your mind to mirth and merriment,

114–15] *as verse* F1; *as prose* POPE 114.1] HIBBARD; *not in* F1; *The servants withdraw.* NEW CAMBRIDGE 125.1] F1 (*Enter a Messenger.*); *Enter the Lord as a Messenger.* HIBBARD 126 SERVINGMAN] F1 (*Mes.*)

114.1 Although F1 provides no exit here, Sly's order would presumably be obeyed. (If the Lord is the 'Messenger' who enters at l. 125.1, he must certainly leave the stage now.)

120 **In peril to incur** to avoid the danger of your bringing upon yourself

123 **it stands** i.e. Sly is sexually aroused
tarry hold back, delay

125.1 Hibbard's conjecture that the Lord assumes the role of the messenger may be right: the Lord would naturally wish to introduce, and later observe the results of, the performance he has organized. There is support of a kind both in the fact that the Lord makes the corresponding announcement in *A Shrew* (and remains with Sly) and in the use of the word 'Presenters' at 1.1.246.1 (see note). On the other hand, 1.1.247 is given by F1 to '1.*Man*', a speech prefix more appropriate to a servant – and there are apparently only three characters 'above' at that time. See also Introduction, p. 41.

127 **pleasant** (Probably) humorous, merry (*OED* 3) rather than 'giving pleasure'. Cf. l. 132, and Henry V's 'We are glad the Dauphin is so pleasant with us', 1.1.259.

129 **sadness . . . blood** Elizabethan medical theory did hold that melancholy caused thickening of the blood, which in turn could cause delirium or temporary insanity ('frenzy').

131 **hear** should hear (a subjunctive use rather than, as Abbott explains it, 370, an irregular sequence of tenses)

132 **frame** prepare, adjust (as later in 1.1.224). Compare our 'frame of mind'.

Which bars a thousand harms, and lengthens life.

SLY Marry, I will. Let them play it. Is not a comonty a Christmas gambold or a tumbling-trick?

PAGE

No, my good lord, it is more pleasing stuff.

SLY What, household stuff?

PAGE It is a kind of history.

SLY Well, we'll see't. Come, madam wife, sit by my side and let the world slip, we shall ne'er be younger. 140

I.1 *A flourish. Enter Lucentio and his man Tranio*

LUCENTIO

Tranio, since for the great desire I had
To see fair Padua, nursery of arts,
I am arrived for fruitful Lombardy,

134 will. Let] F3; will let F1 play it. Is] CAPELL (play't. – Is); play, it is F1; play; is it THEOBALD comonty] F1 (Comontie); commodity POPE 139–40] *as prose* POPE; Well ... see't: | Come ... side, | And ... yonger. | F1

I.1.0.1 *A ... Tranio*] F1 (*omitting 'A' and spelling 'Triano'*); *Act I Sc. I ... Enter ...* POPE
3 for] F1; from THEOBALD; in CAPELL (*conj.* HEATH)

133 **bars** prevents, avoids the risk of. The belief that merriment lengthens life survives in such a saying as 'laugh and be fat'.

134 **comonty** 'Commodity' may well be the word Sly *intended*: it is used in a corresponding passage in *A Shrew* and is found in the anonymous prefatory note to the 1609 Quarto of *Troilus*, where it is asserted that 'were but the vaine names of commedies changde for the titles of Commodities, or of Playes for Pleas', they would be sought for 'the maine grace of their gravities'. Nevertheless emendation is unnecessary: as usual, Sly is confused.

135 **gambold** A regular earlier form of the now normal 'gambol': frolic, brisk game.

137 **household stuff** (Presumably) domestic 'doings'.

138 **history** In the wider sense: 'story' or 'tale'.

140 **let...slip** Proverbial (Tilley W879), and previously used by Sly in Induction 1.5.
we . . . younger Another proverb (Tilley Y36); indeed a cliché.

I.1 The exposition (as Lucentio tells Tranio what he must know but the audience does not yet know); the stilted expression (e.g. ll. 14–16); and the versification (with the stiff movement and the cacophony of 'Lombardy', 'Italy', 'company') would form presumptive evidence of a date of composition, for this section at least, in the early 1590s, were it not for the possibility that Shakespeare is writing in a deliberately 'artificial' style – as in, for example, the play-within-a-play in *Hamlet* – to mark off his 'enclosed' story from the realism of the Induction.

0.1 The 'flourish', or fanfare, of trumpets normally announced that a play was about to begin, even in the public theatre. The name 'Tranio' may have been suggested by that of the resourceful slave in Plautus' *Mostellaria*.

2 **fair Padua, nursery of arts** Padua, already famous for its old university, and a great centre of philosophic and other learning

3 **am arrived** As in modern French, the auxiliary 'be', rather than 'have', was frequently used with verbs of motion in Elizabethan English (Abbott 295).
for Sometimes glossed as 'in' but seems to mean 'before', 'in front of' (i.e. at the gates of), *OED* I. a. Compare, e.g., 'For whose throne 'tis needful . . . to kneel' in *All's Well*, 4.4.3–4. Bond conjectured that it might mean 'for a stay in'.

3–4 **fruitful Lombardy . . . Italy** A proverb had it that Lombardy (probably used loosely, of the north of Italy) was the

The pleasant garden of great Italy,
And by my father's love and leave am armed
With his good will and thy good company,
My trusty servant well approved in all,
Here let us breathe and haply institute
A course of learning and ingenious studies.
Pisa renowned for grave citizens 10
Gave me my being, and my father first,
A merchant of great traffic through the world,
Vincentio, come of the Bentivolii.
Vincentio's son, brought up in Florence,
It shall become to serve all hopes conceived
To deck his fortune with his virtuous deeds;
And therefore, Tranio, for the time I study,
Virtue and that part of philosophy
Will I apply that treats of happiness
By virtue specially to be achieved. 20
Tell me thy mind, for I have Pisa left
And am to Padua come as he that leaves
A shallow plash to plunge him in the deep,

9 ingenious] F1; ingenuous TONSON 1734 13 Vincentio, come] HANMER; *Vincentio's* come F1 17–18 study, Virtue and] F1; study Virtue, and COLLIER

garden of Italy or even of the world (Tilley L414).

7 **approved** tested, reliable

8 **breathe** pause, settle down (*OED* v. 1. 5)
haply Compare Induction 1.133. 'With good luck' seems to be meant here (and conversely in 4.4.53 'happily' is used, where the meaning is 'perhaps').
institute begin – but Lucentio is perhaps being pedantic, for the word also meant 'educate', or 'establish in principles' (*OED* v. 3).

9 **ingenious** As with 'haply' and 'happily', Elizabethans seem to have used interchangeably 'ingenious' (which could mean 'involving intellect', 'intellectual', *OED* I. 1.b) and 'ingenuous' (in the sense of 'befitting a high-born person', *OED* II. 6). Either meaning fits here.

10 **renowned** Probably, but not necessarily, here pronounced as three syllables. The whole line is repeated at 4.2.95. For the sentiment, Boswell-Stone well compares the reference in Greene's *Royal Exchange* (1590) to Pisa 'famous for honorable Citizens' (sig. B3).

11 i.e. gave me, and my father before me

12 **of great traffic** involved in extensive trade (*OED* 'traffic', *sb.* 1.)

13 **come of** descended from
the Bentivolii A famous fifteenth-century family not of Pisa but of Bologna, as Bond points out.

14–16 i.e. it will be fitting for Vincentio's son – indeed, incumbent upon him – to fulfil all the high hopes held for him, by adding virtuous deeds to what fortune has already given.

17 **for the time** while

17–20 Collier's alteration of the F1 punctuation (accepted by New Cambridge), taking 'Virtue' as the object of 'study', makes the sentence unidiomatic and overlooks the parallel of ll. 29–30. Lucentio seems to be saying – again in a stilted way – that he will devote himself to virtue *and* to the study of that particular kind of philosophy that shows how happiness can best be achieved through virtue.

23 **plash** marshy pool

And with satiety seeks to quench his thirst.

TRANIO

Me pardonato, gentle master mine:
I am in all affected as yourself,
Glad that you thus continue your resolve
To suck the sweets of sweet philosophy;
Only, good master, while we do admire
This virtue and this moral discipline, 30
Let's be no stoics, nor no stocks, I pray,
Or so devote to Aristotle's checks
As Ovid be an outcast quite abjured.
Balk logic with acquaintance that you have,
And practise rhetoric in your common talk;
Music and poesy use, to quicken you;
The mathematics and the metaphysics,
Fall to them as you find your stomach serves you.
No profit grows where is no pleasure ta'en.
In brief, sir, study what you most affect. 40

25 *Me pardonato*] F1: Mi perdonate CAPELL (*conj.* HEATH): Mi perdonato CAMBRIDGE
33 Ovid‸] F3: *Ouid*: F1

25 ***Me pardonato*** excuse me; with apologies. Not, of course, perfect Italian, but good enough to give the illusion that the speakers are Italian (and having established this, by occasional phrases throughout the first act, Shakespeare hardly worries about it again later).

26 **in all affected** . . . in all such matters inclined in the same way as you are

29 **admire** The commonest Elizabethan meaning is 'wonder at' but probably here means rather 'revere' (*OED* 3).

30 **moral discipline** study of moral philosophy (what Lucentio has referred to in ll. 18–20).

31 **stoics . . . stocks** Tranio is playing with words, and his pun is not original: 'stoics', the traditionally austere philosophers, practising repression and inviting suffering; 'stocks', persons without sensitivity (the same metaphor as the modern colloquial 'logs'). *OED* 'stock' *sb.* I. 1.c.

32 **devote** devoted, solemnly dedicated (an instance of a word already 'ending' in 't' not adding 'd' or 'ed' in the participial form. Abbott 342)
checks abnegations; principles of austerity. (Aristotle is being loosely classified as a stoic, apparently because he stressed the superiority of the life of contemplation.)

33 i.e. that we should have to renounce Ovid and regard him as an outcast, as one whose doctrine or practice is not acceptable in ordinary society. Tranio is thinking of Ovid as an erotic poet, author of e.g. the *Ars Amatoria*.

34 **Balk logic** chop logic, exchange quibbles (*OED* 'balk' *v.* III.6). The force of Tranio's advice to Lucentio is that such exercises should be tried with acquaintances and in everyday conversation, not confined to academic situations.

36 **quicken** refresh, enliven (as in 'quicken his embraced heaviness | With some delight or other', *Merchant*, 2.8.52–3).

38 **Fall to** partake of
stomach appetite, inclination or mood (probably used metaphorically in sequence with 'fall to' but for most purposes the metaphor was already 'dead').

39 This is at one and the same time an inversion of the proverb 'no pains, no profit' (Tilley P24) and an extension of the literary doctrine that instruction is more likely to strike home if it simultaneously gives pleasure (best known in the form of Horace's *Omne tulit punctum qui miscuit utile dulci*).

40 **most affect** like (or enjoy) best

LUCENTIO

Gramercies, Tranio, well dost thou advise.
If, Biondello, thou wert come ashore,
We could at once put us in readiness,
And take a lodging fit to entertain
Such friends as time in Padua shall beget.
But stay awhile, what company is this?

TRANIO

Master, some show to welcome us to town.

Enter Baptista with his two daughters Katherina and Bianca; Gremio, a pantaloon; and Hortensio, suitor to Bianca. Lucentio and Tranio stand by

BAPTISTA

Gentlemen, importune me no farther,
For how I firmly am resolved you know:
That is, not to bestow my youngest daughter 50
Before I have a husband for the elder.
If either of you both love Katherina,
Because I know you well, and love you well,
Leave shall you have to court her at your pleasure.

42 Biondello, thou wert] F1 (*without the comma*); Biondello now were COLLIER 1853 (*conj. Notes*) 47.3 *suitor*] F2 (*Shuiter*); *sister* F1; *suitors* CAPELL

41 **Gramercies** thank you (a common Elizabethan phrase, now obsolete – from OF *grant merci*)

42 **come ashore** Shakespeare seems to think of Padua as a port, reached by water from Pisa. The Italian geography of *Two Gentlemen* appears similarly to be confused (many editors try to tidy it up for Shakespeare). The criticism would lose some of its force, however, if Shakespeare knew (as Bond suggested that he may have known) of regular trade by river-systems and canals in the northern Italy of his day. Coryate tells in his *Crudities* (1611) of the constant traffic by barge between Padua and Venice, and says that Verona received most of its merchandise by river, not only from Venice but also from Germany.

47.1–3 As Greg noted, a typical authorial direction. The specifying of relationships is characteristic of the process of composition; 'stand by' is the theatrical phrasing of an already professional dramatist. F1 spells the heroine's name 'Katerina' here and often elsewhere, but sometimes it is 'Katherina' or 'Katherine' or even 'Katerine'; the speech prefix is normally '*Kate.*'.

47.2 ***pantaloon*** The stock comic character of, originally, Italian *commedia dell' arte*: the old man verging on dotage. Gremio would appear as the type described in the 'Seven Ages of Man' speech in *As You Like It*, 2.7.158–63: 'the lean and slippered pantaloon, | With spectacles on nose and pouch on side, | His youthful hose, well sav'd, a world too wide | For his shrunk shank; and his big manly voice, | Turning again toward childish treble, pipes | And whistles in his sound'.

50 **youngest** As often, the superlative is used where the comparative, since only two objects are compared, would now be normal ('younger'). Abbott 10.

GREMIO
To cart her rather. She's too rough for me.
There, there, Hortensio, will you any wife?

KATHERINA (*to Baptista*)
I pray you, sir, is it your will
To make a stale of me amongst these mates?

HORTENSIO
'Mates', maid, how mean you that? No mates for you
Unless you were of gentler, milder mould. 60

KATHERINA
I'faith, sir, you shall never need to fear;
Iwis it is not halfway to her heart.
But if it were, doubt not her care should be
To comb your noddle with a three-legged stool,
And paint your face, and use you like a fool.

HORTENSIO
From all such devils, good Lord deliver us!

GREMIO
And me too, good Lord!

TRANIO (*aside to Lucentio*)
Husht, master, here's some good pastime toward;
That wench is stark mad, or wonderful froward.

LUCENTIO (*aside to Tranio*)
But in the other's silence do I see 70

59] *as one line* POPE; Mates ... that? | No ... you, | F1 68 Husht] F1; Hush ROWE 1714

55 **cart** Because a common punishment for prostitutes was being carried through the streets in, or tied to, a cart – sometimes being whipped at the same time.
rough harsh or violent, in temper or manner – as in Petruchio's later 'For I am rough and woo not like a babe', 2.1.136. Gremio's words are often marked as an aside, but Katherine's next lines seem to imply that she has heard them.

56 **will you** do you want, are you seeking?

58 **stale ... mates** The words involve a whole series of quibbles: (1) on 'stalemate', the situation in which a chess player cannot move without putting his king in check and so losing the game; (2) on 'stale' as meaning (a) decoy (for Bianca; compare 3.1.88 and note, and 'stale to catch these thieves', *Tempest*, 4.1.187), (b) laughing-stock, as in *Titus*, 1.1.304, (c) woman of loose morals, or prostitute (originally, perhaps, one used as a decoy), as in *Much Ado*, 2.2.22 and 4.1.64; and (3) on 'mates' as meaning both 'creatures beneath contempt', as in *2 Henry IV*, 2.4.118, and '(potential) husbands'.

62 **Iwis** certainly, indeed (OE *gewis*)
it ... heart i.e. marriage is something she is not even half attracted to

64 **noddle** Colloquial for 'head', generally with the connotation of dullness. (Originally the word meant rather 'back of the head'.) 'To comb (somebody's) head with a three-legged stool' was proverbial (Tilley H470).

65 **paint** i.e. by scratching, and drawing blood

66 Hortensio is adapting the Litany, 'from the crafts and assaults of the devil ... Good Lord, deliver us'.

68 **toward** imminent, about to take place

69 **wonderful froward** extraordinarily (the 'adverbial' form without 'ly', as before) perverse

Maid's mild behaviour and sobriety.
Peace, Tranio.

TRANIO (*aside to Lucentio*)
Well said, master. Mum, and gaze your fill.

BAPTISTA
Gentlemen, that I may soon make good
What I have said, Bianca, get you in,
And let it not displease thee, good Bianca,
For I will love thee ne'er the less, my girl.

KATHERINA
A pretty peat! It is best
Put finger in the eye, an she knew why.

BIANCA
Sister, content you in my discontent. 80
– Sir, to your pleasure humbly I subscribe:
My books and instruments shall be my company,
On them to look and practise by myself.

LUCENTIO (*aside to Tranio*)
Hark, Tranio, thou mayst hear Minerva speak.

HORTENSIO
Signor Baptista, will you be so strange?
Sorry am I that our good will effects
Bianca's grief.

GREMIO Why will you mew her up,
Signor Baptista, for this fiend of hell,
And make her bear the penance of her tongue?

75 said,] F1; said, – CAPELL; said – STEEVENS; said ... KEIGHTLEY 78–9 A ... best | Put ... why.] CAPELL; *as prose* F1; A ... Eye, | And ... why. | ROWE

71 **sobriety** moderation – and modesty

78 **peat** The word, although not found again in Shakespeare, is recorded elsewhere and is explained by *OED* and various editors as meaning 'pet', with the recognition that (as in 'proud peat') it was also used contemptuously, particularly of a spoilt girl. The etymology is unknown. One wonders, however, in view of Katherine's following words, whether it may not here mean 'pout' (or perhaps Shakespeare *wrote* 'pout'?): Bianca has put on a pretty, false, show of distress but would have done better still to force weeping by putting her finger in her eye (a proverbial phrase: Tilley F229).

78–9 **It is best | Put** The omission of 'to' is normal in such phrases (Abbott 351).

81 **pleasure** will
subscribe submit

84 **Minerva** As the goddess of wisdom and some at least of the arts (she was said to have invented the flute).

85 **strange** distant, in manner; cold or unhelpful

87 **mew her up** confine her – as the falcon is confined while 'mewing' (moulting)

88 **for** because of

89 i.e. and make her (Bianca) virtually do penance because of the sharpness of her (Katherine's) tongue

BAPTISTA
Gentlemen, content ye. I am resolved. 90
Go in, Bianca. *Exit Bianca*
And for I know she taketh most delight
In music, instruments, and poetry,
Schoolmasters will I keep within my house
Fit to instruct her youth. If you, Hortensio,
Or Signor Gremio, you, know any such,
Prefer them hither; for to cunning men
I will be very kind, and liberal
To mine own children in good bringing-up.
And so farewell. – Katherina, you may stay, 100
For I have more to commune with Bianca. *Exit*

KATHERINA Why, and I trust I may go too, may I not? What, shall I be appointed hours, as though, belike, I knew not what to take and what to leave? Ha! *Exit*

GREMIO You may go to the devil's dam: your gifts are so good here's none will hold you. – Their love is not so great, Hortensio, but we may blow our nails together, and fast it fairly out. Our cake's dough on both sides.

90 resolved] Q1631 (resolud); resould F1 91 *Exit Bianca*] *not in* F1 98 kind, and liberal] THEOBALD (kind; and liberal); kinde and liberall, F1 102–4] *as prose* POPE; Why, ... not? | ... though | ... take, | Ha. F1; Why, ... not? | ... belike, | ... ha! | CAPELL 106 you. – Their love] F1 (you: Their loue); you: there loue Q1631; you: Our love F3; you. Your love MALONE *conj.*; you. There; love COLLIER 1858; you there. Love SISSON *New Readings*

90 **content ye** (you must) be satisfied; it is no use protesting

97 **Prefer** introduce or recommend (*OED v. trans.* II.4)
cunning skilful (compare Induction 1.89 and note)

101 **commune** discuss

105–6 i.e. only the devil's dam (said to be worse than the devil himself – as in *Errors*, 4.3.44–7) is fit company for Katherine: her capacity for shrewishness is so great that no mere human can endure her, or would try to restrain her. Gremio is adapting the proverbial 'no man holds you' (Tilley M328). Sisson (*New Readings*) interpreted it as 'Here's none will strike a bargain with *you*'.

106 **Their love** A notorious crux, not satisfactorily removed by any emendation yet proposed, although it is true, as New Cambridge argues, both that Gremio uses 'there, there' as an exclamation in l. 56 (and Shakespeare may therefore be making it a mannerism in his speech) and that – on the evidence of *More* – Shakespeare is likely to have spelt either 'their' or 'there' as 'ther' and so have misled scribe or compositor. 'Their love' probably makes adequate sense if taken as 'the love of women' – which is not so important that Gremio and Hortensio cannot afford to wait. (Knight took it to mean the (little) love Baptista and Katherine seem to have for one another.)

107 **but . . . may** that we cannot ('but' meaning 'but that')
blow our nails The phrase does not seem to be proverbial. Apparently it means pass, or waste, time (but similar phrases in other Shakespearian plays and elsewhere refer rather to blowing on one's nails to keep one's hands warm).

108 **fast it fairly out** Either 'still manage to survive' or 'survive during this time of abstention in a becoming, not dishonourable, way (without quarrelling)'.
Our cake's dough on both sides 'My cake's dough' was already a standard

Farewell. Yet, for the love I bear my sweet Bianca, if I can by any means light on a fit man to teach her that wherein she delights, I will wish him to her father. 110

HORTENSIO So will I, Signor Gremio; but a word, I pray. Though the nature of our quarrel yet never brooked parley, know now upon advice it toucheth us both, that we may yet again have access to our fair mistress and be happy rivals in Bianca's love, to labour and effect one thing specially.

GREMIO What's that, I pray?

HORTENSIO Marry, sir, to get a husband for her sister.

GREMIO A husband? A devil. 120

HORTENSIO I say a husband.

GREMIO I say a devil. Think'st thou, Hortensio, though her father be very rich, any man is so very a fool to be married to hell?

HORTENSIO Tush, Gremio; though it pass your patience and mine to endure her loud alarums, why, man, there be good fellows in the world, an a man could light on them, would take her with all faults, and money enough.

GREMIO I cannot tell; but I had as lief take her dowry with this condition – to be whipped at the high-cross every morning. 130

HORTENSIO Faith, as you say, there's small choice in rotten apples. But come, since this bar in law makes us friends, it shall be so far forth friendly maintained till by helping

128 all] F1; all her F4

phrase for 'I've failed' (Tilley C12) but 'on both sides' is added, presumably, either to stress that they have both failed or to mean that they have failed both to get Bianca and to solve the problem of Katherine.

111 **wish** recommend (*OED v. trans.* 6)

113 **brooked** tolerated, or permitted

113–14 **parley** Either 'discussion' or 'conference for the negotiation of terms': both meanings were common.

114 **upon advice** on reflection, on better consideration (a regular Shakespearian use)

toucheth concerns, is relevant to

123 **so very a fool to** so complete a fool as to

126 **alarums** Strictly, calls to arms (OF *alarme*) but derivatively, as elsewhere in Shakespeare, loud noises (particularly if aggressive or hostile).

129 **I cannot tell** I don't know about *that*.

had as lief would just as soon, would as willingly (OE *léof*). The phrase is also found in the comparative and superlative, 'had liefer', and 'had liefest'.

130 **high-cross** the cross set on a pedestal in the market place or centre of the town

132–3 **there's . . . apples** Proverbial (Tilley C358): it's hard to distinguish between things all bad.

133 **bar in law** legal impediment (created by Baptista's exercise of his legal right as parent to prohibit Bianca's marriage until it has his consent)

134 **it . . . maintained** matters will continue to be arranged in a friendly way

Baptista's eldest daughter to a husband we set his youngest free for a husband, and then have to't afresh. Sweet Bianca! Happy man be his dole: he that runs fastest gets the ring. How say you, Signor Gremio?

GREMIO I am agreed, and would I had given him the best horse in Padua to begin his wooing that would thoroughly woo her, wed her, and bed her, and rid the house of her. Come on. 140 *Exeunt Gremio and Hortensio*

TRANIO
I pray, sir, tell me, is it possible
That love should of a sudden take such hold?

LUCENTIO
O Tranio, till I found it to be true,
I never thought it possible or likely.
But see, while idly I stood looking on,
I found the effect of love in idleness,
And now in plainness do confess to thee,
That art to me as secret and as dear 150
As Anna to the Queen of Carthage was,
Tranio, I burn, I pine, I perish, Tranio,
If I achieve not this young modest girl.
Counsel me, Tranio, for I know thou canst;

142 *Exeunt Gremio and Hortensio*] F1 (*Exeunt ambo. Manet Tranio and Lucentio*)

136 **have to't** renew combat

137 **Happy . . . dole** A traditional saying (Tilley M158): may one (of us) have the dole (fate) of a lucky man – but that the saying was considered pointless is proved by Shakespeare's putting it into the mouth of Slender at his stupidest, in *Merry Wives*, 3.4.62.

137–8 **he . . . ring** Another proverb (Tilley R130) and with a quibble (not original): the ring, which would once have been that lifted on the lance of the successful mounted knight at jousting, is also here the wedding ring.

140 **horse** Carrying on the first image in Hortensio's second proverb, of riding at the ring.

141 **woo . . . bed her** A set phrase, or cliché (Tilley W731), to which Gremio adds something, this time ('rid the house of her'). The carrying on of this dialogue largely in ready-made phrases characterizes the commonplace minds of the two men involved and makes less likely any sympathy with them.

148 **love in idleness** Perhaps Lucentio is thinking of the flower so called (the hearts-ease or pansy), the juice of which (according to Oberon in *Dream*, 2.1.170–2) 'on sleeping eyelids laid | Will make or man or woman madly dote | Upon the next live creature that it sees'; perhaps he means that he found that it was while he thought he was least involved (only 'idly looking on') that his heart was most easily won; perhaps both.

150 **secret** intimate and worthy of confidence

151 **As . . . was** Again the stiffness of the simile – in Shakespeare's early manner – catches one's attention more than does its aptness, although it has been suggested that he was thinking not so much of Virgil as of Marlowe's *Dido Queen of Carthage* (to which he also probably alludes in *Hamlet*, 2.2): Dido confesses to her sister Anna her sudden love for Aeneas, and Anna even acts as Dido's messenger to him.

Assist me, Tranio, for I know thou wilt.

TRANIO

Master, it is no time to chide you now;
Affection is not rated from the heart.
If love have touched you, naught remains but so:
Redime te captam quam queas minimo.

LUCENTIO

Gramercies, lad. Go forward, this contents; 160
The rest will comfort, for thy counsel's sound.

TRANIO

Master, you looked so longly on the maid,
Perhaps you marked not what's the pith of all.

LUCENTIO

O yes, I saw sweet beauty in her face,
Such as the daughter of Agenor had,
That made great Jove to humble him to her hand,
When with his knees he kissed the Cretan strand.

TRANIO

Saw you no more? Marked you not how her sister
Began to scold and raise up such a storm
That mortal ears might hardly endure the din? 170

159 *captam*] F1; *captum* F2

157 **is not rated** cannot be cast out by reproof

159 ***Redime . . . minimo*** Not for the last time in the play, the Latin (like the Italian) is inaccurate but whether deliberately (as part of the characterization) or through printer's error or through author's (by slip or through ignorance) it is impossible to say. 'Captam' should be 'captum'. 'Redeem yourself from captivity at the lowest price possible.' Dr Johnson pointed out that Shakespeare's quotation is not direct from Terence's *Eunuchus* (I.i.30) but from the version in the *Brevissima Institutio*, the second part of Lilly's *Grammar*, the text book prescribed for use in Elizabethan schools. (That Shakespeare learnt his Latin from it is best shown by *Merry Wives*, 4.1.)

160 **this contents** this (advice) satisfies me

162 **so longly** Probably 'for such a long time' (from the adjective 'long'); conceivably 'so longingly' (from the verb 'to long (for)'). The word does not occur again in Shakespeare.

163 **marked** noticed

pith centre, core, and so 'essential part', 'essence'

165–7 Another static and purely decorative – even self-conscious – simile and classical allusion. (Shakespeare may be trying to characterize Lucentio and inviting the audience to smile at *him*, but one doubts it.) Jove fell in love with Europa, the daughter of Agenor, King of Tyre; assuming the shape of a snow-white bull, wooed her; and carried her on his back across the sea to Crete. Minos and Rhadamanthus were two of the resultant offspring. It has been said that Shakespeare mistakenly thought Europa was carried *from* Crete but probably he pictures Jove as humbling himself before Europa after they reached Crete. For kissing the ground with one's knees as an image of humility, compare *Richard II*, 3.3.190–1 and *Coriolanus*, 3.2.75.

LUCENTIO
Tranio, I saw her coral lips to move,
And with her breath she did perfume the air.
Sacred and sweet was all I saw in her.

TRANIO (*aside*)
Nay, then 'tis time to stir him from his trance.
– I pray, awake, sir. If you love the maid,
Bend thoughts and wits to achieve her. Thus it stands:
Her elder sister is so curst and shrewd
That till the father rid his hands of her,
Master, your love must live a maid at home,
And therefore has he closely mewed her up, 180
Because she will not be annoyed with suitors.

LUCENTIO
Ah Tranio, what a cruel father's he!
But art thou not advised he took some care
To get her cunning schoolmasters to instruct her?

TRANIO
Ay, marry, am I, sir – and now 'tis plotted.

LUCENTIO
I have it, Tranio.

TRANIO Master, for my hand,
Both our inventions meet and jump in one.

LUCENTIO
Tell me thine first.

TRANIO You will be schoolmaster,
And undertake the teaching of the maid:
That's your device.

LUCENTIO It is. May it be done? 190

TRANIO
Not possible: for who shall bear your part

181 Because she will] F1; Because he will SINGER 1856

177 **curst** waspish; or even 'savage'
shrewd given to shrewishness (as also in 1.2.59)
180 **closely mewed her up** The same image, and almost the same words, as Gremio used at 1.1.87.
181 **Because she** It seems more likely that 'because' is used in the sense 'so that' than that 'she' is F1's error for 'he'.
183 **advised** aware
185 **'tis plotted** i.e. I have a plot that should be the answer.
186 **for my hand** Generally glossed as 'by my hand' but may mean rather 'for my part', 'if I am right'.
187 **our inventions . . . jump in one** Tranio is virtually quoting the proverb 'Good wits jump' (Tilley W578). 'Jump' means 'agree', 'come together' – as in 'till each circumstance of place, time, fortune, do cohere and jump', *Twelfth Night*, 5.1.243–4.

And be in Padua here Vincentio's son,
Keep house and ply his book, welcome his friends,
Visit his countrymen and banquet them?

LUCENTIO

Basta, content thee, for I have it full.
We have not yet been seen in any house,
Nor can we be distinguished by our faces
For man or master. Then it follows thus:
Thou shalt be master, Tranio, in my stead,
Keep house, and port, and servants, as I should; 200
I will some other be – some Florentine,
Some Neapolitan, or meaner man of Pisa.
'Tis hatched, and shall be so. Tranio, at once
Uncase thee; take my coloured hat and cloak.
When Biondello comes, he waits on thee,
But I will charm him first to keep his tongue.

TRANIO

So had you need.
In brief, sir, sith it your pleasure is,
And I am tied to be obedient –
For so your father charged me at our parting: 210
'Be serviceable to my son', quoth he,
Although I think 'twas in another sense –
I am content to be Lucentio,
Because so well I love Lucentio.

They exchange clothes

202 meaner] F1; mean CAPELL 204 coloured] F2 (Coulord); Conlord F1; colour'd F3
214.1] *not in* F1; *after l.* 206 THEOBALD

193 **ply** work busily at, apply himself to. *OED* v^2. 1 (from ME *plye*, aphetic form of *aplye*).

194 **countrymen** fellow-countrymen (presumably, from Pisa)

195 ***Basta*** enough. Shakespeare remembers to throw in another Italian word.
have it full have worked out all the details and now have a complete plan.

200 **port** state, appropriately elevated way of life. So too in 3.1.35.

202 **meaner** *Pace* New Cambridge, Capell's emendation 'mean' is not an improvement either in metre or in sense. If Lucentio is not to pretend to be from some other city, he must disguise himself as from a lower rank of society than the one he really belongs to in Pisa.

204 **Uncase thee** undress; 'strip'
coloured As opposed to the drabber uniform of the servant (Petruchio's servants wear the traditional plain blue coats, 4.1.80).

206 **charm** use (money as the) magic to make...

207 The 'incomplete' line need not imply a deliberate cut or other loss of text. It rather points up the wry and laconic nature of Tranio's reply: money is something the Biondellos of the world understand.

208 **sith** since (OE *siððan*)

209 A proverb said that 'they that are bound must obey' (Tilley B354).

211 **serviceable** diligent in (your) duty as servant

LUCENTIO
Tranio, be so, because Lucentio loves,
And let me be a slave t'achieve that maid
Whose sudden sight hath thralled my wounded eye.
Enter Biondello
Here comes the rogue. Sirrah, where have you been?

BIONDELLO Where have I been? Nay, how now, where are you? Master, has my fellow Tranio stolen your clothes, or you stolen his, or both? Pray, what's the news? 220

LUCENTIO
Sirrah, come hither. 'Tis no time to jest,
And therefore frame your manners to the time.
Your fellow Tranio here, to save my life,
Puts my apparel and my countenance on,
And I for my escape have put on his;
For in a quarrel since I came ashore
I killed a man, and fear I was descried.
Wait you on him, I charge you, as becomes, 230
While I make way from hence to save my life.
You understand me?

BIONDELLO I, sir? Ne'er a whit.

LUCENTIO
And not a jot of Tranio in your mouth.
Tranio is changed into Lucentio.

BIONDELLO The better for him. Would I were so too!

TRANIO So would I, 'faith, boy, to have the next wish after, that Lucentio indeed had Baptista's youngest daughter. But, sirrah, not for my sake but your master's, I advise you use your manners discreetly in all kind of companies. 240

233 I, sir?] F1 (I sir,); Ay, sir, ROWE; Aye, sir; – HALLIWELL Ne'er a whit] F1; ne'er a whit (*aside*) HALLIWELL 237–42] *as prose* F1; So ... after, – | ... daughter. | ... advise you | ... company. | ... *Tranio,* | ... *Lucentio.*| CAPELL 237 would] F3; could F1 'faith] F1; i' faith JOHNSON

216 **t'achieve** F1's elision is followed, although there seems no good reason for the one compositor to print 't'achieue' in this line, and 'to atcheeue' in l. 176.

217 **thralled** enslaved (the literal meaning also of 'enthralled')
wounded i.e. as if by Cupid's arrow

219–22 Attempts to rearrange these lines as verse seem pointless. Prose is appropriate for the servant Biondello; and Lucentio and Tranio soon modulate into prose when talking to him, ll. 236 ff.

224 **frame** adapt

226 **Puts ... my countenance on** wears my clothes and imitates my manner – or, perhaps, if 'countenance' is used as in 5.1.35 and 114, 'assumes my identity'

230 **as becomes** as seems fitting or necessary

233 **Ne'er a whit** not a jot – not at all

237 **'faith** i.e. in (all good) faith

When I am alone, why then I am Tranio, but in all places
else your master Lucentio.

LUCENTIO Tranio, let's go. One thing more rests, that thyself execute, to make one among these wooers. If thou ask me why, sufficeth my reasons are both good and weighty. *Exeunt*

The Presenters above speaks

SERVINGMAN
My lord, you nod, you do not mind the play.

SLY Yes, by Saint Anne, do I. A good matter, surely; comes there any more of it?

PAGE (*as Lady*) My lord, 'tis but begun. 250

SLY 'Tis a very excellent piece of work, madam lady: would 'twere done!

They sit and mark

1.2 *Enter Petruchio and his man Grumio*

PETRUCHIO
Verona, for a while I take my leave,

242 your] F2; you F1 243–6] *as prose* POPE; *Tranio* ... go: | ... execute, | ... why, | ... waighty.| F1 247 SERVINGMAN] F1 (1. *Man.*); *Lord* HIBBARD
1.2.0.1 *Enter* ... *Grumio*] F1; *Sc.ii* ... *Enter* ... CAPELL; *Act II Sc. I Enter* ... ROWE

243–4 **rests, that thyself execute**, remains, to which you must give effect, namely .... This is to take 'execute' as a subjunctive; the alternative possibility is to take it as an imperative and omit the comma after it (Abbott 368).

245 **sufficeth** it sufficeth that, it is enough (for you to know) that. The verb is impersonal (Abbott 297).

246.1 ***Presenters*** Apparently only Sly, the Page, and one other are on the 'upper stage' here, the third being F1's 'Messenger' who may or may not be the Lord (Induction 2.125.1 and note). The designation 'Presenters' is normally given to those who introduce a play within a play, and so it is perhaps more appropriate here if the Lord *is* among them; but, alternatively, the word may be used loosely of those who merely watch, and comment on, the Katherine play. Bond, citing Ford's *Perkin Warbeck*, 3.2 (l. 1411) 'Are the presenters ready?' and *Merry Wives*, 4.6.20 'Must my sweet Nan present the Fairy Queen?', thought the word meant only 'actors'.

246.1 ***speaks*** Presumably, the 'old plural in "s"'.

247 SERVINGMAN See note on Induction 2.125.1.

mind pay attention to, give heed to (*OED v.* 4)

248 **Saint Anne** The Clown in *Twelfth Night* (2.3.111) is the only other Shakespearian character who uses this unexpected oath. Saint Anne, mother of the Virgin Mary, was the patroness of married women.

matter subject matter, theme

252.1 For discussion of the problem whether Sly and company do continue to 'sit and mark', see Introduction, pp. 28–9, 40–3.

1.2.0.1 ***Petruchio*** It is now generally agreed that the pronunciation should be 'Petrutchio', Shakespeare's spelling being a rough phonetic equivalent of the Italian *Petruccio*, a diminutive of *Pietro*.

Grumio The name is that of a character in Plautus. Shakespeare sometimes seems, wilfully, to invite confusion, with his 'Grumio' and 'Gremio'; 'Salarino'

To see my friends in Padua, but of all
My best belovèd and approvèd friend,
Hortensio; and I trow this is his house.
Here, sirrah Grumio, knock, I say.

GRUMIO Knock, sir? Whom should I knock? Is there any
man has rebused your worship?

PETRUCHIO Villain, I say, knock me here soundly.

GRUMIO Knock you here, sir? Why, sir, what am I, sir, that
I should knock you here, sir? 10

PETRUCHIO
Villain, I say, knock me at this gate,
And rap me well, or I'll knock your knave's pate.

GRUMIO My master is grown quarrelsome.
I should knock you first,
And then I know after who comes by the worst.

PETRUCHIO Will it not be?
Faith, sirrah, an you'll not knock, I'll ring it;
I'll try how you can *sol fa* and sing it.
He wrings him by the ears

GRUMIO Help, masters, help, my master is mad!

13–14 My ... first] *as two lines* F1; *as one line* THEOBALD 19 masters] THEOBALD; mistris F1

('Salario') and 'Solanio' – if they are indeed the correct names – in *Merchant*; and the two characters named 'Jaques' in *As You Like It*.

2 **of all** most important of all

3 **approvèd** well-tried, trusty

4 **trow** (have reason to) believe
this One of the doors at the rear of the stage in the Elizabethan public theatre would serve.

7 **rebused** For purposes of the laugh, Grumio both misunderstands Petruchio's words and confuses his own: he means, probably, 'abused' (unless – as G. L. Brook supposes (*g* 306) – he is conflating 'abused' and 'rebuked').

8 **knock me here** A regular Elizabethan use (Abbott 220) of the so-called 'ethic dative' – roughly equivalent to 'knock here for me' – but Grumio chooses to take 'me' as an accusative, as the grammatical object of 'knock'.

11 **gate** Not an inconsistency: the word was frequently used of a door, particularly a large one.

12 **knave's** knavish (the possessive of the noun is used as an adjective – Abbott 430)

12 **pate** head (colloquial – and used normally in contempt or ridicule). So too in 2.1.153. The rhymes will be apparent in this exchange between Petruchio and Grumio, as each tries to emphasize a point; but the versification is 'irregular', to say the least. In fact, the only advantage of setting the lines out as they are in F1 is to draw attention to the rhymes.

14–15 i.e. you mean (or, perhaps, meant) me to deliver the first blow and then I'ld have (or would have had) the worst of it.

17 **ring it** ring (at the door) – but probably not in the modern sense. 'Ring' was used of a circular knocker on a door (*OED sb*[1]. I. 3. b). There is also, of course, a pun on 'wringing' ears (the F1 stage direction at 18.1 spells the word 'rings').

18 ***sol fa*** sing accurately the notes (of the major scale). (The modern idiom would possibly be '*do re mi*' it.) Waldo and Herbert suggest that there is a pun on 'sowl', to seize roughly by the ears.
sing it i.e. when you cry out in pain.

19 **masters** Theobald's emendation of F1's

PETRUCHIO Now knock when I bid you, sirrah villain. 20

Enter Hortensio

HORTENSIO How now, what's the matter? My old friend Grumio, and my good friend Petruchio? How do you all at Verona?

PETRUCHIO
Signor Hortensio, come you to part the fray?
Con tutti le core bene trobatto, may I say.

HORTENSIO *Alla nostra casa bene venuto multo honorata signior mio Petruchio.* – Rise, Grumio, rise. We will compound this quarrel.

GRUMIO Nay, 'tis no matter, sir, what he 'leges in Latin. If this be not a lawful cause for me to leave his service! 30 Look you, sir: he bid me knock him, and rap him soundly, sir. Well, was it fit for a servant to use his master so, being perhaps, for aught I see, two and thirty, a pip out?
Whom would to God I had well knocked at first,
Then had not Grumio come by the worst.

25 *tutti le core*] F1; *tutto il Core* THEOBALD *trobatto*] F1; trovato ROWE 26–8] *all as prose*, this edition; *Alla* ... *Petruchio.* | Rise ... quarrell. F1; Alla ... venuto | Multo ... Petruchio | Rise ... STEEVENS 1778 26 *bene*] F1; *ben* F2 *multo*] F1; *molto* THEOBALD *honorata*] F1; *honorato* F2 27 *Petruchio*] F1; Petrucio KNIGHT 29 he 'leges] F1 (he leges); be *leges* RANN (*conj.* TYRWHITT) 30–1 service! Look you, sir:] This edition (*after* PERRING); seruice, looke you sir: F1; service, – Look you, sir, CAPELL; service, look you, sir, CAMBRIDGE; service, look you, sir. HUDSON 33 pip] ROWE 1714; peepe F1 34–5] *as verse* ROWE 1714; *as prose* F1

'mistris' is adopted with some hesitation; perhaps the compositor wrongly expanded an abbreviation in the manuscript. Alternatively, Grumio in his clowning may be calling on some supposed (non-existent) wife of Petruchio, to protect him from his master.

22 **How do you all** How are you and your family?

25–7 Again, the temptation to correct Shakespeare's Italian has been resisted. (Many editors leave 'Petruchio' in the F1 form while 'correcting' the remainder of the line. To be consistent they should perhaps, with Knight and the Cambridge editors, alter to 'Petrucio', or to 'Petruccio'.) 'With all my heart, well met!' 'Welcome to our house, most honoured Petruchio.'

27 **compound** settle (amicably)

29 **'leges** alleges. Grumio (not being now thought of by Shakespeare as Italian!) doesn't understand Petruchio's 'foreign' language.

33 **two and thirty, a pip out** Grumio is presumably saying that Petruchio is 32 years of age, allowing for a possible error of a 'pip' (a spot on a playing card) and is implying that he *is* one year 'out', because 'to be one-and-thirty' meant 'to be drunk' (Tilley O64) and he can well believe that Petruchio is so. 'One-and-thirty' or 'Bone-ace' was a card game; hence 'pip'. (Perhaps F1's 'peepe' does not mean 'pip' and should be kept, as 'peep', in the sense of 'tiny speck' but that is usually said only of light, as in 'peep of dawn'.)

34–5 Probably the lines are doggerel verse, as printed here, to cap the complaint. F1 does not distinguish them from the prose of the remainder of Grumio's speech but the compositor seems to be saving space in the lower half of this column, presumably because of copy inaccurately 'cast

PETRUCHIO
A senseless villain. Good Hortensio,
I bade the rascal knock upon your gate,
And could not get him for my heart to do it.

GRUMIO Knock at the gate? O heavens! Spake you not these words plain: 'Sirrah, knock me here; rap me here; knock me well, and knock me soundly'? And come you now with 'knocking at the gate'? 40

PETRUCHIO
Sirrah, be gone, or talk not, I advise you.

HORTENSIO
Petruchio, patience, I am Grumio's pledge.
Why, this' a heavy chance 'twixt him and you,
Your ancient, trusty, pleasant servant Grumio.
And tell me now, sweet friend, what happy gale
Blows you to Padua here, from old Verona?

PETRUCHIO
Such wind as scatters young men through the world
To seek their fortunes farther than at home, 50
Where small experience grows. But in a few,
Signor Hortensio, thus it stands with me:
Antonio, my father, is deceased,
And I have thrust myself into this maze,
Happily to wive and thrive as best I may.
Crowns in my purse I have, and goods at home,
And so am come abroad to see the world.

45 this'] DYCE; this F1; this is ROWE; this's CAMBRIDGE 51 grows. But in a few,] HANMER (*subs.*); growes but in a few. F1 55 Happily] F1; Happly ROWE 1714

off'. Grumio is referring back to his earlier, now regretted, decision *not* to strike first (ll. 14–15).

38 **not . . . for my heart** The corresponding modern idiom is 'not for my life'; 'not if my life depended on it'.

44 **pledge** surety or guarantor

45 **this'** Abbott 461 shows that 'this' is often used for 'this is' in Elizabethan texts. The reading 'this'' is therefore an interpretation rather than an emendation.
heavy chance misfortune; regrettable happening

46 **ancient** long-standing (rather than 'old')

47 **what happy gale . . .** Hortensio is adapting, in compliment to Petruchio, 'What wind blows you hither?' (Tilley W441).

51 **in a few** in brief

54 **this maze** the confusing paths (of the world at large)

55 **Happily** So F1, meaning, no doubt, 'with good luck', 'if luck is with me' but some editors prefer to emend to 'haply' – a distinction without a difference. See note on Induction 1.133.
to wive and thrive Behind the expressed hope lie the unexpressed proverbs (Tilley T264 and Y12): 'First thrive and then wive' and 'It is hard to wive and thrive both in a year'.

HORTENSIO

Petruchio, shall I then come roundly to thee
And wish thee to a shrewd ill-favoured wife?
Thou'dst thank me but a little for my counsel; 60
And yet I'll promise thee she shall be rich,
And very rich. But thou'rt too much my friend,
And I'll not wish thee to her.

PETRUCHIO

Signor Hortensio, 'twixt such friends as we
Few words suffice; and therefore, if thou know
One rich enough to be Petruchio's wife –
As wealth is burden of my wooing dance –
Be she as foul as was Florentius' love,
As old as Sibyl, and as curst and shrewd
As Socrates' Xanthippe, or a worse, 70
She moves me not – or not removes at least

59 shrewd] F1 (shrew'd) 69 shrewd] F1 (shrow'd); *so too in l.* 89 71 not –] F1 (not,); not; THEOBALD

58 **come roundly** speak straightforwardly, bluntly. For 'roundly' compare 3.2.216 and note.

59 **wish thee to** put you in the way of
shrewd shrewish
ill-favoured Normally means 'ugly' but there is no other reason for thinking Katherine so and Hortensio himself soon says that she is not (l. 85). Probably 'with some unpleasant attributes', 'ill-natured' – as conceivably in *Merry Wives*, 1.1.271–2, Slender's idiotic comment that bears 'are very ill-favour'd rough things'.

64–5 **'twixt . . . suffice** Petruchio is adapting the proverbial 'Among friends few words are best' (Tilley W796).

67 **burden** musical undersong or bass (rather than 'refrain', a possible meaning). Compare *As You Like It*, 3.2.233–4, 'I would sing my song without a burden; thou bring'st me out of tune' (and Johnson thought that it 'would have been more proper' for the *Shrew* text to read 'wooing song').

68 **foul** ugly
Florentius' love In Gower's *Confessio Amantis* Book I, the knight Florent, to save his life, has to discover the answer to the question 'What do all women most desire?' He is given the right answer by an old 'loathly' and 'foul' hag – namely, to 'be sovereign of man's love' – but the price he has to pay is to marry her. On the wedding night, however, she takes the form of a beautiful young woman; and when released by his faith from magic enchantment, is revealed as in fact the daughter of the King of Sicily. The story is told also in Chaucer's 'Wife of Bath's Tale' but the Arthurian knight of that version has no name. It is seemingly a coincidence that Fletcher's *Women Pleased* (see note on Induction 1.85) is yet another version.

69 **Sibyl** It is not easy to distinguish the various Sibyls of classical mythology; but one of them (the Erythraean or, according to Ovid in *Metamorphoses* XIV, the Cumaean), when invited by the would-be seducer Apollo to choose a gift, asked for as many years of life as she held grains of sand in her hand; but since she did not then ask for youth, he was able to say he would add it only if she yielded to him; she refused, and became proverbial for hideous old age. Compare *Merchant*, 1.2.95–6, Portia's 'If I live to be as old as Sibylla, I will die as chaste as Diana, unless I be obtained by the manner of my father's will'.

70 **Xanthippe** Wife of Socrates, she was notorious (perhaps unfairly) for her 'nagging' and shrewishness.

71 **moves** affects, or disturbs

Affection's edge in me, were she as rough
As are the swelling Adriatic seas.
I come to wive it wealthily in Padua;
If wealthily, then happily in Padua.

GRUMIO Nay, look you, sir, he tells you flatly what his mind is. Why, give him gold enough and marry him to a puppet or an aglet-baby, or an old trot with ne'er a tooth in her head, though she have as many diseases as two-and-fifty horses. Why, nothing comes amiss, so money comes withal. 80

HORTENSIO
Petruchio, since we are stepped thus far in,
I will continue that I broached in jest.
I can, Petruchio, help thee to a wife
With wealth enough, and young and beauteous,
Brought up as best becomes a gentlewoman.
Her only fault, and that is faults enough,
Is that she is intolerable curst,
And shrewd, and froward, so beyond all measure
That, were my state far worser than it is, 90
I would not wed her for a mine of gold.

PETRUCHIO
Hortensio, peace: thou know'st not gold's effect;
Tell me her father's name and 'tis enough.
For I will board her though she chide as loud
As thunder when the clouds in autumn crack.

72 me, were she as] STEEVENS 1778; me. Were she is as F1; me. Were she as Q1631; me: were she as BOSWELL; me. Whe'er she is as RIVERSIDE 73 seas.] F1; Seas, ROWE 1714; seas: CAPELL

72 **Affection's edge** my keen readiness to like her

72–3 **as rough . . . Adriatic seas** A standard comparison, deriving from Horace but by Elizabethan times almost a commonplace.

74 **wive it** 'It' was often used thus after a noun to give the noun the function of a verb (Brook, *g* 81, comparing 'I'll queen it no inch farther' in *Winter's Tale*, 4.4.441). Compare the modern 'lord it' (over somebody).

78 **aglet-baby** a doll-shaped figure such as formed the tag of a lace or was worn as a tag-like ornament on a dress (*OED* 'aglet' I. 2)

78 **trot** hag (*OED sb*[2].)

80 **so** if, provided that

82 **are stepped thus far in** have become so far involved; have 'waded in so far'

83 **that I broached** that which I began by suggesting

88 **intolerable** intolerably (again the form without the now distinctive 'ly' termination)

90 **my state** i.e. my financial condition, my estate

94 **board** go aboard, as when attacking a ship – but the image, a common one, clearly has sexual overtones
chide quarrel, scold, complain angrily

95 **crack** make a loud, explosive noise

HORTENSIO

Her father is Baptista Minola,
An affable and courteous gentleman;
Her name is Katherina Minola,
Renowned in Padua for her scolding tongue.

PETRUCHIO

I know her father, though I know not her, 100
And he knew my deceasèd father well.
I will not sleep, Hortensio, till I see her,
And therefore let me be thus bold with you,
To give you over at this first encounter,
Unless you will accompany me thither.

GRUMIO (*to Hortensio*) I pray you, sir, let him go while the humour lasts. O' my word, an she knew him as well as I do, she would think scolding would do little good upon him. She may perhaps call him half a score knaves or so: why, that's nothing; an he begin once, 110 he'll rail in his rope tricks. I'll tell you what, sir, an she stand him but a little, he will throw a figure in her face, and so disfigure her with it, that she shall have no more eyes to see withal than a cat. You know him not, sir.

HORTENSIO

Tarry, Petruchio, I must go with thee,

111 rope tricks] F1; rhetorick HANMER; rhetricks SISSON (*after* MASON, *who conj.* 'rhetoricks')

103–4 **be . . . encounter** presume so far – take such an extreme liberty – as to say that I will leave you (to visit Baptista and see Katherine) even though we have just met

107 **humour** mood or whim

111 **rope tricks** If emendation is thought necessary, 'rhetricks' is the best yet offered; but 'rope tricks' may well be correct and may mean tricks that can be punished adequately only by hanging. (Compare 'crack-hemp' in 5.1.40, and note.) It may also be Grumio's version – or perversion – either of 'rhetorics' or, as Hibbard suggested, of 'rope-rhethorique' (rope-rhetoric), which is found in Nashe's *Have with you to Saffron-Walden* (1596). Bond saw a possible indecency in 'rope' but the general sense of the phrase must be that Petruchio's railing will be more violent than Katherine's.

112 **stand** stand up to, withstand
figure i.e. rhetorical figure, figure of speech; and even Tilley may have overlooked some possible connection with his proverb T575 'Truth has no need of rhetoric (or "figures")'. Editors have long suspected a secondary meaning, perhaps indecent, but no convincing explanation has been offered. Interestingly, Garrick retained the phrase in his *Catharine and Petruchio* (though he omitted many of Shakespeare's lines) – which may be some kind of evidence that the idiom was still understood in his day.

113 **disfigure** (i) deform or deface (ii) disfigure – render her incapable of any kind of figure

113–14 **no . . . cat** Again the meaning is obscure. There seems to be no point in a pun on 'cat' and 'Kate'; and cats not only have eyes but also 'can see in the dark'. A subsidiary meaning may well be that Petruchio will scratch her eyes out, but there must be more to it than that. Again, Garrick retained the phrase.

For in Baptista's keep my treasure is.
He hath the jewel of my life in hold,
His youngest daughter, beautiful Bianca,
And her withholds from me and other more,
Suitors to her and rivals in my love. 120
Supposing it a thing impossible,
For those defects I have before rehearsed,
That ever Katherina will be wooed,
Therefore this order hath Baptista ta'en,
That none shall have access unto Bianca
Till Katherine the curst have got a husband.

GRUMIO
'Katherine the curst',
A title for a maid, of all titles the worst.

HORTENSIO
Now shall my friend Petruchio do me grace,
And offer me disguised in sober robes 130
To old Baptista as a schoolmaster
Well seen in music, to instruct Bianca,
That so I may by this device at least
Have leave and leisure to make love to her,
And unsuspected court her by herself.

Enter Gremio, and Lucentio disguised as Cambio

GRUMIO Here's no knavery; see, to beguile the old folks, how the young folks lay their heads together! – Master, master, look about you. Who goes there, ha?

119 me and other] HANMER (*subs.*); me. Other F1; me, and others THEOBALD (*conj.* THIRLBY) 120 love.] This edition; Loue: F1; love; COLLIER; love, HERFORD 123 wooed,] CAPELL (*subs.*); woo'd: F1; woo'd^ Q1631; woo'd; ROWE; woo'd. KEIGHTLEY 133 least] F1; last HOSLEY 135.1] F1 (*subs.*); *after 'together' in l.* 137 CAMBRIDGE

116 **keep** Either 'keeping' or 'castle keep' (tower) – an appropriate place in which to guard a treasure or jewel. The noun is not found elsewhere in Shakespeare.

117 **in hold** The double meaning of 'keep' is carried on here: (i) in his keeping; (ii) in prison (as in *Measure*, 4.3.83, 'Put them in secret holds, both Barnardine and Claudio' and *Richard III*, 4.5.3, 'My son George Stanley is frank'd up in hold').

119 **and other** Hanmer's emendation seems inevitable: F1's wording does not make sense. 'Other' as a plural is not unusual in Shakespearian and general Elizabethan usage.

122 **For** because of

122 **rehearsed** related or enumerated (normal Shakespearian meanings: *OED v. trans.* 2, 3)

124 **this order** this plan, these measures

129 **do me grace** do me a kindness, a 'favour'

132 **Well seen** well versed, fully qualified

135.1 The placing of the stage direction here by F1 does not mean that Grumio's next sentence refers to Gremio and Lucentio: on the contrary, the audience smiles because it can see those characters approaching before Grumio sees them and so can observe a better example of young folks conspiring (Lucentio's scheming will in fact foil Hortensio's).

HORTENSIO

Peace, Grumio. It is the rival of my love.
Petruchio, stand by a while. 140

GRUMIO

A proper stripling and an amorous!

Petruchio, Hortensio and Grumio stand aside

GREMIO (*to Lucentio*)

O, very well, I have perused the note.
Hark you, sir, I'll have them very fairly bound,
All books of love; see that at any hand
And see you read no other lectures to her.
You understand me. Over and beside
Signor Baptista's liberality,
I'll mend it with a largess. Take your paper too.
And let me have them very well perfumed,
For she is sweeter than perfume itself 150
To whom they go to. What will you read to her?

LUCENTIO

Whate'er I read to her, I'll plead for you
As for my patron, stand you so assured,
As firmly as yourself were still in place,
Yea, and perhaps with more successful words
Than you, unless you were a scholar, sir.

GREMIO

O this learning, what a thing it is!

GRUMIO (*aside*)

O this woodcock, what an ass it is!

PETRUCHIO (*aside*)

Peace, sirrah.

HORTENSIO (*aside*)

Grumio, mum! – God save you, Signor Gremio. 160

140 Petruchio, stand] F1 (*subs.*); *Petruchio.* Stand CAMBRIDGE *conj.* 141.1] *not in* F1 151 go to] F1; go ROWE

141 **proper stripling** handsome youth – Grumio's amused and ironical description of the decrepit wooer, Gremio

142 **note** bill or account (for the books Lucentio has purchased). Compare *2 Henry IV*, 5.1.18.

143 **fairly** beautifully, handsomely. (Books were normally sold unbound.)

144 **see . . . hand** see to that, for one thing (or 'at all costs'). Compare l. 222 and note.

145 **lectures** lessons or courses of instruction

148 **mend it with a largess** add to it with a gratuity

149 **them** i.e. the books

154 **still in place** always present

158 **woodcock** bird of the snipe family, easily caught and proverbial for stupidity (Tilley S788, W746, W748)

GREMIO And you are well met, Signor Hortensio. Trow you whither I am going? To Baptista Minola. I promised to inquire carefully about a schoolmaster for the fair Bianca, and by good fortune I have lighted well on this young man, for learning and behaviour fit for her turn, well read in poetry and other books – good ones, I warrant ye.

HORTENSIO
'Tis well. And I have met a gentleman
Hath promised me to help me to another,
A fine musician to instruct our mistress.
So shall I no whit be behind in duty 170
To fair Bianca, so beloved of me.

GREMIO
Beloved of me, and that my deeds shall prove.

GRUMIO (*aside*)
And that his bags shall prove.

HORTENSIO
Gremio, 'tis now no time to vent our love.
Listen to me, and if you speak me fair,
I'll tell you news indifferent good for either.
Here is a gentleman whom by chance I met,
Upon agreement from us to his liking,
Will undertake to woo curst Katherine,
Yea, and to marry her, if her dowry please. 180

161–6] *as prose* POPE; And ... *Hortensio.* | ... *Minola,* | ... carefully | ... *Bianca,* | ... well | ... behauiour | ... Poetrie | ... ye. | F1 163 the fair] F1; fair STEEVENS 1793 168 help me] ROWE; helpe one F1

161 **Trow you** An idiomatic use of 'trow'. The phrase is almost equivalent to the modern colloquial 'Would you believe ...?'.

165 **her turn** what she requires; her needs. Compare 2.1.271 and note, and 3.2.131 and note.

173 **bags** i.e. money-bags

174 **vent** 'Utter', 'express', and 'divulge' are all normal meanings but here, perhaps, rather 'talk about at length', or even 'unburden our hearts (by speaking about)', as in 'vent the soul', *OED v.* I. b.

175 **speak me fair** meet me on terms of civility

176 **indifferent** impartially, equally (the adverbial form without 'ly' again)

178 **Upon ... liking** i.e. if we agree on an arrangement (financial) that he can accept. Petruchio has made no such stipulation, in the hearing of the audience (which, if it cares, may assume the agreement to have been made while Petruchio and Hortensio stood aside). In ll. 210–11 later, Hortensio says he has promised that he and Gremio will pay all the expenses of Petruchio's wooing of Katherine. Bond infers that it is Hortensio's method of getting money for himself from Gremio and, later, Tranio (ll. 268–71).

GREMIO
So said, so done, is well.
Hortensio, have you told him all her faults?

PETRUCHIO
I know she is an irksome brawling scold.
If that be all, masters, I hear no harm.

GREMIO
No, say'st me so, friend? What countryman?

PETRUCHIO
Born in Verona, old Antonio's son.
My father dead, my fortune lives for me,
And I do hope good days and long to see.

GREMIO
O sir, such a life with such a wife were strange.
But if you have a stomach, to't a God's name; 190
You shall have me assisting you in all.
But will you woo this wildcat?

PETRUCHIO Will I live?

GRUMIO Will he woo her? Ay, or I'll hang her.

186 Antonio's] ROWE; *Butonios* F1 190 stomach ... name;] F1 (stomacke, too 't a Gods name,) 193 I'll] F1 (Ile); he'll HOSLEY

181 **So said, so done, is well** A variation on the traditional 'no sooner said than done' (Tilley S117): 'it is always good if what is done matches what is said or promised'. Gremio's phrase has also some of the force of the modern colloquial 'I'll believe it when I see it'.

183 **irksome** The word had a stronger meaning in Shakespeare's day; almost 'loathsome' or 'offensive'. Compare *As You Like It*, 3.5.91–4, 'Silvius, the time was that I hated thee; | . . . Thy company, which erst was irksome to me . . .'.

185 **say'st me so** The exact equivalent of the modern 'You don't say!' The omission of 'to' after 'say' was common (Abbott 201).

What countryman? what is your 'country', where do you come from?

186 **Antonio's** That F1's *Butonios* is simply a compositor's error is shown by its use of the correct name not only earlier at l. 620 (1.2.53) but also later at l. 929 (2.1.68).

189 **O sir** Capell's emendation omitting the 'O', although accepted by New Cambridge and defended by a pseudo-bibliographical explanation of the alleged error, is of interest only as showing how eighteenth-century editors tried to confine Shakespeare to ten syllables a line.

189 **were strange** would be extraordinary – but probably with a pun on 'strange' as meaning 'foreign', following Gremio's enquiry about Petruchio's country or city of origin.

190 **stomach, . . . name;** This reading seems closest to F1's version, recorded in the collations; but the alternative (said by Cambridge to have been conjectured by Bubier) 'if you have a stomach to't, a God's name' is tempting. Stomach: appetite for, liking. 'A' is the weakened form of OE *on* (meaning 'in').

193 **or I'll hang her** Behind this perhaps lies a proverb 'Better be half hanged than ill wed' (Tilley H130) of which Feste has another version in *Twelfth Night*, 1.5.18–19, 'Many a good hanging prevents a bad marriage'; but the exact force of Gremio's remark is not clear. There may be a glance at the custom of hanging unwanted animals.

PETRUCHIO

Why came I hither but to that intent?
Think you a little din can daunt mine ears?
Have I not in my time heard lions roar?
Have I not heard the sea, puffed up with winds,
Rage like an angry boar chafed with sweat?
Have I not heard great ordnance in the field,
And heaven's artillery thunder in the skies? 200
Have I not in a pitched battle heard
Loud 'larums, neighing steeds, and trumpets' clang?
And do you tell me of a woman's tongue,
That gives not half so great a blow to hear
As will a chestnut in a farmer's fire?
Tush, tush, fear boys with bugs!

GRUMIO For he fears none.

GREMIO

Hortensio, hark.
This gentleman is happily arrived,
My mind presumes, for his own good and yours.

HORTENSIO

I promised we would be contributors 210
And bear his charge of wooing, whatsoe'er.

GREMIO

And so we will, provided that he win her.

GRUMIO

I would I were as sure of a good dinner.

202 trumpets'] CAPELL; trumpets F1; trumpet's STEEVENS 209 yours] F1; ours THEOBALD (*conj.* THIRLBY)

198 **chafed** irritated or angered, as in *3 Henry VI*, 2.5.126, 'Warwick rages like a chafed bull'. The word is doubly appropriate in the context because it is applicable also to the fury of the sea (compare, e.g., *Winter's Tale*, 3.3.87).

199 **ordnance** artillery, cannon
field battlefield

202 **'larums** alarms – used here (as not in 1.1.126) in the original sense, calls to arms.

206 **fear boys with bugs** (Go away and) frighten boys with bogeymen (another folk-saying: Tilley B703). 'Frighten' was the first meaning of 'fear' used as a transitive verb; the sense surviving today is in Gremio's reply. (Another early sense, 'have doubts concerning', is found in 4.4.10.) 'Bug' survives in the compound 'bugbear' as the name of the imaginary creature invoked to frighten children.

209 **yours** The F1 reading, which needs no justification, has been defended, against the emendation 'ours', by the argument that Gremio is anxious to make Petruchio the responsibility of Hortensio. It may be so, although neither in l. 212 nor in the earlier ll. 190–1 does Gremio show any reluctance to pay his share.

Enter Tranio, brave (as Lucentio), and Biondello

TRANIO Gentlemen, God save you. If I may be bold, tell me, I beseech you, which is the readiest way to the house of Signor Baptista Minola?

BIONDELLO He that has the two fair daughters – is't he you mean?

TRANIO Even he, Biondello.

GREMIO Hark you, sir, you mean not her to – 220

TRANIO Perhaps him and her, sir. What have you to do?

PETRUCHIO Not her that chides, sir, at any hand, I pray.

TRANIO I love no chiders, sir. Biondello, let's away.

LUCENTIO (*aside to Tranio*) Well begun, Tranio.

HORTENSIO Sir, a word ere you go.
Are you a suitor to the maid you talk of, yea or no?

TRANIO
And if I be, sir, is it any offence?

GREMIO
No, if without more words you will get you hence.

TRANIO
Why, sir, I pray, are not the streets as free
For me as for you?

GREMIO But so is not she. 230

TRANIO
For what reason, I beseech you?

GREMIO For this reason, if you'll know,
That she's the choice love of Signor Gremio.

214–16] *as prose* POPE; Gentlemen ... bold | ... way | ... *Minola?* | F1 217 BIONDELLO] F1; *Hortensio* (or *Grumio*) HEATH *conj.*; *Gre*[*mio*] CHALMERS 1823 is't] F1; is't (*aside to* Tra.) MALONE 220 her to –] F1; her too? DELIUS (*conj.* TYRWHITT); her to woo HALLIWELL (*conj.* MALONE)

213.1 ***brave*** finely dressed (sometimes with the implication of showiness or extravagance)

217–18 Either Biondello is playing a prearranged part, or he may be unable to keep quiet. Malone thought that some of the words were an aside to Tranio.

219 **Even he** yes, precisely, he

220–32 These lines may be prose, or (mostly bad) verse. One wonders whether Shakespeare was not experimenting with rhymed prose. In the absence of other evidence, F1's divisions are followed, by and large. See also Introduction pp. 61–3.

220 **her to –** Tyrwhitt's interpretation ('too') hardly makes sense. Tranio interrupts, in his assumed arrogant manner.

221 **What . . . do?** what business is it of yours?

222 **at any hand** in any circumstances. Petruchio is saying that whatever Tranio's intentions may be with Baptista's family, he would be well advised not to meddle with the shrewish daughter.

233 **choice** (i) chosen – as in *Henry VIII*, 1.2.162; and, perhaps, (ii) excellent, as elsewhere in Shakespeare

HORTENSIO
That she's the chosen of Signor Hortensio.

TRANIO
Softly, my masters! If you be gentlemen,
Do me this right: hear me with patience.
Baptista is a noble gentleman,
To whom my father is not all unknown,
And were his daughter fairer than she is,
She may more suitors have, and me for one. 240
Fair Leda's daughter had a thousand wooers,
Then well one more may fair Bianca have;
And so she shall: Lucentio shall make one,
Though Paris came, in hope to speed alone.

GREMIO
What, this gentleman will out-talk us all!

LUCENTIO
Sir, give him head, I know he'll prove a jade.

PETRUCHIO
Hortensio, to what end are all these words?

HORTENSIO (*to Tranio*)
Sir, let me be so bold as ask you,
Did you yet ever see Baptista's daughter?

TRANIO
No, sir, but hear I do that he hath two: 250

242 one more may] F1; may one more F3

238 **all** altogether

239–42 **And . . . have** The lines have not attracted comment although F3 tried to emend the fourth, and Keightley thought a line missing after 239. It seems that Shakespeare's pen has run away with him. The context demands some such meaning as 'And even if his daughter were *not* fair . . . (there would still be nothing to stop her having additional suitors. But in fact she is comparable with Helen herself . . .)'. As Greg once put it, 'There can be no doubt that Shakespeare occasionally wrote a sentence that does not mean what he intended, though at the time of writing he evidently thought that it did. Sometimes it means the exact opposite' (and he cited *Macbeth*, 3.6.8–10). (*The Editorial Problem in Shakespeare*, 2nd edition, Oxford 1951, p. xi, n. 2.)

241 **Leda's daughter** Helen of Troy. Editors suggest that her wooers number a 'thousand' because of Marlowe's Faustus's tribute to her, 'Was this the face that launched a thousand ships . . .?' *A Shrew* is more Marlovian still when it makes Aurelius describe Phylema as 'More fair then was the Grecian *Helena* | For whose sweet sake so many princes dide, | That came with thousand ships to *Tenedos*'.

242 **one more** Not, presumably, a thousand and one, but one more than she already has.

244 **Though Paris came** even if Paris were to come himself. Paris, as the man who stole Helen from her husband (Menelaus), would be a rival to be feared.
speed alone be the only one to succeed

246 **jade** worthless, weak horse, lacking in stamina (i.e. there's no need to restrain Tranio ('Lucentio'); he won't last long anyway)

The one as famous for a scolding tongue
As is the other for beauteous modesty.

PETRUCHIO
Sir, sir, the first's for me, let her go by.

GREMIO
Yea, leave that labour to great Hercules,
And let it be more than Alcides' twelve.

PETRUCHIO
Sir, understand you this of me, in sooth:
The youngest daughter whom you hearken for
Her father keeps from all access of suitors
And will not promise her to any man
Until the elder sister first be wed. 260
The younger then is free, and not before.

TRANIO
If it be so, sir, that you are the man
Must stead us all, and me amongst the rest,
And if you break the ice and do this feat,
Achieve the elder, set the younger free
For our access, whose hap shall be to have her
Will not so graceless be to be ingrate.

HORTENSIO
Sir, you say well, and well you do conceive;
And since you do profess to be a suitor,
You must, as we do, gratify this gentleman, 270

263 stead] F1 (steed) 264 feat] ROWE; feeke F1

253 **let her go by** 'pass' her, leave her out of the question

254–5 **leave . . . Alcides' twelve** i.e. Petruchio is taking on a task even greater than the twelve labours of Hercules (also called Alcides, as the reputed grandson of Alcaeus – though he was probably the son of Zeus, not of Alcaeus' son Amphitryon). The twelve labours given to Hercules seemed impossible to achieve – such as the killing of Hydra – but he performed them all. 'Let it be': 'admit that it would be'.

256 **sooth** truth

257 **hearken for** Either 'enquire after' (*OED* v. 6) or 'seek to capture', 'lie in wait for', 'scheme for' (7), as perhaps in *1 Henry IV*, 5.4.51–2, Prince Hal to his father: 'O God, they did me too much injury | That ever said I heark'ned for your death' ('hearkned to' in F1 and the later Quartos).

263 **stead** benefit, help (often so used by Shakespeare)

264 **break the ice** This is the stock phrase still in use (Tilley I3).
feat The emendation seems essential and is justified on the theory that it was easy for a compositor to misread secretary 'f' as 'long s' and 't' as 'k'.

266 **whose hap shall be** he whose (good) fortune it will be

267 **to be ingrate** as to be ungrateful

268 **conceive** understand, interpret

270 **gratify** reward. Hortensio is making sure that Tranio understands that Petruchio will expect more than gratitude. Compare l. 178 and note.

To whom we all rest generally beholding.

TRANIO

Sir, I shall not be slack; in sign whereof,
Please ye we may contrive this afternoon,
And quaff carouses to our mistress' health,
And do as adversaries do in law, 275
Strive mightily but eat and drink as friends.

GRUMIO *and* BIONDELLO

O excellent motion! Fellows, let's be gone.

HORTENSIO

The motion's good indeed, and be it so.
Petruchio, I shall be your *Bene venuto*. *Exeunt*

2.1 *Enter Katherina, and Bianca (with her hands tied)*

BIANCA

Good sister, wrong me not, nor wrong yourself,
To make a bondmaid and a slave of me.
That I disdain. But, for these other goods,

273 contrive] F1; convive THEOBALD 279 *Bene*] This edition; *Been* F1; *Ben* F2
2.1.0.1] F1 (*Enter Katherina and Bianca*); *Act II Sc. I ... Enter ...* POPE 3 goods] F1; Gawds THEOBALD; gards COLLIER 1853

271 **beholding** indebted, 'obliged'

273 **contrive** Explained by *OED* ('contrive' v^2.) as 'pass or employ time' on the assumption that the word is irregularly derived from *contrivi*, preterite of the Latin *conterere*, to use up or waste. Upton first cited in support *The Faerie Queene*, 2.9.48 ('Three ages such as mortal men contrive') the sense of which is not certain. More convincing than this – and than the citations in *OED* itself – are (in modern spelling) the line quoted by Hudson, from *Damon and Pithias* (1571), 'In travelling countries, we three have contrived | Full many a year' (Malone Society edition, ll. 272–3), and that quoted by Collier from Painter's Romeo and Juliet novella in his *Palace of Pleasure*, 'Julietta knowing the fury of her father ... retired for the day into her chamber, and contrived that whole night more in weeping than sleeping'. Accordingly, emendation to 'contrive this afternoon | To quaff carouses', although tempting (on the supposition that the compositor's eye caught 'And' from the beginning of the next line), is hardly justifiable.

274 **quaff carouses** i.e. drink toasts – but 'carouse' implies drinking 'full bumpers', drinking without restraint

275 **adversaries** lawyers representing opposing parties

277 **motion** proposal

279 ***Bene*** Editors 'correct' to 'ben' – but F1's 'Been' is more likely to be the compositor's error for 'Bene', used twice earlier in this scene (ll. 25, 26). 'Bene (ben) venuto', meaning 'welcome', seems here to be used metaphorically for 'host': Petruchio is to be Hortensio's guest at the drinking.

2.1.1 **yourself** Brook (*g* 76 b) points out that 'Bianca, trying to conciliate her elder sister Katherine, uses the respectful *you*, whereas Katherine uses the impatient *thou*'. (In fact Katherine's idiom changes in ll. 16–17.)

3 **disdain** In the sense of 'ignore' or 'think unworthy of notice' (as probably in *Lucrece* 844) rather than 'scorn'.

goods The emendation 'gawds', although generally accepted, is unsatisfactory: 'gawds' are cheap articles giving facile pleasure. (Nor would it be easy to misread 'gawds' or 'gauds' in secretary hand as 'goods'; New Cambridge is driven back on the unlikely hypothesis of a mishearing.) F1's 'goods', meaning 'possessions' or

Unbind my hands, I'll pull them off myself,
Yea, all my raiment, to my petticoat;
Or what you will command me will I do,
So well I know my duty to my elders.

KATHERINA
Of all thy suitors here I charge tell
Whom thou lov'st best; see thou dissemble not.

BIANCA
Believe me, sister, of all the men alive 10
I never yet beheld that special face
Which I could fancy more than any other.

KATHERINA
Minion, thou liest. Is't not Hortensio?

BIANCA
If you affect him, sister, here I swear
I'll plead for you myself but you shall have him.

KATHERINA
O, then belike you fancy riches more:
You will have Gremio to keep you fair.

BIANCA
Is it for him you do envy me so?
Nay then you jest, and now I well perceive
You have but jested with me all this while. 20
I prithee, sister Kate, untie my hands.

KATHERINA (*striking her*)
If that be jest, then all the rest was so.

Enter Baptista

BAPTISTA
Why, how now dame, whence grows this insolence?

8 charge] F1; charge thee F2 10 all the] F1; all POPE 22 *striking her*] F1 (*'Strikes her', after* 'so')

just 'articles', makes better sense than 'gawds' if Bianca is not speaking ironically and equally good sense if she is.

4 **Unbind** i.e. if you will unbind

8 **charge** F2's 'charge thee' makes the line 'regular' and assumes the normal, transitive, use of 'charge' but is not essential.

10 **all the** Similarly, the omission of 'the' is justifiable only if one believes in the necessity for a metrical strait-jacket.

13 **Minion** spoilt brat – as notably in *Romeo*, 3.5.151–2, 'Mistress minion, you, | Thank me no thankings . . .'.

14 **affect** fancy, care for

15 **but** An exceptional use, where the meaning 'but in any case' seems inadequate. Abbott (126) plausibly suggests 'I'll plead for you myself *if* you shall *not* have him otherwise' and compares 'I should woo hard but be your groom' in *Cymbeline*, 3.6.69.

16 **belike** 'perhaps' or 'presumably'

17 **fair** finely dressed

18 **envy** hate, dislike (not just 'feel jealous of'). The accent fell on the second syllable. Compare Induction 2.63 and note.

– Bianca, stand aside. Poor girl, she weeps.
Go ply thy needle, meddle not with her.
(*To Katherina*) For shame, thou hilding of a
devilish spirit,
Why dost thou wrong her that did ne'er wrong thee?
When did she cross thee with a bitter word?

KATHERINA
Her silence flouts me, and I'll be revenged.
She flies after Bianca

BAPTISTA
What, in my sight? Bianca, get thee in. *Exit Bianca* 30

KATHERINA
What, will you not suffer me? Nay, now I see
She is your treasure, she must have a husband,
I must dance bare-foot on her wedding-day,
And for your love to her lead apes in hell.
Talk not to me, I will go sit and weep,
Till I can find occasion of revenge. *Exit*

BAPTISTA
Was ever gentleman thus grieved as I?
But who comes here?
Enter Gremio; Lucentio as Cambio, in the habit of a mean man; Petruchio, with Hortensio as Litio; and Tranio as Lucentio, with his boy, Biondello, bearing a lute and books

GREMIO Good morrow, neighbour Baptista.

BAPTISTA Good morrow, neighbour Gremio. – God save you, gentlemen. 40

30 *Exit Bianca*] F1 (*Exit*) 36 *Exit*] *not in* F1 38.1–4] F1 (*Enter Gremio, Lucentio, in the habit of a meane man, Petruchio with Tranio, with his boy bearing a Lute and Bookes.*); ROWE *first added Hortensio*

25 **meddle not with** have nothing to do with. Perhaps Baptista here unties Bianca's hands.

26 **hilding** vicious beast (*OED* 1) rather than 'jade' or 'good for nothing', the commoner meanings

28 **cross** oppose, thwart, contradict

29 **flouts** 'mocks' or even 'insults'

31 **suffer me** let me be, let me have anything I want

33 **dance . . . wedding-day** Dancing barefoot was the proverbial fate of an elder sister when a younger married first (Tilley D22).

34 **lead apes in hell** The proverbial fate of an old maid – the undesirable opposite of the married woman's leading children in heaven (Tilley M37). Beatrice has a delightful adaptation of it in *Much Ado*, 2.1.36–41.

38.1 F1's omission of Hortensio is strange. It may be accidental; or perhaps he should not enter until Petruchio presents him at l. 55.
habit dress, garments

38.2 ***mean man*** man not of the upper classes. Compare 1.1.202 and note.

PETRUCHIO

And you, good sir. Pray have you not a daughter
Called Katherina, fair and virtuous?

BAPTISTA

I have a daughter, sir, called Katherina.

GREMIO

You are too blunt, go to it orderly.

PETRUCHIO

You wrong me, Signor Gremio, give me leave.
I am a gentleman of Verona, sir,
That hearing of her beauty and her wit,
Her affability and bashful modesty,
Her wondrous qualities and mild behaviour, 50
Am bold to show myself a forward guest
Within your house, to make mine eye the witness
Of that report which I so oft have heard;
And for an entrance to my entertainment
I do present you with a man of mine,
Cunning in music and the mathematics,
To instruct her fully in those sciences,
Whereof I know she is not ignorant.
Accept of him, or else you do me wrong.
His name is Litio, born in Mantua. 60

BAPTISTA

You're welcome, sir, and he for your good sake.
But for my daughter Katherine, this I know,
She is not for your turn, the more my grief.

PETRUCHIO

I see you do not mean to part with her,

42–3] *as verse* ROWE 1714; *as prose* F1 60 Litio] F1; *Licio* F2

45 **orderly** in the conventional or polite way. The word was then also an adverb (compare 4.3.94), formed from the noun 'order', but is now only an adjective.

46 **give me leave** i.e. if you will pardon my saying so

50 **qualities** gifts of nature (rather than 'accomplishments')

51 **forward** eager (not necessarily with the suggestion of presumption that it has in 3.1.1)

54 **for an entrance** as an entrance-fee
entertainment (hospitable) reception

56 **Cunning** skilled

57 **sciences** subjects, fields of knowledge (i.e. *not* sciences as opposed to 'humanities')

60 **Litio** Hosley has argued that this F1 spelling should be preserved, for the good reason that it is the form used in *Supposes* and also because he believes that it is the old Italian word for garlic. F1 has it again at l. 1349 (3.1.54) but at l. 1846 and elsewhere in what is now Act 4 Scene 2 'Lisio'. ('Licio', favoured in modern editions of the play, does not occur at all in F1.) The pronunciation is probably 'Litzio' or 'Lishio'.

Or else you like not of my company.

BAPTISTA
Mistake me not, I speak but as I find.
Whence are you, sir? What may I call your name?

PETRUCHIO
Petruchio is my name, Antonio's son,
A man well known throughout all Italy.

BAPTISTA
I know him well. You are welcome for his sake. 70

GREMIO Saving your tale, Petruchio, I pray let us that are poor petitioners speak too. Bacare! You are marvellous forward.

PETRUCHIO
O pardon me, Signor Gremio, I would fain be doing.

GREMIO
I doubt it not, sir, but you will curse your wooing.

70 know] F1; knew DYCE 1866 (*conj.* SINGER 1856) 71–3] *as prose* F1; Saving ... pray | ... too. | ... forward. | STEEVENS 1778 72 Bacare] F1; *Baccare* F2; Backare COLLIER 75–86 I doubt ... coming?] *all as prose* POPE; I ... curse | Your wooing neighbors: this is a guift | ... expresse | ... beene | ... any: | ... hath | ... cunning | ... Languages, | ... Mathematickes: | ... seruice.| ... *Gremio*: | ... sir, | ... stranger, | ... comming? | F1 75–6 wooing. Neighbours,] ROWE 1714; wooing neighbors: F1; wooing. Neighbour, THEOBALD

66 **speak but as I find** Another old saying (Tilley S724).

67 **What ... name?** This tautological idiom, used in Shakespeare chiefly by old men, has been thought an indication of old-fashioned speech. (So Brook, citing Bridget Cusack in *Shakespeare Survey* 23, pp. 4–5.) Compare 4.5.55.

70 **know him** Perhaps 'know of him'. Compare ll. 103–4 and note, and 115. (Petruchio tells Hortensio that Baptista 'knew my deceasèd father well' (1.2.101) but Baptista doesn't *know* Antonio well enough to have heard – or apparently care – that he has died.) Steevens aptly compared *Timon*, 3.2.4–5, 'We know him for no less, though we are but strangers to him'.

71 **Saving** with all due respect to

72 **poor petitioners** The adjective regularly goes with the noun, probably because of the customary humility of formal petitions. Compare 2 *Henry VI*, 1.3.23.

Bacare stand back. Probably mock-Latin but not of Shakespeare's invention (Tilley M1183); the joke is found in *Ralph Roister Doister*, 1.2; Lyly's *Midas*, 1.2.3; and John Heywood's *Dialogue conteyning the ... effectual proverbes in the English tonge ... With ... Epigrammes* (1562 and 1566). Heywood gives three versions of the epigram. One is 'Bacare quoth Mortimer to his sow: se | Mortimers sow speakth as good latin as he'; another 'Backare, quoth Mortimer to his sow | Went that sow backe, at that biddyng trow you?' Alternatively, *OED* conjectures that the word may be a corruption of 'back there' or 'backer' – further back. Gremio is also punning on 'forward': (i) the opposite to backward; (ii) presumptuous.

74 **would fain be doing** am anxious to 'get on with it' – but there may be a quibble on 'doing' in the sense of 'having sexual intercourse'

75 **I ... wooing** 'Wooing' does rhyme with 'doing', and Gremio is capping Petruchio's phrase – but it is difficult to make these opening words into a verse line (unless, conceivably, 'sir' is regarded as hypermetrical). F1's verse arrangement of the entire speech must be wrong (and though in F it is *all* set out as verse, the 'wooing' – 'doing' rhyme is lost). As Florence Ashton pointed out, the text is suspect until l. 113. The conventional explanation that lines written in the margin have been mistaken by the

– Neighbours, this is a gift very grateful, I am sure of it. (*To Baptista*) To express the like kindness, myself, that have been more kindly beholding to you than any, freely give unto you this young scholar that hath been long studying at Rheims, as cunning in Greek, Latin, and 80 other languages as the other in music and mathematics. His name is Cambio; pray accept his service.

BAPTISTA A thousand thanks, Signor Gremio. Welcome, good Cambio. (*To Tranio*) But, gentle sir, methinks you walk like a stranger. May I be so bold to know the cause of your coming?

TRANIO

Pardon me, sir, the boldness is mine own
That, being a stranger in this city here,
Do make myself a suitor to your daughter,
Unto Bianca, fair and virtuous; 90
Nor is your firm resolve unknown to me
In the preferment of the eldest sister.
This liberty is all that I request,
That, upon knowledge of my parentage,
I may have welcome 'mongst the rest that woo,
And free access and favour as the rest.
And toward the education of your daughters
I here bestow a simple instrument,

76–7 it. (*To Baptista*) To] This edition; it, to F1; it: To ROWE 77 kindness, myself,] CAMBRIDGE; kindnesse my selfe, F1 78 any,] POPE; any: F1; any‸ Q1631 79 you this] CAPELL (*conj.* TYRWHITT); this F1

compositor for verse would fit Gremio's speech but would hardly cover the problems of the following two. On this page in F1 (215, sig.[S6r]), the 'copy' may have been cast-off inaccurately (and it would be the last of the inner formes in the gathering) and the compositor may be spreading words out.

76 **Neighbours** Gremio is presumably addressing the whole group. If the emendation 'Neighbour' is accepted, he is addressing Baptista. The 'gift' must be Petruchio's earlier 'presenting' of Hortensio/Litio, which Gremio now matches by 'giving' Lucentio/Cambio.
grateful pleasing, acceptable (*OED* I)

80 **Rheims** the famous European university

82 **Cambio** Italian for 'exchange'

85 **walk like a stranger** stand back and keep to yourself, as not being one of the group; or perhaps 'stranger' has the original meaning, 'foreigner'.

92 **In the preferment of** in the priority you give to (*OED* II. b). The word, in a meaning closer to the Latin, was used specifically of priority of right or privilege, particularly in matters of buying and selling. It could also mean 'putting forward', 'advancement' or even 'promotion'.

94 **upon knowledge of** i.e. when you know the facts about

98 **instrument** the lute that Katherine soon breaks over Hortensio's head

And this small packet of Greek and Latin books.
If you accept them, then their worth is great. 100

BAPTISTA
Lucentio is your name? Of whence, I pray?

TRANIO
Of Pisa, sir, son to Vincentio.

BAPTISTA
A mighty man of Pisa, by report;
I know him well. You are very welcome, sir.
(*To Hortensio*) Take you the lute, (*to Lucentio*) and you
the set of books,
You shall go see your pupils presently.
Holla, within!

Enter a Servant

Sirrah, lead these gentlemen
To my daughters, and tell them both
These are their tutors. Bid them use them well.

Exeunt Servant, Hortensio and Lucentio

We will go walk a little in the orchard, 110
And then to dinner. You are passing welcome,
And so I pray you all to think yourselves.

101 BAPTISTA] F1; BAPTISTA (*opening one of the books*) HIBBARD 103 Pisa, by report;] F1 (*Pisa* by report.); *Pisa;* by report ROWE 104 know] F1; knew RANN (*conj.* CAPELL *Notes*) 108 my] F1; my two F2 109.1] THEOBALD (*subs.*); *not in* F1; *Exit Servant, with* Luc[entio] *and* Hor[tensio]. Bi[ondello] *follows.* CAPELL

101 **Lucentio . . . name** The name 'Lucentio' has not yet been mentioned to Baptista – a fact that no audience would notice – but some editors believe that Baptista obtains the name by opening one of the books. They assume these to be either 'those Lucentio had brought with him to Padua for study' (Bond) or presentation copies bearing an inscription giving the donor's name.

103 **mighty** important, influential

103–4 **by report; | I . . . well.** Since later Baptista does not recognize Vincentio, some editors have re-punctuated and read, in effect, 'by report I know him well'. But 'know' may mean only 'know of' – as perhaps in l. 70.

106 **presently** immediately

108 The line is irregular, if one counts by syllables (and F2's addition of 'two' hardly helps), but it is easily spoken as verse, with a pause after 'daughters'. (Bond allowed himself to be persuaded by Walker that 'daughters' was sometimes trisyllabic.)

109.1 Theobald's stage direction may stand. There seems to be nothing to prevent Biondello's remaining on stage while Petruchio bargains with Baptista.

110 **orchard** garden. Elizabethans sometimes distinguished between the 'garden' (for flowers) and the 'orchard' (for herbs and fruit trees) but there was seldom any call for the differentiation.

111 **dinner** the principal meal of the day, served in the late morning, not the evening. (This is made clear by, e.g., the action of *Merry Wives*, 3.3.)
passing i.e. surpassingly; 'most', as in Induction 1.64.

PETRUCHIO
Signor Baptista, my business asketh haste,
And every day I cannot come to woo.
You knew my father well, and in him me,
Left solely heir to all his lands and goods,
Which I have bettered rather than decreased.
Then tell me, if I get your daughter's love,
What dowry shall I have with her to wife?

BAPTISTA
After my death the one half of my lands, 120
And in possession twenty thousand crowns.

PETRUCHIO
And for that dowry I'll assure her of
Her widowhood, be it that she survive me,
In all my lands and leases whatsoever.
Let specialties be therefore drawn between us,
That covenants may be kept on either hand.

BAPTISTA
Ay, when the special thing is well obtained,
That is, her love; for that is all in all.

PETRUCHIO
Why, that is nothing; for I tell you, father,

122 of] F1; for HANMER; on STEEVENS *conj.*

114 A quotation, with slight rearrangement, of a line from a sixteenth-century song, one of many that took the form of a courting dialogue. The song (in one of perhaps many versions) began 'Joan q[uo]d John when wyll this be | tell me when wilt thow marrie me | . . . | saie Joan said John what wilt thow doe | I cannot come every daie to wooe'. It may well have been known to Elizabethan audiences from its use in a jig; and it may have been particularly appropriate to Petruchio because Joan (in one version of the dialogue at least) is determined, like Katherine, to 'have my will in all'. The song is discussed (but without reference to Shakespeare) by John M. Ward, '*Joan qd John* and other Fragments at Western Reserve University', in *Aspects of Medieval and Renaissance Music. A Birthday Offering to Gustave Reese*, ed. Jan LaRue, N.Y. 1966, pp.832–7. The single line 'I cannot come every day to woo' is found also as a refrain in such a song as 'I have house and land in Kent', printed in Thomas Ravenscroft's *Melismata* (1611).

121 **in possession** i.e. in immediate possession, on marriage

123 **widowhood** Presumed (by *OED* also) to mean 'widow's rights' (to be specified in a marriage contract). This use of the *word* is unique but compare the financial arrangements for Bianca's marriage, in ll. 344–6.
be it that she if she should – the common inversion of subject and subjunctive verb in a conditional clause. (Brook *g* 221)

125 **specialties** special legal contracts, under seal (*OED* II. 7)

126 **covenants** formal agreements (here, to do something; often, to refrain from certain actions)

129 **father** By presuming to use the informal term of address that would be appropriate *after* the wedding, Petruchio is, characteristically, taking everything for granted – or pretending to.

I am as peremptory as she proud-minded, 130
And where two raging fires meet together
They do consume the thing that feeds their fury.
Though little fire grows great with little wind
Yet extreme gusts will blow out fire and all.
So I to her, and so she yields to me,
For I am rough and woo not like a babe.

BAPTISTA
Well mayst thou woo, and happy be thy speed!
But be thou armed for some unhappy words.

PETRUCHIO
Ay, to the proof, as mountains are for winds
That shakes not though they blow perpetually. 140

Enter Hortensio (as Litio) with his head broke

BAPTISTA
How now, my friend, why dost thou look so pale?

HORTENSIO
For fear, I promise you, if I look pale.

BAPTISTA
What, will my daughter prove a good musician?

HORTENSIO
I think she'll sooner prove a soldier.
Iron may hold with her, but never lutes.

BAPTISTA
Why then thou canst not break her to the lute?

HORTENSIO
Why no, for she hath broke the lute to me.
I did but tell her she mistook her frets,

130 **peremptory** Probably three syllables, with the stress on the first.

131–4 Petruchio is repeating old adages (e.g. Tilley W424).

137 **thy speed** your fortune; the result for you

139 **to the proof** to the point of invulnerability. 'Proof armour', to which Petruchio refers, is armour 'proved' by testing to be impenetrable.

140 **shakes** Another instance of the 'Northern plural in "s"'

142 **promise** assure (*OED v.* 5. b). So too in l. 285.

143 **prove** turn out to be – but in his reply Hortensio also puns on the sense 'test'.

145 **hold with her** (i) suit her; (ii) resist her, be strong enough to withstand her attacks

145 **lutes** There is perhaps a quibble on 'lute' (*OED sb.*[2]), clay used as a kind of cement.

146 **break her to** The same idiom as 'breaking in' a horse or other animal; but again Hortensio puns on the word in his reply.

148 **mistook her frets** i.e. played the wrong notes by placing her fingers upon the wrong frets (the bars or ridges – then normally made by winding gut around the frame – that regulate the fingering on such a stringed instrument as a lute). This time it is Katherine who quibbles, in the reported reply of l. 151: 'frets' there means 'vexations', causes of anger or 'fuming'.

And bowed her hand to teach her fingering,
When, with a most impatient devilish spirit, 150
'Frets, call you these?' quoth she, 'I'll fume with them'
And with that word she struck me on the head,
And through the instrument my pate made way,
And there I stood amazèd for a while,
As on a pillory, looking through the lute,
While she did call me 'rascal', 'fiddler',
And 'twangling Jack', with twenty such vile terms,
As had she studied to misuse me so.

PETRUCHIO
Now, by the world, it is a lusty wench;
I love her ten times more than e'er I did. 160
O how I long to have some chat with her!

BAPTISTA (*to Hortensio*)
Well, go with me, and be not so discomfited.
Proceed in practice with my younger daughter;
She's apt to learn and thankful for good turns.
– Signor Petruchio, will you go with us
Or shall I send my daughter Kate to you?

PETRUCHIO
I pray you do. I'll attend her here –

Exeunt all but Petruchio

156 'rascal', 'fiddler'] F1 (Rascall, Fidler); rascal fidler CAPELL 167 I'll] F1 (Ile); I will ROWE
167.1 *Exeunt all but Petruchio*] F1 (*Exit. Manet Petruchio.*) *after l.* 166; *after 'do'* HERFORD

149 **bowed** (I) curved

151 **fume** Katherine is playing on the phrase 'fret and fume', meaning 'give way to obvious anger'. The image in 'fume' is found again in the colloquial 'get all steamed up'.

153 **pate** head. See note on 1.2.12.

154 **amazèd** bewildered, astonished

155 **pillory** The comparison is with the wrong-doer firmly held by head and arms in the wooden instrument of punishment. (In the stocks, the legs also were pinioned.)

156 **'rascal', 'fiddler'** 'Rascal' signifies here not 'wrong-doer' but 'mean fellow' or 'one of the rabble'. (The noun was used also of the inferior deer in a herd.) The adjective, with corresponding meaning, was common too; hence the plausible but unnecessary emendation 'rascal fiddler', to match 'twangling Jack'. 'Fiddler' may have three syllables.

157 **Jack** mean fellow, rascal

158 **As . . . studied** as if she had thought deeply how

159 **lusty** In its regular Elizabethan meaning, 'full of life' (perhaps, also, as often, implying admiration for the strength or sense of humour of the one so described).

163 **Proceed in practice with** continue your teaching of ('practice' in the sense, still found, of 'exercise in any art [etc.] . . . for the purpose of attaining proficiency', *OED* 1.3)

164 **apt** ready. 'Apt' and 'turns' sometimes had indecent connotations but Baptista obviously does not intend them.

167 Petruchio speaks the words 'I pray you do. I'll attend her here' as Baptista leaves, and completes the second sentence when Baptista is out of hearing.
attend await

And woo her with some spirit when she comes.
Say that she rail, why then I'll tell her plain
She sings as sweetly as a nightingale. 170
Say that she frown, I'll say she looks as clear
As morning roses newly washed with dew.
Say she be mute and will not speak a word,
Then I'll commend her volubility
And say she uttereth piercing eloquence.
If she do bid me pack, I'll give her thanks,
As though she bid me stay by her a week.
If she deny to wed, I'll crave the day
When I shall ask the banns, and when be marrièd.
But here she comes, and now, Petruchio, speak. 180

Enter Katherina

Good morrow, Kate – for that's your name, I hear.

KATHERINA
Well have you heard, but something hard of hearing:
They call me Katherine that do talk of me.

PETRUCHIO
You lie, in faith, for you are called plain Kate,
And bonny Kate, and sometimes Kate the curst.
But Kate, the prettiest Kate in Christendom,
Kate of Kate Hall, my super-dainty Kate,
For dainties are all Kates, and therefore, Kate,
Take this of me, Kate of my consolation:
Hearing thy mildness praised in every town, 190

185 bonny] F1 (bony); F4 *first spells 'bonny'* 188 Kates] F1; Cates POPE

175 **piercing** moving, affecting – as in *Lear*, 4.3.9–10, 'Did your letters pierce the Queen to any demonstration of grief?'

176 **pack** be gone, take myself off. This intransitive use is lost but compare 'she packed him off' and 'send (someone) packing'.

178 **crave the day** ask her to name the day

182 **heard . . . hard** The Elizabethan pronunciation of 'heard' as 'hard' would have made the pun clearer.
something somewhat

185 **bonny** Perhaps in the widest general sense, 'fine' or 'good', but conceivably 'of fine size' (*OED* 2.a.). It is barely possible that F1's 'bony' means 'bony' or something like 'angular'. (In *As You Like It*, 2.3.8, where Adam calls the Duke's wrestler his 'bonnie priser', some editors, in reverse gear, read 'bony'.)

187 **Kate Hall** May mean only 'the house Kate rules over' or (ironically) 'the house that is known because Kate lives there'. There was a Katharine Hall in the south of England (of no great known importance) and the Cambridge college Catharine Hall (later St. Catharine's College) already existed but there seems to be no point in an allusion to either.

188 **Kates** i.e. cates, delicacies, choice viands. (The words are probably to be construed 'all Kates are dainties', not 'all dainties are Kates'.)

Thy virtues spoke of, and thy beauty sounded,
Yet not so deeply as to thee belongs,
Myself am moved to woo thee for my wife.

KATHERINA
'Moved', in good time! Let him that moved you hither
Remove you hence. I knew you at the first
You were a movable.

PETRUCHIO Why, what's a movable?

KATHERINA A joined stool.

PETRUCHIO Thou hast hit it. Come sit on me.

KATHERINA
Asses are made to bear, and so are you. 200

PETRUCHIO
Women are made to bear, and so are you.

KATHERINA
No such jade as you, if me you mean.

PETRUCHIO
Alas, good Kate, I will not burden thee,
For knowing thee to be but young and light.

194 'Moved', in good time!] This edition; Mou'd, in good time, F1; Mov'd! in good time; ROWE; Mov'd? In good time; THEOBALD 1740 198 joined] F1 (ioyn'd); joint- CAPELL 203 thee,] F1; thee; THEOBALD; thee: CAPELL 204 light.] F1; light – ROWE

191 **sounded** Another pun: (i) proclaimed, spoken of (ii) tested for depth, as with a plummet or plumb-line; hence 'deeply' in the following line. Compare *As You Like It*, 4.1.184–8, 'O . . . that thou didst know how many fathom deep I am in love! But it cannot be sounded: my affection hath an unknown bottom, like the Bay of Portugal'.

192 **belongs** is appropriate

194 **in good time** Best explained by Schmidt, as equivalent to *à la bonne heure*: an exclamation 'used either to express acquiescence, or astonishment and indignation'. Katherine, punning on 'moved', is expressing all three.

196 **movable** (i) an article of furniture that may be moved, as opposed to a 'fixture'; (ii) somebody given to change, and thus inconsistent and unreliable (*OED* 'movable' B 3, 5).

196 ff. Throughout this exchange, verse seems to mingle with prose. The hypothesis that all can be arranged as complete verse lines is quite untenable.

198 **joined stool** stool made (by a joiner) from parts fitted together. 'I took you for a joint-stool' was a stock form of mock-apology for overlooking somebody whom it was desired to ridicule (Tilley M897). Compare, e.g., *Lear*, 3.6.51.

199 **hit it** hit the target, guessed correctly

201 **bear** Petruchio adds two further senses to the one used by Katherine: (i) bear children; (ii) bear the weight of a lover (as in the Nurse's characteristic would-be jest, *Romeo*, 2.5.76).

202 **jade** As in 1.2.246, the animal lacking in stamina. Katherine is being insulting about Petruchio's probable capacity as a lover. (Many emendations, not worth listing, miss that point.)

203 **burden** In addition to the sexual puns similar to those in 'bear' in ll. 200–1, 'burden' can mean (i) lay accusations upon; and (ii) provide a 'burden' or bass in a musical score (compare 1.2.67 and note) – and a song without a bass is 'light'.

204 **For knowing** (I will abstain) because I know. This sense seems to be required by the original punctuation; the alternative is to re-punctuate as in the collations.

KATHERINA
Too light for such a swain as you to catch,
And yet as heavy as my weight should be.

PETRUCHIO
'Should be'? Should – buzz!

KATHERINA
Well ta'en, and like a buzzard.

PETRUCHIO
O slow-winged turtle, shall a buzzard take thee?

KATHERINA
Ay, for a turtle, as he takes a buzzard.

PETRUCHIO
Come, come, you wasp, i'faith you are too angry. 210

KATHERINA
If I be waspish, best beware my sting.

PETRUCHIO
My remedy is then to pluck it out.

207 'Should be'? Should – buzz!] GRANT WHITE (*subs.*); Shold be, should: buzze. F1; Should be! should! buz. ROWE; Should *bee* – should *buz* – BLAIR; Should be? Should buz. CAPELL; Should be? should? buz! KNIGHT 209 he] F1; she BOND (*conj.* KINNEAR)

205 **light** (i) 'light' as opposed to 'heavy' or 'strong'; (ii) not 'weighty', of small consequence; (iii) 'wanton', 'promiscuous'. (The puns were common; and even Portia ventures 'A light wife doth make a heavy husband', *Merchant*, 5.1.130.) Katherine's reply adds a further variation by using 'light' with a favourable connotation: 'nimble' and, perhaps, 'intellectually sharp'.
swain (i) pastoral lover; (ii) clot, country-bumpkin, as in 4.1.114 later and elsewhere in Shakespeare.

206 i.e. not 'clipped' or counterfeit coinage, but 'true metal'; not 'light' where I should be full weight – and not sexually light either.

207 **'Should be' . . . buzz!** F1's 'Shold be, should: buzze' may be re-punctuated in various ways, none of them beyond dispute. (i) Petruchio catches up the phrase 'should be' and retorts that he is interested not in what she *should* be, only in what she is; (ii) 'be' suggests to him 'bee' and so 'buzz like a bee'; but (iii) 'buzz' was also an interjection of impatience: 'nonsense'; and (iv) the noun 'buzz' could mean 'rumour', as in *Lear*, 1.4.326, and so Petruchio may even be implying further that rumour of what she *is* is very different from what she should be.
Well ta'en As the following reference to the buzzard makes clear, not a genuine compliment: rather, 'that's what you would be expected to say'.

207 **buzzard** (i) the inferior, unteachable kind of hawk – which will take the wrong prey; (ii) – as a metaphorical extension of this – anyone or anything stupid; and perhaps also (iii) an insect that buzzes (*OED sb*[2].). The last is apparently the meaning in l. 209, although 'buzzard' as a (dialectal) name for insects (nocturnal) is not recorded until after Shakespeare's day. Hibbard further conjectures that 'buzzard' may mean a person who 'buzzes', spreads rumours (*Richard III*, 1.1.133 lends only doubtful support).

208 **turtle** turtle-dove (the emblem of chaste and faithful love, as Katherine's reply acknowledges)

209 i.e. if a fool of a buzzard takes me, thinking me to be a turtle-dove, he is making a bad miscalculation, as the turtle-dove is mistaken when it catches the insect known as a buzzard (presumably not to the turtle's taste).

210 **wasp** Petruchio is picking up the insect reference in Katherine's retort, but with a further reference to her waspishness, through an adaptation of the adage 'Women are wasps if angered' (Tilley W705).

KATHERINA
Ay, if the fool could find it where it lies.

PETRUCHIO
Who knows not where a wasp does wear his sting?
In his tail.

KATHERINA In his tongue.

PETRUCHIO Whose tongue?

KATHERINA
Yours, if you talk of tales, and so farewell.

PETRUCHIO
What, with my tongue in your tail? Nay, come again.
Good Kate, I am a gentleman – 220

KATHERINA That I'll try.
She strikes him

PETRUCHIO
I swear I'll cuff you if you strike again.

KATHERINA So may you lose your arms.
If you strike me, you are no gentleman,
And if no gentleman, why then no arms.

PETRUCHIO
A herald, Kate? O put me in thy books!

KATHERINA
What is your crest – a coxcomb?

214–15 sting? | In his tail] *as verse* Q1631; *as prose* F1 219–20 What ... again | Good ... gentleman –] POPE (*subs.*); What ... taile. | Nay, ... Gentleman, | F1

214 **his** (Probably) its.

218 **tales** Katherine is at once punning on 'tails' and accusing Petruchio of making up fairy-tales.

219 **my tongue in your tail** The obvious pun again in 'tail-tale' is made clearer if there is emphasis on the two pronouns: Petruchio is feigning to be astonished not only at the indecency he chooses to see in Katherine's reply but also at the incongruity of *his* tongue's being involved in *her* tale.
come again try again – and perhaps 'come back again', if she has moved away as she says 'farewell' in l. 218.

223 **lose your arms** A series of quibbles on 'loose' and 'lose', words which were not always distinguished and indeed overlap in meaning: (i) – as Katherine proceeds to explain – 'lose your right to a coat of arms'; (ii) 'waste (the strength of) your arms'; and possibly (iii) 'loosen your arms' – if he has put them round her, as some editors conjecture. (It seems better for Petruchio *not* to use any kind of physical force here: probably too many stage directions have been introduced involving 'holding' Kate and 'releasing' her.)

226 **herald ... books** One of the functions of a herald was to regulate the use of armorial bearings, e.g. by recording them in a register. Petruchio also asks to be in Katherine's 'good books', in her favour. (Compare *Much Ado*, 1.1.64, 'I see, lady, the gentleman is not in your books', and Tilley B534.)

227 **crest** (i) the device – originally on the knight's helmet – placed above the shield and helmet in a coat of arms; (ii) the tuft of feathers or 'comb' on, e.g., the head of a cock
coxcomb The same word as 'cock's comb' (crest) but in this spelling also meaning

PETRUCHIO
A combless cock, so Kate will be my hen.
KATHERINA
No cock of mine, you crow too like a craven.
PETRUCHIO
Nay, come, Kate, come, you must not look so sour. 230
KATHERINA
It is my fashion when I see a crab.
PETRUCHIO
Why, here's no crab, and therefore look not sour.
KATHERINA
There is, there is.
PETRUCHIO
Then show it me.
KATHERINA Had I a glass, I would.
PETRUCHIO What, you mean my face?
KATHERINA Well aimed of such a young one.
PETRUCHIO
Now, by Saint George, I am too young for you.
KATHERINA
Yet you are withered.
PETRUCHIO 'Tis with cares.
KATHERINA I care not.
PETRUCHIO
Nay, hear you, Kate. In sooth, you scape not so.
KATHERINA
I chafe you if I tarry. Let me go. 240

239 Kate] F1; Kate (*Staying her*) BOSWELL-STONE so.] F1; so. (*Holding her*) COLLIER 1853

the cap of the fool or jester (and often 'fool').

228 **combless** i.e. harmless, gentle. To 'cut down' somebody's comb was to 'take the conceit out of him' (*OED* 'comb' *sb.* 1. 5). But Petruchio may even be thinking of the cuckold's horn as a comb.
so provided that, if

229 **craven** confessed coward; cock that too readily admits defeat (in cock-fighting) and shows it by the drooping comb

231 **crab** (i) the wild apple, notorious for its sourness; and so (ii) any 'sour' or 'sour-faced' person. The 'wit-combat' is losing still more of its momentum.

236 **Well aimed . . . one** i.e. you are surprisingly accurate for somebody so young in years and inexperienced

237 **too young** too strong, with the strength of youth. The same quibble is found in *Much Ado*, 5.1.118–19, 'Had we fought, I doubt we should have been too young for them'.

239 **scape** escape – either from the battle of wits, or (conceivably) physically – but see l. 223 and note. 'Scape' is an aphetic variant of 'escape'.

240 **chafe** (i) annoy, make furious (compare 1.2.198 and note); and perhaps (ii) warm, inflame (ME *chaufen*, OF *chaufer*, to heat)

PETRUCHIO

No, not a whit; I find you passing gentle.
'Twas told me you were rough, and coy, and sullen,
And now I find report a very liar,
For thou art pleasant, gamesome, passing courteous,
But slow in speech, yet sweet as spring-time flowers;
Thou canst not frown, thou canst not look askance,
Nor bite the lip, as angry wenches will,
Nor hast thou pleasure to be cross in talk;
But thou with mildness entertain'st thy wooers,
With gentle conference, soft and affable. 250
Why does the world report that Kate doth limp?
O slanderous world! Kate like the hazel-twig
Is straight and slender, and as brown in hue
As hazel-nuts and sweeter than the kernels.
O let me see thee walk: thou dost not halt.

KATHERINA

Go, fool, and whom thou keep'st command.

PETRUCHIO

Did ever Dian so become a grove
As Kate this chamber with her princely gait?
O be thou Dian, and let her be Kate,
And then let Kate be chaste and Dian sportful. 260

246 askance] F2 (*subs.*); a ſconce F1

242 **coy** disdainful (the commonest meaning in Shakespeare)

243 **very** complete

244 **gamesome** Best explained by citation of Brutus's lines, *Caesar*, 1.2.28–9, 'I am not gamesome: I do lack some part | Of that quick spirit that is in Antony'.

245 **But slow** only, admittedly, slow.

246 **look askance** cast disdainful looks (as against the modern sense of mistrust or doubt).

248 **cross** perverse

249 **entertain'st** receive(st) honourably (rather than 'keep amused')

250 **conference** conversation, talk

253–4 **as brown . . .** Since the Elizabethan lady took great care not to allow the sun to darken her skin, there is probably much irony in Petruchio's praise here.

255 **halt** limp

256 **whom . . . command** i.e. give orders (only) to those (servants) you maintain (Tilley C245, 'Thou dost not bear my charges that thou shouldst command me')

257 **Dian . . . grove** Diana, goddess of chastity, was in one of her functions 'Diana Nemorensis' i.e. of the grove, and was worshipped at a famous shrine in a grove in the Alban hills. Perhaps unnecessarily, Thomson finds in this line a reminiscence of the passage in the first book of the *Aeneid* (ll. 328–9) where Aeneas, in a wood, meets his mother Venus, disguised, 'and wonders if she can be Diana'.
become grace, adorn (rather than 'accord with', the other common meaning)

258 **gait** movement, manner of walking (but the word is not incongruous as it would be in the same phrase today)

260 **sportful** merry, playful, or even 'amorous'. The apparent contrast with 'chaste' suggests to some editors the meaning 'wanton' but there seems to be no authority for that – and it would be very uncomplimentary to Katherine.

KATHERINA
Where did you study all this goodly speech?
PETRUCHIO
It is extempore, from my mother-wit.
KATHERINA
A witty mother, witless else her son.
PETRUCHIO
Am I not wise?
KATHERINA
Yes, keep you warm.
PETRUCHIO
Marry, so I mean, sweet Katherine, in thy bed.
And therefore, setting all this chat aside,
Thus in plain terms: your father hath consented
That you shall be my wife; your dowry 'greed on;
And will you, nill you, I will marry you. 270
Now, Kate, I am a husband for your turn,
For by this light whereby I see thy beauty,
Thy beauty that doth make me like thee well,
Thou must be married to no man but me.
Enter Baptista, Gremio and Tranio (as Lucentio)
For I am he am born to tame you, Kate,
And bring you from a wild Kate to a Kate
Conformable as other household Kates.
Here comes your father. Never make denial;
I must and will have Katherine to my wife.
BAPTISTA Now, Signor Petruchio, how speed you with my 280
daughter?

274.1] F1 (*Enter Baptista, Gremio, Trayno*); *after l.* 279 POPE; *after l.* 277 CAPELL

261 **goodly** fair, elegant
263 **witless . . . son** i.e. her son has no other claim to wit, he would be without wit if he couldn't thus claim some of his mother's (Katherine is, of course, quibbling on 'mother-wit', which really means 'natural intelligence').
265 **keep you warm** i.e. just wise enough to keep yourself warm. Proverbial (Tilley K10) and comparable with the modern 'not sense enough to keep out of the cold'.
270 **will you, nill you** whether you will or not (*ne* + *will*). A stock phrase (Tilley W401), which survives in the modern 'willy, nilly'.
271 **for your turn** to suit you ('turn' in the sense of 'occasion' or 'need' and perhaps also 'disposition' or 'bent'. *OED sb.* V and VI). Compare 1.2.165, and 3.2.131 and note.
274.1 The placing of the direction in F1 indicates another entrance from the back of the deep Elizabethan stage. The audience sees the other characters approaching before Petruchio sees them.
276 **wild Kate** Perhaps there is a quibble on 'wild cat' (to which Rowe emended); certainly in the following line there is the same pun as before on 'Kate' and 'cate'.
280 **speed** fare, succeed

PETRUCHIO

How but well, sir? How but well?
It were impossible I should speed amiss.

BAPTISTA

Why, how now, daughter Katherine, in your dumps?

KATHERINA

Call you me 'daughter'? Now I promise you
You have showed a tender fatherly regard,
To wish me wed to one half-lunatic,
A madcap ruffian and a swearing Jack,
That thinks with oaths to face the matter out.

PETRUCHIO

Father, 'tis thus: yourself and all the world 290
That talked of her have talked amiss of her.
If she be curst, it is for policy,
For she's not froward, but modest as the dove;
She is not hot, but temperate as the morn;
For patience she will prove a second Grissel,
And Roman Lucrece for her chastity;
And to conclude, we have 'greed so well together
That upon Sunday is the wedding-day.

KATHERINA

I'll see thee hanged on Sunday first.

GREMIO Hark, Petruchio, she says she'll see thee hanged first. 300

TRANIO Is this your speeding? Nay then good-night our part.

284 **in your dumps** in low spirits, depressed. The phrase survives only in the impersonal form, 'in *the* dumps'.

285 **promise you** aver (much as in l. 142)

286 **showed** Two forms of the past participle, 'showed' and 'shown', were used in earlier English; only 'shown' survives.

288 **Jack** rascal, as in l. 157

289 **face** brazen

292 **policy** The word probably already had overtones: Machiavellian policy, scheming to attain the desired end by any means, however unprincipled.

293 **froward** perverse, difficult to control (as in 1.1.69, and later)

modest . . . dove A standard comparison (Tilley D573).

294 **hot** violent – but with a quibble on the literal meaning, as the remainder of the line shows. Compare 'hot as the devil'.

295 **Grissel** Griselda, proverbial for wifely obedience no matter what the provocation given by the husband. Chaucer's *Clerk's Tale* is one version of the story likely to have been known to Shakespeare but there were also, e.g., ballads.

296 **Lucrece** The Roman matron who felt so strongly the 'dishonour' of her rape by Tarquin that she killed herself. The composition of Shakespeare's own *Rape of Lucrece* (published in 1594) can probably be dated soon after *The Taming of the Shrew*.

302 **speeding** success. Tranio is catching up Petruchio's 'it were impossible I should speed amiss' (l. 283).

302–3 **good-night our part** i.e. our hopes (of Bianca) are dashed; we can say good-bye to what we hoped to gain.

PETRUCHIO

Be patient, gentlemen, I choose her for myself;
If she and I be pleased, what's that to you?
'Tis bargained 'twixt us twain, being alone,
That she shall still be curst in company.
I tell you 'tis incredible to believe
How much she loves me. O, the kindest Kate,
She hung about my neck, and kiss on kiss 310
She vied so fast, protesting oath on oath,
That in a twink she won me to her love.
O, you are novices! 'Tis a world to see
How tame, when men and women are alone,
A meacock wretch can make the curstest shrew.
– Give me thy hand, Kate, I will unto Venice,
To buy apparel 'gainst the wedding-day.
– Provide the feast, father, and bid the guests.
I will be sure my Katherine shall be fine.

BAPTISTA

I know not what to say, but give me your hands. 320
God send you joy; Petruchio, 'tis a match.

GREMIO *and* TRANIO

Amen, say we. We will be witnesses.

PETRUCHIO

Father, and wife, and gentlemen, adieu,
I will to Venice, Sunday comes apace.
We will have rings, and things, and fine array,

320–1 give ... match] F1 (giue ... hãds, | God ... ioy, *Petruchio*, 'tis a match)

307 **still** always
311 **vied** Perhaps only 'multiplied' (*OED* *v.* 6) but more probably with reference to the gambling use of the word: in card-playing, one 'vied' (staked a certain sum) and 'revied' (raised the bid) (*OED v.* 1, 2). Compare 'out-vied' in l. 387. The meaning may thus be that Kate (allegedly) responded to Petruchio's kisses with even greater passion than his betrayed.
312 **a twink** the twinkling of an eye
313 **a world to see** worth a world to see (a common phrase: Tilley W878)
315 **meacock** cowardly, feeble (the origin of the word is obscure; perhaps (*OED*) the name of a bird)
317 **'gainst** in preparation for, in anticipation of (Abbott 142)
318 **bid** invite
319 **fine** richly dressed
321 **'tis a match** It may be questioned whether this does constitute an Elizabethan common-law marriage, as some commentators assert. Petruchio and Katherine have not exchanged vows, and Katherine has certainly not indicated her willingness to marry.
324 **apace** rapidly
325 Jewellery from Venice was highly esteemed (compare l. 356).

And kiss me, Kate, we will be married o' Sunday.

Exeunt Petruchio and Katherina separately

GREMIO

Was ever match clapped up so suddenly?

BAPTISTA

Faith, gentlemen, now I play a merchant's part,
And venture madly on a desperate mart.

TRANIO

'Twas a commodity lay fretting by you; 330
'Twill bring you gain, or perish on the seas.

BAPTISTA

The gain I seek is quiet in the match.

GREMIO

No doubt but he hath got a quiet catch.
But now, Baptista, to your younger daughter:
Now is the day we long have looked for;
I am your neighbour, and was suitor first.

TRANIO

And I am one that love Bianca more
Than words can witness or your thoughts can guess.

GREMIO

Youngling, thou canst not love so dear as I.

TRANIO

Greybeard, thy love doth freeze.

GREMIO But thine doth fry. 340

326.1 *separately*] THEOBALD (*severally*); *not in* F1 332 in] ROWE 1714; me F1

326 **we . . . Sunday** Again Petruchio seems to be quoting from an old ballad. As Halliwell pointed out, the fourth song in *Ralph Roister Doister* (that in 3.3) is 'I mun be married a Sunday' – which may be an adaptation to a particular situation of a popular refrain.

327 **clapped up** made up, hastily arranged (compare *K. John*, 3.1.234–5, 'No longer than we well could wash our hands, | To clap this royal bargain up of peace').

329 **desperate mart** extremely risky or uncertain market or piece of bargaining; ('mart', from Du. *markt*, commonly pronounced 'mart', *OED sb*[4].)

330 **'Twas . . . you** i.e. it (the goods for sale or exchange – namely Katherine) was a piece of merchandise that was becoming corroded or worn away (*OED* 'fret' *v*. 6, 7), but with a quibble on another sense of 'fret': 'it was wearing *you* out by a process of irritation'.

331 **perish on the seas** i.e. be lost, as goods going abroad, or returning thence, are often lost at sea

332 **in** F1's 'me' is presumably the compositor's misreading of 'ine' or 'inne' (as again at l. 1924 – 4.2.71).

333 **he** i.e. Petruchio, whose 'catch', Katherine, is likely to be anything but 'quiet'.

335 **long have looked for** Gremio again adapts a stock phrase, 'long looked for comes at last' (Tilley L423).

339 **Youngling** young (or younger) man – but with a derogatory implication, 'novice', or, in Schmidt's paraphrase, 'greenhorn'. Compare *Titus*, 2.1.73–4.

Skipper, stand back, 'tis age that nourisheth.

TRANIO

But youth in ladies' eyes that flourisheth.

BAPTISTA

Content you, gentlemen, I will compound this strife.
'Tis deeds must win the prize, and he of both
That can assure my daughter greatest dower
Shall have my Bianca's love.
Say, Signor Gremio, what can you assure her?

GREMIO

First, as you know, my house within the city
Is richly furnishèd with plate and gold,
Basins and ewers to lave her dainty hands; 350
My hangings all of Tyrian tapestry;
In ivory coffers I have stuffed my crowns,
In cypress chests my arras counterpoints,

346 my Bianca's] F1 (*subs.*); *Biancas* F2 353 cypress] F1 (Cypros)

341 **Skipper** one who 'skips' (moves heedlessly, is irresponsible, or wastes time) – much like 'youngling' in l. 339
nourisheth provides the nourishment or necessities (with money)

343 **Content you** be pacified
compound settle

344–5 **deeds . . . dower** 'Deeds': 'actions' (as opposed to talk) but probably also 'legal deeds'; specifically, 'marriage settlements', prescribing the 'dower' (the part of the estate that the husband leaves in his will to his widow for life). 'Dower' is here (but not always) distinguished from the 'dowry' given by the father with the bride.

344 **he of both** whichever of the two of you

345 **assure** guarantee, or, convey by deed to (*OED* 3)

348 ff. In some ways the following speech is curiously similar to lines in Robert Greene's *Friar Bacon and Friar Bungay* (probably written in 1589) where two wooers, Serlsby and Lambert, make their bid for the hand of Margaret. In particular ll. 358–61 resemble Serlsby's would-be tempting offer that 'forty kine with fair and burnished heads, | With strouting dugs that paggle to the ground, | Shall serve thy dairy, if thou wed with me' (Sc.10 ll. 62–5).

349 **plate** utensils of silver (or, often, gold)

350 **lave** wash. The word may already have seemed rather formal: and Gremio is trying to rise to rhetoric.

351 **hangings** Tapestry was used not only for aesthetic pleasure but also as practical covering on walls (compare Induction 1.44 and 2.47–51 and notes).
Tyrian from Tyre, which was famous both as a centre of trade and for the manufacture of a dye, probably crimson (though called 'purple'). Tyrian tapestry would have been expensive and highly esteemed.

352 **crowns** coins (originally those bearing the crown imprint, and of some value)

353 **cypress** the wood prized for its durability and its fragrance (thought to repel moths) – but the F1 spelling 'Cypros' here, together with 'the Cyprus grove' in *Coriolanus*, 1.10.30, suggests (particularly in the context of Tyrian tapestry, Turkey cushions, and Venetian gold) that Shakespeare may have believed that the wood, like the fabric, took its name from Cyprus.
arras counterpoints quilted bed-covers (counterpanes) from Arras (renowned for the colour and weaving of its tapestries). 'Arras' itself is often used as the noun to mean 'Arras tapestry' or, indeed, any tapestry.

Costly apparel, tents, and canopies,
Fine linen, Turkey cushions bossed with pearl,
Valance of Venice gold in needlework,
Pewter and brass, and all things that belongs
To house or housekeeping; then at my farm
I have a hundred milch-kine to the pail,
Six-score fat oxen standing in my stalls, 360
And all things answerable to this portion.
Myself am struck in years, I must confess,
And if I die tomorrow this is hers,
If whilst I live she will be only mine.

TRANIO

That 'only' came well in. Sir, list to me.
I am my father's heir and only son;
If I may have your daughter to my wife,
I'll leave her houses three or four as good
Within rich Pisa walls as any one
Old Signor Gremio has in Padua, 370
Besides two thousand ducats by the year
Of fruitful land, all which shall be her jointure.
What, have I pinched you, Signor Gremio?

356 Valance] F1 (Vallens) 359 pail] F1 (pale)

354 **tents** (apparently) coverings or bed-curtains, but the word is found elsewhere in this sense only in Baret's *Alvearie* 1580, first cited by Halliwell. Baret treats 'tent' as a synonym of 'testerne' – something 'to hang over a bed'.
canopies coverings suspended over the bed or couch (or, elsewhere, over a throne); testers

355 **Turkey** i.e. from Turkey (compare l. 369 and note). Elizabethan trade with Turkey – developed by the Levant company – certainly included carpets, rugs, and silks. Gremio is making his possessions sound as exotic, and valuable, as possible.
bossed embossed; richly embroidered, here with a design picked out in pearls

356 **Valance** hanging drapery, especially that which hangs from the canopy of a bed
Venice gold gold thread from Venice

357 **belongs** The verb after a relative pronoun is often thus singular in form, though the antecedent of the relative is plural (Abbott 247).

359 **milch-kine to the pail** milking-cows, providing milk for the pail or pails (as distinct from those less profitably feeding calves). *OED* 'pail' I. c.

361 **answerable to** corresponding to, in proportion with
portion (inheritable) estate

362 **struck in** affected for the worse by, handicapped by

365 **came well in** came into (the conversation) very appropriately

369 **Pisa walls** The name of a town or city was often thus used in Elizabethan English as an adjective (Abbott 22, 430).

371–2 **two . . . land** fertile land producing two thousand ducats (approximately nine hundred or a thousand pounds – a large sum) of annual income.

372 **her jointure** the estate she will inherit upon my death

373 **pinched** The corresponding modern idiom would be, used of a debate, either 'forced you into a tight corner' or 'cut the ground from under your feet'. Bond explains, perhaps less convincingly, as 'made you wince'.

GREMIO

Two thousand ducats by the year of land?
(*Aside*) My land amounts not to so much in all.
– That she shall have, besides an argosy
That now is lying in Marcellus road.
(*To Tranio*) What, have I choked you with an argosy?

TRANIO

Gremio, 'tis known my father hath no less
Than three great argosies, besides two galliasses 380
And twelve tight galleys. These I will assure her,
And twice as much whate'er thou offer'st next.

GREMIO

Nay, I have offered all, I have no more,
And she can have no more than all I have.
(*To Baptista*) If you like me, she shall have me and mine.

TRANIO

Why then the maid is mine from all the world
By your firm promise; Gremio is out-vied.

BAPTISTA

I must confess your offer is the best,
And let your father make her the assurance,
She is your own; else, you must pardon me. 390
If you should die before him, where's her dower?

TRANIO

That's but a cavil; he is old, I young.

374] F1; *marked 'aside'* KITTREDGE 375 (*Aside*)] NEILSON (*conj.* WARBURTON, MS.); *not marked as aside* F1 not] F1; but THEOBALD 377 Marcellus] F1; Marsellis F2; Marseilles's POPE 390 own; else, ... me.] F1 (owne, else ... me:); own: else ... me; BLAIR; own; else, ... me: CAPELL; own; else, ... me, HERFORD

375 **Aside** Hibbard's direction is acceptable, for Gremio would not wish the limitation of his wealth to be common knowledge. His next offer is in desperate excess of his capacity to pay.

376 **argosy** the largest class of merchant vessel; one of those which 'with portly sail | . . . Do overpeer the petty traffickers, | That curtsy to them . . .' (*Merchant*, 1.1.9–13).

377 **Marcellus road** The roadstead of Marseilles. Again the proper noun is used as an adjective (as in l. 369); and the spelling (not unique in Shakespeare) well indicates the contemporary pronunciation.

378 **choked** A corresponding modern colloquialism might be 'choked you off' or 'shut you up'.

380 **galliasses** larger galleys (one-deck vessels, with both sails and oars)

381 **tight** water-tight, sound (as in *Tempest*, 5.1.224)

382 **twice as much** double

387 **out-vied** out-bid. See l. 311 and note.

389 **assurance** guarantee (compare l. 345 and note).

390 **else** otherwise

392 **cavil** frivolous objection

GREMIO

And may not young men die as well as old?

BAPTISTA

Well, gentlemen,
I am thus resolved: on Sunday next you know
My daughter Katherine is to be married;
Now, on the Sunday following shall Bianca
Be bride (*to Tranio*) to you, if you make this assurance;
If not, to Signor Gremio.
And so I take my leave, and thank you both. *Exit* 400

GREMIO

Adieu, good neighbour. – Now I fear thee not;
Sirrah, young gamester, your father were a fool
To give thee all, and in his waning age
Set foot under thy table. Tut, a toy,
An old Italian fox is not so kind, my boy! *Exit*

TRANIO

A vengeance on your crafty withered hide!
Yet I have faced it with a card of ten.
'Tis in my head to do my master good.
I see no reason but supposed Lucentio
Must get a father, called supposed Vincentio, 410
And that's a wonder: fathers commonly
Do get their children, but in this case of wooing
A child shall get a sire, if I fail not of my cunning.
Exit

394–5 Well, gentlemen | ... know] CAPELL; Well ... resolu'd, | On ... know | F1

393 Again Gremio relies on a platitude (Tilley M609: 'Young men may die, old men must die').

402 **gamester** gambler. Gremio is well aware of the irresponsibility of many of Tranio's 'assurances' (and is perhaps carrying on the card metaphor from 'out-vied').

404 **Set ... table** i.e. be forced to live with you, be dependent on what *you* care to give *him* (a standard phrase: Tilley F572).
toy nonsensical fabrication or supposition (*OED* I. 3. 4)

406 **A vengeance** a curse (an obsolete but once common imprecation)

407 **faced it** outdone (you) – but with the implication that it has been done by bluff. The card-playing image is being continued, in a proverb-like phrase (Tilley C75).

407 **card of ten** card with ten 'pips'. A modern card-player might say that he had 'trumped' Gremio's 'ace' but that does not carry the requisite suggestion of bluff.

409 **see no reason but** can see no alternative to (the plan that) .... For 'supposed' see 5.1.106 note.

412 **get** A quibble: beget.

413 **fail ... cunning** do not fail to use my wits; am successful with my plotting. (The versification in these final lines is highly irregular but emendation seems unnecessary.)

3.1 *Enter Lucentio as Cambio, Hortensio as Litio, and Bianca*

LUCENTIO

Fiddler, forbear, you grow too forward, sir.
Have you so soon forgot the entertainment
Her sister Katherine welcomed you withal?

HORTENSIO

But, wrangling pedant, this is
The patroness of heavenly harmony.
Then give me leave to have prerogative,
And when in music we have spent an hour,
Your lecture shall have leisure for as much.

LUCENTIO

Preposterous ass, that never read so far
To know the cause why music was ordained! 10
Was it not to refresh the mind of man
After his studies or his usual pain?
Then give me leave to read philosophy
And while I pause serve in your harmony.

HORTENSIO

Sirrah, I will not bear these braves of thine.

BIANCA

Why, gentlemen, you do me double wrong
To strive for that which resteth in my choice.

3.1.0.1 *Enter* ...] F1 (*Actus Tertia. Enter Lucentio, Hortentio, and Bianca.*) 4 this is] F1; know this lady is HANMER; this, her sister, is MARSHALL; this Urania is TILLYARD *conj.*; *etc.*

3.1.2 **entertainment** reception (or 'kind reception', used, of course, ironically; compare 2.1.54).

4–5 **this is ... harmony** Line 4 is certainly short, and hard to scan, but it is not hard to say, and makes sense as it stands. Hortensio affirms that 'this' (Bianca) is a patroness of harmony – not, like Katherine, of discord – and by implication a goddess. It must remain uncertain whether Shakespeare was thinking of a particular goddess (perhaps Pallas Athene, Minerva) or muse (perhaps Erato, muse of the lyre; perhaps Polyhymnia, muse of sacred song).

6 **prerogative** the prior right, precedence – which Hortensio claims because Bianca, by the hypothesis of ll. 4–5, is associated with music, not literature.

8 **lecture** lesson

9 **Preposterous** In the literal meaning 'having last that which should be first', but the more general meaning 'perverse' or 'unreasonable' was already common.

10 **To know** as to know

ordained instituted (*OED v. trans.* I. 4) or even 'decreed', 'created by God' (II. 13). Thomson – not inclined to overestimate Shakespeare's classical knowledge – suggests that the sentiment of ll. 9–12 derives from Aristotle's *Politics* (perhaps known to Shakespeare in a Latin translation).

12 **usual pain** customary or regular labours

13 **read** teach

14 **serve in** serve up – contemptuous but not as colloquial as the modern 'dish up'

15 **braves** taunts

17 **resteth in my choice** is for me to decide

I am no breeching scholar in the schools,
I'll not be tied to hours nor 'pointed times,
But learn my lessons as I please myself. 20
And, to cut off all strife, here sit we down,
Take you your instrument, play you the whiles;
His lecture will be done ere you have tuned.

HORTENSIO
You'll leave his lecture when I am in tune?

LUCENTIO
That will be never. Tune your instrument.

BIANCA Where left we last?

LUCENTIO Here, madam:
(*reading*) '*Hic ibat Simois, hic est Sigeia tellus,*
Hic steterat Priami regia celsa senis.'

BIANCA Conster them. 30

LUCENTIO '*Hic ibat*', as I told you before; '*Simois*', I am Lucentio; '*hic est*', son unto Vincentio of Pisa; '*Sigeia tellus*', disguised thus to get your love; '*Hic steterat*', and that Lucentio that comes a-wooing; '*Priami*', is my man Tranio; '*regia*', bearing my port; '*celsa senis*', that we might beguile the old pantaloon.

HORTENSIO Madam, my instrument's in tune.

BIANCA Let's hear. (*He plays*) O fie, the treble jars!

LUCENTIO Spit in the hole, man, and tune again.

19 'pointed] THEOBALD 1740; pointed F1 28–9] *as verse* ROWE 1714; *as prose* F1 28, 31, 40 *Hic*] F1; *Hac* THEOBALD 28, 32, 41 *Sigeia*] F2; *sigeria* F1 38 *He plays*] *not in* F1

18 **breeching scholar in the schools** school pupil who is liable to be breeched or flogged. The 'ing' termination is often thus used in a passive, not an active, sense (Abbott 372).

19 **'pointed** i.e. appointed. So too in 3.2.1.

22 **the whiles** during that time

24 **when I am in tune** when I have tuned my instrument – but Lucentio apparently takes it in a figurative sense, 'when I am normal' or (as we might say) 'not off-key'.

28–9 ***Hic ... senis*** These two Latin lines are a version of Ovid's *Heroides*, I.33–4, 'Here ran the Simois, here is the Sigeian land, here stood the lofty palace [or capital?] of old Priam' (in Turbervile's 1567 translation 'the aged *Priam's* Hawle | and Princely house'). F2's emendation 'sigeia', of F1's 'sigeria', is accepted, not without hesitation: 'sigeria' is repeated in ll. 32 and 41. (Shakespeare may have intended Lucentio's Latin to be bad; or perhaps Shakespeare was quoting from a different text of Ovid (although the 1583 edition reads 'Sigeia') or from memory.) Theobald's emendation 'hac ibat' is not necessary, although 'hac' may be more idiomatic Latin and is the reading both of the 1583 (Vautrollerius) edition of the *Heroides* and of modern texts of Ovid (but then modern editions also read 'haec est' in the second half of the line).

30 **Conster** construe (an older form of the word, stressed on the first syllable)

35 **bearing my port** living in the gentlemanly style appropriate to me. For 'port' compare 1.1.200 and note.

36 **pantaloon** i.e. Gremio, as in 1.1.47.2. See note there.

38 **jars** is discordant or out of tune

39 **Spit in the hole** Elizabethans may well have used this method of making the pegs

BIANCA (*to Lucentio*) Now let me see if I can conster it. '*Hic ibat Simois*', I know you not; '*hic est Sigeia tellus*', I trust you not; '*Hic steterat Priami*', take heed he hear us not; '*regia*', presume not; '*celsa senis*', despair not. 40

HORTENSIO
Madam, 'tis now in tune.
He plays again

LUCENTIO All but the bass.

HORTENSIO
The bass is right, 'tis the base knave that jars.
(*Aside*) How fiery and forward our pedant is!
Now, for my life, the knave doth court my love.
Pedascule, I'll watch you better yet.

BIANCA (*to Lucentio*)
In time I may believe, yet I mistrust.

LUCENTIO (*aside to Bianca*)
Mistrust it not – (*aloud*) for, sure, Aeacides 50
Was Ajax, called so from his grandfather.

BIANCA
I must believe my master; else, I promise you,

42 *steterat*] F2; *staterat* F1 44 *He plays again*] *not in* F1 46–8 How ... yet.] *Continued to Hortensio* ROWE 1714; *Luc.* How ... yet: F1 49 BIANCA In ... mistrust] POPE 1728 (*conj.* THEOBALD *S.R.*): *continued to Lucentio* F1 50 LUCENTIO] POPE 1728 (*conj.* THEOBALD *S.R.*); *Bian.* F1 52 BIANCA] POPE 1728 (*conj.* THEOBALD *S.R.*); *Hort.* F1; *continued to Bianca* ROWE

tighter, to keep the tension on the strings, but Lucentio's advice is not necessarily meant to be helpful. He seems to be misapplying the proverb 'Spit in your hands and take better hold' (Tilley H120).

42 ***steterat*** 'Staterat' is clearly a compositor's error: 'steterat' is correct in F1 in ll. 29 and 33.

46–52 The obviously incorrect distribution of the speech prefixes in F1 (set out in the collations) is not easy to explain. It is true, as New Cambridge suggests, that 'Lu' (for 'Lucentio'), 'Li' (for 'Litio'. i.e. Hortensio) and 'Bi' (for 'Bianca') could be confused – but l. 46 would not have had a speech prefix at all in the MS, unless it were an afterthought or, perhaps, began a new page. Presumably the colon after 'yet' at the end of l. 1343 (l. 48) is the compositor's, in his fruitless attempt to make sense of the lines as wrongly distributed.

48 **Pedascule** Apparently, as Warburton suggested, a contemptuous coinage from 'pedant' on the analogy of 'didaskolos', Greek for 'master' or 'teacher' ('didasculus' in the Latinized form). The 'e' termination probably is meant to indicate the vocative case; certainly a four-syllable pronunciation fits the metre.

49 Bianca is continuing her words to Lucentio, interrupted by Hortensio at l. 44.

50 **Aeacides** Lucentio is now pretending that he is explaining the beginning of the next line (l. 35) from Ovid (following those he pretended to construe), namely '*Illic Aeacides* . . . '. His explanation is correct as far as it goes; but perhaps Shakespeare is being very subtle. As Bond points out, Bianca's hesitation over taking Lucentio's word may be because she knows that the patronymic *Aeacides* does not necessarily designate Ajax; and indeed the very line of Ovid that Lucentio is 'explaining' more probably refers to another grandson of Aeacus, Achilles (and Turbervile translated it 'There fierce *Achylles* pight his Tentes').

I should be arguing still upon that doubt,
But let it rest. – Now, Litio, to you:
Good master, take it not unkindly, pray,
That I have been thus pleasant with you both.

HORTENSIO (*to Lucentio*)
You may go walk, and give me leave awhile:
My lessons make no music in three parts.

LUCENTIO
Are you so formal, sir? Well, I must wait –
(*Aside*) And watch withal, for, but I be deceived, 60
Our fine musician groweth amorous.
He stands aside

HORTENSIO
Madam, before you touch the instrument,
To learn the order of my fingering,
I must begin with rudiments of art,
To teach you gamut in a briefer sort,
More pleasant, pithy, and effectual,
Than hath been taught by any of my trade,
And there it is in writing fairly drawn.

BIANCA
Why, I am past my gamut long ago.

HORTENSIO
Yet read the gamut of Hortensio. 70

BIANCA (*reads*)
'*Gamut*, I am the ground of all accord;

55 master] F1; masters ROWE 1714 61.1 *He stands aside*] *not in* F1 71 *reads*] POPE (*subs.*); *not in* F1

56 **pleasant** merry

57 **give me leave** leave me free, leave us alone – a polite request immediately turned to an impolite one by the following line

60 **withal** as well
but unless

63 **order** method or 'logic'

65 **gamut** Originally 'gamma', the Greek letter 'g', as the name of the lowest note in the old six-note scale (whence l. 71); later, 'gamma-ut', whence 'gamut', also used for the scale generally.

68 **drawn** set out

70 **of Hortensio** Here, of course, and in the following lines, Hortensio drops (with Bianca) the pretence that he is Litio. His 'gamut' takes this form because rhymed mnemonics were commonly used in teaching the scale; but the attempts made to find secondary meanings in the musical terms themselves are too fanciful (see, e.g., Harry Colin Miller, 'A Shakespearean Music Lesson', *Notes and Queries*, 165 (1933), 255–7).

71 ***Gamut*** See note on l. 65 above. 'Gamut' in this sense has been replaced by 'do' or 'doh' as the name of the 'ground' or 'lowest' note; but there is a further quibble on 'ground' as meaning 'basis'.
accord harmony, 'agreement' of sounds

A re, to plead Hortensio's passion;
B mi, Bianca, take him for thy lord
C fa ut, that loves with all affection;
D sol re, one clef, two notes have I;
E la mi, show pity or I die.'
Call you this 'gamut'? Tut, I like it not;
Old fashions please me best; I am not so nice
To change true rules for odd inventions.
Enter a Servant

SERVANT
Mistress, your father prays you leave your books 80
And help to dress your sister's chamber up.
You know tomorrow is the wedding-day.

BIANCA
Farewell, sweet masters both, I must be gone.
Exeunt Bianca and Servant

LUCENTIO
Faith, mistress, then I have no cause to stay. *Exit*

HORTENSIO
But I have cause to pry into this pedant:
Methinks he looks as though he were in love.
Yet if thy thoughts, Bianca, be so humble

72 *A re*] Q1631; *Are* F1 73 *B mi*] POPE; *Beeme* F1 74 *C fa ut*] F1 (*Cfavt*) 75 clef] F1 (Cliffe) 76 *E la mi*] F1 (*Ela mi*) 79 change] F2; charge F1 odd] THEOBALD; old F1; new ROWE 1714 79.1 *Servant*] ROWE; *Messenger* F1 80 SERVANT] ROWE; *Nicke* F1 83.1] CAPELL; *not in* F1; *Ex.* ROWE 84 *Exit*] ROWE; *not in* F1

72–6 'Re', 'mi', 'fa', 'sol', 'la' are the other notes of the scale (so named from the first syllables of successive lines in a Latin hymn). 'Ut', 're', and 'mi' are repeated after C, D, E because a second scale begins at C.

75 **one . . . I** In the musical terminology of the time (as explained e.g. in Morley's probably later text, *A Plaine and Easie Introduction to Practicall Musicke*, 1597). D is correctly said to have two 'notes', because it is the 'sol' of the 'Gamma' scale, and the 're' of the 'C' scale. Indeed this line may be from a genuine musical mnemonic. What Hortensio sees as *his* 'one clef, two notes', however, is not clear. Perhaps the 'one clef' (the symbol that designates pitch) is Hortensio's personal identity, his 'two notes' his real and assumed characters (as Hortensio and Litio); or the second 'note' may be, as the following line suggests, his willingness to die as the alternative to successful wooing.

78 **nice** See note on next line.

79 **change, odd** F1's 'charge' and 'old' do not make sense, and the adjective with 'inventions' must contrast with the 'true' and with 'old fashions'. With the emendations, Bianca's statement means that she is not so difficult to please (or, possibly, so trivial) as to wish to change proven principles for fantastic novelty such as Hortensio's 'gamut'. 'Nice' had many derogatory implications and indeed once meant 'foolish'.

80 **SERVANT** F1's '*Nicke*' (suggesting again that the printer's copy was the author's MS) may be either Shakespeare's passing thought for a name for the character or (more probably) the name of the actor who might play the part. Nicholas Tooley was once the favourite nominee. See Introduction, p. 5.

To cast thy wandering eyes on every stale,
Seize thee that list; if once I find thee ranging,
Hortensio will be quit with thee by changing. *Exit* 90

3.2 *Enter Baptista, Gremio, Tranio as Lucentio, Katherina, Bianca, Lucentio as Cambio, and attendants*

BAPTISTA (*to Tranio*)
Signor Lucentio, this is the 'pointed day
That Katherine and Petruchio should be married,
And yet we hear not of our son-in-law.
What will be said, what mockery will it be
To want the bridegroom when the priest attends
To speak the ceremonial rites of marriage?
What says Lucentio to this shame of ours?

KATHERINA
No shame but mine. I must forsooth be forced
To give my hand, opposed against my heart,
Unto a mad-brain rudesby, full of spleen, 10
Who wooed in haste and means to wed at leisure.
I told you, I, he was a frantic fool,
Hiding his bitter jests in blunt behaviour;

3.2.0.1 *Enter* ...] F1; *Scene II. Enter* ... POPE 0.2 *Lucentio and attendants*] ROWE; *and others, attendants.* F1 10 mad-brain] F1 (mad-braine); mad-brain'd KEIGHTLEY 13 behaviour;] F4; behauiour, F1

88 **stale** *OED* conjectures that the word is derived from AF *estale*, applied to the pigeon used to entice the hawk into a net. Perhaps that is the sense here, but the word came also to mean anyone who allures to deceive (and so particularly a prostitute, especially one serving as a decoy). Compare 1.1.58 and note.

89 **Seize thee that list** let anyone who wants you seize you. (Bianca is now the prey, apparently, not the hunter – which may cast doubt on the first meaning suggested for 'stale'.) For 'list' as a personal verb see 3.2.164 and note.
ranging roving – perhaps as a badly-trained hawk might rove but certainly in the other sense of 'being inconstant', of a fickle woman.

90 **be quit** get even (the modern colloquial 'be quits')

3.2 Lucentio presumably enters with the others at the beginning of this scene, since he cannot easily be brought on later, but see note on ll. 127 ff. On other problems in this scene, see Introduction pp. 11–12.

5 **want** lack

8 **forsooth** in truth. The word lends added contemptuousness to the phrase it 'modifies'.

10 **mad-brain** Although 'mad-brained' occurs in l. 162, emendation is superfluous: this combination of adjective and noun was common (Brook *g* 316).
rudesby unmannerly and disorderly fellow, brute. Olivia uses the word in *Twelfth Night*, 4.1.50 to Sir Toby to express her indignation with the 'ungracious wretch, | Fit for the mountains and the barbarous caves'.
full of spleen of uncertain temper (the spleen as the seat of both melancholy and laughter, both high spirits and irritability. Compare Induction 1.134 and note).

11 Katherine is varying the proverb 'Marry in haste and repent at leisure' (Tilley H196).

12 **frantic** wildly insane

And to be noted for a merry man,
He'll woo a thousand, 'point the day of marriage,
Make friends, invite, and proclaim the banns,
Yet never means to wed where he hath wooed.
Now must the world point at poor Katherine
And say 'Lo, there is mad Petruchio's wife,
If it would please him come and marry her'. 20

TRANIO

Patience, good Katherine, and Baptista too.
Upon my life, Petruchio means but well,
Whatever fortune stays him from his word.
Though he be blunt, I know him passing wise;
Though he be merry, yet withal he's honest.

KATHERINA

Would Katherine had never seen him though!

Exit weeping

BAPTISTA

Go, girl, I cannot blame thee now to weep,
For such an injury would vex a very saint,

14 man,] ROWE; man; F1; man: F4 16 friends, invite, and] F1; friends, invite, yes and F2; friends, invite them, and MALONE; feasts, invite friends, and DYCE 1866; make friends invited, and GRANT WHITE 26.1 *Exit weeping*] F1; *Exit weeping: is follow'd by* Bianca, Gremio, Hortensio, *and Others* CAPELL; *Exit weeping, followed by Bianca and the other women* HIBBARD, *as* NEW CAMBRIDGE

14 **to be noted for** in order to gain a reputation as

16 **friends, invite, and** If alteration is thought necessary, because the line is hard to scan and because the intransitive use of 'invite' is rare (although not unique), Malone's emendation, supposing a simple compositorial error, is preferable to Dyce's 'improvement'.

21 **TRANIO** It will be noticed that Tranio suddenly here (and particularly in l. 70 later) becomes the well-informed old friend of Petruchio – the role previously played by Hortensio. P. A. Daniel, G. I. Duthie, and others have noted that in *A Shrew* the corresponding lines *are* given to Hortensio's counterpart Polidor – some reason for supposing that in *The Shrew* they were originally given to Hortensio. As Duthie also points out, it had become necessary to find a speaker other than Hortensio because *he* has just left the stage (in his disguise as Litio). See Introduction p. 11.

23 **fortune** chance or (even) accident
stays . . . word by delaying him stops him from keeping his word

25 **merry** given to joking
withal i.e. at the same time
honest (Probably) honourable.

26.1 Some modern editors send Bianca (and unspecified 'other women') off the stage here with Katherine. But Katherine is a solitary figure throughout, until she and Petruchio really come together in Act 5; Baptista's exit line refers only to Katherine as leaving; and Bianca's continuing presence on stage is certainly not incongruous. She leaves with the others after l. 126.

27 **to weep** for weeping (Abbott 356)

28 **very** F2's omission of this meaningful word, although adopted by, e.g., New Cambridge and Hibbard, carries no conviction whatever. Shakespeare may be allowed a twelve-syllable line.

Much more a shrew of thy impatient humour.

Enter Biondello

BIONDELLO Master, master, news, and such news as you never heard of! 30

BAPTISTA Is it new and old too? How may that be?

BIONDELLO Why, is it not news to hear of Petruchio's coming?

BAPTISTA Is he come?

BIONDELLO Why, no, sir.

BAPTISTA What then?

BIONDELLO He is coming.

BAPTISTA When will he be here?

BIONDELLO When he stands where I am and sees you there. 40

TRANIO But say, what to thine old news?

BIONDELLO Why, Petruchio is coming in a new hat and an old jerkin; a pair of old breeches thrice turned; a pair of boots that have been candle-cases, one buckled, another laced; an old rusty sword ta'en out of the town armoury, with a broken hilt, and chapeless; with two

29 of thy] F2; of F1 30 news, and such news] F1; old News, and such News ROWE; news, old news, and such news CAPELL; news and such old news COLLIER *conj.* (*Notes*); news, new news, old news, and such news RIDLEY 33 hear] Q1631 (*subs.*); heard F1

29 **of thy** F2's emendation is acceptable and seems necessary for both sense and metre.

humour Perhaps already by the time Shakespeare wrote this play, 'humour' had become a vogue word; it was certainly so by 1597, the date of Chapman's *An Humourous Day's Mirth*, followed in 1598 by Jonson's *Every Man in his Humour*. Medical theory said that a man's character depended on the proportions, in his composition, of the four 'humours' or 'fluids'; and so, by extension, jealousy, e.g., or shrewishness (as here) could be a 'humour'. But a person could be brought out of his 'humour' if, for instance, he could be made to see how absurd it was; and so the word often denoted some deliberately cultivated way of behaviour that could yet be 'cured'. These seem to be the connotations of the word in 4.1.168 and 196.

30–4 Most editors feel the need to insert 'old' somewhere in l. 30 (see collations) because of Baptista's following question. Perhaps, however, that is an ironic comment on the fact that he is one of the last to hear the 'news': 'is it to be new to me and yet is already old to you?' In l. 42, Tranio then picks up *Baptista's* use of the word 'old'.

33 **hear of** The emendation is acceptable here. The F1 compositor probably misread 'heare' as 'heard', the taking of 'e' as 'd' (or vice versa) being the easiest of all misreadings in the secretary hand.

42 **what to** what of, or 'what about'

44 **jerkin** a close-fitting short coat or jacket (often of leather)

45 **have been candle-cases** i.e. have already been discarded as unfit for wear, and used to keep candle-ends in, but have now been resuscitated

47 **chapeless** without the 'chape' or metal plate on the scabbard that protects the point of the sword

broken points; his horse hipped, with an old mothy saddle and stirrups of no kindred; besides, possessed with the glanders and like to mose in the chine, troub- 50 led with the lampass, infected with the fashions, full of windgalls, sped with spavins, rayed with the yellows, past cure of the fives, stark spoiled with the staggers,

48–9 points; his horse hipped, ... kindred; besides] F1 (points: his horse hip'd ... kindred: besides); *rearranged as* points: with an old mothy saddle and stirrups of no kindred: his horse hipped besides, NEW CAMBRIDGE *after* RANN 52 rayed] F1 (raied)

48 **broken points** Generally explained as meaning that the laces that should be holding up Petruchio's breeches are broken (as in *1 Henry IV*, 2.4.207–8) but, following the reference to the chapeless sword, may mean rather that the sword has been broken and now therefore has two jagged tips instead of one sharp point.

hipped with dislocated hip. (Markham in his *Maister-peece*, 1610 – first cited by Halliwell – writes (Bk.2, Ch.71): 'A Horse is said to be hipped when either by straine, blow, or other accident, the hippe bone is removed out of his right place'.)

49 **of no kindred** not related to each other, not a pair

49–50 **possessed with** afflicted with (but probably the image is of 'possession' by an evil spirit or demon)

50 **glanders** a disease, contagious, causing swelling below the jaw and nasal discharge (Markham considers the latter to be its distinguishing feature).

like likely

mose in the chine The 'chine' is the spine, but 'mose' is not elsewhere recorded in the context of equine disability. Emendation to 'mourn' is not easily justified, even though the reference may well be to what is generally known as 'mourning of the chine'. As Madden points out, Biondello is parading his knowledge of stable language such as may not get into print. It may be relevant that 'mose' is found in dialects listed by Wright, as an adjective meaning 'rotten' or 'decayed' (used of fruit and vegetables, for example) and as a verb meaning 'to rot or become mouldy' (of hay, for instance); and Markham (Ch. 41) says that some farriers call 'mourning of the chine' 'the moist malady'. Biondello may mean no more than 'grow weak in the back', 'become bow backed'.

51 **lampass** Another equine disease. This one causes swelling in the roof of the mouth behind the teeth or a film-like growth over the teeth ('an excression of flesh above the teeth', in Markham's account, Bk.2, Ch.26).

fashions A dialectal form (recorded by Wright), or a corruption, of 'farcin(s)', another infectious equine disease, causing tumour-like growths. Markham explains that 'the Farcy (of our ignorant Smiths called the Fashions) ... is a kinde of creeping ulcer' and perhaps Biondello thinks of 'fashions' as the name of the actual swellings.

52 **windgalls** distensions just above the fetlocks

sped with spavins made useless, 'finished' by tumours resulting from inflammation of the hocks. For 'sped' compare the wounded Mercutio's 'I am sped' (*Romeo*, 3.1.88).

rayed Aphetic form of the obsolete 'berayed' (sometimes spelt, erroneously, 'bewrayed') meaning 'disfigured', 'defiled'.

yellows A common name for jaundice in animals.

53 **fives** A corruption of 'avives', the infectious equine disease better known as the strangles (though Markham attempts a distinction between them. In his *Discourse of Horsemanship* (1593; 1602, Ch.23) he explains that the Vives 'bee certain Kernels growing under the horses eare, which come of corrupt bloud').

stark absolutely (an adverb, used generally in an unsympathetic sense, as also in 'stark mad' in 1.1.69. Another surviving example is 'stark naked').

staggers A name for practically any disease (of horses and domestic animals) of which staggering or inability to control movement is the symptom.

begnawn with the bots, weighed in the back and
shoulder-shotten, near-legged before, and with a half-
checked bit and a headstall of sheep's leather which,
being restrained to keep him from stumbling, hath been
often burst, and now repaired with knots; one girth six
times pieced, and a woman's crupper of velour, which
hath two letters for her name fairly set down in studs, 60
and here and there pieced with pack-thread.

BAPTISTA Who comes with him?

BIONDELLO O sir, his lackey, for all the world caparisoned

54 **weighed]** F1 (Waid): sway'd HANMER 55 **near-legged]** F1 (neere leg'd); ne'er legg'd MALONE 55–6 **half-checked]** F1 (halfe-chekt); half-cheek'd HANMER 58 **now repaired]** F1: new-repaired DYCE 1866 (*conj.* WALKER)

54 **begnawn with** gnawed at, eaten away by
bots maggots that afflict the horse's intestines ('little short wormes with great red heads' according to Markham, Ch.73); also the name of the disease they cause.
weighed (Presumably) weighed down and so 'broken-backed' or 'bow-backed' – perhaps Biondello's misunderstanding of the normal 'swayed', used e.g. by Markham. Compare the later 'sway-backed'.

55 **shoulder-shotten** 'Shotten' was originally applied to the (exhausted state of the) fish that has spawned and so the word came to mean 'emaciated' or just 'weak'. Here, then, 'gone in the shoulder'.
near-legged before New Cambridge, protesting that this (defined as 'standing with the forelegs close together') was a virtue in a horse, thought Shakespeare meant to write 'near-legged behind'; Malone thought he probably wrote 'ne'er legged' and explained it, implausibly, as 'founder'd in his fore-feet'. Other attempted explanations are 'knock-kneed' and 'leading off with the near-side leg' (an alleged imperfection in gait).

55–6 **half-checked** As Madden points out, the later Folios saw nothing wrong with F1's word – which is some reason for not accepting the later emendation 'half-cheeked'. (For that matter, 'check' may have been an alternative to 'cheek' as the name for either the optional gear that prevents the bit pulling through the mouth or the 'checker' that prevents the horse from lugging.) The explanation of 'a bit with the bridle attached half-way up the check, thus giving inadequate leverage' derives from Markham but is hardly convincing. Perhaps in the context, of ineffective gear, Biondello means that there was a check on only one end of the bit, which could then not pull through the mouth one way – but could easily pull out the other side.

56 **headstall** the part of the bridle that fits over and round the horse's head
sheep's leather This would be inferior in quality to other skins normally used.

57 **restrained** tightened by pulling or by shortening the grip

58 **now repaired** Retention of the F1 reading supposes the ellipsis of 'is'. Editors who emend to 'new-repaired' take Biondello to say that the headstall had been often broken and as often repaired with knots. There are, however, other means of repairing leather – particularly sewing – which would have been tried first; knots are the last resort.

59 **pieced** repaired, somehow put together again. Similarly in l. 61.
crupper the strap from the saddle which, going under the horse's tail, stops the saddle from moving. Normally it would be of leather; one made of velour would be decorative but less functional.
velour fabric like velvet

60 **two letters for her name** i.e. the woman's initials
fairly set down in studs handsomely formed by metal or jewelled studs

61 **pack-thread** twine for tying or sewing up packs and parcels

63 **lackey** servant or footman, who might be expected to wear the master's livery – but this one is very different.
for all the world in all respects, so far as can be seen
caparisoned The caparison is strictly the

like the horse: with a linen stock on one leg and a kersey boot-hose on the other, gartered with a red and blue list; an old hat, and the humour of forty fancies pricked in't for a feather; a monster, a very monster in apparel, and not like a Christian footboy or a gentleman's lackey.

TRANIO
'Tis some odd humour pricks him to this fashion,
Yet oftentimes he goes but mean-apparelled. 70

BAPTISTA I am glad he's come, howsoe'er he comes.

BIONDELLO Why, sir, he comes not.

BAPTISTA Didst thou not say he comes?

BIONDELLO Who? That Petruchio came?

BAPTISTA Ay, that Petruchio came.

BIONDELLO No, sir, I say his horse comes with him on his back.

BAPTISTA Why, that's all one.

BIONDELLO
Nay, by Saint Jamy,
I hold you a penny, 80
A horse and a man
Is more than one,
And yet not many.

79–83] *as five lines of verse* COLLIER; *as two* ROWE 1714; *as prose* F1

covering, particularly a decorative one, spread over the saddle, and so, generally, the trappings. Hence, 'decked out'.

64 **stock** stocking
kersey (made of) coarse woollen cloth

65 **boot-hose** an over-stocking worn inside the riding boot (and often turned down over the top of it)
list *Either* (any) strip of cloth *or* strip made from the cut-off selvage or border of a piece of cloth (*OED sb.*[3]) – probably the latter.

66 **the humour of forty fancies** Not satisfactorily explained and can hardly be either, as Warburton suggested, a reference to some lost popular ballad or the title of a book of ballads. There are several recorded instances of 'fancy' in the sense of a light artistic creation (including musical); perhaps, then, 'having the decorations of forty different imaginations (previous owners?) instead of one simple feather'.

66–7 **pricked in't for a feather** *Either* picked out as a design *or* pinned on (*OED* III or IV.19) instead of the feather one would expect to be worn on the hat.

68 **footboy** page, boy servant

69 **humour** mood or whim
pricks drives, incites – perhaps a quibble on the word as used by Biondello a few lines earlier

78 **all one** all the same

79–83 Biondello's jingle (printed by F1 as prose) has not been traced but seems unlikely to be extempore. No relevant proverb is recorded.

80 **hold** bet

83 **many** New Cambridge saw a pun on 'meiny', presumably in the sense of 'combination (of people) with a single object'. It seems unlikely.

Enter Petruchio and Grumio

PETRUCHIO Come, where be these gallants? Who's at home?

BAPTISTA You are welcome, sir.

PETRUCHIO And yet I come not well?

BAPTISTA And yet you halt not.

TRANIO Not so well apparelled as I wish you were.

PETRUCHIO

Were it not better I should rush in thus? 90

But where is Kate? Where is my lovely bride?

How does my father? Gentles, methinks you frown,

And wherefore gaze this goodly company

As if they saw some wondrous monument,

Some comet, or unusual prodigy?

BAPTISTA

Why, sir, you know this is your wedding-day.

First were we sad, fearing you would not come,

Now sadder, that you come so unprovided.

Fie, doff this habit, shame to your estate,

An eyesore to our solemn festival! 100

TRANIO

And tell us what occasion of import

Hath all so long detained you from your wife

83.1] F1; Enter *Ferando* baselie attired, and a red cap on his head A SHREW 90 not better] KEIGHTLEY; better F1 thus?] RANN; thus: F1; thus. ROWE; thus: [*Pretends great excitement.*] RIVERSIDE

84 **be** An example of the (frequent) use of 'be', not 'are', as a kind of subjunctive in what Abbott calls 'questions of appeal' (299).

87 **come not well** am not welcome

88 **you halt not** A (double) quibble on 'halt' (in relation to 'come well'): (i) you certainly are not limping (the meaning surviving in 'the halt and the lame'); (ii) you are rushing in, not waiting to be asked.

90 **not better** The addition of 'not' seems to be demanded by the sense (and does improve the metre, assuming that verse begins again here; the preceding lines resist rearrangement as verse, though it has often been attempted). Garrick retained 'were it better' in *Catharine and Petruchio* and presumably gave it some meaning.

92 **Gentles** Gentlemen, and ladies; the term of polite address to people of 'gentle' birth or rank – and somewhat forced in its use by Petruchio here, without being exactly ironical.

93 **goodly** handsome (spoken in flattery and not without irony) rather than 'extensive' as in Induction 2.79

94 **monument** The word might well first suggest to an Elizabethan audience the ornamental figure on a tomb (likely to be 'better' than life, or allegorical, or, e.g., in the form of an angel).

95 **comet . . . prodigy** Comets *were* thought to be prodigies, forewarnings of disaster.

98 **unprovided** inadequately equipped and attended

99 **this habit** these clothes

estate rank and wealth

100 **solemn festival** ceremonious occasion

102 **all so long** An interesting use of 'all' as

And sent you hither so unlike yourself.

PETRUCHIO

Tedious it were to tell, and harsh to hear.
Sufficeth I am come to keep my word,
Though in some part enforcèd to digress,
Which at more leisure I will so excuse
As you shall well be satisfied with all.
But where is Kate? I stay too long from her,
The morning wears, 'tis time we were at church. 110

TRANIO

See not your bride in these unreverent robes,
Go to my chamber, put on clothes of mine.

PETRUCHIO

Not I, believe me; thus I'll visit her.

BAPTISTA

But thus I trust you will not marry her.

PETRUCHIO

Good sooth, even thus. Therefore ha' done with words;
To me she's married, not unto my clothes.
Could I repair what she will wear in me
As I can change these poor accoutrements,
'Twere well for Kate and better for myself.
But what a fool am I to chat with you, 120
When I should bid good morrow to my bride,
And seal the title with a lovely kiss! *Exit*

TRANIO

He hath some meaning in his mad attire.
We will persuade him, be it possible,
To put on better ere he go to church.

108 with all] F1; withall Q1631 122 lovely] F1; loving COLLIER 1853 122 *Exit*] F1; *Exeunt* Pet[ruchio], Gru[mio] *and* Bio[ndello] CAPELL; *Exeunt Petruchio and Grumio* DYCE

an intensive before another adverb ('so very long'). Abbott 28.

105 **Sufficeth** it sufficeth that (the impersonal verb). Compare 1.1.245.

106 **digress** deviate, vary a little (perhaps in both of two senses: 'not do exactly as I said I would' and 'turn aside from my planned route').

108 **with all** The contrast with 'in some part' supports the retention of F1's two words (meaning 'with everything') rather than the interpretation of them as 'withal' (meaning 'with my explanation').

110 **wears** The commonest modern idiom would be 'is slipping away'.

111 **unreverent** not showing the respect due to the occasion

115 **Good sooth** in all good truth, assuredly

116 Petruchio is perhaps adapting the maxim that 'fine clothes make not the gentleman' (Tilley S451).

117 **wear** wear out (in sexual activity)

122 **lovely** loving, amorous (*OED* I. a, b)

123 **meaning** purpose, 'ulterior motive'

BAPTISTA

I'll after him and see the event of this.

Exeunt all except Tranio and Lucentio

TRANIO

But, sir, to love concerneth us to add
Her father's liking, which to bring to pass,
As before imparted to your worship,
I am to get a man, whate'er he be – 130
It skills not much, we'll fit him to our turn –
And he shall be Vincentio of Pisa,
And make assurance here in Padua
Of greater sums than I have promised.
So shall you quietly enjoy your hope
And marry sweet Bianca with consent.

LUCENTIO

Were it not that my fellow schoolmaster
Doth watch Bianca's steps so narrowly,
'Twere good methinks to steal our marriage,
Which once performed, let all the world say no, 140
I'll keep mine own despite of all the world.

126.1] F1 (*Exit*) 127 sir, to love] KNIGHT; sir, Loue F1; Sir, our love POPE; Sir, to our love THEOBALD; sir, to her love MALONE (*conj.* TYRWHITT); to our love COLLIER 1853; to her love GRANT WHITE 129 before] F1; before I F2; I before POPE

126 **event** result, outcome

127 ff. This conversation of Tranio with Lucentio, begun apparently in the middle (although a few seconds earlier Tranio was talking to Baptista) and with no previous indication that Tranio has told Lucentio of his successful 'wooing' of Bianca; the omission of Lucentio from the list of characters who enter at the beginning of this scene, and his silence until now (which both seem to imply that his entry was originally delayed); Hortensio's entry (according to the F1 direction) at l. 182, although he neither speaks nor is referred to in the dialogue; and Tranio's sudden fund of information about Petruchio earlier in the scene all point to some revision or change of mind in this part of the play.

127 **to love** Emendation seems necessary, and Knight's 'to love' makes sense and is plausible: there are several 'to's' in five lines, and the compositor could easily have omitted one of them by haplography. If the F1 reading is retained, the words can only mean that love (in the sense of the wooing of Bianca) makes her father's 'liking' essential.

127 **concerneth us** i.e. it concerneth us, it is in our interests

129 **As before** The addition of 'I' is unnecessary. 'As was indicated to you before'.

131 **skills not much** matters little. A now archaic impersonal use of 'skill' in the sense of 'be of importance' or 'make a difference' (*OED* v[1]. 2 b).

turn need, purpose or convenience (*OED sb.* V. 30). Compare 'to serve our turn', still heard, and similar phrases at 1.2.165 and 2.1.271.

133 **assurance** formal promise or guarantee (as before in 2.1.389 and 398, and later four times in Act 4)

135 **enjoy your hope** enjoy what you have hoped to gain

138 **steps** actions, proceedings (as in Cordelia's 'no unchaste action or dishonoured step', *Lear*, 1.1.227)

so narrowly with such close attention (*OED* I)

TRANIO

That by degrees we mean to look into
And watch our vantage in this business.
We'll overreach the greybeard Gremio,
The narrow prying father Minola,
The quaint musician, amorous Litio,
All for my master's sake, Lucentio.

Enter Gremio

Signor Gremio, came you from the church?

GREMIO

As willingly as e'er I came from school.

TRANIO

And is the bride and bridegroom coming home? 150

GREMIO

A bridegroom, say you? 'Tis a groom indeed,
A grumbling groom, and that the girl shall find.

TRANIO

Curster than she? Why, 'tis impossible.

GREMIO

Why, he's a devil, a devil, a very fiend.

TRANIO

Why, she's a devil, a devil, the devil's dam.

GREMIO

Tut, she's a lamb, a dove, a fool to him.

145 narrow prying] F1; narrow-prying POPE   152 grumbling] F1 (grumlling)

143 **watch our vantage** be alert for an opportunity favourable to us

144 **overreach** outdo (*OED v.* 6), not necessarily in a bad sense although it does probably here imply 'out-scheme' (Gremio, Baptista, and Litio being thought of as underhand plotters)

145 **narrow prying** Most editors hyphenate the words, taking 'narrow' as an adverb and explaining as 'over-inquisitive', 'spying' or 'examining closely'. Alternatively, 'narrow' may be an adjective, meaning 'parsimonious' or 'mean-minded' (*OED a.* 4).

146 **quaint** crafty, scheming (*OED* I b)

149 **As . . . school** Proverbial (Tilley W398).

150 **is** When two singular nouns form a grammatical subject, Shakespeare normally uses a singular verb thus (Abbott 336). So too in l. 248 and 4.1.15.

151 **groom** In the pejorative sense (as perhaps again in l. 215), like the now customary derogatory meaning of 'menial': 'crude fellow', the opposite to 'aristocrat' (*OED sb*[1]. 2). This is implicit in, e.g., 'the base bed of some rascal groom' in *Lucrece* 171 and several other lines in Shakespeare.

153 **Curster** more curst (Elizabethan English, unlike modern, did not avoid this comparative form of adjectives ending in 'st'. Abbott 7).

155 **devil's dam** See 1.1.105–6 and note.

156 **fool** In the sense in which it is generally preceded by 'poor' (like the hunted deer that are 'poor dappled fools' in *As You Like It*, 2.1.22): a term of sympathy, deriving from the belief in the traditional innocent goodwill of the feeble-minded. 'Poor innocent'.

to compared to

I'll tell you, Sir Lucentio: when the priest
Should ask if Katherine should be his wife,
'Ay, by gog's wouns', quoth he, and swore so loud
That all-amazed the priest let fall the book, 160
And as he stooped again to take it up,
This mad-brained bridegroom took him such a cuff
That down fell priest and book, and book and priest.
'Now take them up', quoth he, 'if any list.'

TRANIO
What said the wench when he rose again?

GREMIO
Trembled and shook, for why he stamped and swore
As if the vicar meant to cozen him.
But after many ceremonies done
He calls for wine. 'A health!' quoth he, as if
He had been aboard, carousing to his mates 170
After a storm, quaffed off the muscadel,
And threw the sops all in the sexton's face,

165 rose] F1; rose up F2; arose STEEVENS 1793 166–82] *arranged as* STEEVENS 1793; *as prose* F1; *as sixteen lines of 'verse'* F2 166 shook, for why] ALEXANDER; shooke: for why F1; shooke for why Q1631; shook; for why, ROWE

157 **Sir Lucentio** Schmidt explains that 'Sir' was often 'applied to names of foreigners belonging to the gentry'; but many of his examples have nothing to do with foreigners (e.g. 'Sir Paris' twice in *Romeo*, as addressed by Capulet and Friar Laurence). It is a respectful form of address to one who is not a close personal acquaintance.

158 **Should ask** came to the point (in the marriage service) where he is required to ask. Abbott seems to overlook this usage (it probably has nothing to do with reported speech – Abbott 328).

159 **by gog's wouns** by God's (Christ's) wounds – a common oath and, of course, hideously inappropriate in such a context as the marriage service.

162 **took** gave

164 **them** 'Them' has been taken to refer to the bride's clothes, with the explanation that Petruchio is pretending that he suspected the priest of trying to interfere with Katherine's underwear. (Hibbard mentions the custom of 'removing' the bride's ribbon garters.) One wonders whether even Petruchio would go so far. In any case, 'them' more naturally refers to the nouns of the preceding line, 'priest and book, and book and priest'.

164 **list** desire. The verb, originally impersonal ('me listeth' – it is to my wish) was regularly used as a personal verb even before Elizabethan times, and Shakespeare always uses it so. Compare 3.1.89 and 4.5.7.

165 **rose** Emendation to ensure ten syllables is unnecessary: the line is easily spoken.

166 **for why** because (a frequent Shakespearian use)

167 **cozen** cheat (presumably, by not legally marrying them)

168 **ceremonies** (formal) rites

170 **aboard** on board ship
carousing to drinking (frequent) toasts to (and with). Compare 1.2.274 and note.

171 **muscadel** Also known as 'muscatel': a sweet wine. Petruchio should be passing the wine to others, as part of the ceremonial pledge.

172 **sops** Nares explains that cakes and similar delicacies were blessed and put in the wine presented to the bride; and these were 'sops', matter steeped and softened in liquor. (The derogatory meaning 'dregs' or 'sediment' seems to have been a slightly later development.)

Having no other reason
But that his beard grew thin and hungerly
And seemed to ask him sops as he was drinking.
This done, he took the bride about the neck,
And kissed her lips with such a clamorous smack
That at the parting all the church did echo;
And I seeing this came thence for very shame,
And after me I know the rout is coming. 180
Such a mad marriage never was before.
Hark, hark, I hear the minstrels play.

Music plays.
Enter Petruchio, Katherina, Bianca, Hortensio, Baptista, Grumio, and attendants

PETRUCHIO
Gentlemen and friends, I thank you for your pains.
I know you think to dine with me today,
And have prepared great store of wedding cheer,
But so it is, my haste doth call me hence,
And therefore here I mean to take my leave.

BAPTISTA
Is't possible you will away tonight?

PETRUCHIO
I must away today before night come.
Make it no wonder: if you knew my business, 190
You would entreat me rather go than stay.

182.3 *Grumio*] CAPELL; *not in* F1 *and attendants*] CAPELL (*subs.*); *not in* F1

173 **Having . . . reason** The incomplete line is perhaps odder than many that editors insist on emending. (In fact F1 prints this whole speech as prose.)

174 **hungerly** sparsely, in a hungry-looking way; as if its possessor were in need of nourishment.

175 **ask him** ask of him (Petruchio); ask him for

180 **rout** assemblage, group of people (*OED sb*[1]. I) but the suggestion of disorderliness is already there in most Shakespearian uses, and Gremio may well mean to speak disrespectfully of the wedding party.

182.2 ***Hortensio*** So far as F1 is concerned (since it makes no distinction in stage directions between Hortensio in his own person and Hortensio in disguise), he could come on here as Litio; but the 'real' Hortensio would be more likely to be a wedding guest than the supposed music-master. ('Cambio' is not at the wedding either.) It will be noticed that Hortensio is not given anything to say. For the possible implications, see Introduction pp. 10–13.

185 **cheer** 'refreshments', in the modern idiom; food (and drink)

188, 189 **will away, must away** The verb of motion ('go') is often thus omitted, even in modern usage. Compare 'I must hence'.

190 **Make it no wonder** do not think it extraordinary or think that there must be some unusual explanation.

191 **entreat me . . . go** An example of the omission of the 'to' of the infinitive, common in Elizabethan English. So too in ll. 197 and 204.

And, honest company, I thank you all
That have beheld me give away myself
To this most patient, sweet, and virtuous wife.
Dine with my father, drink a health to me,
For I must hence, and farewell to you all.

TRANIO
Let us entreat you stay till after dinner.

PETRUCHIO It may not be.

GREMIO Let me entreat you.

PETRUCHIO It cannot be. 200

KATHERINA Let me entreat you.

PETRUCHIO I am content.

KATHERINA Are you content to stay?

PETRUCHIO
I am content you shall entreat me stay –
But yet not stay, entreat me how you can.

KATHERINA Now if you love me, stay.

PETRUCHIO Grumio, my horse.

GRUMIO Ay, sir, they be ready, the oats have eaten the horses.

KATHERINA
Nay then, do what thou canst, I will not go today, 210
No, nor tomorrow, not till I please myself.
The door is open, sir, there lies your way,
You may be jogging whiles your boots are green.
For me, I'll not be gone till I please myself.
'Tis like you'll prove a jolly surly groom

199 GREMIO] F1 (*Gra.*) 210] *as one line* this edition; Nay then, | Doe ... to day, | F1
211 tomorrow, not] F1; tomorrow, nor F4; to-morrow NEW CAMBRIDGE

207 **my horse** (Probably) my horses. Compare Induction 1.58 and note.

208–9 **the oats . . . horses** Obscure. It is difficult to accept that the words mean only that the horses have eaten their fill of oats and are therefore ready. If they had eaten too much they would not be in a fit condition to start; and conceivably Grumio is alleging that they ought to be ready, since they've had so *few* oats. Heath's explanation is 'the horses were so poor that the oats were the more substantial creature of the two'. No relevant proverb is recorded.

210 **Nay . . . today** There is no difficulty in taking this as one line. 'Nay then', like forms of address, is strictly 'extra-metrical', an addition to the normal ten syllables.

211 **not till** Sisson (*New Readings*) has ably defended the F1 reading. It means 'I won't go tomorrow or any other day – not until I please to go'.

212 'Here is the door and there is the way' was a common saying (Tilley D556).

213 **jogging . . . green** Proverbial (Tilley B536) for going while one can, not waiting until it is too late. 'Green': 'new' or 'unmarked'.

215 **jolly** self-confident; arrogant (*OED* II. 6) **groom** See note on l. 151.

That take it on you at the first so roundly.

PETRUCHIO

O Kate, content thee, prithee be not angry.

KATHERINA

I will be angry; what hast thou to do?
– Father, be quiet: he shall stay my leisure.

GREMIO

Ay marry, sir, now it begins to work. 220

KATHERINA

Gentlemen, forward to the bridal dinner.
I see a woman may be made a fool
If she had not a spirit to resist.

PETRUCHIO

They shall go forward, Kate, at thy command.
– Obey the bride, you that attend on her.
Go to the feast, revel and domineer,
Carouse full measure to her maidenhead,
Be mad and merry, or go hang yourselves;
But for my bonny Kate, she must with me.
Nay, look not big, nor stamp, nor stare, nor fret, 230
I will be master of what is mine own.
She is my goods, my chattels, she is my house,
My household stuff, my field, my barn,
My horse, my ox, my ass, my any thing,
And here she stands, touch her whoever dare!

216 **take it on you** assume it is for you to make all the decisions; presume too far
roundly unceremoniously, without waiting for an invitation (as in 1.2.58 and 4.4.104 and in *As You Like It*, 5.3.10.)

218 **what hast thou to do?** what has it to do with you? What business is it of yours?

219 **Father, be quiet** Katherine assumes – perhaps wrongly – that Baptista is about to interrupt.
stay my leisure wait until *I* am ready (to go)

220 **it begins to work** things are beginning to happen – or even, in the modern colloquialism, 'it's on!'.

226 **domineer** revel, feast riotously (*OED* 2, deriving the word from Du. *domineren*, to feast luxuriously)

229 **for** as for

230 Petruchio here begins the pretence that he is rescuing Katherine from those who wish to detain her against her will. If, incidentally, as some editors suggest, Katherine is behaving in the way he alleges (in this line) that the others are behaving, he can hardly simultaneously have his arm around her – as they also suggest. (It is not Petruchio's way to address *Kate* in words like those of ll. 230–1.)

230 **big** haughty, defiant
stare look wildly

232–4 Petruchio is here almost parodying the words of the marriage service and of the tenth commandment ('Thou shalt not covet thy neyghbours house, neyther shalt thou covet thy neyghbours wyfe, nor his man servaunt, nor his mayde, nor his oxe, nor his asse, nor any thing that is thy neyghbours' – in the wording of the Bishops' Bible, Exodus 20:17); he claims

I'll bring mine action on the proudest he
That stops my way in Padua. – Grumio,
Draw forth thy weapon, we are beset with thieves,
Rescue thy mistress if thou be a man.
– Fear not, sweet wench, they shall not touch thee, Kate; 240
I'll buckler thee against a million.

Exeunt Petruchio, Katherina, and Grumio

BAPTISTA
Nay, let them go, a couple of quiet ones.

GREMIO
Went they not quickly, I should die with laughing.

TRANIO
Of all mad matches never was the like.

LUCENTIO
Mistress, what's your opinion of your sister?

BIANCA
That being mad herself, she's madly mated.

GREMIO
I warrant him, Petruchio is Kated.

BAPTISTA
Neighbours and friends, though bride and bridegroom wants
For to supply the places at the table,
You know there wants no junkets at the feast. 250
Lucentio, you shall supply the bridegroom's place,
And let Bianca take her sister's room.

241.1 *and Grumio*] CAPELL (*subs.*); *not in* F1

to be defending what is now lawfully his (Katherine) from those who sinfully covet it.

236 **bring mine action** (i) take physical action; (ii) start legal proceedings (for, e.g., theft, or 'assault and battery')
the proudest he the proudest, most self-assured, man ('he' was often thus used for 'man'. Abbott 224).

241 **buckler** defend, by serving as a shield

246 **madly mated** mated with – married to and matched by – a madman

247 **warrant him** (am prepared to) guarantee, so far as he is concerned
Kated Gremio's jocular equivalent of 'mated' – mated with (and matched or overmatched by) a Kate (not the kind that is a household delicacy). Commentators have found in it a medical image – in catching Kate, he has caught a disease – but it seems improbable, in spite of the alleged parallel with *Much Ado*, 1.1.73–4 ('caught the Benedick').

248 **wants** are wanting, are missing (and again the singular verb is used where there are two singular subjects).

249 **supply** fill, take. So too in l. 251.

250 **there wants no** there is no lack of. Here the verb is singular, following 'there' and *preceding* a plural subject (Abbott 335).
junkets In the general sense, 'sweetmeats' (cakes and so on). Nowadays, of course, the word is used mainly of one particular kind of sweet dish.

252 **room** allotted place (i.e. the bride's, as Tranio's comment makes clear)

TRANIO
Shall sweet Bianca practise how to bride it?

BAPTISTA
She shall, Lucentio. Come, gentlemen, let's go. *Exeunt*

4.1 *Enter Grumio*

GRUMIO Fie, fie on all tired jades, on all mad masters, and all foul ways! Was ever man so beaten? Was ever man so rayed? Was ever man so weary? I am sent before to make a fire, and they are coming after to warm them. Now were not I a little pot and soon hot, my very lips might freeze to my teeth, my tongue to the roof of my mouth, my heart in my belly, ere I should come by a fire to thaw me; but I with blowing the fire shall warm myself, for, considering the weather, a taller man than I will take cold. Holla, ho, Curtis! 10

Enter Curtis

CURTIS Who is that calls so coldly?

GRUMIO A piece of ice. If thou doubt it, thou mayst slide from my shoulder to my heel with no greater a run but my head and my neck. A fire, good Curtis.

CURTIS Is my master and his wife coming, Grumio?

4.1.0.1 *Enter Grumio*] F1; *Act IV Sc. I . . . Enter . . .* POPE 3 rayed] F1 (raide) 11 is that] F1; is thats Q1631; is it that F3; is't that HOSLEY

4.1.1 **jades** useless horses, with no stamina (as before in 1.2.246)

2 **ways** roads or pathways

3 **rayed** defiled, dirtied (see 3.2.52 and note)

5 **a little pot . . . hot** Proverbial (Tilley P497); a small pot that boils quickly: a small person but quickly angry. Grumio is apparently small (l. 23) and is wryly and ironically taking consolation from the fact.

6 **my tongue . . . mouth** Perhaps, as Noble thinks, suggested by Psalm 137:6: 'let my tongue cleave to the roof of my mouth'.

7 **come . . . me** find a fire good enough to make me warm

8 **blowing the fire** A quibble based on the maxim 'Let them that be acold blow at the coal' (Tilley C460) and carrying on the implications of 'soon hot': 'fanning my anger'.

9 **taller** A quibble on 'tall' in (i) the modern sense and (ii) the other common Elizabethan meanings of 'strong', 'valiant', and 'well able to look after himself' – often used ironically.

11 **is that** is that who *or* is it that

so coldly Another quibble (i) with so little enthusiasm (ironical, for Grumio is presumably shouting loudly); (ii) like one who is cold (and doesn't wish to remain so).

13 **no greater a run but** no longer a 'take-off' than (Grumio is so iced-up that Curtis need not 'get speed up' before beginning the slide from shoulder to heel).

15 **Is** For the singular verb, see, e.g., 3.2.150 and note.

GRUMIO O ay, Curtis, ay – and therefore fire, fire, cast on no water.

CURTIS Is she so hot a shrew as she's reported?

GRUMIO She was, good Curtis, before this frost; but thou know'st winter tames man, woman, and beast: for it hath tamed my old master, and my new mistress, and myself, fellow Curtis. 20

CURTIS Away, you three-inch fool, I am no beast.

GRUMIO Am I but three inches? Why, thy horn is a foot, and so long am I at the least. But wilt thou make a fire, or shall I complain on thee to our mistress, whose hand – she being now at hand – thou shalt soon feel, to thy cold comfort, for being slow in thy hot office?

CURTIS I prithee, good Grumio, tell me how goes the world? 30

GRUMIO A cold world, Curtis, in every office but thine – and therefore fire. Do thy duty, and have thy duty, for my master and mistress are almost frozen to death.

CURTIS There's fire ready, and therefore, good Grumio, the news.

GRUMIO Why, 'Jack boy, ho boy!' and as much news as wilt thou.

21 myself] F1; thyself HANMER 23 CURTIS] Q1631; *Gru.* F1 36–7 wilt thou] F1; thou wilt Q1631

16–17 **fire . . . water** A deliberate misquotation of a popular round or catch, 'Scotland's burning . . . Fire, fire! Cast on water! . . .'; Grumio, frozen, needs the fire – anything but the water.

18 **hot** passionate, vile-tempered (compare 2.1.294); but 'hot' seems also to have been used simply as an intensive.

20 **winter . . . beast** The proverb really is (Tilley A64) 'Winter and wedlock tame both man and beast'. Grumio omits 'wedlock', leaving Curtis to supply it, and adds 'woman', to make it plain that winter has tamed even Katherine. But his sequence 'man-woman-beast' 'master-mistress-himself', when he also calls Curtis his 'fellow', leaves room for Curtis's assumed indignation at being by implication called a 'beast'.

23 **three-inch fool** Another allusion, apparently, to Grumio's lack of size; compare ll. 5, 9. Grumio's reply turns it into an indecency.

24 **thy horn is a foot . . .** (Presumably) the cuckold's horn that you wear is a foot long (and I must therefore have a potential of more than three inches to have given it to you).

28 **cold comfort** A standard phrase (Tilley C542) for 'satisfaction' that is the reverse of encouraging.

hot office In the literal sense: the duty of making a fire.

32 **Do thy duty, and have thy duty** The normal form of the saying was 'do thy duty and take thy due' – but Grumio cannot resist the opportunity of another quibble since 'duty' can also mean 'due' (recompense or reward), as in Tindale's translation of Matthew 20:4, 'Take that which is thy duty', cited by *OED* (2).

36 **'Jack boy, ho boy!'** As Curtis implies in his

CURTIS Come, you are so full of cony-catching.

GRUMIO Why therefore fire, for I have caught extreme cold.
Where's the cook, is supper ready, the house trimmed, 40
rushes strewed, cobwebs swept, the servingmen in their
new fustian, the white stockings, and every officer his
wedding-garment on? Be the Jacks fair within, the Jills fair
without, the carpets laid, and everything in order?

CURTIS All ready, and therefore, I pray thee, news.

GRUMIO First, know my horse is tired, my master and
mistress fallen out.

CURTIS How?

GRUMIO Out of their saddles into the dirt, and thereby
hangs a tale. 50

CURTIS Let's ha't, good Grumio.

GRUMIO Lend thine ear.

CURTIS Here.

42 the] F1; their F3; and HOSLEY

rejoinder, Grumio's mind is full of 'catches'. This one went 'Jack boy, ho boy, news! | The cat is in the well, | Let us ring now for her knell, | Ding, dong, bell.' This is then presumably Grumio's way of saying that there is no news (none that he is yet ready to give). There may conceivably be a quibble on 'well' and 'wilt'; but again it is hard to believe that there is one on 'cat' and 'Kate'. The music of the 'catch' is given in Thomas Ravenscroft's *Pammelia. Musicks Miscellanie* (1609); it is anonymous but seems to date from the sixteenth century and to have become traditional by the 1590s. It is printed in Appendix B of this edition, from Naylor's transcription. (Another is in Peter Warlock's edition of *Pammelia*, London, 1928.)

38 **cony-catching** the catching of the cony (or 'bunny'); the deceit practised by the confidence-man. But there is, of course, a pun on 'catch' in the other sense: Grumio has already quoted from two.

39 **caught** The past tense of 'catch' in yet another sense.

40 **trimmed** made trim, put in order (*OED* v. II. 2)

41 **rushes strewed** i.e. on the floor. This was the normal floor-covering; carpets were expensive and were used as coverings for beds, chests or tables (see l. 44 note).

42 **fustian** A cloth, coarse and therefore cheap and appropriate for servants (and probably blue: compare l. 80).

the . . . stockings Emendation to 'their' seems unnecessary, for Grumio refers to *the* white stockings as something special, something the servants had been specially ordered to wear, like the 'wedding-garment' of the following line.

officer Probably slightly higher in the scale than the menial servants: one who had some administrative responsibility.

42–3 **his wedding-garment on** Noble sees a reminiscence of Matthew 22:12, 'Friend, how camest thou in hither, not having a wedding garment?'

43 **Jacks, Jills** (i) lads and lasses – referring here to the servants; (ii) 'jacks' as containers (often of coated leather) for liquor; 'jills' or 'gills', smaller vessels, holding half a pint or less and, because they were usually metal, likely to need polishing on the outside.

44 **carpets** woollen tablecloths (*OED* 1) rather than floor-coverings

49–50 **thereby hangs a tale** A stock phrase, of course (Tilley T48).

GRUMIO (*cuffing him*) There.

CURTIS This 'tis to feel a tale, not to hear a tale.

GRUMIO And therefore 'tis called a sensible tale; and this cuff was but to knock at your ear and beseech listening. Now I begin. Inprimis we came down a foul hill, my master riding behind my mistress –

CURTIS Both of one horse? 60

GRUMIO What's that to thee?

CURTIS Why, a horse.

GRUMIO Tell thou the tale. But hadst thou not crossed me, thou shouldst have heard how her horse fell, and she under her horse; thou shouldst have heard in how miry a place, how she was bemoiled, how he left her with the horse upon her, how he beat me because her horse stumbled, how she waded through the dirt to pluck him off me; how he swore, how she prayed, that never prayed before; how I cried, how the horses ran 70 away, how her bridle was burst; how I lost my crupper – with many things of worthy memory, which now shall die in oblivion, and thou return unexperienced to thy grave.

CURTIS By this reckoning he is more shrew than she.

GRUMIO Ay, and that thou and the proudest of you all shall find when he comes home. But what talk I of this? Call forth Nathaniel, Joseph, Nicholas, Philip, Walter, Sugarsop, and the rest. Let their heads be slickly combed, their

54 *cuffing him*] *not in* F1 55 'tis] F1; is ROWE 1714 58 Inprimis] F1; Imprimis F4
79 slickly] F1 (slickely); sleekly ROWE 1714

56 **sensible** Yet another quibble: (i) making sense; (ii) perceptible by the senses; and perhaps (iii) easily understood.

58 **Inprimis** Grumio, comically, is aiming at impressiveness by the use of legal jargon. There is no need to emend: F1 has 'inprimis' again in 4.3.131 and also in very similar circumstances in *Two Gentlemen*, 3.1, where it is twice used by Launce. 'In the first place'.

foul muddy

60 **of** on (as often: Abbott 175)

63 **crossed** (i) cut across, interrupted; (ii) thwarted

66 **bemoiled** daubed with mud, bemired. 'Bemoil' is not recorded elsewhere in Shakespeare; 'moil' is used by Spenser, for one.

71 **burst** broken, snapped (as in 3.2.58)

72–4 **of worthy memory . . . grave** i.e. which are worth recording but, since I haven't time to tell of them, must be forgotten – and you must die without ever having profited from knowledge of them

75 **reckoning** calculation (compare 'reckoned up' in Induction 2.90) and, perhaps, calling to account

77 **what** why (a common use)

79 **the rest** A dozen or more are named in this scene but they do not all appear on stage.

slickly smoothly, skilfully. (The words 'slick' and 'sleek' are closely related.)

blue coats brushed, and their garters of an indifferent knit; let them curtsy with their left legs, and not presume to touch a hair of my master's horse-tail till they kiss their hands. Are they all ready? 80

CURTIS They are.

GRUMIO Call them forth.

CURTIS Do you hear, ho? You must meet my master to countenance my mistress.

GRUMIO Why, she hath a face of her own.

CURTIS Who knows not that?

GRUMIO Thou, it seems, that calls for company to countenance her. 90

CURTIS I call them forth to credit her.

Enter four or five Servingmen

GRUMIO Why, she comes to borrow nothing of them.

NATHANIEL Welcome home, Grumio.

PHILIP How now, Grumio.

JOSEPH What, Grumio.

NICHOLAS Fellow Grumio.

NATHANIEL How now, old lad.

GRUMIO Welcome, you! – How now, you! – What, you! – Fellow, you! And thus much for greeting. Now, my spruce companions, is all ready, and all things neat? 100

NATHANIEL All things is ready. How near is our master?

92.1] F1; *after l.* 93 CAPELL 97 NICHOLAS] F1 (*Nick.*)

80 **blue coats** The normal servant uniform. **indifferent** Perhaps (i) plain, not extreme, moderate (compare Hamlet's 'I am myself indifferent honest', 3.2.122–3); (ii) not differing, uniform (cf. 1.2.176); or even (iii) immaterial – i.e. Grumio doesn't care what knit the garters are: he may be making much the same point as Benedick was to make when he listed the qualities desirable in a woman and ended 'and her hair shall be of what colour it please God' (*Much Ado*, 2.3.29–30).

81 **left legs** Said to be a token of deference; to curtsy with the right leg was to imply defiance.

82–3 **kiss their hands** Another, somewhat extreme, submissive greeting – such as would not normally be expected.

86–7 **countenance** pay respect to – but Grumio, of course, chooses to take it in the sense of 'face'.

90 **calls** A second person singular verb (alternative to 'callest') that is perhaps the old Northern form.

92 **credit** do credit to (*OED v.* 5) – but Grumio cannot resist the pun again and pretends to believe that it means 'offer financial credit'.

101 **spruce** brisk in manner or smart in appearance; perhaps both.

102 **All things is ready** 'Is' has been taken as another example of the singular verb where the subject is thought of as a collective noun; but more probably Nathaniel's is a 'smart' answer. Grumio can idiomatically ask 'is all ready, and all things neat?' because the singular 'is' with the first subject implies the plural 'are' with the second; Nathaniel mockingly answers as if Grumio had made an error.

GRUMIO E'en at hand, alighted by this; and therefore be
not – Cock's passion, silence, I hear my master.

Enter Petruchio and Katherina

PETRUCHIO
Where be these knaves? What, no man at door
To hold my stirrup nor to take my horse?
Where is Nathaniel, Gregory, Philip?

ALL SERVINGMEN Here, here sir, here sir.

PETRUCHIO
'Here sir, here sir, here sir, here sir'!
You logger-headed and unpolished grooms! 110
What? No attendance? No regard? No duty?
Where is the foolish knave I sent before?

GRUMIO
Here sir, as foolish as I was before.

PETRUCHIO
You peasant swain, you whoreson malt-horse drudge,
Did I not bid thee meet me in the park
And bring along these rascal knaves with thee?

GRUMIO
Nathaniel's coat, sir, was not fully made,
And Gabriel's pumps were all unpinked i'th' heel;
There was no link to colour Peter's hat,
And Walter's dagger was not come from sheathing; 120
There were none fine but Adam, Ralph, and Gregory,
The rest were ragged, old, and beggarly,

103 GRUMIO] F3; *Gre.* F1 121 Ralph] F1 (*Rafe*)

104 **Cock's passion** (by) God's (Christ's) passion (on the Cross) – an asseveration coming naturally from a servant.

110 **logger-headed** blockheaded (Shakespeare elsewhere uses the noun 'loggerhead', meaning 'dolt').

113 Tilley believed that Grumio was cleverly alluding to the proverb 'He that sends a fool expects one' (F488); such a retort would certainly give fuel to Petruchio's indignation.

114 **peasant swain** country bumpkin ('swain' in the sense of 'farm labourer', *OED* 4, not 'pastoral lover')
whoreson son of a whore (an adjective)
malt-horse drudge Each word is found elsewhere as a term of reproach; 'malt-horse' – considered the embodiment of slowness and stupidity because it plods its way on the treadmill, grinding malt – in *Errors*, 3.1.32 ('malthorse, . . . coxcomb, idiot, patch'); and 'drudge', for 'menial' or 'slave', several times.

115 **park** As in 'deer-park'.

117 ff. That Grumio here speaks formally in verse may well be an indication that he is playing a part, in league with Petruchio.

118 **pumps** light shoes
unpinked not ornamented by pinking, not pierced with eyelet holes (*OED* 'pink' *v.* 3) – a frivolous excuse, of course, as are Grumio's other explanations.

119 **link** blacking (made from the 'links' or torches of tow and pitch)

120 **sheathing** being fitted with a sheath

121 **fine** elegant, well-presented

Yet, as they are, here are they come to meet you.

PETRUCHIO

Go, rascals, go and fetch my supper in. *Exeunt Servingmen*

(*Singing*) *Where is the life that late I led?*

Where are those – ? – Sit down, Kate, and welcome.

(*Humming*) *Soud, soud, soud, soud.*

Enter Servants with supper

Why, when, I say! – Nay, good sweet Kate, be merry.

– Off with my boots, you rogues! You villains, when!

(*Singing*) *It was the friar of orders grey,* 130

As he forth walkèd on his way –

– Out, you rogue! You pluck my foot awry.

Take that (*he kicks the Servant*) and mend the plucking of the other.

– Be merry, Kate. – Some water here! What ho!

Enter one with water

125 *Singing*] THEOBALD; *not in* F1 125–6 *Where ... those*] *all as a song* THEOBALD; *all in Roman type as dialogue* F1; *first line, only, as song* CAPELL 127 *Humming*] HANMER; *not in* F1 127 *Soud ... soud.*] F1 (Soud ... ſoud); Food ... food! NEW CAMBRIDGE 130 *Singing*] ROWE; *not in* F1 (*but the two lines 'It ... way' are italicized*) 133 *he kicks the Servant*] This edition, *as* COLLIER 1853; *not in* F1; *Strikes him* ROWE 133 of] F1; off ROWE 134.1] F1; *Water presented (after l.* 139) CAPELL

125 ***Where ... led*** The first line of a ballad, also quoted by Pistol in *2 Henry IV*, 5.2.139, and – as Malone explained – appropriate because on the theme of the newly-wedded man's loss of freedom. There are several references to the ballad (and answers to it) but neither full text nor music survives.

126 ***Where are those*** – Almost certainly the beginning of the second line of the ballad ('Where are those pleasant days?') and not merely another indignant demand, which Petruchio leaves unfinished as he turns, in pretended deference, to Katherine. (The evidence is given in *A Handful of Pleasant Delights*, ed. Hyder E. Rollins, Cambridge, Mass., 1924, p. 88.)

127 ***Soud, soud ...*** Taken to be an indication that Petruchio hums or continues singing to himself, rather than an expression of fatigue (Malone) or F1's error (thrice repeated) for 'food!'. Petruchio has already ordered his supper and, impatient though he is, that may be another reason for rejecting also Hilda Hulme's emendation 'sond' (an old word for 'a serving of food', not recorded after 1440).

128, 129 **when** A common exclamation of impatience – as is 'Out' in l. 132.

130–1 Petruchio sings the opening words of another ballad, apparently one of the many bawdy variations on the popular theme of the seduction by the Friar of the Nun. Two early forms of this ballad or carol (no later than the early sixteenth century) are discussed by P. J. Croft, 'The "Friar of Order Gray" and the Nun', *Review of English Studies*, 32 (1981), 1–16; and Croft sees 'the dramatic significance' of Petruchio's singing it here as being its theme of 'male domination and female submission'. In the full form of the carol, the Friar's seducing of the nun under the pretence of teaching her the gamut, the singing of Latin hymns, and other devotional exercises has the further interest of being a parallel to the wooing of Bianca by Hortensio and Lucentio in the music and Latin 'lessons' of 3.1. The ballad may even have given Shakespeare the 'idea' for that scene.

132 **pluck awry** jerk my foot in the wrong direction (as you try to pull off the boot)

133 **mend** improve, do a better job with (taking off the other boot)

Where's my spaniel Troilus? Sirrah, get you hence,
And bid my cousin Ferdinand come hither.
– One, Kate, that you must kiss and be acquainted
with.
– Where are my slippers? Shall I have some water?
– Come, Kate, and wash, and welcome heartily.
– You whoreson villain, will you let it fall? 140

KATHERINA
Patience, I pray you, 'twas a fault unwilling.

PETRUCHIO
A whoreson, beetle-headed, flap-eared knave!
– Come, Kate, sit down, I know you have a stomach.
Will you give thanks, sweet Kate, or else shall I?
– What's this? Mutton?

SERVINGMAN Ay.

PETRUCHIO Who brought it?

PETER I.

PETRUCHIO
'Tis burnt, and so is all the meat.
What dogs are these! Where is the rascal cook? 150
How durst you villains bring it from the dresser
And serve it thus to me that love it not?
There, take it to you, trenchers, cups, and all.
You heedless jolt-heads and unmannered slaves!
What, do you grumble? I'll be with you straight.
Exeunt Servants

140] *'Strikes him' added by* CAPELL 155.1 *Exeunt Servants*] *not in* F1

136 **cousin Ferdinand** We never find out whether Petruchio has such a relative or not. Conceivably the servants know that there is no such person, for F1 provides no exit here, and editors spoil the joke by inserting one. Similarly by altering F1's placing of the stage direction after l. 134, they reduce Petruchio's irrationality in his ignoring of what is already there; and by introducing a direction that the servant lets the ewer fall at l. 139, they again give reason for Petruchio's anger when it most lacks reason. (Perhaps he does spill the water himself.)

139 **wash** Eating with the fingers made hand-washing doubly desirable.

142 **beetle-headed** thick-headed (from 'beetle', the name of a large mallet, with a heavy head). 'As dull as a beetle' is also recorded.

142 **flap-eared** with ears like a donkey

143 **a stomach** an appetite (as in 1.1.38 and 1.2.190)

144 **give thanks** say grace

151 **dresser** *Either* the table or kitchen sideboard on which meat was served up *or* the person who prepares that meat.

153 **trenchers** wooden plates

154 **heedless** careless, not taking proper care
jolt-heads blockheads. Petruchio certainly has a remarkable range of synonyms for this.

155 **be with you straight** i.e. come out and 'attend' to you, discipline you,

KATHERINA
I pray you, husband, be not so disquiet.
The meat was well, if you were so contented.

PETRUCHIO
I tell thee, Kate, 'twas burnt and dried away,
And I expressly am forbid to touch it,
For it engenders choler, planteth anger, 160
And better 'twere that both of us did fast,
Since, of ourselves, ourselves are choleric,
Than feed it with such over-roasted flesh.
Be patient, tomorrow 't shall be mended,
And for this night we'll fast for company.
Come, I will bring thee to thy bridal chamber. *Exeunt*

Enter Servants severally

NATHANIEL Peter, didst ever see the like?

PETER He kills her in her own humour.

Enter Curtis

GRUMIO Where is he?

CURTIS
In her chamber, making a sermon of continency to her, 170
And rails, and swears, and rates, that she, poor soul,
Knows not which way to stand, to look, to speak,
And sits as one new risen from a dream.
Away, away, for he is coming hither. *Exeunt*

165 for company] F1; in company HOSLEY 166.1 *Enter . . . severally*] F1; *Manent* seruingmen and eate vp all the meate. A SHREW 168.1] CAPELL (*subs.*); *Enter Curtis a Seruant* (*after* 'Where *is he?*') F1 169–70 Where . . . to her] *as prose* F1; Where . . . he? | In . . . to her | POPE; Where is he? | In . . . chamber, | Making . . . her: | CAPELL 171–4] *as verse* POPE; *as prose* F1 174 *Exeunt*] *not in* F1

immediately (rather than 'be even with you', less appropriate from Petruchio to a servant)

160 **engenders choler** Not Petruchio's invention but an accepted Elizabethan medical theory. 'Choler' (anger) was hot and dry.

162 **of ourselves** in ourselves; by our make-up

165 **for company** as one way of keeping each other company

166.1 ***severally*** not together; (probably) at different doors

168 **kills . . . humour** brings her out of her 'humour' (shrewishness), and ensures that it cannot survive, by beating her at her own game. For 'humour' compare l. 196 later in this scene, and see note on 3.2.29.

170–4 It is odd that Curtis should speak in verse (there seems little doubt that the last four lines of his speech, at least, *are* verse). Perhaps the purpose is to make the transition to Petruchio's formal soliloquy.

170 **continency** self-control (generally; not only in sexual behaviour)

171 **rates** reproves vehemently
that so that, with the result that

Enter Petruchio

PETRUCHIO

Thus have I politicly begun my reign,
And 'tis my hope to end successfully.
My falcon now is sharp and passing empty,
And till she stoop she must not be full-gorged,
For then she never looks upon her lure.
Another way I have to man my haggard, 180
To make her come and know her keeper's call:
That is, to watch her, as we watch these kites
That bate and beat and will not be obedient.
She ate no meat today, nor none shall eat.
Last night she slept not, nor tonight she shall not.
As with the meat, some undeservèd fault
I'll find about the making of the bed,
And here I'll fling the pillow, there the bolster,
This way the coverlet, another way the sheets.
Ay, and amid this hurly I intend 190
That all is done in reverent care of her.

175 **politicly** in a cunning or clever way – showing the skill in management that a potential ruler should show

177 ff. **My falcon . . .** In what follows, Petruchio outlines the different stages in training the haggard (the wild female hawk), each corresponding to a step in his taming of Katherine. (The terminology is the exact technical language of falconry.) Once tamed, the wild hawk was the best.
sharp craving for food (and therefore eager to find it)

178 **stoop** (learns to) make straight for the lure or the prey. Before training, the haggard would easily be diverted from the true prey by practically anything in sight, as the following line explains.
full-gorged fully fed

179 **her lure** The lure is the falconer's mock-bird, made of feathers but containing food, which the haggard is being trained to aim at; and the proverb said that 'In time all haggard hawks will stoop to lure' (Tilley T298).

180 **man my haggard** train my hawk – but Petruchio is quibbling on 'man' because the bird trained is always the female.

182 **watch** keep awake, prevent from sleeping (an invariable part of falconry)

182 **kites** Falconers despised kites, which were said to have no courage; and indeed 'these kites' is used also in other contexts as an expression of contempt.

183 **bate** flutter their wings from nervousness, and flutter away (OF *batre*, later *battre*; *OED v*[1]. 2)
beat flap their wings (probably, in anger and more forcefully than when merely bating)

190 **hurly** commotion and strife (almost certainly a later word than the surviving 'hurly-burly')
intend Twice earlier in this play, and often elsewhere in Shakespeare, the word as in modern English is equivalent to 'mean' or 'propose'; but another meaning in Elizabethan usage (found, e.g., in *Richard III*, 3.7.45) is 'pretend' (*OED* VI. 22). The ambiguity, in a soliloquy, is unfortunate; it would be good to know whether Shakespeare really saw Petruchio as imagining that everything he did showed consideration (and more) for Kate.

191 **reverent** showing every respect. See 4.5.48 and note.

And, in conclusion, she shall watch all night,
And if she chance to nod I'll rail and brawl,
And with the clamour keep her still awake.
This is a way to kill a wife with kindness,
And thus I'll curb her mad and headstrong humour.
He that knows better how to tame a shrew,
Now let him speak; 'tis charity to show. *Exit*

4.2 *Enter Tranio as Lucentio, and Hortensio as Litio*

TRANIO Is't possible, friend Litio, that Mistress Bianca doth fancy any other but Lucentio? I tell you, sir, she bears me fair in hand.

HORTENSIO Sir, to satisfy you in what I have said, stand by and mark the manner of his teaching. 5

They stand aside. Enter Bianca, and Lucentio as Cambio

LUCENTIO
Now, mistress, profit you in what you read?

BIANCA
What, master, read you? First resolve me that.

4.2.0.1] F1; *Act IV Sc. II Enter* ... STEEVENS 1–3] *as prose* this edition; Is't ... *Bianca* | ... *Lucentio*, | ... hand.| F1 4 HORTENSIO] F2; *Luc.* F1 4–5] *as prose* this edition; Sir, ... said, | ... teaching. | F1 5.1 *They stand aside*] *not in* F1 5.1–2 *Enter* ...] ROWE (*subs.*); *Enter Bianca.* F1 6, 8 LUCENTIO] F2; *Hor.* F1 7 you? First] THEOBALD (*subs.*); you first, F1

192 **watch** stay awake (the intransitive use of the verb, as against the transitive in l. 182).

193 **brawl** be noisy, raise a clamour (*OED* v^1. 2)

194 **still** constantly, without respite

195 **kill ... with kindness** Proverbial (Tilley K51) for spoiling, ruining, or even literally killing by excessive consideration – but Petruchio is speaking ironically and means almost the opposite: cure by not showing kindness at all.

196 **humour** disposition or (eccentric) behaviour. See note on 3.2.29.

197–8 The rhyme is possible because 'shrew' was formerly pronounced 'shrow'. Indeed F1 so spells it in the final couplet of the play (and has 'shrow'd' at 1.2.69 and 1.2.89); and in Peele's *Arraignment of Paris*, 4.3.820–1, it is spelt 'shroe' (and rhymes with both 'so' and 'below').

198 **'tis charity to show** to speak up, share such knowledge, is to perform an act of charity. ('Charity' is used in one of its wider senses, 'Christian love' or 'benevolence'.)

4.2.2–3 **bears me fair in hand** leads me on with (false) hopes and expectations. For this sense, compare *Much Ado*, 4.1.302, and *Measure*, 1.4.50–5, 'The Duke ... | Bore many gentlemen ... | In hand, and hope of action; but we do learn | ... His givings-out were of an infinite distance | From his true-meant design'.

5.1 Apparently F1 omits Lucentio's entrance here because of its error in the speech prefix of l. 4, giving him, instead of Hortensio, ll. 4–5.

6, 7, 8 **read** study – with quibbles on the literal meaning, and on 'teach' (as in 3.1.13).

7 **resolve me that** answer that for me, satisfy me about that. 'Me' is the old dative (Abbott 220).

LUCENTIO

I read that I profess, *The Art to Love.*

BIANCA

And may you prove, sir, master of your art.

LUCENTIO

While you, sweet dear, prove mistress of my heart. 10

They move away. Tranio and Hortensio come forward

HORTENSIO (*to Tranio*) Quick proceeders, marry! Now tell me,
I pray, you that durst swear that your mistress Bianca
loved none in the world so well as Lucentio –

TRANIO

O despiteful love, unconstant womankind!
I tell thee, Litio, this is wonderful.

HORTENSIO

Mistake no more, I am not Litio,
Nor a musician as I seem to be,
But one that scorn to live in this disguise
For such a one as leaves a gentleman
And makes a god of such a cullion. 20
Know, sir, that I am called Hortensio.

TRANIO

Signor Hortensio, I have often heard
Of your entire affection to Bianca,
And since mine eyes are witness of her lightness,

8 I ... *Love.*] ROWE (*subs.*); I reade, that I professe the Art to loue. F1 10.1] *not in* F1 11–13] *as prose* F3; Quicke ... pray, | you ... *Bianca* | Lou'd me ... *Lucentio.* | F1; Quick ... *Bianca* (*as prose*) | Lov'd ... *Lucentio.* F2 13 none] ROWE; me F1 Lucentio –] DYCE 1866; *Lucentio.* F1; Lucentio ... KEIGHTLEY 18 scorn] F1; scorns COLLIER

8 **that I profess** that which I have made my profession
The Art to Love Ovid's *Ars Amatoria.* Indeed there may be in this line a witty reversal of Ovid's own protestation (*Amores*, II.xviii, l. 19 ff.) that *he* professes what he teaches (in the same work).

9–10 **art . . . dear . . . heart** A series of quibbles on 'art', 'hart', 'deer', and 'dear'.

11 **proceeders** Hortensio is catching up Bianca's 'master of your art' and thinking of 'Master of Arts' – one of the degrees to which in an English university one 'proceeds', from the Bachelor's degree. There may therefore even be an implicit pun on 'bachelor'.
marry By Mary (as in Induction 2.99).

13 **none . . . Lucentio** – Even if Rowe's emendation 'none' for F1's 'me' is adopted, the passage does not make sense unless one assumes that Tranio interrupts. (There is no direct grammatical object of Hortensio's 'tell'.)

15 **wonderful** to be 'wondered' at, a cause for amazement

18 **scorn** The verbal form has been explained as singular, 'attracted' by the original subject 'I'; alternatively it may surely be the regular plural, 'one *of those* that scorn'.

20 **such a cullion** such a despicable rascal (as the schoolmaster, Cambio)

23 **entire** unalloyed

24 **lightness** light behaviour, unfaithfulness

I will with you, if you be so contented,
Forswear Bianca and her love for ever.

HORTENSIO
See how they kiss and court! Signor Lucentio,
Here is my hand, and here I firmly vow
Never to woo her more, but do forswear her,
As one unworthy all the former favours 30
That I have fondly flattered her withal.

TRANIO
And here I take the like unfeigned oath
Never to marry with her though she would entreat.
Fie on her, see how beastly she doth court him!

HORTENSIO
Would all the world but he had quite forsworn!
For me, that I may surely keep mine oath,
I will be married to a wealthy widow,
Ere three days pass, which hath as long loved me
As I have loved this proud disdainful haggard.
And so farewell, Signor Lucentio. 40
Kindness in women, not their beauteous looks,
Shall win my love, and so I take my leave,
In resolution as I swore before. *Exit*

⌈*Lucentio and Bianca come forward again*⌉

TRANIO
Mistress Bianca, bless you with such grace
As 'longeth to a lover's blessèd case!
Nay, I have ta'en you napping, gentle love,
And have forsworn you with Hortensio.

BIANCA
Tranio, you jest – but have you both forsworn me?

31 her] F3; them F1 35 forsworn!] F1–4 (forsworn‸); forsworn her ROWE 1714
36 oath,] ROWE; oath. F1; oath: F4 43 *Exit*] *not in* F1 43.1] *not in* F1

31 **fondly** foolishly
34 **beastly** An adverb, again in the same form as the adjective and perhaps more easily so because the adjective already ends in 'ly' (so too 'friendly' in l. 108). 'In a beastly manner', 'lasciviously'.
35 i.e. I wish that everybody else had given up completely and that he were the only choice she had – and my only rival.
38 **which** who. Elizabethan English did not always observe the distinction between the 'personal' and 'impersonal' relative.
39 **haggard** Hortensio is thinking of the untamed female hawk's readiness to be diverted by anything that crosses its path.
45 **'longeth to** belongs to, is appropriate for
46 **ta'en you napping** The modern 'caught you napping' (by overhearing the conversation with Lucentio). Tilley N36–7.

TRANIO
Mistress, we have.

LUCENTIO Then we are rid of Litio.

TRANIO
I'faith, he'll have a lusty widow now 50
That shall be wooed and wedded in a day.

BIANCA
God give him joy!

TRANIO Ay, and he'll tame her.

BIANCA
He says so, Tranio.

TRANIO
Faith, he is gone unto the taming-school.

BIANCA
The taming-school? What, is there such a place?

TRANIO
Ay, mistress, and Petruchio is the master
That teacheth tricks eleven-and-twenty long,
To tame a shrew and charm her chattering tongue.

Enter Biondello

BIONDELLO
O master, master, I have watched so long
That I am dog-weary, but at last I spied 60
An ancient angel coming down the hill
Will serve the turn.

TRANIO What is he, Biondello?

60 I am] F1; I'm POPE

50 **lusty** merry, lively (as in 2.1.159) – but probably here does also mean 'lustful'.

51 **That . . . day** Hortensio did not say that (see l. 38). One would assert confidently that Tranio was improving on the truth for comic purposes if it were not for his unexpected knowledge in ll.54–6 of Hortensio's other intention. See Introduction pp. 12, 23–4.

57 **eleven-and-twenty** i.e. 31 – and the allusion is apparently to the card-game 'one-and-thirty' of 1.2.33 (see note). Presumably when Petruchio teaches taming he is not 'one pip out' but exactly right, 'spot on'.

58 **charm** stop, silence, as if by a magic spell

60 **dog-weary** worn out (we still say 'dog-tired'). Tilley D441.

61 **ancient angel** (i) guardian angel (ii) with a quibble on the name of the gold coin – worthy old fellow. Singer aptly quoted Cotgrave's 1611 definition of 'angelot' as 'an old angel, by metaphor, a fellow of th' old, sound, honest, and worthie stamp' (as opposed to debased later coinage). Emendation to 'angle' (bait) or 'engle' (dupe) is therefore gratuitous.

62 **serve the turn** serve the purpose, do well enough

BIONDELLO

Master, a marcantant or a pedant,
I know not what, but formal in apparel,
In gait and countenance surely like a father.

LUCENTIO

And what of him, Tranio?

TRANIO

If he be credulous and trust my tale,
I'll make him glad to seem Vincentio,
And give assurance to Baptista Minola
As if he were the right Vincentio. 70
Take in your love, and then let me alone.

Exeunt Lucentio and Bianca

Enter a Pedant

PEDANT

God save you, sir.

TRANIO And you, sir. You are welcome.

63 marcantant] F1; mercantant POPE; mercatante CAPELL; mercatant DELIUS 71] *continued to Tranio* F2; *Par.* Take ... alone. F1 in] THEOBALD; me F1 71.1 *Exeunt ... Bianca*] *not in* F1

63 **marcantant** Not, *pace* Capell (*Notes*, 1783) and New Cambridge, the compositor's blunder but Biondello's version of 'mercatante' on the false analogy (probably deliberately so) of 'pedant'. (Perhaps the stress is on the second syllable.) Editors are too anxious to emend here (as in l. 60) if only to make Biondello's speeches 'better' verse. (They may even be prose, which is what one would expect; but F1 prints as verse and apparently not for reasons of 'cast-off' copy.)
pedant schoolmaster (without the pejorative connotation that soon becomes normal)

65 **countenance** general demeanour and appearance (*OED sb.* 1 & 2). Compare 1.1.226.

67 **trust my tale** accept unquestioningly the story I plan to tell him

68 **seem** pretend to be

71 F1 gives this line to a mysterious '*Par*'. New Cambridge (p. 115) records a conjecture by Greg that it was an abbreviation of the name of the actor playing the pedant (mentioned in the following stage direction) – written in the margin and misunderstood by the compositor as a speech prefix. Greg himself (*The Shakespeare First Folio*, p. 119) is content to put the (anonymous) conjecture in a footnote – and to refer to New Cambridge.

71 **in** Theobald's emendation is acceptable, F1's 'me' being either an easy misreading of 'ine' and/or an example of dittography ('me' occurs later in the line).
let me alone i.e. leave me, confidently, to my own resources

71.2 ***Pedant*** This stage direction may be only a casual authorial one, perhaps implying no more than 'Pedant or whatever he is', although he continues to be 'Pedant' in stage directions and speech prefixes. In *A Shrew* the character is a merchant, and Hosley deduces from ll. 89–90 that he must be a merchant here too; but that does not necessarily follow: even schoolmasters might carry bills of exchange.

Travel you far on, or are you at the farthest?

PEDANT

Sir, at the farthest for a week or two,
But then up farther, and as far as Rome,
And so to Tripoli, if God lend me life.

TRANIO

What countryman, I pray?

PEDANT

Of Mantua.

TRANIO

Of Mantua, sir? Marry, God forbid!
And come to Padua, careless of your life?

PEDANT

My life, sir? How, I pray? For that goes hard. 80

TRANIO

'Tis death for anyone in Mantua
To come to Padua. Know you not the cause?
Your ships are stayed at Venice, and the Duke,
For private quarrel 'twixt your Duke and him,
Hath published and proclaimed it openly.
'Tis marvel, but that you are but newly come,
You might have heard it else proclaimed about.

PEDANT

Alas, sir, it is worse for me than so,
For I have bills for money by exchange

73 far on, or] F1 (farre on, or); farrer on, or HIBBARD 78 Mantua, sir? Marry,] F1 (*Mantua* Sir, marrie); Mantua? Sir, marry, HIBBARD

73 **far on** F1's 'farre' has been taken to be the equivalent of 'farrer', recorded by *OED* as an old form of the comparative, meaning 'farther'. It is found in that sense in *Winter's Tale*, 4.4.423. But throughout the F text of *Shrew*, 'farre' is the regular spelling of 'far', and it is used by (probably) three different compositors. It occurs again only two lines below, in l. 75.

at the farthest as far as you plan to go

75–6 A very curious route, to put it mildly. It is difficult to see how Rome is farther 'up' than Padua on the way from Mantua. See too l. 83 and note. Tripoli may be either the North African city and state or Tripoli(s) in Syria.

77 **What countryman . . .?** Where do you come from? (as in 1.2.185)

80 **goes hard** Probably 'is bad', 'is not to be taken lightly' (as in *Two Gentlemen*, 4.2.2) but perhaps 'is not to be lost without a struggle', which would be comparable with 4.4.105.

83 **stayed** held. No doubt there was nothing to prevent merchants in Mantua from owning ships but Mantua is not a seaport. In Shakespeare's Italy it seems possible to get from any city to another by water. But compare 1.1.42 and note.

the Duke Presumably, of Venice, and thought of as the ruler of Padua also.

86–7 **'Tis . . . about** The sense is clearer than the syntax. 'If it were not that you have only just arrived, it would be strange that you hadn't already heard it announced everywhere.'

88 **worse . . . than so** even worse than that

89 **bills . . . exchange** A bill of exchange entitled the bearer to cash payment on a given date.

From Florence, and must here deliver them. 90

TRANIO

Well, sir, to do you courtesy,
This will I do, and this I will advise you:
First tell me, have you ever been at Pisa?

PEDANT

Ay, sir, in Pisa have I often been,
Pisa renownèd for grave citizens.

TRANIO

Among them know you one Vincentio?

PEDANT

I know him not, but I have heard of him:
A merchant of incomparable wealth.

TRANIO

He is my father, sir, and sooth to say,
In count'nance somewhat doth resemble you. 100

BIONDELLO (*aside*) As much as an apple doth an oyster, and all one.

TRANIO

To save your life in this extremity,
This favour will I do you for his sake,
And think it not the worst of all your fortunes
That you are like to Sir Vincentio:
His name and credit shall you undertake,
And in my house you shall be friendly lodged.
Look that you take upon you as you should.
You understand me, sir. So shall you stay 110
Till you have done your business in the city.
If this be courtesy, sir, accept of it.

PEDANT

O sir, I do, and will repute you ever
The patron of my life and liberty.

TRANIO

Then go with me, to make the matter good.

101 and] F1 (&); but HOSLEY

91 **courtesy** a favour. So too in l. 112.
95 An odd repetition of Lucentio's phrase at 1.1.10. See note on that line.
101 Proverbial (Tilley A291).
102 **all one** no matter for that – but the phrase is an almost meaningless 'filler'.
107 **credit** reputation, or standing
107 **undertake** put on, assume
109 **take upon you** accept your responsibilities, do what is required
113 **repute** consider
115 **make the matter good** carry out the plan

This, by the way, I let you understand:
My father is here looked for every day
To pass assurance of a dower in marriage
'Twixt me and one Baptista's daughter here.
In all these circumstances I'll instruct you. 120
Go with me to clothe you as becomes you.

Exeunt

4.3 *Enter Katherina and Grumio*

GRUMIO
No, no, forsooth, I dare not for my life.

KATHERINA
The more my wrong, the more his spite appears.
What, did he marry me to famish me?
Beggars that come unto my father's door
Upon entreaty have a present alms;
If not, elsewhere they meet with charity.
But I, who never knew how to entreat,
Nor never needed that I should entreat,
Am starved for meat, giddy for lack of sleep,
With oaths kept waking, and with brawling fed; 10
And that which spites me more than all these wants,
He does it under name of perfect love,
As who should say, if I should sleep or eat,
'Twere deadly sickness or else present death.
I prithee go and get me some repast,

121 me] F1; me sir F2
4.3.0.1 *Enter* ...] *Actus Quartus. Scena Prima. Enter* ... F1; *Act IV Sc. III Enter* ... STEEVENS

116 **by the way** as we go along. (So too in *As You Like It*, 3.2.395.)
117 **looked for** expected (as in modern usage)
118 **pass assurance** make a legal conveyance, make a formal agreement
120 **circumstances** details
4.3 That F1 chooses to begin 'Act 4' here is barely worthy of mention. The act-division is a literary one, superimposed on a play that would not have been *written* in Acts at all, or acted in them: what is now '4.2' is an adequate 'break' between 4.1 and 4.3 and any other would ruin the continuity.
1 **forsooth** in truth
2 **The ... appears** the greater the wrong done to me, the greater seems to grow his desire to do harm. 'Spite' had a stronger meaning in this earlier use. Similarly in l. 11: 'injures', 'hurts'.
5 **a present** an immediate (so too in l. 14)
9 **meat** food
13 **As who should say** as if to say, as if it meant

I care not what, so it be wholesome food.

GRUMIO

What say you to a neat's foot?

KATHERINA

'Tis passing good, I prithee let me have it.

GRUMIO

I fear it is too choleric a meat.
How say you to a fat tripe finely broiled? 20

KATHERINA

I like it well, good Grumio, fetch it me.

GRUMIO

I cannot tell, I fear 'tis choleric.
What say you to a piece of beef and mustard?

KATHERINA

A dish that I do love to feed upon.

GRUMIO

Ay, but the mustard is too hot a little.

KATHERINA

Why then the beef, and let the mustard rest.

GRUMIO

Nay then, I will not: you shall have the mustard,
Or else you get no beef of Grumio.

KATHERINA

Then both, or one, or anything thou wilt.

GRUMIO

Why then the mustard without the beef. 30

KATHERINA

Go, get thee gone, thou false deluding slave (*she beats him*)
That feed'st me with the very name of meat.
Sorrow on thee and all the pack of you
That triumph thus upon my misery!
Go, get thee gone, I say.

16 **so it be** In modern idiom, 'so long as it is'. 'So' meaning 'provided that' (Brook *g* 201, Abbott 133).

17 **neat's** ox's

19 **too choleric** too inclined to promote choler. (This may be Grumio's invention, but choleric people were certainly advised by the medical texts to avoid mustard (ll. 23–5) and the dry or overcooked meat of 4.1.156–63.)

22 **cannot tell** can't be certain

26 **let the mustard rest** do without the mustard (in modern idiom, 'skip the mustard')

32 **very name** mere name, name and nothing else

Enter Petruchio and Hortensio with meat

PETRUCHIO
How fares my Kate? What, sweeting, all amort?

HORTENSIO
Mistress, what cheer?

KATHERINA Faith, as cold as can be.

PETRUCHIO
Pluck up thy spirits, look cheerfully upon me.
Here, love, thou seest how diligent I am,
To dress thy meat myself, and bring it thee. 40
I am sure, sweet Kate, this kindness merits thanks.
What, not a word? Nay then, thou lov'st it not,
And all my pains is sorted to no proof.
Here, take away this dish.

KATHERINA I pray you let it stand.

PETRUCHIO
The poorest service is repaid with thanks,
And so shall mine before you touch the meat.

KATHERINA
I thank you, sir.

HORTENSIO
Signor Petruchio, fie, you are too blame.
Come, Mistress Kate, I'll bear you company.

PETRUCHIO (*aside to Hortensio*)
Eat it up all, Hortensio, if thou lovest me. 50
(*To Katherina*) Much good do it unto thy gentle heart!
Kate, eat apace. And now, my honey love,
Will we return unto thy father's house,

48 too blame] F1; to blame Q1631

36 **sweeting** sweetheart
all amort Originally, as derived directly from French *à la mort*, 'in the state of death'; later, 'spiritless', 'depressed' (and often reduced to 'amort').

37 **what cheer?** how are you? A common greeting, but one that does not expect an answer.

38 **Pluck up thy spirits** As commonplace a phrase as our 'cheer up' (Tilley H323).

40 **dress** prepare

43 **pains** trouble (treated as a general noun and singular)
is sorted to no proof has been contrived to no good effect; has turned out to be futile

48 **too blame** too much at fault. Editors substitute 'to' for F1's 'too' but Shakespeare seems often to have thought of 'blame' as an adjective meaning 'blameworthy'. Compare particularly *Errors*, 4.1.47, in the F1 text (l. 1033) 'And I too blame have held him heere too long' where clearly 'too blame' is a parallel to 'too long'.

51 A common blessing, found again in *Merry Wives*, 1.1.83, and in the form 'much good dich thy good heart' in *Timon*, 1.2.70.

52 **apace** freely, without hesitation (rather than 'with speed')

And revel it as bravely as the best,
With silken coats and caps, and golden rings,
With ruffs and cuffs, and farthingales, and things;
With scarfs and fans, and double change of bravery,
With amber bracelets, beads, and all this knavery.
What, hast thou dined? The tailor stays thy leisure,
To deck thy body with his ruffling treasure. 60

Enter Tailor

Come, tailor, let us see these ornaments.

Enter Haberdasher

Lay forth the gown. – What news with you, sir?

HABERDASHER

Here is the cap your worship did bespeak.

PETRUCHIO

Why, this was moulded on a porringer;
A velvet dish. Fie, fie, 'tis lewd and filthy.
Why, 'tis a cockle or a walnut-shell,
A knack, a toy, a trick, a baby's cap.

61.1] F1; *after 'gown' in l.* 62 DYCE 63 HABERDASHER] ROWE; *Fel.* F1

54 **as bravely** as handsomely dressed (unlike the attire he wore for the wedding)

56 **ruffs** The starched linen or muslin neck-wear, like high collars, fashionable in the Elizabethan period.
cuffs Probably the bands, often of lace, sewn on to the sleeves for ornament.
farthingales The wide petticoats, stretched over cane or whalebone framework, worn by Elizabethan women of the higher classes.

57 **bravery** rich costume, finery

58 **this knavery** The word generally means 'roguish tricks', and *OED* finds no parallel to the apparently different use here. A paraphrase might be 'all these useless frills'. Interestingly, Petruchio begins to speak in rhyme in ll. 55–6 and here and in the following couplet modulates into double rhyme. The effect is of jocular insincerity.

59 **stays** waits on

60 **ruffling** adorned with (too many) ruffles (*OED* 1 : a 'ruffle' is an ornamental strip of lace). The tailor's 'treasures' might be expected to have all the trimmings Petruchio listed in the preceding lines. Schmidt's paraphrase 'rustling' is thus not really correct.

61.1 The haberdasher has begun his entry before Petruchio notices him – or deigns to notice him. Haberdashers were in the sixteenth century makers of, and dealers in, caps; the modern meaning is not found until the seventeenth century.

63 **HABERDASHER** F1's '*Fel*' is as likely to be an abbreviation of 'Fellow' as of an actor's name. See Introduction, p. 6.
cap headgear (caps were not necessarily distinguished from hats and included the head-coverings worn indoors)
bespeak order

64 **porringer** bowl or food-basin (used for porridge and children's food in particular)

65 **A velvet dish** i.e. it is only a dish made of velvet
lewd and filthy vulgar (*OED* 'lewd' 3) or worthless (*OED* 6) and disgusting (*OED* 'filthy' 4) – but Petruchio's use of epithets is, of course, somewhat strained.

66 **a cockle** i.e. like, and no more valuable than, a cockle-shell (the empty shell of the mollusc)

67 **knack** trinket (as in 'knick-knack')
toy trifle. The word was used of anything worthless (*OED sb.* II. 5) and particularly of a valueless small article that was purely ornamental (*OED* 7).
trick Much the same as 'toy' and 'knack': 'mere bauble'.

Away with it; come, let me have a bigger.

KATHERINA

I'll have no bigger, this doth fit the time,
And gentlewomen wear such caps as these. 70

PETRUCHIO

When you are gentle, you shall have one too,
And not till then.

HORTENSIO That will not be in haste.

KATHERINA

Why sir, I trust I may have leave to speak,
And speak I will. I am no child, no babe;
Your betters have endured me say my mind,
And if you cannot, best you stop your ears.
My tongue will tell the anger of my heart,
Or else my heart concealing it will break,
And rather than it shall, I will be free
Even to the uttermost, as I please, in words. 80

PETRUCHIO

Why, thou say'st true, it is a paltry cap,
A custard-coffin, a bauble, a silken pie:
I love thee well in that thou lik'st it not.

KATHERINA

Love me or love me not, I like the cap,
And it I will have, or I will have none.

PETRUCHIO

Thy gown? Why, ay. Come, tailor, let us see't.

⌈*Exit Haberdasher*⌉

81 is a] Q1631; is F1 86 gown?] ROWE 1714; gowne, F1 86.1] *not in* F1; *after l.* 85 CAMBRIDGE

69 **doth fit** is appropriate for; i.e. the cap is fashionable.

72 **HORTENSIO** The line is not necessarily the aside that Hanmer and others have thought it to be: although Hortensio does not normally criticize Katherine to her face, ll. 163–5 show that he is in Petruchio's plot, and he has elsewhere made clear to Katherine his opinion of her. The words are more effective as a spontaneous comment, one he cannot resist.

75 **endured me say** tolerated my saying

82 **custard-coffin** coffin-like crust of pastry in which a custard could be baked. Hardin Craig suggests that there may be a quibble on 'costard', slang for 'head' (actually the name of a large apple).

82 **silken pie** pie made of silk – as previously it was a dish made of velvet. But Petruchio never repeats himself, even if he contradicts himself (and like Whitman is proud of it).

86.1 The haberdasher presumably leaves now, when Petruchio abruptly abandons discussion of the cap and turns to the tailor. (In *A Shrew*, Ferando orders the haberdasher to go, before the tailor enters.) Alternatively, it would do no harm if he remained silent on stage enjoying the tailor's discomfiture. (F1 does provide an exit for the tailor, after l. 165.)

O mercy, God, what masquing stuff is here?
What's this? A sleeve? 'Tis like a demi-cannon.
What, up and down carved like an apple tart?
Here's snip, and nip, and cut, and slish and slash, 90
Like to a censer in a barber's shop.
Why, what a devil's name, tailor, call'st thou this?

HORTENSIO (*aside*)
I see she's like to have neither cap nor gown.

TAILOR
You bid me make it orderly and well,
According to the fashion and the time.

PETRUCHIO
Marry, and did; but if you be remembered,
I did not bid you mar it to the time.
Go, hop me over every kennel home,
For you shall hop without my custom, sir;
I'll none of it. Hence, make your best of it. 100

KATHERINA
I never saw a better-fashioned gown,

88 like a] Q1631; like F1

87 **masquing stuff** material fit only for masques (or, perhaps, masquerades). Some theatrical costumes must have been made then, as now, for appearance, not quality, although others were elaborate and expensive.

88 **demi-cannon** Literally, half-cannon, but still a cumbersome one, of about six and a half inches bore. Artillery was often intricately embellished, and that too is relevant to Petruchio's classification of the sleeve.

89 **up and down . . . tart** The 'slashing' on the sleeve (slits, to reveal brighter fabric beneath) reminds Petruchio of the slits in the pastry on top of apple tarts (still customary, to let the steam escape as the apples cook).

91 **censer** Both here and in the only other line in which the word appears in Shakespeare (*2 Henry IV*, 5.4.20), the precise meaning is uncertain. A 'censer' was the vessel in which incense was burnt, and perhaps the reference is to a carved, fretwork, top.

92 **a devil's name** in the devil's name

94 **bid** bade (a recognized alternative form of the past tense)
orderly in an orderly, not careless, way

96 **and did** i.e. so I did
be remembered remember. This use of 'to be remembered', now archaic, was common in the sixteenth century (*OED* I. 6.c). In comparable circumstances today, 'if I might remind you' would have the same tone.

97 **mar it to the time** Petruchio's antithesis to the tailor's 'make it . . . according to . . . the time'. 'To time' could mean 'for ever' and perhaps 'to the time' has that as a secondary meaning here.

98 **hop me** The 'ethic dative' again: you can hop, so far as I am concerned. A similar use of 'hop' survives in the modern colloquialism 'You can go hopping to hell'. New Cambridge sees a pun in the following line on 'hop' and 'hope'.
kennel street gutter

100 **make your best of it** make the best use you can of it (to get some value from it)

More quaint, more pleasing, nor more commendable.
Belike you mean to make a puppet of me.

PETRUCHIO
Why, true, he means to make a puppet of thee.

TAILOR
She says your worship means to make a puppet of her.

PETRUCHIO
O monstrous arrogance!
Thou liest, thou thread, thou thimble,
Thou yard, three-quarters, half-yard, quarter, nail,
Thou flea, thou nit, thou winter-cricket thou!
Braved in mine own house with a skein of thread? 110
Away, thou rag, thou quantity, thou remnant,
Or I shall so be-mete thee with thy yard
As thou shalt think on prating whilst thou liv'st.
I tell thee, I, that thou hast marred her gown.

TAILOR
Your worship is deceived: the gown is made
Just as my master had direction;
Grumio gave order how it should be done.

106–7] F1 (*subs.*); *as one line* CAPELL

102 **quaint** neat, elegant. Compare *Much Ado*, 3.4.22, 'a fine, quaint, graceful, and excellent fashion'.

103 **Belike** it seems; presumably
puppet i.e. a figure manipulated at will like one in a puppet-show; but 'puppet' was also used as a term of contempt, particularly for a woman (*OED* 1), and Petruchio in l. 104 chooses to take it in that sense and to assume that Katherine was addressing the tailor. The tailor corrects him in l. 105.

106–7 F1 prints thus, as two lines. Printing the two as one line does nothing to improve the versification.

108 **nail** As a measure of length for cloth: a quarter of a quarter of a yard, two and a quarter inches.

109 **nit** (the egg of a) louse
winter-cricket cricket (insect) that appears in the winter

110 **Braved** defied – but with a quibble. One would normally expect to be 'braved' by a tailor in the other sense: 'fitted out', 'decked out'. The pun is explicit in ll. 124–5.
with a skein of thread Continuing the quibble: (i) defied *by* one who is only a skein of thread; (ii) fitted out *with* a mere skein.

111 **rag** Again a quibble: (i) torn-off piece of cloth (ii) worthless rascal, as in *Merry Wives*, 4.2.113 and *Timon*, 4.3.270 (some editors uncomprehendingly emended to 'rogue' in both).
quantity (Apparently) small quantity, mere fragment (*OED* II. 8.b).

112 **be-mete** *OED*, while noting the existence of OE *bemetan*, thinks that the word was probably re-formed by Shakespeare. If so, it was for the sake of the pun on 'mete': (i) measure; (ii) deal out punishment. Noble may be right in seeing also an allusion to Matthew 7:2 'and with what measure ye mete, it shalbe measured to you againe'.
yard (i) the measure, carrying on the insult of l. 108; (ii) yard-stick

113 **think on prating** *Either* 'think hard before you prate (talk idly)' *or* 'you will always remember this prating' – in either case with a pun on 'prat' in the colloquial sense of 'beat about the buttocks', as in *Merry Wives*, 4.2.162.

GRUMIO I gave him no order, I gave him the stuff.

TAILOR
But how did you desire it should be made?

GRUMIO Marry, sir, with needle and thread. 120

TAILOR
But did you not request to have it cut?

GRUMIO Thou hast faced many things.

TAILOR I have.

GRUMIO Face not me. Thou hast braved many men; brave not me: I will neither be faced nor braved. I say unto thee, I bid thy master cut out the gown, but I did not bid him cut it to pieces. Ergo thou liest.

TAILOR Why, here is the note of the fashion to testify.

PETRUCHIO Read it.

GRUMIO The note lies in 's throat if he say I said so. 130

TAILOR (*reads*) 'Inprimis, a loose-bodied gown.'

GRUMIO Master, if ever I said 'loose-bodied gown', sew me in the skirts of it and beat me to death with a bottom of brown thread. I said 'a gown'.

PETRUCHIO (*to the Tailor*) Proceed.

TAILOR 'With a small compassed cape.'

GRUMIO I confess the cape.

TAILOR 'With a trunk sleeve.'

GRUMIO I confess two sleeves.

TAILOR 'The sleeves curiously cut.' 140

131 *reads*] CAPELL (*subs.*); *not in* F1 Inprimis] F1; Imprimis F3

118 **stuff** material

122, 125 **faced** A similar quibble to that on 'braved' in l. 110 and in ll. 124–5: (i) put 'facing' or trimming on a garment; (ii) stood up to, defied.

124 **braved** See note on l. 110. See also Introduction, pp. 14–15, 58–9.

127 **Ergo** Latin for 'therefore'; well known as a term in logic, when drawing a conclusion from premisses.

128 **note of the fashion** document setting out what fashion or style was required – but Grumio in l. 130 must quibble on the meaning 'musical note'.

130 **lies in 's throat** (i) is sounded from his throat (as a musical note) – and is a mere sound; (ii) is a despicable lie (proverbial – Tilley T268 – and frequent in Shakespeare, e.g. *Hamlet*, 2.2.568).

131 **loose-bodied** Apparently with a quibble on 'loose body', meaning harlot (harlots wore loose gowns), for in *A Shrew* the lines appear as: '*Tailor*. Item a loose bodied gowne. | *San*. Maister if ever I said loose bodies gowne . . .'. The joke seems to have been recalled but not the exact words.

133 **bottom** skein or ball (*OED* II. 15)

136 **compassed** cut (on the bias) to form a circle; flared

137 **confess** admit to

138 **trunk sleeve** wide sleeve (perhaps what is now known as a 'bishop sleeve' rather than the 'bell sleeve')

140 **curiously** (i) carefully; (ii) – and this would be the natural meaning in the context – in an elaborate or intricate pattern

PETRUCHIO Ay, there's the villainy.

GRUMIO Error i'th' bill, sir, error i'th' bill! I commanded the sleeves should be cut out, and sewed up again, and that I'll prove upon thee, though thy little finger be armed in a thimble.

TAILOR This is true that I say; an I had thee in place where, thou shouldst know it.

GRUMIO I am for thee straight. Take thou the bill, give me thy mete-yard, and spare not me.

HORTENSIO God-a-mercy, Grumio, then he shall have no odds. 150

PETRUCHIO (*to the Tailor*)
Well sir, in brief, the gown is not for me.

GRUMIO You are i' the right, sir, 'tis for my mistress.

PETRUCHIO
Go, take it up unto thy master's use.

GRUMIO Villain, not for thy life! Take up my mistress' gown for thy master's use?

PETRUCHIO
Why sir, what's your conceit in that?

GRUMIO O sir, the conceit is deeper than you think for. Take up my mistress' gown to his master's use? O fie, fie, fie! 160

PETRUCHIO (*aside*)
Hortensio, say thou wilt see the tailor paid.
(*To the Tailor*) Go take it hence, be gone, and say no
more.

147 where, thou] Q1631; where thou F1 155 mistress'] F1 (Mistresse) 158–60] *as prose* this edition; Oh ... for: | ... vse. | Oh ... F1 159 mistress'] F1 (Mistris)

142 **Error i'th' bill** A semi-legal phrase, using 'bill' now in the sense of legal document. A criminal charge, for instance, would fail if there were a provable error in the formal indictment.

144 **prove upon thee** prove against thee – but with specific reference to trial by combat.

146–7 **in place where** in the 'right' place; where we could indeed fight it out

148 **for thee** ready for you; prepared to oppose you

bill (i) the document (the 'note' of l. 128); (ii) the weapon (a halberd)

149 **mete-yard** measuring stick (the 'yard' of l. 112)

150 **God-a-mercy** A corruption of 'May God have mercy'. Hortensio is deliberately using somewhat inflated language, in mock concern for the tailor.

151 **odds** advantage (and clearly the tailor will have none if he has only a piece of paper with which to fight)

154 **take ... use** pick it up and take it away and let your master cut his losses by making any use of it he can. But Grumio, of course, pretends that 'take up' means 'lift up'.

157 **conceit** (i) meaning; (ii) fanciful notion

HORTENSIO (*aside to the Tailor*)
Tailor, I'll pay thee for thy gown tomorrow;
Take no unkindness of his hasty words.
Away, I say, commend me to thy master. *Exit Tailor*

PETRUCHIO
Well, come my Kate, we will unto your father's,
Even in these honest mean habiliments.
Our purses shall be proud, our garments poor,
For 'tis the mind that makes the body rich;
And as the sun breaks through the darkest clouds, 170
So honour peereth in the meanest habit.
What, is the jay more precious than the lark
Because his feathers are more beautiful?
Or is the adder better than the eel
Because his painted skin contents the eye?
O no, good Kate; neither art thou the worse
For this poor furniture and mean array.
If thou account'st it shame, lay it on me,
And therefore frolic: we will hence forthwith
To feast and sport us at thy father's house. 180
(*To Grumio*) Go call my men, and let us straight to him,
And bring our horses unto Long-lane end;
There will we mount, and thither walk on foot.
Let's see, I think 'tis now some seven o'clock,
And well we may come there by dinner-time.

KATHERINA
I dare assure you, sir, 'tis almost two,

172 What, is] THEOBALD; What is F1; What; is POPE 178 account'st] ROWE (*subs.*); accountedst F1

164 **Take no unkindness of** do not infer any ill feeling (towards yourself) from
hasty angry and ill-considered (*OED* 4)

167 **honest mean habiliments** respectable and unpretentious clothes

168 **proud** a subject for pride (*OED* I. 5) or perhaps 'rich', 'full' – an extension of the senses listed under II.6 and 7. In either case, the word is used as an opposite of 'poor'.

171 **peereth** peeps through

172 **What,** Taken to be an exclamation (and a comma added); but Bond explains it as 'how'.

175 **painted** richly patterned (not 'highly coloured')

177 **furniture** equipment
array attire

178 **lay it on me** attribute it to me, put the blame at my door

179 **frolic** be merry, 'relax'

184 **some seven o'clock** (Presumably) about seven o'clock ('some' being used adverbially, as it still is in a few phrases, such as 'some seven days ago'). Abbott 21.

185 **dinner-time** the time for the main dinner, served at midday or as early as 11 a.m. Compare 2.1.111 and note.

And 'twill be supper-time ere you come there.

PETRUCHIO

It shall be seven ere I go to horse.
Look what I speak, or do, or think to do,
You are still crossing it. Sirs, let't alone, 190
I will not go today; and ere I do,
It shall be what o'clock I say it is.

HORTENSIO (*aside*)

Why, so this gallant will command the sun. *Exeunt*

4.4 *Enter Tranio as Lucentio, and the Pedant, booted but dressed like Vincentio*

TRANIO

Sir, this is the house; please it you that I call?

PEDANT

Ay, what else? And but I be deceived
Signor Baptista may remember me
Near twenty years ago in Genoa,
Where we were lodgers at the Pegasus. 5

TRANIO

'Tis well, and hold your own in any case

193 *Exeunt*] *not in* F1

4.4.0.1] This edition; *Enter Tranio, and the Pedant drest like Vincentio.* F1; *Act V Sc. IV Enter...* HANMER 1 Sir] THEOBALD; Sirs F1 5] *continued to Pedant* THEOBALD; *Tra.* Where ... F1

187 **supper-time** time for the late afternoon or evening meal, about 6 p.m.

189 **Look what** 'Look' seems to be used, in such constructions, as a kind of intensifier (and some editors put a comma after it). 'No matter what'.

190 **still** always, constantly

crossing contradicting *or* doing the opposite to

191 **ere I do** i.e. before I go at all. Capell, unnecessarily, emended 'and' to 'or'.

193 **so** at this rate (and Petruchio does 'command the sun', in a sense, in 4.5.7)

4.4 The fact that nothing whatever comes of the fear that Baptista may remember having met the Pedant; the strange F1 stage direction at l. 18.1, which seems to imply that the Pedant has not previously been on the stage in this 'scene'; and the repetition by F of the speech prefix '*Tra.*' before l. 19 – all make one wonder whether ll. 1–18 may not have been a false start. (The theory that they are an afterthought may not explain the first of these peculiarities; but see note on l. 6.) Crossings-out in the manuscript, leading to misalignment, may account for the misattribution in F of l. 5 to Tranio.

0.1–2 This is a combination of F1's opening stage direction with part of that at l. 18.1 (l. 2200).

0.1 ***booted*** in his travelling boots, not in socially appropriate footwear

1 **please it you** is it your pleasure that? This is the impersonal use of 'please', and it is followed by the subjunctive ('call').

2 **but** unless (followed by the subjunctive verb, 'be'). Abbott 120.

4 **Near** nearly

5 **Pegasus** i.e. at an inn with the sign of Pegasus (the famous winged horse of classical mythology). Shakespeare's foreign towns tend to have inns with popular English inn-signs, notably 'the Elephant' in *Twelfth Night*, 3.3.39 and 'the Centaur' in *Errors*, 2.2.2.

6 **'Tis well** (Presumably) 'well thought of', 'a good point'; but Bond suggested that the Pedant's preceding lines were a

With such austerity as 'longeth to a father.
Enter Biondello

PEDANT
I warrant you. But sir, here comes your boy.
'Twere good he were schooled.

TRANIO
Fear you not him. – Sirrah Biondello, 10
Now do your duty throughly, I advise you.
Imagine 'twere the right Vincentio.

BIONDELLO
Tut, fear not me.

TRANIO
But hast thou done thy errand to Baptista?

BIONDELLO
I told him that your father was at Venice,
And that you looked for him this day in Padua.

TRANIO
Thou'rt a tall fellow, hold thee that to drink.
⌈*He gives Biondello money*⌉
(*To the Pedant*) Here comes Baptista. Set your
countenance, sir.
Enter Baptista, and Lucentio as Cambio. The Pedant stands bare-headed
– Signor Baptista, you are happily met.
– Sir, this is the gentleman I told you of. 20

17.1] *not in* F1 18.1–2] This edition; *Enter Baptista and Lucentio: Pedant booted and bare headed.* F1 19 Signor] F1 (*Tra.* Signior)

feigned reminiscence, to show how skilfully he could assume the character of Vincentio, and if that is so, Tranio is congratulating him on his acting – and could even speak l. 5, as in F1, as an embellishment of the Pedant's story.
hold your own play your (own) part as well as you can

7 **austerity** judicial severity or, perhaps, gravity (*OED* 2 and compare *OED* 'austere' *a.* 5)
'longeth belongeth; is natural or appropriate (as in 4.2.45)

8 **warrant you** promise you that; guarantee it

9 **schooled** given his instructions, taught what he has to do (as a horse is still 'schooled')

10 **Fear you not him** don't be perturbed or dubious about him (i.e. he can be relied on). Similarly in l. 13.

11 **throughly** fully, perfectly ('thorough' in comparable contexts is only a variant of 'through')
advise With a rather stronger sense than today's: 'warn', 'tell you for your own good'.

16 **looked for** expected (as in 4.2.117)

17 **tall** worthy (again with the normal ironic tinge). Compare 4.1.9 and note.
hold thee that take that for yourself

18 **Set your countenance** i.e. put on the expression of gravity (the 'austerity' that ''longeth to a father' of l. 7).

18.2 ***bare-headed*** As a sign of respect to Baptista.

I pray you stand good father to me now,
Give me Bianca for my patrimony.

PEDANT

Soft, son! – Sir, by your leave: having come to Padua
To gather in some debts, my son Lucentio
Made me acquainted with a weighty cause
Of love between your daughter and himself;
And for the good report I hear of you,
And for the love he beareth to your daughter,
And she to him, to stay him not too long,
I am content, in a good father's care, 30
To have him matched; and, if you please to like
No worse than I, upon some agreement
Me shall you find ready and willing
With one consent to have her so bestowed;
For curious I cannot be with you,
Signor Baptista, of whom I hear so well.

BAPTISTA

Sir, pardon me in what I have to say,
Your plainness and your shortness please me well.
Right true it is your son Lucentio here
Doth love my daughter, and she loveth him, 40
Or both dissemble deeply their affections,
And therefore if you say no more than this,
That like a father you will deal with him,
And pass my daughter a sufficient dower,

23] *as one line* F1; Soft, son. | Sir ... HANMER 33 ready and willing] F1; most ready and most willing F2

21 **stand** prove yourself to be

23 **Soft** steady! The opening two words of the line, as a kind of exclamatory term of address, are regarded as 'extra-metrical', as are such phrases as 'my lord'.
having come Strictly, the participle is unattached; but as in everyday speech still, the first person 'I' to which it relates is taken to be implied by the 'my' of 'my son'.

25 **weighty cause** important matter

27, 28 **for** because of

29 **stay** delay

31 **like** approve (of the match)

32–3 The metre limps rather badly in these two lines. Perhaps 'agreement' was stressed on the first syllable; or conceivably l. 32 should read 'then upon some agreement', 'then' having been omitted by haplography (F1 spells 'No worse then I' in the first half of the line). It seems, however, – and ll. 23–4 may be relevant here too – that Shakespeare wishes to give the impression that the Pedant is stumbling along, playing his part with difficulty.

34 **With one consent** in unanimity

35 **curious** The word has sometimes a vaguely pejorative sense (as in one modern meaning, 'over-inquisitive') and seems to be equivalent here to 'over-careful', 'too demanding', 'pernickety'.

44 **pass** grant to, formally settle on
dower See 2.1.344–5 and note.

The match is made, and all is done;
Your son shall have my daughter with consent.

TRANIO

I thank you, sir. Where then do you know best
We be affied and such assurance ta'en
As shall with either part's agreement stand?

BAPTISTA

Not in my house, Lucentio, for you know 50
Pitchers have ears, and I have many servants.
Besides, old Gremio is hearkening still,
And happily we might be interrupted.

TRANIO

Then at my lodging, an it like you.
There doth my father lie; and there this night
We'll pass the business privately and well.
Send for your daughter by your servant here;
My boy shall fetch the scrivener presently.
The worst is this, that at so slender warning
You are like to have a thin and slender pittance. 60

BAPTISTA

It likes me well. Cambio, hie you home,
And bid Bianca make her ready straight;
And, if you will, tell what hath happened:
Lucentio's father is arrived in Padua,

61–2 It . . . home, | And . . . straight;] POPE; It . . . well: | *Cambio* . . . straight: | F1 63 will, tell] ROWE; will tell F1

45 Another 'short' line. Perhaps the four heavy stresses, and the monosyllables, are intended to give the effect of emphasis and conclusiveness.

48 **be** The subjunctive: 'may be'.
affied formally betrothed

48–9 **such . . . stand** and such legal guarantees be given as are consistent with what the two parties involved have now agreed on

51 **Pitchers have ears** Proverbial (still): Tilley P363 ('Small pitchers have wide ears'). Originally there was a pun on the 'ears' (handles) of the jar, but not all who use the proverb are aware of it.

52 **hearkening still** always eavesdropping

53 **happily** haply, perhaps. Compare Induction 1.133 and 1.1.8 and notes.

55 **lie** lodge, stay

56 **pass** transact

57 **your servant** i.e. the supposed Cambio, the hired tutor. Perhaps – in accordance with l. 74 – Tranio should wink at Lucentio here (although one is not told how the audience could be sure to see it).

58 **My boy** Biondello
scrivener notary (one authorized to draw up legal contracts) rather than merely 'professional scribe'
presently immediately

60 **pittance** allowance of food and drink; 'rations' (*OED* 2)

61 **It likes me** The impersonal use of 'like' (Abbott 297).

62 **make her** make herself

And how she's like to be Lucentio's wife.

BIONDELLO

I pray the gods she may, with all my heart.

⌈*Exit Lucentio*⌉

TRANIO

Dally not with the gods, but get thee gone.
– Signor Baptista, shall I lead the way?
Welcome! One mess is like to be your cheer.
Come sir, we will better it in Pisa. 70

BAPTISTA

I follow you. ⌈*Exeunt all except Biondello*⌉

Enter Lucentio as Cambio

BIONDELLO Cambio.

LUCENTIO What say'st thou, Biondello?

BIONDELLO You saw my master wink and laugh upon you?

LUCENTIO Biondello, what of that?

BIONDELLO Faith, nothing; but h'as left me here behind to expound the meaning or moral of his signs and tokens.

LUCENTIO I pray thee moralize them.

65] *'Exit Lucentio' added by* BOND (*conj.* NICHOLSON) 66 BIONDELLO] F1; *Lucentio* ROWE 66.1 *Exit Lucentio*] F1 (*Exit*); *om.* MALONE (*conj.* TYRWHITT); *Lucentio retires (after l.* 68) DYCE 1866 67] *'Exit Biondello' added by* CAMBRIDGE 67.1] F1 *has S.D. 'Enter Peter'* 71 *Exeunt ... Biondello*] F1 (*Exeunt*) 71.1] F1 (*Enter Lucentio and Biondello*); *Re-enter Biondello* CAMBRIDGE 72 Cambio.] F1; *Cambio,* – (*calling* Lucentio *back*) – CAPELL 77 h'as] HANMER; has F1; 'has ROWE; ha's THEOBALD

65–72 There is some difference of opinion on what exactly happens here. F1 gives l. 66 to Biondello, followed by an 'Exit'. Rowe and many later editors give the line to Lucentio (Cambio) and believe that it is he who then goes off, temporarily, in obedience to Baptista's command (ll. 61–2). They are probably wrong on the first point, for there is other evidence that it is Biondello who speaks the line, in that Tranio, in his rejoinder to it, picks up 'I pray the gods' with his 'Dally not with the gods' and orders the speaker of l. 66 to be gone – an instruction appropriate for his own supposed servant, Biondello, but not for Baptista's, Cambio. Probably it is 'Cambio' who leaves the stage (and whether after l. 65 or l. 66 hardly matters); and F's '*Enter Lucentio and Biondello*' at 71.1 (l. 2258) may be taken to mean no more than that Lucentio there rejoins Biondello. F's stage direction '*Enter Peter*' after l. 67 (l. 2253), however, remains a mystery. It is omitted in this edition on the reasoning that it is a false start for the re-entry of Lucentio a few lines later. (Bond suggested that a servant enters and whispers to Tranio that a meal is ready; New Cambridge that 'Peter' is an actor's name.) Biondello need not leave the stage at all (but may well stand aside); he explains to Lucentio in ll. 77–8 why he has stayed behind.

69 **mess** serving or portion of food; course (*OED sb.* I. 1)

your cheer the hospitality you will receive

70 **in Pisa** i.e. when you visit me in my real home, in Pisa

79 **moralize them** interpret them, 'draw the moral' from them

BIONDELLO Then thus: Baptista is safe talking with the deceiving father of a deceitful son. 80

LUCENTIO And what of him?

BIONDELLO His daughter is to be brought by you to the supper.

LUCENTIO And then?

BIONDELLO The old priest at Saint Luke's church is at your command at all hours.

LUCENTIO And what of all this?

BIONDELLO I cannot tell, except they are busied about a counterfeit assurance. Take you assurance of her, *cum* 90 *previlegio ad impremendum solem*. To th' church take the priest, clerk, and some sufficient honest witnesses. If this be not that you look for, I have no more to say, but bid Bianca farewell for ever and a day. (*Going*)

LUCENTIO Hear'st thou, Biondello –

BIONDELLO I cannot tarry. I knew a wench married in an afternoon as she went to the garden for parsley to stuff a rabbit; and so may you, sir; and so adieu, sir. My master hath appointed me to go to Saint Luke's to bid the priest be ready to come against you come with your 100 appendix. *Exit*

89 except] F2; expect F1 90–1 *cum ... solem*] F1; *Cum privilegio ad Imprimendum solum* F2 91 church take] F1; church; take REED (*conj.* TYRWHITT); church! – take COLLIER 92–4 If ... day] *as prose* WARBURTON; If ... say, | But ... day. | F1 94 *Going*] *not in* F1 100 to come against] F1; against KEIGHTLEY

80 **safe** i.e. out of the way, safely taken care of

89 **except** *Either* 'except that' (*OED conj.* 1) *or* 'unless' (*OED* 2).

90 **counterfeit assurance** legal contract that will be invalid (because one of the parties to it – the Pedant – is not the person he claims to be)

Take you assurance of her make legal your claim to her (by marrying her)

90–1 ***cum ... solem*** Again Biondello's Latin is less than perfect. The phrase *cum privilegio ad imprimendum solum*, meaning 'with the right for printing, only' became the Elizabethan printer's regular formula for 'with the sole right [i.e. monopoly] to print'. The bridegroom's right to the bride is similarly to be a monopoly. Some editors have seen a pun on 'printing' in the sense of 'stamping one's own image on a woman by getting her with child' but an audience would need to be alert to detect it.

92 **sufficient** adequate (in number) or competent for legal purposes

94 **for ever and a day** The phrase was already standard (Tilley D74).

95 Lucentio presumably begins an instruction to Biondello but is not allowed to finish it.

100 **against you come** no later than, and in anticipation of, your coming

101 **appendix** appendage, adjunct (i.e. wife). The word was sometimes used of a person but Biondello is carrying on the witticism of his earlier lines 90–1.

LUCENTIO

I may and will, if she be so contented.
She will be pleased, then wherefore should I doubt?
Hap what hap may, I'll roundly go about her;
It shall go hard if Cambio go without her.

Exit

4.5 *Enter Petruchio, Katherina, and Hortensio*

PETRUCHIO

Come on, a God's name, once more toward our father's.
Good Lord, how bright and goodly shines the moon!

KATHERINA

The moon? The sun; it is not moonlight now.

PETRUCHIO

I say it is the moon that shines so bright.

KATHERINA

I know it is the sun that shines so bright.

PETRUCHIO

Now by my mother's son, and that's myself,
It shall be moon, or star, or what I list,
Or e'er I journey to your father's house.
(*To Hortensio*) Go on and fetch our horses back again.
– Evermore crossed and crossed, nothing but crossed! 10

HORTENSIO (*to Katherina*)

Say as he says, or we shall never go.

KATHERINA

Forward, I pray, since we have come so far,
And be it moon, or sun, or what you please;

4.5.0.1 *Enter … Hortensio*] F1; *Act IV Sc. V Enter …* STEEVENS

104 **Hap what hap may** Proverbial (Tilley C529).
roundly go about her demand her answer, without hesitation or indecisiveness. For 'roundly', compare 1.2.58, 3.2.216 and note.

105 **It shall go hard** i.e. it will not be for lack of trying

4.5 Petruchio, Katherine, and Hortensio have obviously set out to walk to 'Long-lane end' as Petruchio planned at 4.3.182–3. The horses and servants await them there, but at l. 9 Petruchio threatens to have the horses taken back to the house. There is no need to import servants into this scene; see note on l. 9.

1 **our father's** i.e. Baptista's house, in Padua

2 **goodly** beautifully

7 **list** please. Compare 3.2.164 and note.

8 **Or e'er I journey** before ever I'll consider making the journey

9 It may be argued that such an instruction could be issued only to servants (who are therefore brought on the stage by most editors, although F1 sees no need for them). In the context, since the threat is not serious anyway, the words are appropriately addressed to Hortensio.

And if you please to call it a rush-candle,
Henceforth I vow it shall be so for me.

PETRUCHIO
I say it is the moon.

KATHERINA I know it is the moon.

PETRUCHIO
Nay, then you lie. It is the blessèd sun.

KATHERINA
Then, God be blessed, it is the blessèd sun,
But sun it is not, when you say it is not,
And the moon changes even as your mind: 20
What you will have it named, even that it is,
And so it shall be so for Katherine.

HORTENSIO
Petruchio, go thy ways, the field is won.

PETRUCHIO
Well, forward, forward, thus the bowl should run,
And not unluckily against the bias.
But soft, company is coming here.
Enter Vincentio
(*To Vincentio*) Good morrow, gentle mistress, where away?
– Tell me, sweet Kate, and tell me truly too,
Hast thou beheld a fresher gentlewoman?
Such war of white and red within her cheeks! 30
What stars do spangle heaven with such beauty
As those two eyes become that heavenly face?

18 is] Q1631; in F1   22 be so] F1; be, so, ROWE; be, so BOND   23] F1 (*subs.*); *as aside* CAPELL

14 **rush-candle** a candle (not of good quality) 'made by dipping the pith of a rush in tallow or other grease' (*OED*)

20 **moon . . . mind** Katherine also implies that his mind changes as often as the moon traditionally changed (Tilley M1111) and that he is insane (the very word 'lunatic' derives from the old belief that the moon caused madness).

23 **go thy ways** (well done and) carry on

25 **unluckily against the bias** unnaturally against the bias instead of with it (the bias being the weighting of one side of the bowl that causes the bowl to swerve back to that side)

27 **where away?** where are you going?

29 **fresher** more blooming, looking more radiantly youthful (*OED adj.* II.9.b). Baldwin has suggested (ii. 274) that the choice of opposite epithets throughout this exchange (e.g. 'fresher' and 'budding' versus 'reverend') may have begun from schoolboy memories of Erasmus's *Libellus de conscribendis epistolis*.

30 **war** contest. The thought is commonplace, unless, as Bond suggests, Shakespeare intends a metaphorical reference to the Wars of the Roses.

32 **become** suit (in the sense of 'look well in', 'are becoming in'). Again the sentiment is a commonplace, though with slightly more meaning than it would have today: the eyes had in the human frame or microcosm the place corresponding to that of the 'heavenly' stars in the universe or macrocosm.

– Fair lovely maid, once more good day to thee.
– Sweet Kate, embrace her for her beauty's sake.

HORTENSIO (*aside*) A will make the man mad, to make the woman of him.

KATHERINA
Young budding virgin, fair, and fresh, and sweet,
Whither away, or where is thy abode?
Happy the parents of so fair a child;
Happier the man whom favourable stars 40
Allots thee for his lovely bedfellow.

PETRUCHIO
Why, how now, Kate, I hope thou art not mad:
This is a man, old, wrinkled, faded, withered,
And not a maiden, as thou say'st he is.

KATHERINA
Pardon, old father, my mistaking eyes
That have been so bedazzled with the sun
That everything I look on seemeth green.
Now I perceive thou art a reverend father;
Pardon, I pray thee, for my mad mistaking.

PETRUCHIO
Do, good old grandsire, and withal make known 50
Which way thou travellest; if along with us,
We shall be joyful of thy company.

35–6 the woman] F1; a woman F2 38 Whither] F1 (Whether) where] F2; whether F1

35 **A** A common colloquial and unemphatic form of 'he'.

35–6 **the woman** Conceivably, as Hibbard suggests, Shakespeare means 'make him play the part of a woman *as on the stage*' but such interpretation is not essential. In any case emendation is unnecessary.

37 **budding** blooming

38 **where** F2's emendation is accepted; F1's 'whether' may be explained either as dittography (F1 spells 'Whither' at the beginning of the line as 'Whether') or as a misunderstanding ('where' was also a spelling of the clipped form of 'whether' now sometimes represented as 'whe'er').

40 **whom** to whom. The thought of ll. 39–41 would seem to be commonplace, but Steevens cites a probable direct source in Golding's translation of Ovid's *Metamorphoses* (IV. 392–7). The point of the allusion – though it would be too subtle for even an Elizabethan audience, surely – may be the reversal of the roles: Golding's Ovid writes 'far more blist than these is shee | Whome thou vouchsafest for thy wife and bedfellow for too bee'.

41 **Allots** Another instance of the 'plural in "s"'.

47 **green** A quibble on the two senses (i) the colour; (ii) immature, young.

48 **reverend** to be revered, worthy of reverence. So too in l. 60. 'Reverent' and 'reverend', as Onions and *OED* certify, were not clearly distinguished at the time and probably only the preferences of different compositors explain why 'reverent' is twice found in this scene where modern usage would demand 'reverend'; and 'reverend' is used at 4.1.191 where the meaning is 'reverent'.

VINCENTIO
Fair sir, and you my merry mistress,
That with your strange encounter much amazed me,
My name is called Vincentio, my dwelling Pisa,
And bound I am to Padua, there to visit
A son of mine, which long I have not seen.

PETRUCHIO
What is his name?

VINCENTIO Lucentio, gentle sir.

PETRUCHIO
Happily met, the happier for thy son.
And now by law, as well as reverend age, 60
I may entitle thee my loving father.
The sister to my wife, this gentlewoman,
Thy son by this hath married. Wonder not,
Nor be not grieved: she is of good esteem,
Her dowry wealthy, and of worthy birth;
Beside, so qualified as may beseem
The spouse of any noble gentleman.
Let me embrace with old Vincentio,
And wander we to see thy honest son,
Who will of thy arrival be full joyous. 70

VINCENTIO
But is this true, or is it else your pleasure,
Like pleasant travellers, to break a jest
Upon the company you overtake?

HORTENSIO
I do assure thee, father, so it is.

54 **encounter** salutation, greeting

55 **My ... Vincentio** For the old-fashioned idiom, see 2.1.67 and note.

62–3 So far as the text of the play goes, Petruchio does not know that Lucentio has already ('by this') married Bianca, and in fact Lucentio has not yet married her; and Hortensio who confirms Petruchio's assertion (l. 74), ought to assume that Lucentio would never become her husband: Tranio, whom he supposes to be Lucentio, forswore her in Hortensio's presence, at 4.2.32–3. Perhaps Shakespeare was simply careless; but this is part of the cumulative evidence that Hortensio's role was different in some earlier version of the play. See Introduction, pp. 10–13. (In *A Shrew* Ferando–Petruchio similarly somehow knows of the impending marriages of Katherine's sisters and says he has promised them that she will 'be there'.)

64 **esteem** reputation, standing

66 **so qualified** with such (good) qualities
beseem befit, be commendable in

69 **wander** Perhaps merely 'travel', 'go' (which would not be unique in Shakespeare's uses of the word) but more probably with some sense of 'deviate' (*OED v. intr.* I. 3): Vincentio's plans are being altered by the news of his son's wedding.

70 **of** with, at

72 **pleasant** fun-seeking, light-hearted

72–3 **break a jest | Upon** play a practical joke on

PETRUCHIO
Come, go along and see the truth hereof, 75
For our first merriment hath made thee jealous.
Exeunt all but Hortensio

HORTENSIO
Well, Petruchio, this has put me in heart.
Have to my widow, and if she be froward,
Then hast thou taught Hortensio untoward. *Exit*

5.1 *Gremio enters alone and stands aside. Then enter Biondello, Lucentio (no longer in disguise), and Bianca*

BIONDELLO Softly and swiftly, sir, for the priest is ready.
LUCENTIO I fly, Biondello; but they may chance to need thee at home, therefore leave us. *Exeunt Lucentio and Bianca*
BIONDELLO Nay, faith, I'll see the church a' your back, and then come back to my master's as soon as I can. *Exit* 5

GREMIO
I marvel Cambio comes not all this while.
Enter Petruchio, Katherina, Vincentio, and Grumio, with attendants

PETRUCHIO
Sir, here's the door, this is Lucentio's house.

76.1] F1 (*Exeunt*) 78 she be] F2; she F1 79 untoward] This edition; to be vntoward F1
5.1.0.1–2] F1 (*Enter Biondello, Lucentio and Bianca, Gremio is out before*); *Act V ... Enter ...* THEOBALD 3 *Exeunt ... Bianca*] F1 (*Exit*); *after l.* 5 ROWE 4 a'] F1 (a); o' ROWE 1714
5 master's] CAPELL; mistris F1; Master THEOBALD 5 *Exit*] *not in* F1

76 **merriment** Carrying on the idea of l. 72: 'practical joking'.
jealous suspicious, mistrustful (*OED* 5 a, b)

77 **put me in heart** given me courage

78 **Have to** forward to; now for
froward perverse, unreasonable.

79 F1's 'to be' in this line seems superfluous, metrically and otherwise; and 'be' must be added to F's version of the preceding line to make sense. Presumably an interlineation or marginal addition of 'be' was misunderstood and the word introduced to the wrong one of two lines. 'Untoward' is taken to be an adverb and to mean 'unluckily' (*OED* 3): Petruchio's demonstration to Hortensio of how to tame a wife has come at a most unlucky time for any widow who proposes to be 'froward'.

5.1.0.1 F1's '*Gremio is out before*' has the look of an author's stage direction. Gremio, always suspicious but never quick-witted enough to see the full truth, fails to recognize Lucentio now that he is no longer disguised as Cambio and so is once again left lamenting (ll. 127–8).

4 **a' your back** Presumably, at your back; i.e. I'll see you enter the church (so that the door is at your back). 'On your back' hardly makes sense (although Lacey, in his adaptation *Sauny the Scot*, has Jamy (corresponding to Biondello) say 'I have seen the Church on their Back', and Lacey normally alters what is obscure). The phrase seems to be used for the sake of the purely verbal quibble on 'back' in the following line.

5 **master's** Both here and in l. 47, an abbreviation for 'master's' has apparently been misunderstood by the F1 compositor as an intended abbreviation for 'mistress's' (or perhaps, here, 'mistress').

My father's bears more toward the market-place;
Thither must I, and here I leave you, sir.

VINCENTIO
You shall not choose but drink before you go. 10
I think I shall command your welcome here,
And by all likelihood some cheer is toward.

He knocks

GREMIO They're busy within, you were best knock louder.

Pedant looks out of the window

PEDANT What's he that knocks as he would beat down the gate?

VINCENTIO Is Signor Lucentio within, sir?

PEDANT He's within, sir, but not to be spoken withal.

VINCENTIO What if a man bring him a hundred pound or two to make merry withal?

PEDANT Keep your hundred pounds to yourself, he shall need none so long as I live. 20

PETRUCHIO (*to Vincentio*) Nay, I told you your son was well beloved in Padua. – Do you hear, sir? To leave frivolous circumstances, I pray you tell Signor Lucentio that his father is come from Pisa and is here at the door to speak with him.

PEDANT Thou liest. His father is come from Padua and here looking out at the window.

VINCENTIO Art thou his father?

PEDANT Ay sir, so his mother says, if I may believe her. 30

PETRUCHIO (*to Vincentio*) Why how now, gentleman! Why,

27 from Padua] F1; to Padua POPE; from – Mantua (*as aside*) CAPELL; from Pisa MALONE (*conj.* TYRWHITT); from Mantua HALLIWELL (*conj.* MALONE) here] F1; is here KNIGHT (*conj.* LETTSOM)

8 **bears more toward** is rather in the direction of; is closer to

11 **your welcome** hospitality for you

12 **cheer is toward** good 'entertainment' (food and drink) is in preparation, will be forthcoming

13.1 F1's 'out of the window' does not presuppose any elaborate staging or even the imitation of a house front. Any 'upper stage' area would serve, as for Brabantio's comparable exchange with Roderigo in the opening minutes of *Othello*. Bond thought that use of the upper stage here would make it even less likely that Sly and other 'presenters' remained there during the whole play.

23–4 **To . . . circumstances** to abandon pointless detail, to get down to what matters

27 **from Padua** Perhaps not the best of jokes but editors are not entitled to improve Shakespeare by introducing 'a much better jest' or 'a much better comic effect' (e.g. by making the Pedant give himself away by naming Mantua). The Pedant is not obliged to tell Vincentio anything, and 'Padua' will serve: he has 'come from' where he is and has been for a while.

30 Another standard – and weak – joke (see, e.g., Tilley M1193).

this is flat knavery, to take upon you another man's name.

PEDANT Lay hands on the villain: I believe a means to cozen somebody in this city under my countenance.

Enter Biondello

BIONDELLO (*aside*) I have seen them in the church together. God send 'em good shipping! But who is here? Mine old master Vincentio? Now we are undone and brought to nothing.

VINCENTIO Come hither, crack-hemp. 40

BIONDELLO I hope I may choose, sir.

VINCENTIO Come hither, you rogue. What, have you forgot me?

BIONDELLO Forgot you? No, sir. I could not forget you, for I never saw you before in all my life.

VINCENTIO What, you notorious villain, didst thou never see thy master's father, Vincentio?

BIONDELLO What, my old worshipful old master? Yes, marry, sir, see where he looks out of the window.

VINCENTIO Is't so, indeed? 50

He beats Biondello

BIONDELLO Help, help, help! Here's a madman will murder me. *Exit*

PEDANT Help, son! Help, Signor Baptista! (*He leaves the window*)

PETRUCHIO Prithee, Kate, let's stand aside and see the end of this controversy.

Enter Pedant from the house, with Servants; Baptista, and Tranio as Lucentio

TRANIO Sir, what are you that offer to beat my servant?

VINCENTIO What am I, sir? Nay, what are you, sir? O im-

47 master's] F2 (*subs.*); Mistris F1 48 old worshipful old] F1; worshipful old Q1631 52 *Exit*] *not in* F1 53 *He leaves the window*] *not in* F1; *Exit, from above* CAPELL 55.1–2] F1 (*Enter Pedant with seruants, Baptista, Tranio*)

32 **flat** downright; 'sheer'

34 **cozen** cheat

35 **under my countenance** by taking my name (and relying on my good reputation)

37 **good shipping** happy journeying (the equivalent of our 'bon voyage') or, simply, 'good luck' (*OED* 'shipping' 3. b.)

40 **crack-hemp** rogue fit only for hanging; one who would stretch the rope on the gallows

41 **choose** make my own decision, on which way I proceed, whether I come or go

46 **notorious** manifest; remarkable (a common Shakespearian usage)

56 **offer** presume

mortal gods! O fine villain! A silken doublet, a velvet hose,
a scarlet cloak, and a copatain hat! O, I am undone, I am
undone: while I play the good husband at home, my son 60
and my servant spend all at the university.

TRANIO How now, what's the matter?

BAPTISTA What, is the man lunatic?

TRANIO Sir, you seem a sober ancient gentleman by your habit, but your words show you a madman. Why, sir, what 'cerns it you if I wear pearl and gold? I thank my good father, I am able to maintain it.

VINCENTIO Thy father? O villain, he is a sail-maker in Bergamo.

BAPTISTA You mistake, sir, you mistake, sir. Pray, what 70
do you think is his name?

VINCENTIO His name? As if I knew not his name! I have brought him up ever since he was three years old, and his name is Tranio.

PEDANT Away, away, mad ass, his name is Lucentio, and he is mine only son, and heir to the lands of me, Signor Vincentio.

VINCENTIO Lucentio? O, he hath murdered his master! Lay hold on him, I charge you, in the Duke's name. O, my
son, my son! Tell me, thou villain, where is my son 80
Lucentio?

TRANIO Call forth an officer.

Enter an Officer

Carry this mad knave to the jail. Father Baptista, I charge

82.1] *not in* F1; *Enter One with an* Officer. CAPELL; *Exit Servant, who returns with an Officer.* RIVERSIDE (*adapting* DYCE)

58 **fine** elegant, expensively dressed
hose (pair of) breeches. 'Doublet and hose' was the normal Elizabethan dress for men.

59 **copatain** *OED* takes this to be a variant of 'copintank', and to mean a kind of high-crowned hat, sometimes pointed, sometimes flat or rounded, commonly worn in Shakespeare's day (the 'sugar-loaf hat').

60 **husband** A quibble, the second meaning being that of one who 'husbands', economizes, saves money.

66 **what 'cerns it you** in what way does it concern you; it is none of your business.

67 **maintain** afford

68–9 **Bergamo** Bergamo is not a sea-port. Perhaps Shakespeare's geography is at fault (but compare 1.1.42 and note); or perhaps 'a sailmaker in Bergamo' is a stock joke, like the Swiss navy or Wigan Pier. Alternatively, Bergamo may be an appropriate birthplace for a Tranio *either* because, as Hibbard suggests, it was the traditional home of Harlequin, the intriguing clown of Italian farce, *or* because, as Coryate tells us in his *Crudities* (1611), its language was 'esteemed the rudest and grossest of all Italy' (p.349).

you see that he be forthcoming.

VINCENTIO Carry me to the jail?

GREMIO Stay, officer, he shall not go to prison.

BAPTISTA Talk not, Signor Gremio; I say he shall go to prison.

GREMIO Take heed, Signor Baptista, lest you be cony-catched in this business. I dare swear this is the right Vincentio. 90

PEDANT Swear if thou dar'st.

GREMIO Nay, I dare not swear it.

TRANIO Then thou wert best say that I am not Lucentio.

GREMIO Yes, I know thee to be Signor Lucentio.

BAPTISTA Away with the dotard, to the jail with him!

Enter Biondello, Lucentio, and Bianca

VINCENTIO Thus strangers may be haled and abused. O monstrous villain!

BIONDELLO O, we are spoiled, and yonder he is! Deny him, forswear him, or else we are all undone. 100

Exeunt Biondello, Tranio, and Pedant, as fast as may be

LUCENTIO (*kneeling*)
Pardon, sweet father.

VINCENTIO Lives my sweet son?

BIANCA
Pardon, dear father.

BAPTISTA How hast thou offended?
Where is Lucentio?

LUCENTIO Here's Lucentio,
Right son to the right Vincentio,
That have by marriage made thy daughter mine,

96.1] F1 (*subs.*); *Enter* Lucentio *and* Bianca ROWE; *after l.* 98 CAPELL 100.1] F1 (*subs.*); *after l.* 101 CAPELL 102–3 How ... offended? | Where is Lucentio?] CAPELL (*subs.*); *one line* F1 103–4 Here's Lucentio, | Right ... Vincentio,] CAPELL; *one line* F1

84 **forthcoming** Generally explained as 'ready to be produced (for trial) when required' but it is not clear why this should be Baptista's responsibility.

89–90 **cony-catched** made a 'bunny', victimised, by a confidence trick (as in 4.1.38)

96 **dotard** imbecile (cf. 'in his dotage')

96.1 Again the placing of the stage direction in F1 ensures that the audience, seeing the approach of Biondello and the others before the characters already on stage see them, enjoys the joke first.

97 **haled** dragged around
abused wronged, treated shamefully

99 **spoiled** ruined, undone

100.1 ***as fast as may be*** The phrase occurs also in a stage direction in *Errors*, 4.4.144.1; compare also, in the 'Bad Quarto' of *Romeo*, '*Enter Juliet somewhat fast, and embraceth Romeo*' (10.10). For Sly's intervention at this point in *A Shrew*, see Introduction p. 2.

While counterfeit supposes bleared thine eyne.

GREMIO Here's packing, with a witness, to deceive us all!

VINCENTIO

Where is that damned villain, Tranio,

That faced and braved me in this matter so?

BAPTISTA

Why, tell me, is not this my Cambio? 110

BIANCA

Cambio is changed into Lucentio.

LUCENTIO

Love wrought these miracles. Bianca's love

Made me exchange my state with Tranio,

While he did bear my countenance in the town,

And happily I have arrived at the last

Unto the wished haven of my bliss.

What Tranio did, myself enforced him to;

Then pardon him, sweet father, for my sake.

VINCENTIO I'll slit the villain's nose that would have sent me to the jail. 120

BAPTISTA (*to Lucentio*) But do you hear, sir, have you married my daughter without asking my good will?

VINCENTIO Fear not, Baptista, we will content you, go to, but I will in to be revenged for this villainy. *Exit*

BAPTISTA And I to sound the depth of this knavery. *Exit*

115 at the last] F1; at last F2

106 **counterfeit supposes** Close to tautology: false assumptions of identity or impersonations. Shakespeare has presumably taken the word 'supposes' from the title of the main source for his subplot, George Gascoigne's translation of Ariosto's *I Suppositi* (Gascoigne asks his audience to 'understand, this our Suppose is nothing else but a mystaking or imagination of one thing for an other'). Indeed Shakespeare is borrowing closely here: behind l. 104 lies Gascoigne's phrase 'the right *Philogano* the right father of the right *Erostrato*'. On the source, see Introduction, pp. 43–7.

bleared thine eyne dimmed your eyes, hoodwinked you (a standard phrase). 'Eyne' (or 'eyen') is the older form of the plural of 'eye'.

107 **packing** conspiracy, underhand plotting (*OED vbl sb*[2]. a)

with a witness with clear evidence, without a doubt (but the phrase has the force of the different modern idiom 'with a vengeance')

109 **faced and braved** stood up to and defied. Compare 4.3.122–5.

113 **state** rank (and its appurtenances, particularly clothes)

114 **bear my countenance** assume my identity. Compare l. 35.

121 **do you hear** The modern idiom would be 'listen!'.

123 **go to** An exclamation of impatience (and generally annoyance); here equivalent to 'stop worrying'.

125 **sound the depth** discover (as with a plummet) the full extent. Compare 2.1.191 and note.

LUCENTIO Look not pale, Bianca, thy father will not frown.
Exeunt Lucentio and Bianca

GREMIO
My cake is dough, but I'll in among the rest,
Out of hope of all but my share of the feast. *Exit*

KATHERINA Husband, let's follow, to see the end of this ado. 130

PETRUCHIO First kiss me, Kate, and we will.

KATHERINA What, in the midst of the street?

PETRUCHIO What, art thou ashamed of me?

KATHERINA No, sir, God forbid, but ashamed to kiss.

PETRUCHIO Why then, let's home again. (*To Grumio*) Come, sirrah, let's away.

KATHERINA Nay, I will give thee a kiss. Now pray thee, love, stay.

PETRUCHIO
Is not this well? Come, my sweet Kate.
Better once than never, for never too late. *Exeunt* 140

5.2 *Enter Baptista, Vincentio, Gremio, the Pedant, Lucentio with Bianca, Hortensio with the Widow, Tranio, Biondello, and Grumio, followed by Petruchio and Katherina. The Servingmen bring in a banquet*

126.1 *Exeunt Lucentio and Bianca*] F1 (*Exeunt*) 128 *Exit*] ROWE; *not in* F1 140 never too] F1 (neuer to); never is too KEIGHTLEY; never's too HUDSON 1880
5.2.0.1–4] F1 (*Actus Quintus. Enter Baptista, Vincentio, Gremio, the Pedant, Lucentio, and Bianca. Tranio, Biondello Grumio, and Widdow: The Seruingmen with Tranio bringing in a Banquet.*); *Act V Sc. II Enter* ... STEEVENS

127 **My cake is dough** I've lost, for certain. Compare 1.1.108 and note.

128 **Out of hope of all but** with no expectation of anything except

131 **kiss me, Kate** The reminiscence of 2.1.326 is presumably intentional.

135 ***to Grumio*** Dyce (1866), citing 'sirra Iras' in *Antony*, 5.2.228 as evidence that a woman could be addressed as 'sirra', thought that Petruchio's words were spoken to Kate.

140 **Better . . . late** better sometime than never (Petruchio's variant of 'better late than never', Tilley L85); for it is never *too* late to mend (Tilley M875).
Exeunt Apparently the Officer is still on stage until this point. A producer may prefer to send him off sooner, but his presence may be relevant to Katherine's hesitation in l. 134.

5.2 The F1 stage direction is unusual in two ways: the repetition of Tranio's name (although that would be an easy slip if the carrying in of the 'banquet' were an afterthought), and the omission of Hortensio, Petruchio, and Katherine. Such features point to an authorial stage direction rather than away from it: Hortensio's name might easily be left out by oversight (after all the Widow is included), and Katherine's and Petruchio's because they were on the stage at the end of the preceding 'scene'. Conceivably they do not leave it (although F says they do). More probably they do go off and come on again after the others, thus not really breaking

LUCENTIO

At last, though long, our jarring notes agree,
And time it is when raging war is done
To smile at scapes and perils overblown.
My fair Bianca, bid my father welcome,
While I with selfsame kindness welcome thine.
Brother Petruchio, sister Katherina,
And thou, Hortensio, with thy loving widow,
Feast with the best, and welcome to my house.
My banquet is to close our stomachs up
After our great good cheer. Pray you sit down, 10
For now we sit to chat as well as eat.

PETRUCHIO

Nothing but sit and sit, and eat and eat!

BAPTISTA

Padua affords this kindness, son Petruchio.

PETRUCHIO

Padua affords nothing but what is kind.

HORTENSIO

For both our sakes I would that word were true.

PETRUCHIO

Now, for my life, Hortensio fears his widow.

2 done] ROWE; come F1; gone COLLIER 1853

the so-called 'rule of immediate re-entry'. That Grumio has reappeared without an interval would surely not be noticed, in the group of servants, but he could be held back to follow Petruchio and Katherine on if it were thought desirable.

0.4 ***banquet*** Not a formal meal, but a 'supper' including fruit and wine, which is being provided by the groom, Lucentio, in his own house, after the formal ceremonies (including the wedding feast) have been concluded.

1 **long** only after a long time
jarring notes agree notes that (formerly) jarred (now) sound in concord

2 **done** F1's 'come' must be a compositorial error; perhaps the compositor has carried a few lines in his head and unwittingly transposed 'come' from the 'welcome' of l. 4.

3 **scapes** escapes from danger. Compare 2.1.239 and note.
overblown that have blown over, passed away overhead as a storm passes (*OED* 'overblow' *v. intr.* 2)

5 **kindness** Probably there is a quibble on 'kin' and 'kind'; goodwill, and the sense of kinship now appropriate after the marriage.

8 **with the best** on the best (food)

9 **close our stomachs up** There may be a reference to a belief in an actual physiological process, or 'stomachs' may again mean 'appetites'. (In Fletcher's *The Woman's Prize*, 3.2, the husband being disciplined is allowed only 'a kiss or two | To close my stomach'.) Either way, the 'banquet' (the 'supper' of fruit and sweetmeats) is to act like the modern coffee with cheese or 'after-dinner mints'.

10 **great good cheer** i.e., presumably, the full wedding feast (which would have been at Baptista's home)

13 **affords** habitually provides or 'runs to'

16 **for my life** upon my life – then, as now, an almost meaningless asseveration.
fears is afraid of – but the Widow takes it to mean 'frightens'. Compare 1.2.206.

WIDOW

Then never trust me if I be afeard.

PETRUCHIO

You are very sensible, and yet you miss my sense:
I mean Hortensio is afeard of you.

WIDOW

He that is giddy thinks the world turns round. 20

PETRUCHIO

Roundly replied.

KATHERINA Mistress, how mean you that?

WIDOW

Thus I conceive by him.

PETRUCHIO

Conceives by me! How likes Hortensio that?

HORTENSIO

My widow says, thus she conceives her tale.

PETRUCHIO

Very well mended. Kiss him for that, good widow.

KATHERINA

'He that is giddy thinks the world turns round' –
I pray you tell me what you meant by that.

WIDOW

Your husband, being troubled with a shrew,
Measures my husband's sorrow by his woe.
And now you know my meaning. 30

KATHERINA

A very mean meaning.

WIDOW Right, I mean you.

18 **sensible** (i) sensitive; (ii) reasonable
my sense my meaning

20 Proverbial (Tilley W870): 'people judge everything by themselves' – i.e. *you* (Petruchio) are afraid of *your* wife. Katherine has no doubt what is here meant, of course, and the Widow is not unwilling to expound it (ll. 28–30).

21 **Roundly** (i) emphatically (much as in the other uses of the word in the play) but also, with a quibble, (ii) in a roundabout or indirect way, by indirect insult

22 **conceive by him** (reply because of what I) take him (Petruchio) to mean, and to be – as Hortensio assumes (l. 24); certainly not 'conceive a child by him' – as Petruchio pretends to believe.

25 **mended** remedied (Petruchio is alleging that Hortensio has attempted to cover up the Widow's rudeness).

29 **his** his own – i.e. Petruchio's
woe The rhyme is further indication that 'shrew' was – or could be – pronounced 'shrow'.

31 **mean** 'cheap and nasty', characteristic of somebody of low degree – but in l. 32 Katherine uses the word in another sense, 'moderate' (compare the mathematical 'mean'), unless one believes with Hilda Hulme that it is there equivalent to 'chaste'.

KATHERINA
And I am mean, indeed, respecting you.

PETRUCHIO To her, Kate!

HORTENSIO To her, widow!

PETRUCHIO
A hundred marks, my Kate does put her down.

HORTENSIO That's my office.

PETRUCHIO
Spoke like an officer – ha' to thee, lad.
He drinks to Hortensio

BAPTISTA
How likes Gremio these quick-witted folks?

GREMIO
Believe me, sir, they butt together well.

BIANCA
Head and butt? An hasty-witted body 40
Would say your head and butt were head and horn.

VINCENTIO
Ay, mistress bride, hath that awakened you?

BIANCA
Ay, but not frighted me; therefore I'll sleep again.

37 ha' to thee] F1 (ha to the) 39 butt together] F1 (But together); butt Heads together ROWE 1714 40 Head and butt?] ROWE 1714 (*subs.*); Head, and but‸ F1

32 **respecting you** in comparison with you

33, 34 **To her** A variation of the cry with which an Elizabethan 'sportsman' urged on an animal, e.g. inciting a hound to begin the pursuit of the chosen deer (Madden, p. 44). Here, indeed, the women are being equated with animals.

35 **A hundred marks** No small wager: a mark was thirteen shillings and four pence.
put her down (Metaphorically) defeat her, get the better of her – but Hortensio chooses to take it literally. The same quibble is used more pertinently in *Much Ado*, 2.1.252–5, as Steevens pointed out.

36 **office** function or privilege (as husband)

37 **officer** officer of the law. The point of the rejoinder is presumably that Hortensio will see that (his wife's) legal 'duties' are performed.
ha' to ie. here's to.

39 **butt together** butt each other, like cattle. (Hibbard well compares *LLL*, 5.2.251–2.)

40 **Head and butt?** i.e. can you afford to talk of butting (heads) together? (Gremio has not used the word 'head', which some editors duly supply, but has clearly implied it.) It does not help to take 'butt' in the sense of 'bottom', 'tail'.

40 **An hasty-witted body** somebody quick-witted or (perhaps) one inclined to jump to conclusions

41 **head and horn** the (traditional) horned head of the cuckold – but it is odd that Bianca should aim this jest at Gremio, of all people, unless she is equating Gremio, who has lost her to another, with a wronged husband.

42 Vincentio is commenting on the unexpectedness of Bianca's intervention: she has not previously spoken in this scene. It is not really clear why she should be the one to take umbrage at Gremio's 'butt together'; but perhaps she has indeed been dozing, has just awakened, and hits out, without any knowledge of what has gone before.

PETRUCHIO

Nay, that you shall not, since you have begun.
Have at you for a better jest – or two.

BIANCA

Am I your bird? I mean to shift my bush,
And then pursue me as you draw your bow.
You are welcome all.

Exeunt Bianca, Katherina, and Widow

PETRUCHIO

She hath prevented me. Here, Signor Tranio,
This bird you aimed at, though you hit her not; 50
Therefore a health to all that shot and missed.

TRANIO

O sir, Lucentio slipped me like his greyhound,
Which runs himself, and catches for his master.

PETRUCHIO

A good swift simile, but something currish.

TRANIO

'Tis well, sir, that you hunted for yourself.
'Tis thought your deer does hold you at a bay.

BAPTISTA

O, O, Petruchio! Tranio hits you now.

44] F1 (Nay that you shall not since you haue begun:); Nay, that ... not; since ... begun, CAPELL 45 better] F1; bitter CAPELL (*conj.* THEOBALD) two] F3; too F1 48.1] ROWE; *Exit Bianca* F1

44–5 The F1 text is here followed (taking 'too' to mean 'two'), though most editors punctuate differently and also emend 'better' to 'bitter'. The general sense is not affected by the alterations.

45 **Have at you** i.e. be prepared (for), be on your guard (against) – the warning that one intends to take aim and fire (hence Bianca's reply)

46 **your bird** i.e. the bird, sitting in a bush, that you intend to shoot down with your arrow (and can shoot only if it remains still)

47 **pursue me** follow me (on foot), since you cannot hit the moving target

48 **You are welcome all** Bianca remembers, belatedly, that she is, after all, the hostess; and she leads the ladies out.

49 **prevented** anticipated; forestalled
Signor Tranio For a few lines (49–62) Tranio suddenly seems again (as in 3.2) to become an equal of Petruchio and Lucentio; nor for that matter did Tranio really 'miss' Bianca (as Petruchio well knows from the previous scene, though Tranio has to make the point again in ll. 52–3).

52 **slipped** released (from the leash)

54 **swift** quick-witted, and having to do with speed – but nevertheless, as Petruchio goes on to say, having less in common with a (swift) greyhound than with a cur.
something somewhat

56 **your deer** Tranio is carrying on the image of the hound hunting the deer; the deer now stands at bay, ready to defend itself against attack. There is also, no doubt, the inevitable quibble on 'dear': your loved one.

57 **hits you** i.e. scores a hit against you – but there follows a sequence of puns on the literal sense.

LUCENTIO
I thank thee for that gird, good Tranio.

HORTENSIO
Confess, confess, hath he not hit you here?

PETRUCHIO
A has a little galled me, I confess; 60
And as the jest did glance away from me,
'Tis ten to one it maimed you two outright.

BAPTISTA
Now, in good sadness, son Petruchio,
I think thou hast the veriest shrew of all.

PETRUCHIO
Well, I say no. And therefore for assurance
Let's each one send unto his wife,
And he whose wife is most obedient,
To come at first when he doth send for her,
Shall win the wager which we will propose.

HORTENSIO
Content. What's the wager?

LUCENTIO Twenty crowns. 70

PETRUCHIO
Twenty crowns?
I'll venture so much of my hawk or hound,
But twenty times so much upon my wife.

LUCENTIO
A hundred then.

HORTENSIO Content.

PETRUCHIO A match, 'tis done.

HORTENSIO
Who shall begin?

62 two] ROWE; too F1 65 for] F2; fir F1

58 **gird** Another quibble: (i) a sharp blow; (ii) a taunt, a mocking remark.

60 **A** he (compare 4.5.35 and note)
galled me made me sore, by chafing (the quibbles on literal and metaphorical meanings continue)

63 **sadness** seriousness

65 **for assurance** The F2 reading is adopted (and taken to mean 'to put the matter to the test') but F1's 'sir assurance' is not impossible as a mocking title for Baptista.

68 **To come** by coming, in that she will come (what Abbott, 356, calls the 'gerundive use of the infinitive')

72 **of** on (Abbott 174)

74 **match** wager

LUCENTIO That will I.
Go, Biondello, bid your mistress come to me.
BIONDELLO I go. *Exit*
BAPTISTA (*to Lucentio*)
Son, I'll be your half Bianca comes.
LUCENTIO
I'll have no halves; I'll bear it all myself.
Enter Biondello
How now, what news?
BIONDELLO Sir, my mistress sends you word 80
That she is busy, and she cannot come.
PETRUCHIO
How? 'She's busy, and she cannot come'?
Is that an answer?
GREMIO Ay, and a kind one too.
Pray God, sir, your wife send you not a worse.
PETRUCHIO
I hope better.
HORTENSIO
Sirrah Biondello, go and entreat my wife
To come to me forthwith. *Exit Biondello*
PETRUCHIO O ho, entreat her!
Nay, then she must needs come.
HORTENSIO I am afraid, sir,
Do what you can (*enter Biondello*) yours will not be
entreated.
Now where's my wife? 90
BIONDELLO
She says you have some goodly jest in hand.
She will not come; she bids you come to her.

75–6 That ... I. | Go ... me.] F1; That ... Go | Biondello ... me STEEVENS 1793 82–3 How? 'She's ... come'? | Is ... answer?] CAPELL; *as one line* F1 86–8 Sirrah ... wife | To ... her! | Nay ... come] CAPELL; *as prose* F1 88–90 I ... sir, | Do ... entreated. | Now ... wife?] CAPELL; I ... can | Yours ... wife? | F1

78 **be your half** take half the wager you have made; bear half the risk (in certainty of getting half the winnings)

85 **hope** Probably in the stronger sense: 'expect' (confidently).

89 Biondello's entrance should not be relocated: again the audience enjoys the fun of seeing him returning alone while Hortensio is still scoffing at Petruchio.

91 **goodly** excellent (the common ironical use of the adjective)

PETRUCHIO

Worse and worse; 'she will not come'! O vile,
Intolerable, not to be endured!
Sirrah Grumio, go to your mistress,
Say I command her come to me. *Exit Grumio*

HORTENSIO

I know her answer.

PETRUCHIO What?

HORTENSIO She will not.

PETRUCHIO

The fouler fortune mine, and there an end.

Enter Katherina

BAPTISTA

Now, by my holidame, here comes Katherina.

KATHERINA

What is your will, sir, that you send for me? 100

PETRUCHIO

Where is your sister, and Hortensio's wife?

KATHERINA

They sit conferring by the parlour fire.

PETRUCHIO

Go fetch them hither. If they deny to come,
Swinge me them soundly forth unto their husbands.
Away, I say, and bring them hither straight.

Exit Katherina

LUCENTIO

Here is a wonder, if you talk of a wonder.

HORTENSIO

And so it is. I wonder what it bodes.

PETRUCHIO

Marry, peace it bodes, and love, and quiet life,

93–4] STEEVENS 1793 (*subs.*); Worse ... come: | Oh ... indur'd: | F1 96 *Exit Grumio*] F1 (*Exit*) 105.1] *not in* F1 106 of a wonder] F1; of wonder DYCE 1866 (*conj.* WALKER); of wonders HUDSON 1880 (*conj.* LETTSOM)

98 **there an end** that's the end of the matter; there would be no more to say

99 **holidame** An alternative form of 'halidom' (holiness), frequently used as a mild asseveration: 'by everything I hold sacred'. The 'dame' suffix was apparently due to the mistaken belief that the word designated the Virgin Mary.

103 **deny** refuse

104 **Swinge me them ...** whip them, or beat them, out .... 'Me' is again the ethic dative, 'for me'.

107 **bodes** presages; promises or threatens

An awful rule, and right supremacy;
And, to be short, what not that's sweet and happy. 110

BAPTISTA
Now fair befall thee, good Petruchio!
The wager thou hast won, and I will add
Unto their losses twenty thousand crowns,
Another dowry to another daughter,
For she is changed, as she had never been.

PETRUCHIO
Nay, I will win my wager better yet,
And show more sign of her obedience,
Her new-built virtue and obedience.
Enter Katherina, Bianca, and Widow
See where she comes, and brings your froward wives
As prisoners to her womanly persuasion. 120
Katherine, that cap of yours becomes you not.
Off with that bauble, throw it under foot.
She complies

WIDOW
Lord, let me never have a cause to sigh
Till I be brought to such a silly pass!

BIANCA
Fie, what a foolish duty call you this?

LUCENTIO
I would your duty were as foolish too!
The wisdom of your duty, fair Bianca,
Hath cost me a hundred crowns since supper-time.

122.1] *not in* F1 128 me a] CAPELL; me fiue F1; me an ROWE; me one COLLIER 1853

109 **awful** full of awe; awe-inspiring; involving awesome respectfulness
right true, appropriate
110 **what not that's** everything that is
111 **fair befall thee** may good luck be yours always (a form of congratulations here)
115 **as . . . been** as if she had never been (what she was); as if she were a different being
117, 118 **obedience** One of the two occurrences of the word may be an error, another example of dittography; but emendation, *if* necessary, can only be guesswork, and the sense is clear.
122 **bauble** The word Petruchio contemptuously used of the same cap or another at 4.3.82 (although F1 this time spells it 'bable').
124 **pass** course of action
128 **a hundred** Capell's emendation of F1's 'fiue' is accepted here, as it is by Sisson (*New Readings*), since this was the amount of the wager (l. 74) and 'a' in the secretary hand could easily be misread as 'v'; but 'five' is not necessarily wrong: gamblers habitually exaggerate their losses.

BIANCA

The more fool you for laying on my duty.

PETRUCHIO

Katherine, I charge thee tell these headstrong women 130
What duty they do owe their lords and husbands.

WIDOW

Come, come, you're mocking; we will have no telling.

PETRUCHIO

Come on, I say, and first begin with her.

WIDOW

She shall not.

PETRUCHIO

I say she shall: 'and first begin with her'.

KATHERINA

Fie, fie, unknit that threatening unkind brow,
And dart not scornful glances from those eyes
To wound thy lord, thy king, thy governor.
It blots thy beauty, as frosts do bite the meads,
Confounds thy fame, as whirlwinds shake fair buds, 140
And in no sense is meet or amiable.
A woman moved is like a fountain troubled,
Muddy, ill-seeming, thick, bereft of beauty,
And while it is so, none so dry or thirsty
Will deign to sip or touch one drop of it.
Thy husband is thy lord, thy life, thy keeper,

130–1] *as verse* ROWE 1714; *as prose* F1 132 you're] F3; your F1

129 **laying** wagering, laying a bet

136 **unkind** With the usual quibble: (i) unfriendly; (ii) unnatural, not according to the law of nature – that law being, in Katherine's version, for the wife to be submissive.

138 **governor** Presumably another quibble, on the official title 'Governor' and on the literal meaning, one who governs or rules.

139 **blots** puts a blot on, defaces
meads meadows (the word was probably already poetic).

140 **Confounds** In view of the following simile, means 'overthrows', 'destroys' (*OED* 1) rather than 'brings into question'.

140 **fame** reputation
shake i.e. destroy by tossing violently

141 **meet** fitting

142 **moved** angry

143 **ill-seeming** ugly, unpleasant in appearance
thick The opposite of transparent; 'not clear'.

144 **none so dry** nobody – no matter how dry (alternatively explained – Abbott 281 – as a kind of ellipsis: there is nobody so dry *that* he will . . .).

Thy head, thy sovereign: one that cares for thee,
And for thy maintenance; commits his body
To painful labour both by sea and land,
To watch the night in storms, the day in cold, 150
Whilst thou liest warm at home, secure and safe,
And craves no other tribute at thy hands
But love, fair looks, and true obedience –
Too little payment for so great a debt.
Such duty as the subject owes the prince,
Even such, a woman oweth to her husband;
And when she is froward, peevish, sullen, sour,
And not obedient to his honest will,
What is she but a foul contending rebel
And graceless traitor to her loving lord? 160
I am ashamed that women are so simple
To offer war where they should kneel for peace;
Or seek for rule, supremacy, and sway
When they are bound to serve, love, and obey.
Why are our bodies soft, and weak, and smooth,
Unapt to toil and trouble in the world,

148 maintenance; commits] F1 (maintenance. Commits); maintenance, commits GRANT WHITE; maintenance commits CAMBRIDGE

147 **head** In the sense of head of a state or institution – a not unexpected Biblical reminiscence, of Ephesians 5:23, 'For the husband is the head of the wyfe, even as Christe is the head of the Churche'. Shakespeare may also have in mind in this section of Katherine's speech both the marginal gloss in the Geneva Bible ('so the husband ought to nourish, governe & defend his wife from perils') and the words of the marriage service.

148 **maintenance; commits** As the collations demonstrate, it is possible to punctuate here in different ways. No doubt, as New Cambridge argues, the F1 compositor could easily have been misled if in his 'copy' the word 'commits' began with that form of the secretary letter 'c' that is theoretically a capital but was also used by many Elizabethans as an alternative form of the initial minuscule; but it does not follow that 'maintenance commits' must be correct. The F full stop is often the equivalent of the modern colon or semicolon. Either interpretation makes perfectly good sense. W. S. Walker (iii.70) first pointed out that ll. 147–51 may have been suggested by one of Erasmus's *Colloquies* (but it had not yet been translated into English).

149 **painful** involving the taking of pain; onerous (rather than 'causing pain')

150 **watch** be on watch; watch through

151 **secure** Perhaps, as in modern use, 'safe', but more probably in the older sense, closer to the Latin *securus*: 'free from worry or apprehension'.

155–6 **Such . . . husband** Another near-quotation from the Bible, Ephesians 5:24: 'as the Churche is subject unto Christe, likewyse the wyves to their owne husbandes in all thinges'.

157 **peevish** In a stronger sense than the modern usage: 'perverse', 'obstinate'.

159–64 The lines – and particularly 'kneel for peace' – remind one of More's speech about rebellion in that part of the manuscript of *Sir Thomas More* thought to be in Shakespeare's handwriting.

161 **so simple** so simple-minded as

162 **offer** undertake, declare

166 **Unapt** unfitted

But that our soft conditions, and our hearts,
Should well agree with our external parts?
Come, come, you froward and unable worms,
My mind hath been as big as one of yours, 170
My heart as great, my reason haply more,
To bandy word for word and frown for frown;
But now I see our lances are but straws,
Our strength as weak, our weakness past compare,
That seeming to be most which we indeed least are.
Then vail your stomachs, for it is no boot,
And place your hands below your husband's foot.
In token of which duty, if he please,
My hand is ready, may it do him ease.

PETRUCHIO
Why, there's a wench! Come on, and kiss me, Kate. 180

LUCENTIO
Well, go thy ways, old lad, for thou shalt ha't.

VINCENTIO
'Tis a good hearing when children are toward.

LUCENTIO
But a harsh hearing when women are froward.

167 **conditions** dispositions, character (*OED* II. 11–13)
168 **agree with** correspond to; not be in opposition to
169 **unable** powerless, weak
170 **big** arrogant, haughty (as also in 3.2.230)
one of yours either of yours; that of either of you (Bianca and the Widow).
171 **heart** Probably, here, as the seat of courage.
more i.e. stronger
172 **bandy** strike back and forth, as with tennis balls
174 **as weak** i.e. as straws
past compare i.e. we are so weak that no comparison is possible: there is nothing weaker.
175 The syntax is cryptic but the meaning reasonably clear: '(our weakness is greater than anything one can think to compare it with) in that we strive hardest to pretend to that very quality – strength – of which we have least'.
176 **vail your stomachs** lower your pride. 'Vail' was not used only of the lowering of a flag and is therefore not necessarily metaphorical here; 'stomach' has one of its narrower senses, as in *Henry VIII*, 4.2.33–5, 'a man | Of an unbounded stomach, ever ranking | Himself with princes'. (It can also mean 'anger' or 'malice'.)
176 **it is no boot** there is no remedy, nothing else you can do ('boot' in the meaning either of 'profit' or of 'amends')
179 **may it do him ease** *Either* 'and may it give him comfort' *or* 'if it will . . .'.
180 **kiss me, Kate** The third use of the phrase.
181 **go thy ways** Literally '(you may) go on your way' ('ways' is an old genitive) but the phrase is a form of congratulation, equivalent to 'well done'.
ha't have it (the prize), carry the day – and apparently rhymes with 'Kate'.
182 **a good hearing** something good to hear (as opposed to 'a harsh hearing' in the following line)
toward The opposite of 'froward' (used several times before and in the following line): obedient, co-operative.

PETRUCHIO

Come, Kate, we'll to bed.
We three are married, but you two are sped. 185
(*To Lucentio*) 'Twas I won the wager, though you hit
the white,
And being a winner, God give you good night!
Exeunt Petruchio and Katherina

HORTENSIO

Now go thy ways, thou hast tamed a curst shrew.

LUCENTIO

'Tis a wonder, by your leave, she will be tamed so.
Exeunt

187.1] ROWE; *Exit Petruchio* F1 189.1] *not in* F1

185 **sped** brought to the *wrong* conclusion or result; defeated (*OED* 'speed' *v.* I. 7. b)

186 **the white** the white circle at the centre of the archer's target, the 'bull's eye', but with a quibble on 'Bianca', which in Italian means 'white'

187 **being a winner** since I am a winner (I am therefore leaving now, not trusting to my luck any further – a sentiment which perhaps modifies the general sense of triumph?)

189 **by your leave** with your pardon; if you don't mind my saying so

APPENDIX A

THE following are the Christopher Sly 'scenes' in *The Taming of a Shrew* for which there are no equivalents in the First Folio text. The spelling has been modernized.

(1)

These lines would come at a point corresponding to 2.1.141 (except that Ferando's marriage with Kate has already been arranged). 'Sim' is Simon, the Lord; 'the fool' is Sander (Grumio). In *A Shrew* Sly has asked in the Induction 'Is there not a fool in the play?' and his last comment before the 'play' began has been 'Come, Sim, where be the players? Sim, stand by Me and we'll flout the players out of their coats'. (*A Shrew* has nothing corresponding to the Sly lines at the end of 1.1.)

Then Sly speaks

SLY Sim, when will the fool come again?

LORD He'll come again, my lord, anon.

SLY Gi's some more drink here. Sounds, where's the tapster? Here, Sim, eat some of these things.

LORD So I do, my lord.

SLY Here, Sim, I drink to thee.

LORD My lord, here comes the players again.

SLY O brave, here's two fine gentlewomen. (C1[v])

[In fact, it is Valeria (Tranio) who enters with Kate.]

(2)

After 4.4. The marriages are those of Kate's sisters.

SLY Sim, must they be married now?

LORD Ay, my lord.

Enter Ferando and Kate and Sander

SLY Look, Sim, the fool is come again now. (E4)

(3)

After 5.1.100 (but it is the Duke/Vincentio, not Tranio or Baptista, who has threatened the imprisonment). Phylotus is the merchant who impersonates the father of Aurelius/Lucentio.

Phylotus and Valeria runs away
Then Sly speaks

SLY I say we'll have no sending to prison.

LORD My lord, this is but the play, they're but in jest.

SLY I tell thee, Sim, we'll have no sending to prison, that's flat. Why, Sim, am not I Don Christo Vary? Therefore *I* say they shall not go to prison.

LORD No more they shall not, my lord; they be run away.

SLY Are they run away, Sim? That's well. Then gi's some more drink, and let them play again.

LORD Here, my lord.

Sly drinks and then falls asleep (F2)

(4)

Following 5.1, after all other characters have left the stage. Presumably the 'boy' is one of the servants summoned by the Lord, since in *A Shrew* the boy/wife has departed before the entertainment begins (but the reporter's memory may be at fault here).

Sly sleeps

LORD

Who's within there? Come hither, sirs. [*Enter servants*] My lord's
Asleep again: go take him easily up,
And put him in his own apparel again,
And lay him in the place where we did find him,
Just underneath the alehouse side below,
But see you wake him not in any case.

BOY

It shall be done, my lord. Come help to bear him hence.

Exit (F3)

(5)

After the 'play' is ended and the characters in it have gone off.

Then enter two bearing of Sly in his own apparel again, and leaves him where they found him, and then goes out. Then enter the Tapster

TAPSTER

Now that the darksome night is overpast,
And dawning day appears in crystal sky,
Now must I haste abroad. But soft, who's this?
What, Sly? O wondrous, hath he lain here all night?
I'll wake him; I think he's starved by this
But that his belly was so stuffed with ale.
What now, Sly, awake for shame!

SLY Sim, gi's some more wine. What's all the players gone?
Am not I a lord?

TAPSTER A lord with a murrain. Come, art thou drunken still?

SLY Who's this? Tapster? O Lord, sirrah, I have had the bravest dream tonight that ever thou heardest in all thy life.

TAPSTER Ay, marry, but you had best get you home, for your wife will course you for dreaming here tonight.

SLY Will she? I know now how to tame a shrew: I dreamt upon it all this night till now, and thou hast waked me out of the best dream that ever I had in my life. But I'll to my wife presently and tame her too an if she anger me.

TAPSTER

Nay tarry, Sly, for I'll go home with thee,
And hear the rest that thou hast dreamt tonight.

Exeunt omnes (G2–G2[v])

APPENDIX B

4.1.36: 'Jack boy, ho boy, news': the music as arranged by E. W. Naylor.

INDEX TO THE COMMENTARY

An asterisk indicates that the note supplements information given in *OED*.

a, 1.2.190; 4.3.92; 4.5.35; 5.1.4; 5.2.60
a hundred, 5.2.128
abandoned, Ind.2.113
aboard, 3.2.170
abused, 5.1.97
accomplished, Ind.1.109
accord, 3.1.71
action, Ind.1.107; 3.2.236
admire, 1.1.29
Adriatic seas, 1.2.72–3
adversaries, 1.2.275
advice, 1.1.114
advise, advised, 1.1.183; 4.4.11
Aeacides, 3.1.50
affect, affected, 1.1.26, 40; 2.1.14
affection's edge, 1.2.72
affied, 4.4.48
affords, 5.2.13
against, 4.4.100
aglet baby, 1.2.78
agree with, 5.2.168
agreement, 4.4.32–3
alarums, 1.1.126; 1.2.202
Alcides, 1.2.254–5
all, 1.2.238; 3.2.102
all one, 3.2.78; 4.2.102
allots, 4.5.41
aloft, Ind.2 *headnote*
alone, 4.2.71
amazed, 2.1.154
amends, Ind.2.95
amort, 4.3.36
ancient, Ind.2.29; 1.2.46
ancient angel, 4.2.61
Anna, 1.1.151
answerable, 2.1.361
antic, Ind.1.98
apace, 2.1.324; 4.3.52
Apollo, Ind.2.33, 55–8
appendix, 4.4.101
apple, apples, 1.1.132–3; 4.2.101
apple tart, 4.3.89
approved, 1.1.7; 1.2.3
apt, 2.1.164
aptly fitted, Ind.1.84
argosy, 2.1.376
arms, 2.1.223
arras, 2.1.353
array, 4.3.177
art, 4.2.9–10
Art to Love, 4.2.8
as, Ind.1.67, 105
as fast as may be, 5.1.100–1
as who should, 4.3.13
ashore, 1.1.42
ask him, 3.2.175
askance, 2.1.246
assurance, 2.1.389; 3.2.133; 4.2.118; 4.4.90; 5.2.65
assure, 2.1.345
at any hand, 1.2.144, 222
attend, 2.1.167
austerity, 4.4.7
awful, 5.2.109

Bacare, 2.1.72
baggage, Ind.1.3
bags, 1.2.173
balk logic, 1.1.34
balm, Ind.1.45
bandy, 5.2.172
banquet, Ind.1.36; 5.2.0.4
bar in law, 1.1.133
bare-headed, 4.4.18.2
bars, Ind.2.133
Barthol'mew, Ind.1.102
Basta, 1.1.195
bate, 4.1.183
bauble, 5.2.122
be, 3.2.84; 4.4.48
be remembered, 4.3.96
be with you, 4.1.155
bear, bears, *vb.* 2.1.201; 4.2.2–3; 5.1.114
bears more toward, 5.1.8
bear-herd, Ind.2.18
beastly, 4.2.34
beat, 4.1.183
because, 1.1.181
beck, Ind.2.32
become, becomes, 1.1.14–16, 230; 2.1.257; 4.5.32
beetle-headed, 4.1.142
beggar, Ind.1.39
begnawn, 3.2.54

beholding, 1.2.271
being a winner, 5.2.187
belike, Ind.1.72; 2.1.16; 4.3.103
belongs, 2.1.192
be-mete, 4.3.112
bemoiled, 4.1.66
Bene, 1.2.279
Bentivolii, 1.1.13
Bergamo, 5.1.68–9
beseem, 4.5.66
bespeak, 4.3.63
bestraught, Ind.2.23
bestrew, Ind.2.38
better once than never, 5.1.140
bias, 4.5.25
bid, 2.1.318; 4.3.94
big, 3.2.230; 5.2.170
bill, 4.3.142, 148
bills (of exchange), 4.2.89
bird; 5.2.46
bleared, 5.1.106
blots, 5.2.139
blow our nails, 1.1.107
blowing the fire, 4.1.8
blue coats, 4.1.80
board, 1.2.94
bodes, 5.2.107
bonny, 2.1.185
books, 2.1.226
boot, 5.2.176
booted, 4.4.0.1
boot-hose, 3.2.65
bossed, 2.1.355
bots, 3.2.54
bottom, 4.3.133
bowed, 2.1.149
boy, Ind.1.12
brave, bravely, Ind.1.37; 1.2.213.1; 4.3.54
braved, *vb.* 4.3.110, 5.1.109
bravery, 4.3.57
braves, *sb.* 3.1.15
brawl, 4.1.193
break (her to), 2.1.146
break a jest, 4.5.72–3
break the ice, 1.2.264
breathe, breathed, Ind.1.14; Ind.2.46; 1.1.8
breeching, 3.1.18
bring mine action, 3.2.236
brooked, 1.1.113
brown, 2.1.253–4
buckler, 3.2.241
budding, 4.5.37
bugs, 1.2.206
burden, 1.2.67; 2.1.203
burst, Ind.1.6; 4.1.71
Burton-heath, Ind.2.17
but, 1.1.107; *2.1.15; 2.1.245; 3.1.60; 4.1.13
butt together, 5.2.39
buttery, Ind.1.99
buzz, 2.1.207
*buzzard, 2.1.207
by the way, 4.2.116
by your leave, 5.2.189

cake's dough, 1.1.108; 5.1.127
call your name, 2.1.67
Cambio, 2.1.82
came from school, 3.2.149
came well in, 2.1.365
candle-cases, 3.2.45
canopies, 2.1.354
cap, 4.3.63
caparisoned, 3.2.63
card of ten, 2.1.407
cardmaker, Ind.2.18
carouse, carouses, 1.2.274; 3.2.170
carpets, 4.1.44
cart, 1.1.55
cat, 1.2.113–14; 2.1.276
caught, 4.1.39
cavil, 2.1.392
cease, Ind.2.12
censer, 4.3.91
ceremonies, 3.2.168
'cerns, 5.1.66
chafe, chafed, 1.2.198; 2.1.240
change, 3.1.79
chapeless, 3.2.47
charge, 2.1.8
charity, 4.1.198
charm, 1.1.206; 4.2.58
checks, 1.1.32
cheer, 3.2.185; 4.4.69; 5.1.12
chide, 1.2.94
chine, 3.2.50
choice, 1.2.233
choice in rotten apples, 1.1.132–3
choked, 2.1.378
choler, 4.1.160
choleric, 4.3.19
choose, 5.1.41
Cicely Hacket, Ind.2.87
circumstance, 4.2.120

clapped up, 2.1.327
clef, 3.1.75
close, *adv.* Ind.1.124
close up, *vb.* 5.2.9
cockle, 4.3.66
Cock's, 4.1.104
cold bed, Ind.1.7–8
cold comfort, 4.1.28
coldest fault, Ind.1.17
coldly, 4.1.11
coloured, 1.1.204
combless, 2.1.228
come again, 2.1.219
come of, 1.1.13
come roundly, 1.2.58
come to woo, 2.1.114
come well, 3.2.87
comet, 3.2.95
commanded, Ind.1.122
commune, 1.1.101
comonty, Ind.2.134
compassed, 4.3.136
compound, 1.2.27; 2.1.343
conceit, 4.3.157
conceive, 1.2.268; 5.2.22
concerneth, 3.2.127
conditions, 5.2.167
conference, 2.1.250
confess, 4.3.137
confounds, 5.2.140
congealed, Ind.2.129
Conqueror, Ind.1.4
conserves, Ind.2.3, 7
conster, 3.1.30
content, *vb.* 1.1.90, 160; 2.1.343
continency, 4.1.170
*contrive, 1.2.273
cony-catched, 5.1.89–90
cony-catching, 4.1.38
countenance, *sb.* 1.1.226; 4.2.65; 4.4.18; 5.1.35, 114
countenance, *vb.* 4.1.86–7
counterfeit, 4.4.90; 5.1.106
counterpoints, 2.1.353
countryman, countrymen, 1.1.194; 1.2.185; 4.2.77
couple, Ind.1.15
course, Ind.2.45
courtesy, Ind.1.111; 4.2.91
covenants, 2.1.126
coxcomb, 2.1.227
coy, 2.1.242
cozen, 3.2.167; 5.1.34
crab, 2.1.231
crack, 1.2.95
crack-hemp, 5.1.40
crave, 2.1.178
craven, 2.1.229
credit, *sb.* 4.2.107
credit, *vb.* 4.1.92
crest, 2.1.227
cried upon it, Ind.1.20
cross, *adj.* 2.1.248
cross, crossing, *vb.* 2.1.28; 4.1.63; 4.3.190
crowns, 2.1.352
crupper, 3.2.59
cuffs, 4.3.56
cullion, 4.2.20
cum previlegio, 4.4.90–1
cunning, Ind.1.89; 1.1.97; 2.1.56, 413
cup, Ind.2.2
curious, 4.4.35
curiously, 4.3.140
curst, curster, 1.1.177; 3.2.153
custard-coffin, 4.3.82
*cypress, 2.1.353
Cytherea, Ind.2.47–51

dance barefoot, 2.1.33
Daphne, Ind.2.55–8
deeds, 2.1.344–5
deep-mouthed, Ind.1.15
deer, 5.2.56
demi-cannon, 4.3.88
denier, Ind.1.7
deny, 5.2.103
desperate, 2.1.329
devils, 1.1.66
devil's dam, 1.1.105–6
devote, 1.1.32
Dian(a), 2.1.257
diaper, Ind.1.54
digress, 3.2.106
dinner, dinner-time, 2.1.111; 4.3.185
discipline, 1.1.30
disdain, 2.1.3
disease, Ind.1.59
disfigure, 1.2.113
(to) do, 1.2.221; 3.2.218
do it, 4.3.51
do me grace, 1.2.129
do you hear, 5.1.121
dog-weary, 4.2.60
doing, 2.1.74

domineer, 3.2.226
door is open, 3.2.212
dotard, 5.1.96
doublets, Ind.2.8
dower, 2.1.344–5
drawn, 3.1.68
dress, 4.3.40
dresser, 4.1.151
droop, Ind.2.25
drudge, 4.1.114
Duke, 4.2.83
dulcet, Ind.1.48
dumps, 2.1.284
duty, Ind.1.79; 4.1.32

eleven-and-twenty, 4.2.57
else, 2.1.390
embossed, Ind.1.14
encounter, 4.5.54
endured, 4.3.75
entertainment, 2.1.54
entertain'st, 2.1.249
entire, 4.2.23
entrance, 2.1.54
envious, Ind.2.63
envy, 2.1.18
ergo, 4.3.127
estate, 3.2.99
esteem, *sb.* 4.5.64
esteemed, Ind.1.119
Europa, 1.1.165–7
even, 1.2.219
event, 3.2.126
ewer, Ind.1.54
excellent, Ind.1.86
except, 4.4.89
eyne, 5.1.106

face, faced, 2.1.289, 407; 4.3.122; 5.1.109
'faith, 1.1.237
fair, 2.1.17
fair befall thee, 5.2.111
fairly, 1.2.143; 3.2.60
falcon, 4.1.177
fall to, 1.1.38
fame, 5.2.140
fancies, fancy, *sb.* Ind.1.41; 3.2.66
far on, 4.2.73
fare, Ind.2.99
farthest, 4.2.73
farthingales, 4.3.56
*fashions, 3.2.51
fast, *vb.* 1.1.108
fault, Ind.1.17
fay, Ind.2.79
fear, *vb.* 1.2.206; 4.4.10; 5.2.16
feeze, Ind.1.1
Fel., 4.3.63
Ferdinand, 4.1.136
field, 1.2.199
figure, 1.2.112
filthy, 4.3.65
fine, 2.1.319; 4.1.121; 5.1.58
finger in the eye, 1.1.78
fire, fire, 4.1.16–17
fit, fitted, Ind.1.84; 4.3.69
fives, 3.2.53
flap-eared, 4.1.142
flat, 5.1.32
flattering, Ind.1.41
Florentius, 1.2.68
flourish, 1.1.0.1
flouts, 2.1.29
fondly, 4.2.31
fool, 3.2.156
footboy, 3.2.68
for, 1.1.3, 88; 1.2.122; 3.2.229; 4.3.148; 4.4.27–8
for all the world, 3.2.63
for assurance, 5.2.65
for company, 4.1.165
for ever and a day, 4.4.94
for my hand, 1.1.186
for my life, 5.2.16
for the time, 1.1.17
for why, 3.2.166
forsooth, 3.2.8; 4.3.1
forthcoming, 5.1.84
fortune, 3.2.23
forward, 2.1.51
foul, 1.2.68; 4.1.58
frame, *vb.* Ind.2.132; 1.1.224
frantic, 3.2.11
frenzy, Ind.2.129
fresher, 4.5.29
frets, 2.1.148
fretting, 2.1.330
friar of orders grey, 4.1.130–1
frivolous circumstances, 5.1.23–4
frolic, 4.3.179
from Padua, 5.1.27
froward, 1.1.69; 2.1.293; 4.5.78
full-gorged, 4.1.178
fume, 2.1.151
furniture, 4.3.177

fustian, 4.1.42

'gainst, 2.1.317
gait, 2.1.258
galled, 5.2.60
galliasses, 2.1.380
gambold, Ind.2.135
gamesome, 2.1.244
gamester, 2.1.402
gamut, 3.1.65, 70, 71
gate, 1.2.11
gentle sirs, gentles, Ind.1.63; 3.2.92
get, 2.1.412
giddy, 5.2.20
gird, 5.2.58
give me leave, 2.1.46; 3.1.57
give thanks, 4.1.144
give you over, 1.2.103–4
glanders, 3.2.50
go about her, 4.4.104
go by, Ind.1.7; 1.2.253
go hard, goes hard, 4.2.80; 4.4.105
go thy ways, 4.5.23; 5.2.181
go to, 5.1.123
God-a-mercy, 4.3.150
Gog's wounds, 3.2.159
gold, 2.1.349
good hearing, 5.2.182
good shipping, 5.1.37
good sooth, 3.2.115
good-night, 2.1.302–3
goodly, Ind.2.79; 2.1.261; 3.2.93; 4.5.2; 5.2.91
goodman, Ind.2.103
goods, 2.1.3
governor, 5.2.138
Gramercies, 1.1.41
grateful, 2.1.76
gratify, 1.2.270
great good cheer, 5.2.10
Greece, Greet, Ind.2.91
green, 3.2.213; 4.5.47
Grissel (Griselda), 2.1.295
groom, 3.2.151
Grumio, 1.2.0.1

ha't, 5.2.181; (1.1.195)
ha' to, 5.2.37; (1.1.136; 4.5.78)
haberdasher, 4.3.61.1
habiliments, 4.3.167
habit, 2.1.38.1; 3.2.99
Hacket, Ind.2.19–20, 87
haggard, 4.1.177 ff.; 4.2.39
haled, 5.1.97
half, 5.2.78
half-checked, 3.2.55
halt, 2.1.255; 3.2.88
hang her, 1.2.193
hangings, 2.1.351
hap, 1.2.266; 4.4.104
haply, happily, Ind.1.133; 1.1.8; 1.2.56; 4.4.53
happy man be his dole, 1.1.137
hasty, 4.3.164
hasty-witted, 5.2.40
have at you, 5.2.45
have it full, 1.1.195
have to, 4.5.78
have to't, 1.1.136
he, 3.2.236
he of both, 2.1.344
head, 5.2.147
head and butt, 5.2.40
head and horn, 5.2.41
headborough, Ind.1.9–10
headstall, 3.2.56
heard, 2.1.182
hearken for, 1.2.257
hearkening, 4.4.52
heart, 5.2.171
heavy, 2.1.206
heavy chance, 1.2.45
heedless, 4.1.154
her, 4.4.62
herald, 2.1.226
Hercules, 1.2.254–5
high-cross, 1.1.130
hilding, 2.1.26
hipped, 3.2.48
his, 2.1.214
history, Ind.2.138
hit it, 2.1.199
hits you, 5.2.57
hold, *vb.* 1.1.105–6; 2.1.145; 3.2.80; 4.4.6, 17
holidame, 5.2.99
honest, 3.2.25; 4.3.167
honourable, Ind.1.107
hop, 4.3.98
hope, *sb.* 3.2.135
hope, *vb.* 5.2.85
horn, 4.1.24
horse, Ind.1.58; 3.2.207
hose, 5.1.58
hot, 2.1.294; 4.1.18, 28
house, Ind.2.84

household, Ind.2.137
how do you, 1.2.22
humour, Ind.2.12; 1.2.107;3.2.29, 66, 69; 4.1.168, 196
hungerly, 3.2.174
hurly, 4.1.190
husband, *sb.* 5.1.60
husbanded, Ind.1.65

idle, Ind.2.12
ill-favoured, 1.2.59
ill-seeming, 5.2.143
in a few, 1.2.51
in despite, Ind.1.125
in good time, 2.1.194
in hand, 4.2.2–3
in happy time, Ind.1.87
in hold, 1.2.117
in peril to, Ind.2.120
in place, 1.2.154
in's throat, 4.3.130
in tune, 3.1.24
indifferent, 1.2.176; 4.1.80
*infused, Ind.2.15
ingenious, 1.1.9
ingrate, 1.2.267
inprimis, 4.1.58
institute, 1.1.8
intend, 4.1.190
invite, 3.2.16
Io, Ind.2.52–4
irksome, 1.2.183
is out before, 5.1.0.1
Iwis, 1.1.62

Jack, Jacks, 2.1.157, 288; 4.1.43
Jack boy, 4.1.36
jade, 1.2.246; 2.1.202; 4.1.1
jarring notes agree, 5.2.1
jars, *vb.* 3.1.38
jealous, 4.5.76
jerkin, 3.2.44
Jeronimy, Ind.1.7
Jills, 4.1.43
jogging, 3.2.213
joined stool, 2.1.198
jointure, 2.1.372
jolly, 3.2.215
jolt-heads, 4.1.154
Jove (Jupiter), Ind.2.52–4; 1.1.165–7
jump, 1.1.187
junkets, 3.2.250

Kate Hall, 2.1.187
Kated, 3.2.247
kates, 2.1.188
Kat(h)erina, 1.1.47.1
keep, *sb.* 1.2.116
keep, *vb.* 2.1.256
kennel, 4.3.98
kersey, 3.2.64
kill with kindness, 4.1.195
kills, 4.1.168
kindly, Ind.1.12, 63
kindness, 5.2.5
*kindred, Ind.2.26
kiss hands, 4.1.82–3
kiss me, Kate, 5.1.131; 5.2.180
kites, 4.1.182
knack, 4.3.67
knavery, 4.3.58
knave's, 1.2.12
kneel for peace, 5.2.159–64
know, 2.1.70, 103–4

lackey, 3.2.63
lampass, 3.2.51
'larums, 1.2.202
lave, 2.1.350
lay it, 4.3.178
laying, 5.2.129
lead apes in hell, 2.1.34
leave, 5.1.23–4
lecture, lectures, 1.2.145; 3.1.8
Leda's daughter, 1.2.241
leet, Ind.2.85
left legs, 4.1.81
'leges, 1.2.29
let it be, 1.2.255
let the world slide (slip), Ind.1.5; Ind. 2.140
lewd, 4.3.65
lie, 4.4.55
lief, 1.1.129
light, 2.1.205
lightness, 4.2.24
like, *vb.* 4.4.31, 61
like to, 3.2.50
liking, 1.2.178
link, 4.1.119
list, *sb.* 3.2.65
list, *vb.* 3.1.89; 3.2.164; 4.5.7
Litio, 2.1.60
little pot, 4.1.5
logger-headed, 4.1.110
Lombardy, 1.1.3–4

long, 5.2.1
'longeth, 4.2.45; 4.4.7
longly, 1.1.162
looked for, 2.1.335; 4.2.117; 4.4.16
look what, 4.3.189
loose, lose, 2.1.223
loose-bodied, 4.3.131
love in idleness, 1.1.148
lovely, 3.2.122
lowly, Ind.1.111
Lucrece, 2.1.296
lure, 4.1.179
lustful, Ind.2.36
lusty, 2.1.159; 4.2.50
lute, 2.1.145
lyingest, Ind.2.22

mad-brain, 3.2.10
made it good, Ind.1.16
madly mated, 3.2.246
maintain, maintained, 1.1.134; 5.1.67
maintenance, 5.2.148
make the matter good, 4.2.115
malt-horse, 4.1.114
man, *vb.* 4.1.180
Mantua, 4.2.83
many, 3.2.83
marcantant, 4.2.63
Marcellus, 2.1.377
Marian Hacket, Ind.2.19–20
marked, 1.1.163
marks, *sb.* 5.2.35
married o' Sunday, 2.1.326
marry, Ind.2.99; 4.2.11
marry in haste, 3.2.11
mart, 2.1.329
masquing stuff, 4.3.87
master's, 5.1.5
match, 5.2.74
mate, 1.1.58
matter, 1.1.248
maze, 1.2.54
Me pardonato, 1.1.25
meacock, 2.1.315
meads, 5.2.139
mean, meaner, 1.1.202; 2.1.38.2; 4.3.167; 5.2.31
meaning, 3.2.123
meat, 4.3.9
meddle, 2.1.25
meet, 5.2.141
mend, 1.2.148; 4.1.133; 5.2.25
merest, Ind.1.20
merriment, 4.5.76
merry, Ind.1.94; 3.2.25
mess, 4.4.69
mete-yard, 4.3.149
mew, mewed, 1.1.87, 180
mighty, 2.1.103
milch-kine, 2.1.359
mind, 1.1.247
Minerva, 1.1.84
minion, 2.1.13
modesty, Ind.1.65, 91
monument, 3.2.94
moon (changes), 4.5.20
moralize, 4.4.79
more, 5.2.171
*mose, 3.2.50
motherwit, 2.1.263
motion, 1.2.277
movable, 2.1.196
moved, 5.2.142
moves, 1.2.71
muscadel, 3.2.171

nail, 4.3.108
napkin, Ind.1.124
napping, 4.2.46
narrow prying, 3.2.145
narrowly, 3.2.138
naturally, Ind.1.84
near, 4.4.4
neat's, 4.3.17
ne'er a whit, 1.1.233
nice, 3.1.79
Nicke, 3.1.80
nill, 2.1.270
nit, 4.3.109
no boot, 5.2.176
noddle, 1.1.64
none so dry, 5.2.144
not for my heart, 1.2.38
note, 1.2.142; 4.3.128
noted, 3.2.14
notes, 3.1.75
notorious, 5.1.46
nourisheth, 2.1.341

oats, 3.2.208–9
obedience, 5.2.117, 118
odds, 4.3.151
o'er-run, Ind.2.63
of, Ind.2.80; 4.1.60; 4.5.70; 5.2.72
of all, 1.2.2

of no kindred, 3.2.49
of ourselves, 4.1.162
offer, 5.1.56; 5.2.162
office, Ind.1.70; Ind.2.32; 4.1.28; 5.2.36
officer, 4.1.42; 5.2.37
old, 3.2.30–4
one of yours, 5.2.170
or e'er, 4.5.8
orchard, 2.1.110
ordained, 3.1.10
order, 1.2.124; 3.1.63
orderly, 2.1.45; 4.3.94
ordnance, 1.2.199
our, Ind.2.72
out of hope, 5.1.128
out-vied, 2.1.387
overblown, 5.2.3
over-eyeing, Ind.1.92
overleather, Ind.2.11
overreach, 3.2.144
Ovid, 1.1.33
oyster, 4.2.101

pack, 2.1.176
pack thread, 3.2.61
packing, 5.1.107
Padua, 1.1.2
pail, 2.1.359
pain, pains, 3.1.12; 4.3.43
painful, 5.2.149
paint, painted, 1.1.65; 4.3.175
pair of stocks, Ind.1.2
pantaloon, 1.1.47.2; 3.1.36
Par., 4.2.71
Paris, 1.2.244
park, 4.1.115
parley, 1.1.113–14
part, 2.1.302–3
pass, *sb.* 5.2.124
pass, *vb.* 4.2.118; 4.4.44, 56
passing, Ind.1.64; 2.1.111
passion, Ind.1.94; 4.1.104
past compare, 5.2.174
pate, 1.2.12; 2.1.153
paucas pallabris, Ind.1.5
peasant, 4.1.114
*peat, 1.1.78
pedant, 4.2.63, 71.2
Pedascule, 3.1.48
peereth, 4.3.171
peevish, 5.2.157
Pegasus, 4.4.5
Peter, 4.4.65–72
peremptory, 2.1.130
Petruchio, 1.2.0.1
pictures, Ind.1.44; Ind.2.47–51
pieced, 3.2.59
piercing, 2.1.175
pillory, 2.1.155
pinched, 2.1.373
pip, 1.2.33
Pisa walls, 2.1.369
pitchers have ears, 4.4.51
pith, 1.1.163
pittance, 4.4.60
place where, 4.3.146–7
plash, 1.1.23
plate, 2.1.349
pleasant, Ind.2.127; 3.1.56; 4.5.72
please it you, 4.4.1
pleasure, 1.1.81
pledge, 1.2.44
plotted, 1.1.185
pluck, 4.1.132
ply, 1.1.193
'pointed, 3.1.19
points, 3.2.48
policy, 2.1.292
politicly, 4.1.175
poor petitioners, 2.1.72
porringer, 4.3.64
port, 1.1.200; 3.1.35
portion, 2.1.361
possessed (with), 3.2.49–50
possession, 2.1.121
practice, 2.1.163
practise, Ind.1.33
prating, 4.3.113
prefer, 1.1.97
preferment, 2.1.92
preposterous, 3.1.9
prerogative, 3.1.6
present, presently, 2.1.106; 4.3.5; 4.4.58
present, *vb.* Ind.2.85
Presenters, 1.1.246.1
prevented, 5.2.49
pricked, pricks, 3.2.66, 69
proceed, 2.1.163
proceeders, 4.2.11
profess, 4.2.8
profit, 1.1.39
promise, 2.1.142, 285
proof, 2.1.139; 4.3.43
proper, 1.2.141

proud, 4.3.168
prove, 2.1.143; 4.3.144
pumps, 4.1.118
puppet, 4.3.103
pursue me, 5.2.47
put her down, 5.2.35
put me in heart, 4.5.77

quaint, 3.2.146; 4.3.102
qualified, 4.5.66
qualities, 2.1.50
quantity, 4.3.111
quarts, Ind.2.86
quicken, 1.1.36
quit, 3.1.90

rag, 4.3.111
ranging, 3.1.89
rascal, 2.1.156
rated, rates, *vb.* 1.1.157; 4.1.171
rayed, 3.2.52; 4.1.3
Re, mi, 3.1.72–6
read, 3.1.13; 4.2.6
rebused, 1.2.7
reckoned up, Ind.2.90
reckoning, 4.1.75
Redime, 1.1.159
rehearsed, 1.2.122
repute, 4.2.113
resolve, 4.2.7
respecting you, 5.2.32
rest, rests, 1.1.243–4; 4.3.26
restrained, 3.2.57
reverence, Ind.1.50
reverend, reverent, 4.1.191; 4.5.48
Rheims, 2.1.80
Richard Conqueror, Ind.1.4
right, 5.2.109
ring, *sb.* 1.1.137–8
ring it, 1.2.17
road, 2.1.377
roe, Ind.2.46
room, 3.2.252
rope tricks, 1.2.111
rough, 1.1.55
roundly, 1.2.58; 3.2.216; 4.4.104; 5.2.21
rout, 3.2.180
rudesby, 3.2.10
ruffling, 4.3.60
ruffs, 4.3.56
run, 4.1.13
rush-candle, 4.5.14
rushes, 4.1.41

sack, Ind.2.2
sadness, Ind.2.129; 5.2.63
safe, 4.4.80
Saint Anne, 1.1.248
Saint Jeronimy, Ind.1.7
saving, 2.1.71
say'st me so, 1.2.185
scape, scapes, 2.1.239; 5.2.3
schooled, 4.4.9
schools, 3.1.18
sciences, 2.1.57
score, Ind.2.21
scrivener, 4.4.58
secret, 1.1.150
secure, 5.2.151
seem, 4.2.68
seen, 1.2.132
Semiramis, Ind.2.37
sense, 5.2.18
sensible, 4.1.56; 5.2.18
serve in, 3.1.14
serviceable, 1.1.211
Sessa, Ind.1.5
set, 4.4.18
set down, 3.2.60
severally, 4.1.166.1
shake, 5.2.140
sharp, 4.1.177
sheathing, 4.1.120
sheep's leather, 3.2.56
*sheer, Ind.2.21
shift, Ind.1.123
should, 3.2.158
shoulder-shotten, 3.2.55
show, showed, 2.1.286; 4.1.198
shrew, 4.1.197–8
shrewd, 1.1.177; 1.2.59
Sibyl, 1.2.69
Sigeian, 3.1.28–9
silken, 4.3.82
simple, Ind.1.132
since once, Ind.1.80
Sir, 3.2.157
sirrah, Ind.1.71; 5.1.135
sith, 1.1.208
skills, 3.2.131
skipper, 2.1.341
sleep, Ind.1.32
slickly, 4.1.79
slide, Ind.1.5
slipped, 5.2.52

Sly, Ind.1.0.1
small, Ind.2.1
so, Ind.1.79; 1.2.80; 2.1.228; 4.3.16, 193
so said, 1.2.181
so simple, 5.2.161
sobriety, 1.1.71
soft, 4.4.23
sol fa, 1.2.18
solemn, 3.2.100
some, 4.3.184
something, 2.1.182; 5.2.54
sooth, 1.2.256
sops, 3.2.172
sorted, 4.3.43
Soto, Ind.1.85
soud, 4.1.127
sound, 5.1.125
sounded, 2.1.191
spavins, 3.2.52
speak as I find, 2.1.66
speak me fair, 1.2.175
specialties, 2.1.125
sped, 3.2.52; 5.2.185
speed, *sb.* 2.1.137
speed, *vb.* 1.2.244; 2.1.280
speeding, 2.1.302
spit in the hole, 3.1.39
spite, 4.3.2
spleen, Ind.1.134; 3.2.10
spoiled, 5.1.99
sportful, 2.1.260
spruce, 4.1.101
staggers, 3.2.53
stale, stalemate, 1.1.58; 3.1.88
stand, stands, Ind.2.123; 1.2.112; 4.4.21, 48–9
stare, 3.2.230
stark, 3.2.53
state, 1.2.90; 5.1.113
stay, stays, stayed, 3.2.23, 219; 4.2.83; 4.3.59; 4.4.29
stead, 1.2.263
stepped, 1.2.82
steps, 3.2.138
still, 1.2.154; 2.1.307; 4.1.194; 4.3.190; 4.4.52
stock, 3.2.64
stockings, 4.1.42
stocks, 1.1.31
stoics, 1.1.31
stomach, 1.1.38; 1.2.190; 4.1.143; 5.2.9, 176
stoop, 4.1.178
straight, Ind.1.49; 4.1.155
strange, 1.1.85; 1.2.189
stranger, 2.1.85
stripling, 1.2.141
struck, 2.1.362
studied, 2.1.158
stuff, Ind.2.137; 4.3.87, 118
subscribe, 1.1.81
suffer, 2.1.31
sufficeth, 1.1.245; 3.2.105
sufficient, 4.4.92
suits, Ind.1.103
supper-time, 4.3.187
supply, 3.2.249
swain, 2.1.205; 4.1.114
sweet, Ind.1.35, 46
sweeting, 4.3.36
swift, 5.2.54
swinge, 5.2.104

table, 2.1.404
tail, 2.1.219
take, 4.3.164
take it on you, 3.2.216
take upon you, 4.2.109
tale, tales, 2.1.218; 4.1.49–50
tall, taller, 4.1.9; 4.4.17
tarry, Ind.2.123
tell, 1.1.129; 4.3.22
tents, 2.1.354
that, 4.1.171
there an end, 5.2.98
thick, 5.2.143
think on, 4.3.113
this', 1.2.45
thralled, 1.1.217
three-inch, 4.1.23
three-legged stool, 1.1.64
throughly, 4.4.11
tight, 2.1.381
'tis well, 4.4.6
to, 3.2.27, 156
to come, 5.2.68
to her, 5.2.33, 34
to the time, 4.3.97
tongue, 4.1.6
too blame, 4.3.48
took, 3.2.162
toucheth, 1.1.114
toward, 1.1.68; 5.1.12; 5.2.182
toy, 2.1.404; 4.3.67
traffic, 1.1.12

train, Ind.1.12.2
Tranio, 1.1.0.1; 3.2.21
trapped, Ind.2.39
trenchers, 4.1.153
trick, 4.3.67
trimmed, Ind.2.37; 4.1.40
Tripoli, 4.2.75–6
trot, 1.2.78
trow, 1.2.4, 161
trunk sleeve, 4.3.138
trust, 4.2.67
Turkey, 2.1.355
turn, turns, 1.2.165; 2.1.164, 271; 3.2.131; 4.2.62
turtle, 2.1.208
twink, 2.1.312
two and thirty, 1.2.33
Tyrian, 2.1.351

unable, 5.2.169
unapt, 5.2.166
uncase, 1.1.204
under, 5.1.35
undertake, 4.2.107
unkind, 5.2.136
unluckily, 4.5.25
unpinked, 4.1.118
unprovided, 3.2.98
unreverent, 3.2.111
untoward, 4.5.79
usual, 3.1.12
usurp, Ind.1.128

vail, 5.2.176
valance, 2.1.356
vantage, 3.2.143
velour, 3.2.59
vengeance, 2.1.406
Venice, 2.1.325, 356
vent, 1.2.174
Venus, Ind.2.47–51
veriest, Ind.1.98
very, 1.1.123; 2.1.243; 4.3.32
vied, 2.1.311

walk, 2.1.85
wander, 4.5.69
waning age, Ind.2.61
want, wants, Ind.1.101; 3.2.5, 248, 250
wanton, Ind.2.50
war, 4.5.30
warm, 2.1.265
warrant, 3.2.247; 4.4.8
wash, 4.1.139
wasp, 2.1.210
watch, 3.2.143; 4.1.182, 192; 5.2.150
ways, 4.1.2
wear, wears, 3.2.110, 117
wed and bed, 1.1.141
wedding-garment, 4.1.42–3
weighed, 3.2.54
weighty, 4.4.25
welcome, 5.1.11
welkin, Ind.2.43
well ta'en, 2.1.207
what, 4.1.77; 4.3.172
what 'cerns it you? 5.1.66
what cheer? 4.3.37
what not that's, 5.2.110
what to, 3.2.42
when, 4.1.128, 129
where, 4.5.38
where away? 4.5.27
Where is the life? 4.1.125
which, 4.2.38
whiles, 3.1.22
white, 5.2.186
whom, 4.5.40
whoreson, 4.1.114
widowhood, 2.1.123
will, Ind.1.106; 1.1.56; 2.1.270
Wincot, Ind.2.20
windgalls, 3.2.52
winding, Ind.1.12.1
window, 5.1.13.1
winter, 4.1.20
winter-cricket, 4.3.109
wish, 1.1.111; 1.2.59
wit, Ind.2.75
with, 4.3.110
with a witness, 5.1.108
with one consent, 4.4.34
with the best, 5.2.8
withal, 3.1.60; 3.2.25, 108
witless, 2.1.263
wive and thrive, 1.2.55
wive it, 1.2.74
woman, 4.5.36
wonder, 3.2.190
wonderful, 4.2.15
woodcock, 1.2.158
work, 3.2.220
world to see, 2.1.313
worse than so, 4.2.88

worthy memory, 4.1.72–4

Xanthippe, 1.2.70

yard, 4.3.112
ye, Ind.2.83
yellows, 3.2.52
yet, Ind.1.93; Ind.2.65
young, 2.1.237
youngling, 2.1.339
your best, 4.3.100
yourself, 2.1.1

www.worldsclassics.co.uk

MORE ABOUT **OXFORD WORLD'S CLASSICS**

American Literature

British and Irish Literature

Children's Literature

Classics and Ancient Literature

Colonial Literature

Eastern Literature

European Literature

Gothic Literature

History

Medieval Literature

Oxford English Drama

Poetry

Philosophy

Politics

Religion

The Oxford Shakespeare
